Praise for *When Lions* \

"A well-written and well-researched book on the Detroit Lions of the 1950s. They were arguably the best team of that decade, rivaling the Cleveland Browns. Bak goes into great detail on players of that era, giving unique insight into the team. I highly recommend this book."
—Ken Crippen, president of the Professional Football
Researchers Association

"Whether you remember those Lions teams of the 1950s or not, this book is required reading for every fan of the Detroit Lions. It will remind you that there was a time when the Detroit Lions really were the kings of the NFL."
—*Michigan Historical Review*

"Thanks to Bak's research and storytelling, *When Lions Were Kings* is a tremendous read. In addition to describing the Lions' exploits during their most spectacular decade, Bak provides an enormous amount of interesting detail on fans, wives, girlfriends, mascots, water boys, night clubs, and Detroit itself. He's written a cultural history as well as a football history."
—Bill McGraw, longtime *Detroit Free Press* reporter, editor, and sportswriter

"At long last, Richard Bak has provided us with a definitive and colorful retrospective of the Detroit Lions in their decade of dominance. You'll thank him for placing readers inside Briggs Stadium to watch Bobby Layne, Doak Walker, Joe Schmidt, Yale Lary, and a cast of characters march up and down the field to gridiron glory."
—Bill Dow, Detroit journalist and sports historian

"A much-needed blast from the past that talks about one of the most successful dynasties in team sports history—that thought alone might give Lions fans hope that a once incredible past could maybe turn into a very real future."
—*Holland Sentinel*

"A story of pigskin passion for sports fans of all ages."
—*Detroit Free Press*

"Richard Bak's *When Lions Were Kings* is a look at an era of pro football in Detroit that has only rarely been duplicated by other cities' teams. Bak's ability to weave local history, landmarks, and social events into the story of a dynasty that could have been far better than it actually was is remarkable. There are no other books about Detroit's four major sports teams that capture an era of greatness such as the Lions experienced in the 1950s."
—John Makar, Michigan Sports Hall of Fame

RICHARD BAK

WHEN
Lions

A PAINTED TURTLE BOOK

DETROIT, MICHIGAN

WE WERE

Kings

The Detroit Lions

AND THE

Fabulous Fifties

ISBN 978-0-8143-5099-7 (paperback)
ISBN 978-0-8143-3427-0 (jacketed hardcover)
ISBN 978-0-8143-3428-7 (ebook)

Library of Congress Control Number: 2020938188

On cover: Quarterback Bobby Layne is protected by guards
Dick Stanfel (*left*) and Jim Martin (*right*) in this posed photograph from
the Detroit Lions' training camp in 1953. (*Detroit News*).

Cover design by Brad Norr Design.

Wayne State University Press rests on Waawiyaataanong,
also referred to as Detroit, the ancestral and contemporary homeland of
the Three Fires Confederacy. These sovereign lands were granted by the
Ojibwe, Odawa, Potawatomi, and Wyandot Nations, in 1807, through
the Treaty of Detroit. Wayne State University Press affirms Indigenous
sovereignty and honors all tribes with a connection to Detroit. With our
Native neighbors, the press works to advance educational equity and
promote a better future for the earth and all people.

Wayne State University Press
Leonard N. Simons Building
4809 Woodward Avenue
Detroit, Michigan 48201–1309

Visit us online at wsupress.wayne.edu

Topps® and Bowman trading cards used courtesy of
The Topps Company, Inc.

**For Tom and Charles DeLisle,
who were there**

Contents

Introduction: Riding High................................ 2

1 | **Two from Texas**.. 12

2 | **We Can Win with Parker**............................ 34

3 | **World Beaters**... 55

4 | **Pro Football at Its Best**............................ 82

5 | **Gridiron Heroes**.................................... 115

6 | **One of Those Things**.............................. 140

7 | **Sorry, Buddy**.. 183

8 | **Tackling Jim Crow**................................. 209

9 | **Muggings and Mayhem**........................... 228

10 | **Pro Bowls and Army Legs**...................... 256

11 | **The Last Great Season**.......................... 265

12 | **Cardboard Lions**................................. 293

13 | **Goodbye, Two-Minute Guy**................... 301

14 | **Football in a Box**................................ 313

15 | **End of a Perfect Thing**......................... 322

Appendixes

A. Detroit Lions Season Results, 1950–59.......... 333

B. Detroit Lions Composite Roster, 1950–59....... 338

Notes.. 341

Index.. 365

WHEN LIONS WERE KINGS

Riding High

Detroit has always liked professional football. Detroit is a lusty, thriving, vigorous city, and it has found a soul mate in the lusty, thriving, vigorous game.

—Tex Maule, *Sports Illustrated* (1958)

The picture is etched eternally in the memory of thousands of Detroiters lucky enough to be there that cold, bright Sunday afternoon: a silver-helmeted Joe Schmidt, carried aloft by hordes of jubilant fans, clutching a football and bobbing like a cork on a sea of topcoats and varsity jackets. The date is December 29, 1957, and the Detroit Lions have just demolished the Cleveland Browns, 59–14, at Briggs Stadium to capture the championship of the National Football League. Symbolically, Schmidt and the Lions are at the apex of a dynasty that has just given Detroit its third pro football title in six seasons.

"The fans picked me up at midfield and carried me around for a few minutes before they finally put me down," recalled the Hall-of-Fame middle linebacker and defensive captain, today one of the few surviving members of the team. "I think they were after the ball more than anything. To tell you the truth, I was kind of embarrassed."

"Embarrassed" has become the operative word for the once-proud franchise. Sixty-plus seasons have come and gone since the Lions last reigned as champions, one of the longest ongoing title droughts in all of professional sports. Despite the NFL's greatly expanded playoff system, during this period the team has won just a single postseason contest. With all of the frustration surrounding the franchise since Schmidt's impromptu ride—particularly during the Matt Millen era, when the Lions became the first team ever to post a 0–16 season record and shamed fans at Ford Field wore paper bags over their heads—it's easy to forget there once was a time when the Lions were kings.

During a stretch of seven seasons, 1951 through 1957, Detroit won four division titles and narrowly missed grabbing two others on the final Sunday of the season. This was an era when the regular season meant everything, long before the modern tournament-style system of determining a champion diluted the importance of finishing first. The Lions played six postseason games—special divisional tiebreakers with Los Angeles in 1952 and San Francisco in 1957 and title games with Cleveland in 1952, 1953, 1954, and 1957—and triumphed in all but one. Detroit's five postseason victories and three NFL championships made it the most successful big-money team of the decade. In particular, the 1953 championship game and the 1957 playoff—the first featuring a classic Bobby Layne last-licks scoring drive and the other an unprecedented second-half comeback—rank among the most memorable games in league history.

Cleveland, the league's other titan, also won three championships during the decade, but its postseason record during this period was a lackluster 4–5. In head-to-head competition between the two rivals, it was no contest. Detroit won all four regular-season matches and three of four title games with the Browns, accounting for a 7–1 record and an .875 winning percentage. Including pre-season games, which in those days were played more competitively in order to please sponsors and help sell the sport to the public, Detroit compiled a 17-4-1 (.810) record against Paul Brown's Browns. On home turf, the Lions were invincible. The Browns played 10 games at Briggs Stadium during the '50s—six exhibitions, two regular-season games, and two title games—and lost every time. The 1957 championship game rout in Detroit was the worst defeat in franchise history and of Paul Brown's career. "God, we hated that town," one Cleveland player moaned.

Detroit's regular-season record of 68-48-4 during the 1950s, a .586 winning percentage dragged down by a couple of terrible seasons at the very end of the decade, trailed Cleveland, the New York Giants, and the Chicago Bears in the composite standings. However, the Giants won just one title and the Bears none. Given Detroit's sterling postseason record and how thoroughly it dominated the era's other powerhouse, the case can easily be made that the Lions were *the* team of the fabulous '50s, or at least for the bulk of it. "We got sort of a superior feeling," Layne once said of this sweet spot in Lions history.

The very capable Tobin Rote quarterbacked the Lions to their last championship while filling in for the injured Layne. However, it's the fast-living blond quarterback from Texas who remains the centerpiece of Lions lore during the Eisenhower decade.

Schmidt once described what it was like hitting the nightspots with "Sweet Bobby," Layne's favorite nickname. "It was like walking into a room with Babe Ruth—everybody knew him, table down front, drinks for everyone and big tips to the musicians. You'd have a good time but pay for it the next day."

Whether out on the field or out on the town, there never was any doubt about who was in charge. "In our team meetings at the Stadium Bar across from the stadium, Bobby would say, 'Look, guys, there's one chief, and I'm the chief and y'all the Indians,'" said Hall-of-Fame safety Yale Lary. "He was all the way the chief."

Disdaining a face mask and most pads, Layne oozed self-confidence, especially with time running out and the game on the line. "We'd get the ball with two minutes to go in those days," recalled end Dorne Dibble, "and you could almost feel the other team starting to panic. *Oh, here it comes now.* And the defensive backs would start playing off of you, which gave us even more confidence. They were afraid. It was electricity, just like a bolt of lightning. He'd come in the huddle and say, 'No holding, no offside, everybody block, you've got six points.'"

A giant sign reinforced Layne's larger-than-life image. "In the early '50s, there was a huge billboard across Michigan Avenue, facing Briggs Stadium, and when I was a kid it blew me away every time I was downtown," recalled longtime fan Tom DeLisle. "The double-sized board had the huge figure of Bobby Layne, in his blue Lions number 22, with a football in his hand. The ball moved back and forth, back and forth, behind Bobby's helmet, as if he were passing a pigskin the size of a '52 DeSoto. The sight of it was awfully impressive."

Layne wasn't perfect, but he was authentic, which is always more interesting. The feeling among many is that if he had stuck around town the Lions would've won another championship or two. "He was the greatest quarterback this game has ever known," head coach Buddy Parker said. "He called the plays.

He was a good field general. He got the most out of his players. He was a passer and a runner and—most of all—he was a winner."

Co-starring in the backfield with Layne for six seasons was all-purpose All-American halfback Doak Walker, whose good looks and aw-shucks demeanor made him the perfect pitchman for such products as Dr. Pepper, Beech-Nut gum, and Vitalis hair tonic. "He wasn't the fastest guy in the world," a teammate said. "But he had quickness and a change of pace and change of direction. He had football savvy."

Like Layne, his best friend since their high school days together in Texas, Walker had a burning belief in himself and the habit of rising to the occasion. He was genuinely shy and humble, and as fearless and incorruptible as any cowboy galloping across television screens in the '50s. "People had more than respect for Doak," Schmidt said. "It was more like adoration. You could never find anything bad to say about the guy."

That wasn't the case with Layne and some of his rowdier teammates. The Lions of the '50s were a colorful lot, prized by even out-of-town writers. Deep into another decade, Jim Murray of the *Los Angeles Times* still considered them his favorite football team of all. "They were a living example of the power of positive drinking," he wrote in 1966. "Bob Hoernschemeyer would stiff-arm half the Ann Arbor police department on Saturday night, and all of the Green Bay Packers the next day."

Parker insisted he didn't care what his players were up to. "Maybe they all lived it up early in the week," he said. "But they were ready to play on Sunday. They were always ready to play on Sunday. That's all that counts—Sunday."

But even Parker could take only so much, impulsively quitting at a preseason "Meet the Lions" banquet in 1957. He'd had enough, he declared. He couldn't handle the team anymore. Long-time assistant George Wilson took over and almost immediately had to deal with two curfew breakers, Layne and Tom "The Bomb" Tracy, getting arrested after a long night of drinking. Undeterred by the public tumult over Parker's abrupt departure and Layne's trial, the Lions would go on to capture another title in heart-stopping style.

During the 1950s, Detroit was considered by many to be the best football town in the country. For much of the decade, the Lions trailed only the Los Angeles Rams—a warm-weather club playing inside a much larger stadium—in home attendance. Standing-room-only crowds were the norm at Briggs Stadium. Visiting teams, who received a set percentage of the gate, were appreciative of the support as they always left town with a much larger check than the league-mandated $20,000 minimum. In 1955, the Lions sold 36,434 season tickets, a league record they extended each year through the end of the decade. Two years later, they became the first pro football franchise to rake in $1 million at the gate, a significant achievement at a time when ticket sales were still the predominant source of revenue.

In addition to the captivating Layne, the Lions featured three Heisman Trophy winners, nationally recognized glamor boys who arrived in Detroit with their own built-in fan base: Walker from Southern Methodist University, end Leon Hart from Notre Dame, and halfback Howard "Hopalong" Cassady from Ohio State. The Lions also had the game's biggest player, Les Bingaman, a surprisingly nimble middle guard and champion beer drinker whose weight at times came perilously close to 375 pounds. Once, in a celebratory moment, several teammates tried carrying "Bingo" off the field. A couple of players grabbed each beefy leg while a few others pushed from underneath. The effort collapsed in a heap, burying several Lions.

"I'll never forget this," the appreciative Bingaman said. "I'm just too big a hero for all of you."

"Those were just wonderful teams," recalled Marc Larco, whose father, Pete, made sure his favorite players were replenished with hot liquids after chilly late-season practices at Briggs Stadium. Pete opened Larco's Inn on West McNichols near Livernois in 1950, and the Italian restaurant with the savory chophouse menu and generously sized portions soon became a popular hangout for Lions players.

Marc had permission to leave school early every day. "I went to the restaurant, where my father had prepared this enormous pot of soup. We'd put the pot in the back of the station wagon and I'd drive to the stadium, where they would let me drive right onto the field. Practice would stop and two football players would come and take out the pot and everyone had soup." Appreciative players sang a little ditty: "Hooray for Petey Larco, he brings us minestrone."

By 1954, the Lions enjoyed a robust national following. In a single one-month period that fall, five major large-circulation magazines—*Collier's*, *Look*, *Saturday Evening Post*, *Sports Illustrated*, and *Time*—published features about the defending two-time champions, who were attempting to become the first NFL team ever to win three straight titles. The coverage reflected the Lions' popularity and the country's soaring interest in the NFL, with *Time* making Layne the first pro football player ever to appear on its cover. The Lions, a solid draw on the road as well as at home, led the league in total attendance in 1953 and again in 1954. One Sunday, they drew 93,751 fans to Memorial Coliseum for a game with the Rams, establishing what was then an NFL single-game attendance record.

In a decade that saw television radically reshape the way Americans followed sports, Layne and his silver-and-blue teammates helped sell the NFL to a country just settling into the happy habit of watching pro football on Sunday afternoons. As broadcasts grew in number and reach, viewers who had never been within a thousand miles of Briggs Stadium grew familiar with such favorites as halfback Bob "Hunchy" Hoernschemeyer and "Chris's Crew," the fine defensive secondary led by Jack Christiansen. Fans from Oklahoma City to Miami angrily shook their snack tables at such made-for-TV villains as tackle Gil "Wild Hoss" Mains, who transferred his outlaw image to the wrestling ring in the offseason, and cornerback Jimmy "The Hatchet" David, whose small size and toothless grin belied a rascally playing style.

Layne's grandmother, for one, was fascinated by the medium's ability to bring to life players she had previously only heard or read about. "After the first season television beamed the Lions' games back to Texas, I came home and dropped in on my grandmother," he said. "We had won the championship, so I thought grandma might have some kind words for me. But all she kept talking about was her hero, Les Bingaman."

Detroit at midcentury was at its peak of population and influence. The industrial goliath had been the Arsenal of Democracy during World War II, churning out tanks, planes, and munitions for the Allies. Now it was back to being the Motor City, with several million cars and trucks rolling off the line each year. To the outside world, postwar Detroit was the city of Henry Ford, Walter Reuther, Joe Louis, Hal Newhouser, Gordie Howe, Soupy Sales, Jimmy Hoffa, Al Kaline, Jackie Wilson, radio's Lone Ranger and Green Hornet—and, of course, Bobby Layne and Doak Walker. It was home to the world's mightiest corporation and the country's most powerful union. It was the city that created the middle class, the place where vote-hungry politicians always visited on Labor Day, the town that gave the rest of the country a parade and a Lions-Packers game to watch every Thanksgiving. Serious consideration was given to locating the still-to-be-built Pro Football Hall of Fame inside brand-new Cobo Hall. "It was a hell of a city," was the sentiment of more than one old Lion from the era.

At the same time, Detroit was grappling with problems that would lead to its long eclipse. High-paying unskilled factory jobs were drying up as automation took its toll. Freshly constructed freeways were tearing apart established neighborhoods and accelerating the flow of residents, businesses, and tax dollars to the suburbs. The core city was decaying, including the area around Briggs Stadium.

Race relations were dangerously fractious. Despite the city's black population reaching 400,000 during the decade (compared to 50,000 in 1920, when Detroit had its first NFL franchise), it was an overwhelmingly white audience at the ballpark. The Lions reflected that demographic, fielding just five black players during the decade, most of whom had brief, inconsequential careers. In fact, the 1952 and 1953 squads are the last to win NFL titles with an all-white roster. There were no minority coaches or executives, no black shareholders, not even a black waterboy. The league as a whole was slowly desegregating, but it was still disproportionately white.

Leaving aside the racial component, pro football was still a much different sport in the 1950s than it is today. There were only a dozen teams, all but two located in the East and the Midwest. They played a 12-game schedule and crowned a champion by Christmas week. There were no domed stadiums or artificial turf. Briggs Stadium didn't even have an organist, much less an exploding scoreboard. All games were played outside in the elements, in snow, sleet, rain, and scorching heat, and on fields that often resembled mud pits, skating rinks, or dust bowls. A white painted football was used for all night games, the underpowered lights in most parks making long throws and kicks look like herculean egg tosses. Passes and players regularly caromed off the H-shaped goalposts positioned on the goal line. There were no nets keeping kicked balls from sailing into the stands, resulting in mad scrambles among spectators.

The game was nastier, played by men who had in some cases killed other men in wartime. Until 1955, a ball carrier who was knocked down was allowed to get up and continue running until he was completely stopped, a rule that encouraged piling on and cheap shots. Head slaps, clothesline tackles, and blind-blocking were perfectly legal, as was grabbing a ball carrier by his face mask. Face masks weren't even mandatory until midway through the decade, though some players, such as Layne, Walker, and Bingaman, took advantage of a grandfather provision in the new rule to continue playing without one.

Although the NFL played two-platoon football, the age of specialists had yet to fully arrive. Small rosters meant there was no room for a punter or placekicker who couldn't do anything else. "Today the players are bigger and faster, but we were more complete players then," said Vince Banonis, who played center and linebacker for three seasons under Parker. "A lot of guys now go through a whole season without throwing a block or making a tackle. You have specialists for everything—one guy does nothing but return punts, another plays only on third down."

On Parker's Lions, linemen and backs were expected to play both ways when needed and to be able to fill in at two or three different positions. Walker, one of the smallest players in the league, not only ran, caught, passed, and punted the ball out of his left halfback position, he returned kicks, booted extra points and field goals, flew down the field on kickoffs, and occasionally took a turn in the secondary. In 1952, Jim Doran was voted the Lions' Most Valuable Player by his teammates for his sterling work on defense. The following year in the title game, the pass-rushing end switched sides and became a pass-catching end, scoring the touchdown that won another championship.

Just as important as one's versatility was the ability to carry on through excruciating pain. Tackle Lou Creekmur alone suffered 17 concussions and 13 broken noses while never missing a game in 10 seasons. "You never admitted to anything," recalled halfback Lew Carpenter's wife, Ann. "If you wanted to stay on the team you got dressed and went out there." Players competed for the 396 available jobs each season during much of the '50s, a fraction of the 2,016 regular-roster and practice-squad spots in today's NFL.

"There was a different mentality then," Schmidt said. "You played when you were hurt or you were out of a job." The small rosters, which gradually increased from 33 to 36 men during the decade, meant players suited up with fractured jaws, broken fingers, and twisted backs, even with part of their foot missing. Schmidt remembered guard Stan Campbell once trying to get rid of a corn.

"The doctors were treating it," he said, "but it kept getting worse. Finally, someone on the team suggested a home remedy that consisted of pouring acid on the corn. Campbell was one of those guys who wanted to prove he was one of the boys, so he tried the home remedy. The acid burned the flesh but the corn disappeared. The only trouble was that Campbell's foot almost disappeared, too. It was so raw you could see the bone, but Campbell suited up for every game even though he could hardly walk. He didn't want anyone to think he was chicken."

Helmet-to-helmet hits were widely admired. One collision was so memorably violent that Layne was still marveling over it years later. In a Detroit-Pittsburgh contest in 1953, cornerback Bob Smith drew a bead on Steelers fullback Fran Rogel.

"Rogel was one of those squat, hard runners who dished out plenty of punishment and was as rough as they come," Layne recalled. "Smith and Rogel hit head-on in the first half . . . and the noise of the tackle must have registered on one of those earthquake charts. I don't know how either one of them managed to get up, but they did, and they stayed and played the rest of the day."

Pride, competitiveness, peer pressure, and the fear of being replaced kept players from quitting for the day after "getting their bell rung." Concussions, many of them undiagnosed, could pile up during a man's career, leading to devastating results in retirement. Smith died in 2002 after several years of battling dementia, just one of a scandalously high number of former players whose gray matter was turned into fluffy cotton candy by years of butting heads.

Broadcast revenues, the lifeblood of modern sports, were still minimal then. Owners remained heavily dependent on ticket sales, a reality that depressed salaries—as well as the players who earned them. While a handful of highly paid players, the stars on whose shoulder pads the modern 32-team NFL was built, were being paid upwards of $20,000 a year by the mid-'50s, some Lions made as little as $5,500, about the same as a union auto worker with overtime. Nearly every player and coach worked an off-season job, and some moonlighted during the season in order to make ends meet. There was no pension plan. Players bought their own shoes.

Television changed the game, bringing unimaginable riches to owners and players. During the Lions' 1952 title run, the club received $113,000 in TV revenue, a now-laughable amount that was better than most teams and accounted for the major chunk of that year's profits. Some generously pegged the franchise's value at about $1 million. Today, the Lions are worth an estimated $1.8 billion, with broadcast rights and other revenue streams bringing in nearly $400 million annually. Even with a nine-figure payroll, profits run to about $75 million each year.

Lost in the windfall of dollars has been an almost quaint lack of self-awareness. In the locker room after the 1957 title contest, Frank Gatski asked Schmidt if he could have the ball that he had gripped so dearly in a sea of grasping hands. The retiring center said he would like to have it as a memento of his final game. "Well, he's an old Browns player," Schmidt told reporters. "He loved it as much, or more than any of us today, beating his old team."

Years later, Schmidt asked Gatski about the ball. Was the historic pigskin displayed under glass in a den or museum? Perhaps he gifted it to a favorite grandchild or sold it to a collector for top dollar? Gatski, an avid outdoorsman who lived in West Virginia, said his hunting dog found the ball one day and gave it a good chewing, after which he just tossed it in the trash. If Gatski's second tongue had been Latin instead of Polish, he might have added, "Sic transit gloria." Glory fades.

The Lions' 59–14 wipeout of the Browns was the exclamation point to years of dominating play. In those heady moments, nobody present would have dared predict that, long after most of them had passed on to that great grandstand in the sky, their grandchildren would still be waiting for the team to win its next championship.

What muted the Lions' once mighty roar? Many say the trade that sent Layne to Pittsburgh upset the team's chemistry. Others point to the uninspired steward-ship of William Clay Ford, who bought out feuding shareholders to become sole owner. Then there are the jinxes to consider. The so-called Bobby Layne curse holds that the quarterback, angry over being traded, put a whammy on the team. The other curse involves portentous timing, not revenge. Ford bought the team on the day John F. Kennedy was assassinated in Dallas. That the president was gunned down in the city that produced Layne and Walker, the shining stars of the Lions' most lustrous era, adds to the dark irony.

Tom DeLisle and his father were among the fans sharing in the pandemo-nium at Briggs Stadium that distant Sunday. It was the youngster's first Lions game, and he was spoiled.

"Watching that mob parade around the field with Joe Schmidt on their shoul-ders, I naturally assumed we would have decades to come of similar results and celebrations," he said. "Hell, I was a wild-eyed kid. I probably said, 'Hey Dad, let's come back next year!' We all thought it would never end."

CHAPTER

1

Two FROM *Texas*

> Bobby Layne and Doak Walker, two of the greatest names in Southwestern football, will be reunited in professional ranks next fall. . . . Walker and Layne have been close friends for years. Even while playing against each other in college they continued that friendship. Texans who could have imagined what would have happened had both these grid greats gone to the University of Texas or SMU, now can think about what's going to happen next fall when Bobby and Doak pool their talents for McMillan at Detroit.
>
> —*Dallas Morning News*, April 8, 1950

It says a lot about the quality of high school football in Texas and its pipeline to the National Football League that current Detroit Lions quarterback Matthew Stafford, one of the premier players in the game—a man who once signed the richest contract in league history and reached 40,000 career yards faster than any other passer—is only the third-most famous Lion ever to graduate from Highland Park High School in Dallas. A framed, yellowing mission statement from the two legends who continue to tower over him is exhibited on a wall of the school's Highlander Stadium, right by the soda machine dispensing cans of Dr. Pepper.

The statement is signed by Bobby Layne and Doak Walker, co-captains of Highland Park High's 1943 squad. Among their numbered goals is this pledge: "We want to be better men because of our experience in football, and it is hoped that football will be better because we have played."

The "Blonde Blizzard," as the yearbook staff dubbed Layne, and "The Doaker" were stars wherever they laced their cleats. But it was in Detroit where the two Texans, arriving simultaneously in 1950, achieved their greatest fame. "Playing with Bobby made it all a little easier," Walker reflected years later. "In a way, it was like playing at Highland Park. Bobby would drop back, look one way, then throw across the field to a spot where he knew I would be when the ball arrived. We'd been doing it since we were kids."

Layne and Walker were born just a couple of weeks apart, though the streetwise Layne always seemed a few years older than his better-behaved buddy. ("He didn't do the things I did," Bobby said.) Robert Lawrence Layne came into the world on December 19, 1926. Ewell Doak Walker Jr. followed on New Year's Day, 1927. Their childhoods could hardly have been more different.

Layne spent his early years on a farm in Brown County in west-central Texas, milking cows, chopping wood, and swinging from the hayloft. He had two older sisters, as well as a younger brother who died of spinal meningitis as a baby. His father, Sherman, was a farmer and former semipro baseball player.

One morning in 1935, Bobby's mother, Beatrice, got everybody into the family car for a trip to visit relatives in nearby Brownwood. Beatrice drove while Sherman, feeling a little under the weather, rode in the passenger seat. The kids sat in the back of the crowded coupe. They were riding along when Sherman coughed, then suddenly fell backward, pinning Bobby. Beatrice sped to the nearest filling station, but by then Sherman Layne was dead of a heart attack. He was 36.

"I'm not sure he ever completely got over being trapped like that when his father died," Bobby's future wife, Carol, later said. "But he never talked about it much at all. It was only once after we'd been married for a while that he told me what had happened to his father and his life after that."

His mother, deciding she could not afford to raise three children by herself, sent him to live with his Aunt Lavinia and Uncle Wade Hampton. They were good people, unable to have children, and they legally adopted Bobby and raised him as their own. He called them Mom and Dad and grew into adulthood considering them his real parents. Meanwhile, his biological mother and sisters moved to California and had sporadic contact with him over the years. He financially supported them at times. He never once said a derogatory word about his real mother, despite any feelings of neglect he may have had. Bobby's mother and sisters outlived him, not bothering to attend his funeral.

Barstool psychoanalysts might point to that nightmarish episode on the road to Brownwood as being the reason young Bobby Layne grew up living for the moment. Every day was a gift, so it should be enjoyed to the hilt. They might also find in the boy's abandonment an explanation for his incessant need for companionship. He dreaded being alone for almost any reason. Throughout his entire adult life, he was most content when huddled with teammates on some playing field or surrounded by friends inside a nightclub, gatherings that doubled as large surrogate families.

Growing up in Highland Park, an upper-middle-class community not yet swallowed by Dallas, Doak wasn't a cowboy, and he never pretended to be. His parents were respected educators in the local school system, not ranchers, and being posed around horses and cattle by insistent photographers during his collegiate glory days made him feel a little silly. "I'll try," he'd say, "but heck, I can't ride. I'm a town boy."

Instead, along with countless other kids around the country in the 1930s, he vicariously experienced the Old West through the adventures of his favorite radio hero. Each live broadcast of *The Lone Ranger* began with the blood-stirring notes of the "William Tell Overture" and the announcer's famous introduction: "*A fiery horse with the speed of light, a cloud of dust and a hearty Hi-Yo Silver! The Lone Ranger!*" The youngster didn't care that the thrilling serial originated from WXYZ's studio inside Detroit's Maccabees Building, several hundred miles away, and that Silver's galloping hoofbeats were actually a sound-effects man pounding bathroom plungers into a box of gravel. It was enough to know that with the "Masked Man of the Plains" and Tonto on the job, good triumphed over evil—always. Inside the Walker home, everyday morality and humble heroism were prized virtues.

Much of the family's life revolved around the neighborhood Methodist church, where Doak's father taught Sunday school. The Walkers would "open the church on Monday and close it on Sunday," Doak recalled. "Prayer meeting Monday night, youth night on Tuesday, choir practice; something was going on seven days a week."

However, the senior Walker also encouraged his son in sports, especially football, an open-air religion in Texas. By the time Doak was three years old he was drop-kicking footballs over the clothesline and learning the fundamentals of the single wing. In fourth grade, he was assigned to write a composition about a great man from history. While others chose Thomas Edison or George Washington, Doak wrote his essay about Harry Shurford, star fullback of the Southern Methodist University team. Doak's father taught him to be competitive, but he stressed sportsmanship above all, a lesson to be applied in every aspect of life.

Doak was heroic even as a kid, said Dick Davis, a close friend since kindergarten. Davis remembered his buddy once saving him from drowning in a neighbor's pool. "Wherever we were, he was the most popular guy in school," Davis said. "And the main reason was, he was truly an outstanding person, but he never acted like it. There was no conceit, no arrogance. He would be the last person in the world to act like a big shot—and that came from the home. Doak's father literally raised him to be an all-American. I don't mean an all-American football player. I mean an all-American boy."

Doak became acquainted with Bobby after the Hamptons moved into a house on Purdue Street in Highland Park. Walker lived four blocks away on Stanford. They became fast friends. "He was a year ahead of me and was a gangly, awkward kind of guy in high school," Doak remembered.

Walker lettered in five sports in high school and was offered a minor-league contract by the New York baseball Giants, but the outfielder's true love was football. Layne, on the other hand, was more interested in the diamond than the gridiron. Whatever sport they played, what helped bond the two was their competitive drive, though the two displayed it differently.

"With Bobby, it was all up front—he'd bite your arm off to win," said Davis. "It was maybe more subtle with Doak, but just as intense. If you beat him pitching horseshoes, he'd go off and practice for weeks and then come back and invite you to a rematch."

"It's true that we were almost opposite personalities," Walker said. "We came from different backgrounds. I had had such a wonderful childhood, and Bobby had a hard life. . . . But we were just always great friends, and we also seemed to always provide inspiration for each other when we played together. We always had a feeling, starting in high school, that if we played together we could accomplish anything, no one could beat us."

Layne entered the University of Texas on a baseball scholarship in 1944 while Walker finished his final semester of high school. They enlisted in the Merchant Marine together in February 1945, going to basic training in Florida and radio school in New York. A few months later the war was over and they returned to their original plan of playing together at Texas. However, their high school coach was now an assistant coach at Southern Methodist, and Doak was persuaded to enroll at SMU. Over the next few years, Layne and Walker became stars at their respective schools as college football reached new heights of popularity in the postwar era.

At Texas, Layne played tailback and fullback in Dana X. Bible's single-wing offense, a now archaic run-heavy formation that used the quarterback principally as a blocker. When Bible switched to the T formation, he installed Layne at quarterback to take advantage of his talents as a runner and passer.

Layne also was an outstanding pitcher, compiling a 39–7 win-loss record in college. For a time he seriously considered a diamond career, and in the summer of 1948 even played a few weeks with the Lubbock Hubbers in the low minors. However, his passion for the game evaporated on the long bus rides. While on campus, he met Carol Krueger, the daughter of a prominent and wealthy Lubbock surgeon. They married in 1946, and thanks to his father-in-law's holdings and investments Bobby never had to worry about money.

Walker spent a year in the peacetime army after his freshman season at SMU, then returned to the lineup in 1947. Across three autumns, the multi-talented halfback led the Mustangs to a pair of South West Conference titles and two bowl game appearances. The Cotton Bowl was expanded to accommodate the crowds that came to watch No. 37 perform. "Doak isn't fast," SMU coach Marty Bell said. "He's not a great runner. He's not a great kicker. He's not a great passer. He's not a great blocker. But he is still the greatest football player I've ever seen." As a junior, Walker won the 1948 Heisman Trophy as college football's best player, a year after receiving the Maxwell Award from the Maxwell Club of Philadelphia as the country's top amateur athlete.

Doak literally became the face of Saturday afternoons, appearing on the covers of dozens of periodicals, including *Look*, *Life*, and *Collier's*. His campus sweetheart and future bride, Cotton Bowl queen Norma Peterson, sometimes appeared alongside him. The photogenic couple, the football hero and his girl, was a cuddly affirmation of postwar America's return to normalcy.

Doak was the perfect ambassador. When he heard that coaches were considering him for All-America honors his senior year, despite having missed a good part of the season to injury and illness, he wrote a letter to *Collier's* sports editor Bill Fay, requesting that more worthy candidates take his place. "It was an unselfish act of sportsmanship without precedent in 60 years of All-America tradition," Fay wrote admiringly. The magazine honored Doak's wish but still put him and Norma on its cover and saluted Walker as "Player of the Year—for Sportsmanship."

The Boston (soon to be New York) Bulldogs drafted Walker as a junior in 1948, as did the Cleveland Browns of the All-America Football Conference (AAFC). Alvin "Bo" McMillan, coach and general manager of the Detroit Lions, traded halfback Johnny Rauch to the Bulldogs for Walker's rights. Although he hadn't finished his college eligibility, Doak was free to play in the NFL because of his year in the army. McMillan twice brought Walker to Detroit in 1949—once for a boosters banquet in February and then to host a kids' clinic in August—in bald attempts to get him to sign a contract.

Walker, described as "a refreshing combination of naivete and sophistication," knew to keep his options in pro football open. He completed his senior year at SMU. But his hopes of a bidding war between Detroit and Cleveland for his services evaporated when the two leagues agreed to merge in December 1949. NFL commissioner Bert Bell instructed teams to arbitrate any conflicting player claims or they would be resolved by a coin flip.

On January 21, 1950, McMillan gave Cleveland coach Paul Brown a second-round draft pick in exchange for the exclusive rights to Walker. One month later, Doak signed a three-year deal to play for the Lions. Ewell Sr. initially was against his son playing anywhere on Sunday, but he came around.

"The way my father rationalized it in his own mind," said Doak, "was that people who attended football games on Sunday could be doing a lot worse things. That was his analysis of pro football—good, clean family entertainment, especially if his son was playing."

At the same time that Walker was finishing his college career, Layne was wrapping up his second NFL season. The Chicago Bears had acquired his rights from Pittsburgh and made him their top pick in the 1948 draft. Bears owner and coach George Halas really didn't have a spot for a third quarterback, not with old pro Sid Luckman and rookie Johnny Lujack already on the roster, and so Layne spent most of the '48 season on the bench. After the season, Halas reluctantly sent Layne to the New York Bulldogs for $50,000 and two first-round draft picks. Halas was to receive the money in four annual installments of $12,500. It was widely seen as a steal for Halas, but he always rued the deal. Within three years Luckman and Lujack both retired, leaving Halas with a nagging case of what-might-have-been.

The 1949 Bulldogs were horrible, winning only once all year. Layne took a pounding. "Nobody can pass when they're on the seat of their pants," he said, "and I'd never been hit so hard and so often." Layne opened the season at a solid 205 pounds and went home to Texas a 175-pound rag doll, but not before first impressing McMillan with his performance in a late-season game at Briggs Stadium. On December 4, 1949, Layne carved up a well-regarded Detroit secondary with 25 completions and three touchdown passes as the Bulldogs dropped a one-point decision, 28–27.

McMillan saw something he wasn't finding in his quarterbacking carousel of Fred Enke, Frank Tripucka, and Clyde LeForce. McMillan was close friends with Marty Bell, and Walker's college coach helped sell McMillan on the idea of reuniting Doak and Layne in the Detroit backfield.

In early April 1950, McMillan traded veteran fullback Camp Wilson to the Bulldogs for Layne. Wilson announced he would retire rather than move to New York, but the Bulldogs were willing to take a player to be named later. The heart of the deal was the Lions' agreement to take over the two remaining payments the cash-strapped Bulldogs still owed Halas.

"The board of directors didn't want Layne here," recalled Nick Kerbawy, the gregarious one-time Lansing schoolteacher whom McMillan hired in 1948 to handle publicity for the team. "The owners jumped all over Bo. But he reached into his pocket, pulled out his contract, and laid it on the table. He never said another word, but the owners knew what he meant. They gave in. That's how we got Bobby Layne."

"It was a great day when I heard the news," Walker said. "Bobby and I always had hoped to play together again but it hadn't worked out in college. I don't know who was more tickled about the Detroit deal, Bobby or me." Layne was at a basketball game in Austin when he got the phone call telling him he was going to the Lions. "Naturally, I was happy to know Doak and I would play together in Detroit," he recalled. "It would be a fresh start with a club which wanted a championship team."

In time, Walker and Layne would be referred to as "the terrible Texans" in the sporting press for the way they wrecked their opponents around the NFL. For now they were just two high-profile members of what were the terrible Lions.

When Layne and Walker came to the Lions in 1950, "Dynamic Detroit" ranked among the great cities of the nation. At the time, there were only four more populous—New York, Chicago, Philadelphia, and Los Angeles—and none more industrious. Approaching its postwar peak of nearly two million residents, Detroit was a thriving, historically important riverfront community with many fine schools, hospitals, churches, shops, restaurants, parks, and private clubs, ringed by leafy and desirable suburbs. At its core, it remained a lunch-bucket town. "It not only makes automobiles," the *New York Times* observed when the city celebrated its 250th birthday in 1951, "it lives, breathes, and feels automobiles, and as such is the only place in the world where a man in a bar can hear two other men passionately arguing about carburetors or gear ratios or the fuel consumption of an engine."

Some 300,000 Detroiters worked in manufacturing, many in low-skilled but decent-paying jobs. Detroit Diesel, Ford Rouge, Pontiac Motors, Kelsey-Hayes, Chrysler Stamping, Timken Axle, Fisher Body, Dodge Main, Kelvinator, Congress Tool & Die, Briggs Manufacturing, McLouth Steel, Hudson Motor, Chevy Gear & Axle, Great Lakes Steel, and the 3.5-million-square-foot Packard factory complex on East Grand Boulevard were just a few of the plants meeting weekly payrolls. At the midpoint of the American Century, the minimum wage was 75 cents an hour, the average annual salary for all workers was $3,800, and nearly half of all men 65 years and older were still in the workforce. Only 6 percent of the population had a bachelor's degree (compared to 35 percent today). A twenty-something pro gridder making eight or ten thousand dollars for five months' work, with a college diploma and valuable connections to fall back on, was someone to be envied.

The Detroit Football Company, owners of the Detroit Lions, had industrialists, attorneys, and financiers on its roster of stockholders, including members of the locally prominent Briggs, Fisher, and Ford families. The syndicate had been formed by seven sportsmen in January 1948 to buy the floundering Lions franchise from Chicago department store tycoon Fred Mandel, who had bought it from the original owner, WJR radio magnate G. A. "Dick" Richards, just before the war. By 1954, there were 141 shareholders. Some saw the team as a plaything they could show off to friends. Others regarded their investment as being more of a civic obligation, though of course nobody wanted to lose money on the endeavor.

The Detroit Football Company was managed by a 12-man board of directors headed by an unpaid team president. Some of the original and long-serving directors were Ernest Kanzler, Edsel Ford's brother-in-law; future U.S. senator

Philip Hart, the team's general counsel until becoming Michigan's lieutenant governor in 1955; and D. Lyle Fife, owner of the electrical supply firm bearing his name.

Fife was named Lions president in 1948, but he resigned the following year after a messy divorce and subsequent marriage to his mistress. In the tightly knit social circles in which the hard-partying Fife and his contemporaries moved, it wasn't the fact that he stepped out on his wife of many years that was the problem. After all, many powerful men kept rooms in the city for that purpose. The problem was that his indiscretions were public and directors had to constantly hear about "that other woman" from their wives. Battle lines were drawn at cocktail parties, garden teas, and country clubs in Grosse Pointe, Bloomfield Hills, and Palm Beach. Appearances were everything in society. It was rumored that the man who replaced Fife as Lions president, Edwin J. "Andy" Anderson, once engineered the trade of a long-time Lions starter when the lineman began seeing his opera-loving youngest daughter.

Anderson, a nattily dressed man known for his remarkably furry eyebrows and feathered Alpine hats, was president of the Goebel Brewery Company of Detroit. He understood football, having centered the Beloit College team with distinction in the mid-1920s. He always tried to keep an even keel, in business, sports, and the many civic activities he and his socialite wife, Sunny, were involved in. Whenever he felt his blood pressure begin to climb he would excuse himself, go to the washroom, undo his cuffs, and run cold water over both wrists. Plenty of cold water flowed during Anderson's tenure as Lions president, as there was regular infighting between the faction of shareholders who supported him and the smaller group backing Fife.

Bo McMillan was asked to take over the moribund Lions and turn the franchise around. The folksy, soft-spoken Texan, a former three-time All-American quarterback at Centre College in Kentucky, had experienced great success as a college coach and enjoyed what amounted to a lifetime job at Indiana University, where he also was athletic director. Bo was a football legend, often described as the best after-dinner speaker in the country. In February 1948, the lure of a new challenge and the security of a guaranteed five-year contract at a reported $30,000 per year enticed him to leave Indiana for the dual position of coach and general manager of the Lions.

McMillan said it would take three years before he could stock the team with the players he wanted and begin to make it competitive again. The Lions posted a 2–10 record his first season, followed by a 4–8 mark in 1949. Attendance was dreadful, fans were loudly impatient, the team was losing money, and owners were antsy. Nonetheless, McMillan stressed staying the course. Progress had been incremental, but better times were ahead, he promised, thanks to an influx of new talent for the 1950 season.

In addition to acquiring Walker and Layne, McMillan had already landed Leon Hart, one of the most publicized players of the postwar era. Hart, co-captain of Notre Dame's national championship squad, had just won the Heisman and Maxwell trophies and was voted "Athlete of the Year" by the Associated Press. In fact, McMillan, who seemed to be everywhere and know everybody, was the man who presented Hart with the Heisman in New York.

In the 1949 NFL draft, Hart was selected as the "bonus" choice—an annual lottery, created to inject some excitement into otherwise drab proceedings, that this time was won by the Lions. McMillan was ecstatic about getting college football's "superman." During Hart's four years with Frank Leahy's "Fighting Irish," Notre Dame was undefeated and won three national titles. Lining up at left end on offense, Hart was the ideal target for the short, high passes that kept drives going, often rumbling for impressive yardage after making the catch. Working at right end on defense, he simply overwhelmed blockers and backs. Given that the average 18-year-old boy in 1950 was 5-foot-7, Hart's size was enormous for the era. The Polish Catholic kid from Turtle Creek, Pennsylvania, was 6-foot-5 and roughly 265 pounds, with gunboat feet.

In contrast to Layne, who never bothered to take the one science class he needed to get his diploma, Hart studiously maintained an 85 average in his coursework in mechanical engineering. "A lot of college stars show up in our camp waving their newspaper clippings," one member of Detroit's staff said when Hart reported for training. "Hart isn't like that. He is cooperative, anxious to learn, and a good sport. He's going to be all right."

Lions' owners were hoping their investment would grow into something more than "all right." Before organizing the Detroit Football Company in 1948, several of the syndicate's members had explored the idea of obtaining a local franchise in the AAFC, with serious talk at one point of relocating the Chicago Hornets to Detroit. The AAFC, which had teams in several cities in direct competition with established NFL clubs, began play with eight teams in 1946 and offered fans an exciting, entertaining brand of football. But the spiraling cost of vying for players, plus the competitive imbalance of the AAFC (the Cleveland

Browns won the championship in each of the league's four seasons), drove owners to finally agree to a peace agreement that would merge the rival leagues into one truly national pro circuit.

When owners from both leagues assembled in January 1950 to discuss restructuring, they sought to place teams that had a "natural rivalry" in the same conference, where they would play each other twice each season. Although as sports towns Detroit and Cleveland had a healthy rivalry dating back decades, particularly in baseball, the teams were placed in separate conferences and weren't scheduled to meet in the regular season until 1952. However, they would meet annually in the preseason—and, as it turned out, regularly in the postseason.

The reconstituted NFL (which awkwardly tried calling itself the National-American Football League before finally dropping the name change in March 1950) grew from 10 to 13 clubs by taking in three former AAFC teams: Cleveland, Baltimore, and San Francisco. The Western Division, which the Lions had played in since joining the league in 1934, was renamed the National Conference. The Eastern Division was now called the American Conference. The league would shrink by one club starting with the 1951 season. From that point through the end of the decade the NFL would be a 12-team circuit playing a 12-game schedule, though the final roster of franchises wasn't stabilized until 1953.

With Layne, Walker, and Hart, McMillan was building, brick by brick, the foundation of a competitive club. Observers around the league were taking note. "Detroit is sure to have its strongest team in many years," George Halas said. The bricklaying continued as the NFL held a dispersal draft of former AAFC players in June 1950. Lions history to this point was filled with such phonetic challenges as Emil Uremovich, Sam Tsoutsouvas, Ivan "Buzz" Trebotich, and Alex Wojciechowicz, surnames seemingly assembled from a spilled sack of Scrabble tiles. (Indeed, Wojciechowicz was known as "the 13-letter man.") To these could now be added the names of John Prchlik and Bob Hoernschemeyer.

Prchlik, the son of Czech immigrants, was a brainy 235-pound Cleveland native and the only accordion-playing tackle from Yale in pro ball. He was one of three Lions (tackle Gus Cifelli and end Cloyce Box were the others) working on his law degree, often bringing thick books to study on road trips. Hoernschemeyer, a multisports prep star at Cincinnati's Elder High, preferred smacking the line to hitting the books. As a 17-year-old tailback playing for McMillan at Indiana in 1943, he set a long-standing single-game NCAA record for freshmen with six touchdown passes and 458 yards of total offense against Nebraska. After flunking out of the Naval Academy, he turned pro with the Chicago Rockets in 1946 and later played with the Brooklyn Dodgers, leaving the AAFC as its all-time leader in combined rushing and passing yardage.

Hoernschemeyer ("as good as his name is long," said one Chicago sportswriter) was nicknamed "Hunchy." His moniker actually was a corruption of his surname, but it also referenced his hunched-over, battering-ram running style. A shade under six feet, and weighing about 190 pounds, Hoernschemeyer usually played right halfback with the Lions but often lined up at fullback. He was arguably the best third-down back in the league in the early '50s. Need two tough yards? Give the ball to Hunchy. Hoernschemeyer piled up first downs and concussions. His relatively early death—he was 54 when he lost a two-year bout to cancer—likely spared him from the fate of many of his brain-traumatized contemporaries, who grew old no longer recognizing their own children.

"I think we had the best backfield in the league," Hoernschemeyer once said of the six seasons he, Walker, and Layne spent together, "because Doak could throw running one way and I could throw running the other way on the option run-pass. Bobby gave it hell. That put a little bit of stress on the defense." Hoernschemeyer would prove deadly on the halfback option, with all but one of his 11 completions as a Lion going for touchdowns.

In late July, the Lions opened camp at Michigan Normal College in Ypsilanti, eight miles outside Ann Arbor and 35 miles west of Detroit. Known today as Eastern Michigan University, the teachers college had an enrollment of 2,600 students in 1950. The Lions utilized four practice fields and a fieldhouse donated by industrialist Walter O. Briggs Sr. Players bunked in a dormitory and hiked a half mile over a steep hill to and from practice.

McMillan's new quarterback impressed from the get-go. "A slim, blond gridder from Texas has commanded the attention of football observers at the Detroit Lions' training camp at Michigan Normal College," Bob Latshaw wrote in the *Detroit Free Press*. "Practice has just begun, but Bobby Layne left little doubt that he was a 'major leaguer' during the first workouts. Handling the ball expertly as a T-quarterback, Layne's accurate passing and 'take charge' ability that's necessary for a good quarterback were immediately apparent. Coaches are reluctant to pass judgment on players early, but the Lions' staff is elated over the way Layne moved in."

Walker needed to make a slight adjustment to life in the pay-for-play league. "Playing with the Lions wasn't that much of a change for me, as far as football went," Doak once reflected, "but it was a big change as far as the players' attitude was concerned. I'd walk into the locker room after a practice, and people would be sitting around smoking and having a beer. That was a very different atmosphere from the one I was accustomed to."

Layne had enjoyed his taste of the nightlife during his time in Chicago and New York, and he immediately started sampling what his new surroundings had to offer. Halfback Wally Triplett, the only black player on the Lions, explored some of Detroit's many jazz clubs with Layne. "Bobby would put a hundred-dollar bill on the bar and tell the waitress, 'When you use it up, call me a cab,'" Triplett said.

John "Pep" Panelli, a second-year fullback and linebacker out of Notre Dame, was Layne's roommate in training camp and an occasional carousing companion. "He did like to have his fun," Panelli said. One Sunday after a game, he and Layne went to a club where Layne kept the band playing until well past closing. It was about four in the morning when Panelli suggested they leave so they could get some rest.

"Yeah," said Layne, thinking of the band. "Let them get some rest."

To Panelli, his new teammate's competitiveness was as impressive as his endurance. "I never met a person in my life more competitive," he said. "He was naturally that way on the field but also at just about anything. We'd play golf during training camp between the morning and afternoon sessions and he'd always have to bet a buck or two. I might win in golf but he'd come back at me in gin rummy and get his money back."

On August 19 at Pittsburgh's Forbes Field, Layne and Walker performed as Detroit teammates for the first time. The game was tough, but the flight to Pittsburgh was a gut-wrenching ordeal. Several Lions emptied their stomachs as the chartered airliner flew almost the entire way through a violent electrical storm. Perhaps the air-sickness affected the rookies' play, as Walker and Leon Hart "appeared baffled as they made their pro debuts," reported United Press. "The Steelers constantly throttled the Lions' passing attack except in the final period when Johnny Greene snagged Bobby Layne's pass. The play covered 76 yards." The Steelers won the Saturday night game, 17–14.

The following Friday evening in Akron, Ohio, the Cleveland Browns thoroughly outclassed McMillan's rookie-laden lineup, 35–14. The score wasn't indicative of how badly Detroit was outplayed. It took only two plays for Otto Graham to quarterback the Browns to their first touchdown, and only 10 minutes for Paul Brown's veterans to amass a 21–0 lead.

The Lions finally began to jell a bit in their third exhibition, a four-point loss to the Redskins before 50,000 fans in the Cotton Bowl. At home in familiar surroundings, Doak Walker, the "Pride of Dallas," grabbed a half dozen passes for 123 yards from Layne, who missed on only one of his 15 throws while finding a third Texan, Cloyce Box, for two touchdowns. A fourth straight loss followed, this time a smack-down by Philadelphia, the defending NFL champions.

To the immense relief of Layne, who took defeat harder than anybody in the clubhouse, the Lions finally broke into the win column in their last exhibition, beating the Chicago Cardinals in Birmingham, Alabama. Even then, the perennial last-place Lions couldn't seem to escape the cellar. A hotel elevator returning a dozen players to their rooms after their pregame meal slipped its cable and plunged four floors into the basement, an experience as memorably harrowing as the stormy flight to Pittsburgh three weeks earlier. The Lions couldn't wait to leave Birmingham. The night before, thieves with a pass key quietly entered several rooms and stole more than $1,000 from sleeping players and coaches.

After an especially eventful preseason, the 1950 edition of the Detroit Lions launched the regular season on September 17 in Green Bay. There were 21 newcomers on the roster, and practically every last one of them had a hand in the 45–7 thrashing of the Packers. In his first outing as a Lion that officially counted, Layne hit on 10 of 18 passes for 232 yards, including a 50-yard touchdown pitch to Box, as the Lions matched a franchise high for points scored. It was the first time Detroit had won in Wisconsin in a full decade. Walker broke in with a paltry two yards on two carries but gained 85 yards on three receptions, fumbling after one catch into the end zone where teammate Johnny Greene recovered for a touchdown. Packers quarterback Tobin Rote started and had a subpar showing in his pro debut. But it was nowhere near as disastrous as fellow rookie Tom O'Malley, who completed four of 15 passes and threw six interceptions in his first—and last—NFL game.

Heavy rain turned the pigskin into a greased bladder. The teams combined for nine fumbles and eight interceptions, with the Lions returning two bobbles and one pick for touchdowns in the slop. The extra-long cleats the Lions wore for better footing affected Walker's placekicking. He missed three of his first four extra-point attempts, twice hitting the crossbar. After that disastrous start, he wouldn't miss another conversion the rest of the season.

"We may not win the championship," McMillan declared after the game, "but we'll be knocking at the door." Hart remembered the rout as hardly being an endorsement of McMillan's confusing and complicated offense. "We won that game on sheer talent, not the system."

The Lions hosted the Steelers the following week at the University of Detroit's Dinan Field, the Lions' original home for their first four seasons and backup venue when Briggs Stadium was booked. The Detroit defense yielded just one first down in the opening half, but the game remained scoreless at intermission. Pittsburgh opened a 7–0 lead in the third quarter. Layne, "the T-formation quarterback with the itchy feet," piled up yardage all afternoon, gaining 118 yards on 15 carries.

But it was Walker who stole the show. He rushed 16 times for 87 yards, including a 28-yard scamper off a fake punt. In the fourth quarter he made a spectacular scoring catch of a Layne pass, then tacked on the conversion to tie the game at 7–7. In the closing minutes, he punted deep into Pittsburgh territory. The return man fumbled, the Lions recovered, and shortly thereafter Walker kicked the game-winning field goal. All in a day's work for "the fabulous Doak Walker."

The undefeated Lions next played the New York Yanks in a Friday night contest at the Polo Grounds. McMillan was engaged in the classic undersell, but *New York Times* columnist Arthur Daley wasn't buying it. "Bo is a benevolent-appearing gentleman with snow-white hair and an innocent face," Daley wrote in his "Sports of *The Times*" column.

He inspires trust and confidence. What is more, he could charm a bird out of a tree. When McMillan coached at Indiana University and was winning laurels as the Coach of the Year, he used to moan in his beguiling Southern drawl about "mah pore lil' boys." His poor little boys murdered everyone. Now he is coaching the Lions and hasn't changed his tune one bit. . . .

But when Bo starts to give that pore-lil'-boys spiel about Detroit, it's time to holler, "Whoa!" Let's start with Leon Hart, the mastodon from Notre Dame. A year ago the college authorities chopped some twenty pounds off his actual weight just so he wouldn't scare foes in advance. But the 6-foot-4-inch giant has gotten even bigger. When he stepped on the scales at the All-Star camp, the beam shuddered to a halt at 282 pounds. Pore lil' boy, eh? Other midgets operating under the McMillan aegis are Lou Creekmur, 240 pounds; Thurman McGraw, 235, and Joe Watson, also 235. What's that again, Bo?

But the big guy on the Lions is Doak Walker, the magazine cover boy from Southern Methodist University and the All-America everything. He weighs a stunning 173 pounds. But he's a mighty handy man to have on the premises. . . . The ex-Mustang is not flashy but he's solid and it's his sturdy consistency which does the damage. The Lions are owned by a syndicate of millionaires and they may very well be the "sleeper" in their division.

In his rundown of Detroit's heft, Daley inexplicably left out the ground-tilting poundage of middle guard Les Bingaman, who was parked like a stalled DeSoto in the center of Detroit's defensive line. "Bingo," now in his third pro season, was the largest man in the game. His chest measured 55 inches and his waist was 50 inches. His exact weight was a mystery because the Lions didn't have a scale that registered more than 300 pounds. As the stale joke went, he simply was a "Big-a-man."

"There never has been another pro lineman shaped quite like the elliptical Bingaman," Bill Fay marveled in *Collier's*. "He stands six feet three inches tall and measures four feet two inches around the waist. Among the myriad and highly mobile offensive and defensive specialists populating pro line-ups, Bingo enjoys a truly unique distinction—he's the only player in the National Football League who specialized in not moving. Instead of charging across the scrimmage line, Bingo squats and waits. When blockers approach, he cuffs them aside with large and suety fists, or just takes a deep breath and throws his stomach at them. Either way, the bodies pile up around Bingo like corpses in a Mickey Spillane novel. The resultant congestion makes Bingo's sector virtually invulnerable to forays by enemy ball carriers."

"A great player, with a brilliant football mind," Walker said of Bingaman. "And for five yards, as fast as anyone on the field. He was a great help to me when I first came up, and I learned a lot from him. He would get down in the line and tell guys to move left or move right, and they would. When he got 'em all situated, they were usually in the right place to stop the play."

Some veterans, resentful of Walker's publicity, were a little rough at first, but Bingaman was generous. "He's the one who told me that you could always tell whether I was running to the right or left because my knuckles turned white when I lined up in a certain stance," Doak said. "So I changed my stance."

Bingaman, one of the hardest-working players on the team, wasn't always that forthcoming. He grew up in Tennessee, a product of the Great Depression, and later starred at the University of Illinois. His father, also of imposing size, had died in an accident when Les was five, so he learned early to never take anything for granted. He arrived in camp every summer terrified he would lose his job.

"In one preseason scrimmage," said Layne, "he was breaking up every play I tried to run. He seemed to know exactly what was coming." Bingaman and Layne were close friends—they called each other "Slim"—but all the big guard would tell Bobby afterward was that a rookie back was inadvertently tipping off the plays.

"Look, tell me what he's doing," Layne said. "It might help straighten out the offense."

"Oh, no," said Bingaman, shaking his head. "Not until they make the final squad cut. Then I'll tell you."

Playing alongside Bingaman was McGraw, a 6-foot-4 tackle nicknamed "Fum" (a childhood mispronunciation of Thurman), who was McMillan's second-round choice out of Colorado A&M. McGraw used the strength and agility he had developed as a wrestler to ward off blockers and blow up plays. McGraw grew up on a ranch in western Colorado and was said to have once wrestled a horse to the ground. He denied it. "I was shoeing the darned thing," he explained. "I guess I lifted his leg a little too high and the next thing I knew it was flat on its back."

Creekmur, from the College of William & Mary, was picked up in the AAFC dispersal draft. He lined up at guard on offense his first two years in Detroit and often played tackle on defense, typically in short-yardage and goal-line situations. Creekmur and McGraw both impressed as rookies and were selected to play in the inaugural Pro Bowl at the end of the season.

After getting drubbed by the Yanks, 44–21, for their first loss of the season, the Lions returned home to beat San Francisco, 24–7. It was the third time in four outings that the defense had limited the opposition to a single score. Two members of the secondary, cornerback Bob Smith and safety Don Doll, were due praise for their work. Smith, a hard-nosed Texan, was a fine pass defender, powerful tackler, and first-rate punter, though he split his kicking duties with Walker in 1950. The previous season, Smith had corralled nine enemy passes, including a 102-yard return of a Sid Luckman throw on Thanksgiving Day that was the longest in NFL history.

Doll, a Sacramento native who starred at Southern Cal, had 11 interceptions as a Lions rookie in 1949. That year he set a league record with 301 yards on interception returns and also led the loop in kickoff return yardage. The smallish back detailed how he handled bigger men bearing down on him: "I just throw a shoulder into 'em and hit 'em low. If they are over two tons I aim for their shoelaces." Doll would have a tremendous season in 1950, picking off a dozen passes, one short of the NFL record, and being named First Team All-Pro for the second straight year.

Excitement was building as local sports fans, who had just watched the Tigers finish three games behind the Yankees in a doozy of a pennant race, shifted their attention from baseball to football. The Lions' unaccustomed spot at the top of the standings resulted in the largest home crowd in three years coming out to see the Lions play the Los Angeles Rams on October 15. Thirty-three thousand got their money's worth, as the lead changed hands six times. The Lions were ahead by a point when Bob Waterfield, who always did well against the Lions, booted a 10-yard field goal near the end to give Los Angeles a 30–28 victory.

The Lions next took the long flight to California, where across two Sundays they experienced the extremes of losing, from heartbreak to humiliation. At San Francisco, a missed extra point by Layne, who had assumed kicking chores after Walker injured his ankle during the game, was the difference in a 28–27 loss to the previously winless 49ers. At Los Angeles, the Rams annihilated the Lions, 65–24. "I was looking for a place to hide," Leon Hart admitted years later. "Having never known defeat in four years at Notre Dame, it kind of shakes you up a little."

It actually could have been worse. The high-octane Rams, who a week earlier had scored 70 points against Baltimore, posted 41 points against the Lions in the third quarter alone before easing off the gas. The demoralized Lions returned home to drop a 35–21 decision to the Bears, despite Layne's club-record 374 yards through the air.

Detroit fans focused their derision on the usual suspects, the head coach and the quarterback, though the blame for the Lions' swoon could be laid at the feet of many. The offensive line often broke down, putting Layne in jeopardy. However, the quarterback admitted to having a soft spot for Chet Bulger, an eight-year veteran playing out the string with one final season in Detroit.

"Bulger was banged up in both legs and couldn't bend his left knee," he recalled. "But if Chet could get near you he would block you, and if he couldn't block you he would grab you. And he was the most polite tackle in the league. He played on the left side of the line, which is the blind side for a right-handed quarterback. If somebody breaks through a guy can get killed. But Bulger wasn't about to let them kill me. When I was back to pass and heard him shout, 'Look out, Bobby!' I knew that someone was coming and I had time to duck."

With the club reeling, a rebellion brewed in the ranks. There was a growing lack of respect for McMillan and a widening gulf between him and his three assistants, Aldo Forte, George Wilson, and Buddy Parker. The major issue was McMillan's playbook. The offense was a cumbersome hybrid of the Split-T and single wing, with numbered plays that bore no relation to each other. "We all knew we had good personnel," Hart said. "But the system was killing us."

Another complaint was McMillan's authoritative manner, which worked well enough with teenagers on campus but irked worldly veterans. Layne's biggest gripe was McMillan calling plays from the bench, an impossible restraint on his playmaking. "I have to feel I'm on my own to get the job done," the quarterback protested. There was no allowance in McMillan's system for changing a play at the line of scrimmage. Said Hart: "I remember asking Coach McMillan, 'How are we calling audibles?' He said, 'What's an audible?' I couldn't believe it."

Despite his issues with McMillan as a coach, Hart regarded him as a fine man who had the best interests of his players at heart. "Bo was a wonderful guy," he said. "I signed for $15,000 and got a $3,000 bonus. I thought that was all the money in the world. I remember my wife was expecting our first child. We had a two-room apartment at the Lee Plaza. I didn't like it at all.

"So we decided we'd try to buy a house. I didn't have any money yet, so I had to get an advance. I saw Bo and asked him for a $5,000 advance to use as a down payment. He said, 'I can't think of a better reason to give you an advance.' So he did, and we were able to buy a house at Seven Mile and Schaefer, on Hartwell Street. It was a side-door colonial that was very comfortable for the first couple of years."

After losing four in a row, the streaky Lions then went on a three-game tear, averaging 39 points per game in beating the Packers, Yanks, and Colts. In the 24–21 win over the Packers, Walker accounted for every point with three touchdown receptions, a field goal, and three conversions. He scored the winning touchdown on an 8-yard pass from Fred Enke in the final minutes. One Detroit paper called it "a typical Doak Walker day."

Walker was impressing every team he went up against, putting to rest criticism that he was too small to handle the bigger brutes of the NFL. The Doaker would end the year with 128 points on 11 touchdowns, 38 extra points, and eight field goals. His total led all scorers and was just 10 shy of Packers great Don Hutson's all-time record.

"Doak Walker is my ideal of the perfect physical specimen," said Dan Towler of the Rams. "He is just like a rubber band. Regardless of how they pound him or stretch him, he always pops right back up in there at his very best." The NFL fielded 108 rookies in 1950, but it was Walker who added the Associated Press's Rookie of the Year award to his lengthening list of laurels. He also was named a First Team All-Pro by every newspaper and wire service.

On Thanksgiving Day, the Lions continued to set club records, this time for points and yardage, in a 49–14 rubout of the Yanks. The two clubs combined for 1,032 yards of total offense, with Detroit getting 591 of them. To the delight of the midsized crowd and the limited number of viewers watching "video" over the fledgling ABC network (Red Grange and Joe Hasel called the action), players flew up and down the field, with Hoernschemeyer flying the farthest.

In the fourth quarter, Hunchy took off running from the Detroit 4-yard line and didn't stop motoring until he had reached New York's end zone. To this day, no Lions back has surpassed Hoernschemeyer's 96-yard sprint. Overall, he picked up 198 yards on the ground against the Yanks, erasing Dutch Clark's previous franchise high of 194. On the day, Detroit rushed for a team-record 377 yards and four touchdowns.

Cloyce Box, a 6-foot-4, 220-pounder from West Texas State whom McMillan had purchased from Washington for $250, had a breakout game against the Yanks. He caught four passes for 123 yards, with three of them going for touchdowns, including a 65-yarder. At 27, Box was in his second season with the Lions, having lost several years to wartime service.

"I probably was the worst halfback in the history of the league," he said of his rookie season, a year in which he won most of the wind sprints and "generally just fooled around." He averaged just two yards a rush in limited duty in Detroit's backfield in 1949 and was even less impressive on defense. But as a receiver he showed great promise with his size, speed, and flypaper fingers.

McMillan's assistant, former Bears end George Wilson, helped convert Box, a prep hoops star who hadn't played his first football game until he was 18, into one of the game's most dangerous receivers.

"I was just about the first real wide receiver—at least the way you'd think of them now," Box recalled. "The game was just opening up, but there still wasn't all that much to it. I'd run the same pattern just about every time. I wasn't that skilled a player, but I was fast. Back then, that was about all you really needed to get by."

Box followed up his three-touchdown day against the Yanks with one of the most awesome single-game performances ever turned in by an NFL receiver. On December 3 at Baltimore, he grabbed 12 passes for 302 yards, just one yard under the league record, as the Lions rolled to a 45–21 victory. Four of the receptions went for touchdowns, covering 81, 67, 42, and 22 yards. Box's 50 receptions and 1,009 receiving yards in 1950 would be the most of any Lions receiver during the decade. The tallies gave him 11 touchdowns for the year, the same as Walker. Both men tied Bill Dudley's team mark for six-pointers.

The Lions' modest winning streak temporarily silenced some critics. But McMillan continued to struggle for respect, even from youngsters. One bitterly cold afternoon toward the end of the season, he had the team out for three hours at Jayne Field, a public park on the Hamtramck border that the team used for practice. A group of kids impatiently waited for the practice to end so they could flood the field and go ice skating. Finally, one of them got a hose and started spraying the ground.

"Get off the field," McMillan ordered. "Can't you see we're practicing?"

"You guys have had enough practice the way you play," the kid retorted. "Why don't you let us have some fun before the players freeze to death."

The Lions went into their finale at Wrigley Field needing at least a tie to post their first winning season since the end of the war. The Bears needed a win to keep pace with the first-place Rams. Playing on a slippery field, the Lions were held without a touchdown for the first time all season, with George Blanda's fourth-quarter field goal providing the difference in Chicago's 6–3 victory. The following Sunday, in a pair of divisional playoffs, the Rams beat the Bears, 24–14, and Cleveland edged the New York Giants, 8–3, to advance to the championship game. On a bone-chilling Christmas Eve in Cleveland, the Browns won the title, 30–28, on Lou Groza's last-minute field goal.

The loss to the Bears left the Lions with a final 6–6 record. They had started and finished strong, but the four-game sag in the middle had ruined the season.

Nonetheless, there were solid grounds for optimism. The victory total matched that of McMillan's first two seasons combined, and there was a nucleus of young, talented players in place. Layne, Walker, Hoernschemeyer, and Box had rewritten the Lions' record book in almost every single-game and single-season category while rookies Hart, Creekmur, and McGraw had impressed on both sides of the line. The club was progressing according to McMillan's timetable. Bo's squad was on the verge of achieving something great, but the man who deserved a good share of the credit wouldn't be around to see it.

CHAPTER

2

———

WE CAN *Win* WITH *Parker*

We know that Buddy is a championship coach. He puts as much work into a season as most people do in three. We saw him work with the Cards. . . . If a coach was ever a winner, he is.

—Pat Harder, 1951

Bo McMillan was a goner, in every sense of the word. During the last half of the 1950 season, a cabal of disgruntled players and disillusioned directors agitated behind the scenes for his dismissal, with even his assistants questioning whether they could continue working for him. At the same time, rogue cells were silently proliferating inside the beleaguered coach's body. Fifteen months after leaving Detroit, McMillan would be dead.

The Lions' first .500 season since 1945 wasn't enough to save McMillan's job. On the evening of December 11, 1950, the day after the finale against the Bears, eight directors gathered at the Detroit Athletic Club and unanimously agreed to seek his resignation. Word of the secret meeting leaked out, but nothing could be decided until Edwin Anderson returned from California a few days later to iron out the legal and financial wrinkles. Anderson, who had become close friends with McMillan, later said that it took him three and a half hours to fire the coach, who kept repeating, "You can't do this to me."

Anderson assured Bo that he would be paid for the remaining two years of his contract, as well as any money due him from broadcasting gigs and other work—a total amount in the range of $60,000 to $70,000. Bitter over his ouster but satisfied with his severance (the equivalent of more than $600,000 in today's dollars), McMillan announced at a press conference on December 19 that he was stepping down as head coach and general manager.

"It is difficult to do your best work when members of your own official family are sniping at you all the time," he told reporters, adding that he had no apologies for the Lions' showing.

"We lost three tough close games which actually meant the difference between our 6–6 record and playing Cleveland next Sunday for the title. Six points was the total spread in those three games. We lost to Los Angeles by two, we lost to the Chicago Bears by three, and we lost to San Francisco by one. If we had won those three games, we would have been divisional champions. That's how close we came. It has been stated that I had the best material in the league this year. That is ridiculous. We had some fine boys, but most of them were brand new to pro ball. They still have to reach their peak of effectiveness."

Two weeks after McMillan quit, Bobby Layne admitted to being one of the dissenters behind his ouster. Doak Walker, Cloyce Box, Leon Hart, and Johnny Greene had also privately huddled with directors. Layne had told owners he wouldn't play another year under McMillan. Apprised of the quarterback's comments (which Layne later denied making), McMillan responded that such criticism came with the job. "After all," he said, "we don't go out on the football field to make love."

Asked for their opinion of who should replace Bo, the players endorsed his top assistant. We can win with Buddy Parker, they said.

Raymond K. "Buddy" Parker was at home in Kemp, Texas, where he operated a lumber yard with his father, when Anderson phoned him the day after McMillan quit. "I'm tickled to death to get the job," said Parker, who agreed to a one-year deal for $12,000. "I'm getting a very fine club to work with." He became the team's ninth head coach in 17 years. Only one had lasted as long as four seasons.

Parker was a solidly built six-footer equipped with a proper Texan's drawl, squint, and rectitude. He had just turned 37, but he'd already been in pro ball for 15 years, his time split between Detroit and the Chicago Cardinals. He first came to the Lions in 1935, an unheralded back out of small Centenary College in Louisiana, and as a rookie helped Detroit win its first NFL title. The Lions beat the New York Giants in the mud and sleet at Dinan Field, 26–7. Parker scored the last touchdown of the game and also intercepted a pass. He was traded to the Cards in 1937 and gradually moved into the coaching ranks.

"Buddy was a great professional coach," Hart said. "He knew how to handle professional athletes. Buddy's philosophy would be summed up as: 'You better shape up or ship out. We hired you to play, so play.' He put in a system that was workable. He had good assistants, all along the line. And they all had the respect of the players because they knew what they were doing."

Parker retained backfield coach George Wilson and line coach Aldo Forte as assistants and hired Earl Brown, who had just been fired after a forgettable three-year stint as head coach at Auburn University, as ends coach. Theirs was a harmonious relationship, more of a co-partnership than a traditional top-down hierarchy. Parker was apt to credit his assistants and players when things went well and take responsibility when they didn't. That said, he expected every man to pull his own weight.

"Buddy never gave halftime speeches," remembered one old Lion. "His way of motivating was, if we weren't playing well, someone would disappear. A backup guy, just to get everyone's attention."

Parker was one of the most superstitious people in all of sports, which was saying something. He made no apologies for his aversion to the number 13. Rooms and seats had to be selected with the greatest care, lest some combination of numbers or letters add up to that number. Once his wife, Jane, came up from Texas to visit him in Chicago. She found a room at the Ridgeland Apartments. It was during the war and housing was in very short supply.

"I naturally thought Buddy would be anxious to see me for the first time in six weeks," she said, "but he refused to come home when I told him we had Room 319. 'Do you want to ruin me?' he yelled over the phone. 'Three and one and nine equal thirteen. Move out or I'll sleep in the park.'" Jane was finally able to calm him down after she had the hotel manager nail a new room number— 711—on the door of their third-floor apartment.

Buddy naturally kept a wary eye on the calendar, and at times it was hard to dismiss his paranoia. It was a fact that within the next couple of seasons, his father would die and Doak Walker would suffer a freak accident that almost ended his career. Both occurred on Friday the 13th.

"This job is a real challenge," Parker said upon taking over coaching duties. He felt the team was a legitimate title contender, but the first step was simplifying . . . everything.

"McMillan knew football backwards and forwards," he said, "but he had play numbers that nobody could get straight except him. Hell, the coaches never could remember what the plays were, much less the quarterback. He had a 'ninety-eight' where the left halfback went into right guard, then he had an 'eighty-seven' where the quarterback threw a pass. Nothing had anything to do with anything. Bo also believed in long practices. He'd have the whole squad out on the field for three or four hours, but half the time he had them standing around him while he told them about football. There were a lot of things I wanted to do some day when I got to be head coach, and short practices, on the field, was at the top of the list."

Reflecting his long-held belief that murdering each other on Wednesday never won a game on Sunday, during the season Parker kept full-contact scrimmaging to a minimum. Practices were limited to 90 minutes, and the drills were conducted briskly. As the season wore on, practices were cut to an hour. "When we're on the field, we run; we do our talking in the clubhouse," he said.

Simplicity would remain Parker's mantra throughout his head-coaching career. He believed you didn't outmaneuver your opponents, you out-blocked and out-tackled them. "The trouble with most coaches is they want to make the game too damn complicated," he said. "You sit at home in your study running the projector, and everything looks great on paper. But the players aren't on paper. They're out on the field, and out on the field you don't have much time."

Parker wanted to win now, and he felt that veterans, generally less prone to making mental mistakes, were the quickest way to achieve that goal. "Buddy liked seasoned pros because he already knew what they could do," Hart said. One of those seasoned pros was Vince Banonis, the first of several former Cardinals Parker would bring to Detroit as players or coaches over the coming seasons.

Banonis, a strapping 6-foot-1 and 220 pounds, was the only Detroit native on the Lions squad. He was one of six children, including five boys, born to Lithuanian immigrants. His father, Pete, worked 45 years in Henry Ford's auto plants. Just a few years after Parker had starred in the NFL title game at Dinan Field, Banonis was covering the same ground as an All-American center and linebacker for the University of Detroit. Banonis was captain of the College All-Stars in their 1942 game against the Chicago Bears.

"That was my biggest thrill," he said. "Being introduced between the goal-posts before 100,000 people at Soldier Field, and then running onto the field." Banonis signed a $2,500 contract with the Cardinals, where his linebacking partner was player-coach Parker. "I had the brawn," he said, "and Buddy had the brains."

Chicago captured back-to-back Western Division titles in 1947–48. The Cardinals won the championship in 1947, beating Philadelphia at icy Comiskey Park, then lost a rematch the following year in a blizzard at Shibe Park. Banonis credited Parker for much of the Cardinals' success. "He was just an assistant coach then and he didn't get much of the glory. But he actually was the brains behind that Chicago team. I know. I played on it."

In 1949, Parker shared head-coaching duties with Phil Handler, and then assumed solo command when Handler quit at midseason. Despite finishing with a winning record, Parker abruptly resigned, frustrated over interference from the front office. In 1950, he came to Detroit as McMillan's assistant. Now he was back to running the whole show again, and he was quick to surround himself with familiar faces.

The Lions needed a fullback. Paul Brown offered to trade him Emerson Cole, his number-two fullback, plus a first-string tackle for Doak Walker. "No, thanks," Buddy told Cleveland's coach. "We're not interested in trading a chocolate cake for two doughnuts."

Just a few days before the regular season opened, Parker sent John Panelli and Detroit's second pick in the 1952 draft to the Cardinals for veteran fullback Pat Harder. The popular Panelli broke down when told of the trade, but Harder was ecstatic. The 29-year-old holdout, who refused to play another season under coach Curly Lambeau, took less money for the opportunity to join Banonis and Parker on the Lions.

"Old Sarge," a nickname that was an acknowledgment of Harder's leadership on the gridiron and a nod to his stint in the Marines during World War II, was as hard-boiled as they come. At the University of Wisconsin, he was the inspiration for the college cheer: "Hit 'em again—Harder, Harder!" He led the NFL in scoring three straight seasons in the late 1940s and was a driving force in the Cards' success. After several grueling pro campaigns he still was a punishing runner and dependable placekicker, despite a watery right knee that constantly gave him trouble. The burly back with the "educated elbows" also was one of the most feared blockers in the league. "When Harder hits a guy and he don't wind up on his back, then Pat needs a rest," Parker said. "He usually murders them."

People around the league were still talking about Harder's devastating hit on Cleveland end Len Ford the previous October. Ford, who had starred at the University of Michigan, had been slugging Cardinals all afternoon when Harder finally decided that enough was enough. "I'm going to teach that fucker a lesson," he announced in the huddle. He told the linemen to purposely let Ford through so he could have a clear shot at him. The ball was snapped, Ford rushed in, and Harder uncoiled from his crouched position and pulverized his antagonist with a perfectly timed elbow to the face. It broke Ford's jaw, shattered both cheekbones, and knocked out six teeth. Ford underwent reconstructive surgery and missed the next nine weeks of the 1950 season.

Sam Greene later assessed the impact of acquiring Harder and Banonis. The pair "helped to inflame the Lions with a winning spirit," Greene wrote in the *Detroit News*. "Infectious was the championship air of the two veterans. They had ridden the crest with the Cardinals and, by conversation and example, they made the young Lions think in title terms."

The other Browns end on the field the day Harder demolished Ford—another rugged ex-Marine named Jim Martin—also was obtained by Parker via trade. Martin's upper left arm sported a souvenir of his wartime service: a large inked image of a dragon pierced by a knife, accompanied by the motto "Death Before Dishonor." Tattoos were a fairly rare sight inside locker rooms then, even with the large number of ex-servicemen, so Martin's body art stood out.

Like Harder and Banonis, Martin was a proven winner. He'd been an integral member of Notre Dame's postwar national champions, starring alongside a couple of his new Lions teammates, Hart and tackle Gus Cifelli. Martin, a prep swimming star in Cleveland and the heavyweight boxing champion of Notre Dame, left his hometown for Detroit, but not before first flattening light-heavyweight champ Joey Maxim in some altercation.

Martin cost Parker his number-one pick in the 1952 draft, but he was still paying dividends more than a decade later. During his 11 seasons with the Lions, the man alternately called "Jarhead" and "Jughead" because of his "*ooh*-rah!" backstory and prominent ears was an all-around handyman, playing nearly every line position on offense and defense as well as linebacker. In addition, Martin handled kickoffs, long-range field goals, and late in his career blossomed into a full-time placekicker. In a 1960 game against Baltimore, the "poor man's Lou Groza" became the first kicker in NFL history to boot two field goals of more than 50 yards in the same game. In 1963, at the age of 39, he came out of retirement to kick a league-leading 24 field goals for the Baltimore Colts. Martin played one final season with Washington before finally retiring for good. A few years later, he served as the special teams coach for the Lions. "He was a low-key guy," remembered tight end Charlie Sanders, "but you didn't want to mess with him."

Banonis, Harder, and Martin gave Parker's young Lions a nucleus of men who knew firsthand what it took to win a pro football title. Two other players on the roster, both plucked out of the AAFC player pool in 1950, had experienced a championship with Cleveland's undefeated 1948 squad, though only one had actually contributed playing time. Fullback Ollie Cline was Marion Motley's backup that season while John Prchlik had drawn a weekly paycheck sitting on the bench the entire time.

Parker's first class of draftees included players who would become integral cogs of the emerging Detroit powerhouse. Jack Christiansen was a sixth-round pick who benefited from Thurman McGraw's vigorous recommendation. They had been teammates at Colorado A&M. Christiansen, whose father died when he was two, grew up in an Oddfellows orphanage in Colorado, after which the organization helped pay his way through school. The stalky Christiansen concentrated on track (he could run the 100-yard dash in 9.6 seconds) and didn't even play football until his junior year of college.

Christiansen was a rarity in that he came to the pros having played defense exclusively in college. Parker was absolutely fine with that. "You can always get someone to run with the ball," he said, "but good defensive backs are hard to find." Although still a raw talent learning the intricacies of pass defense, Christiansen impressed coaches with his blend of intelligence and meanness. "He wouldn't be afraid if he were covering Satan himself," said one Lions assistant.

There also was a matching set of 6-foot-2 ends, Jim Doran and Dorne Dibble. Doran, an Iowa standout, "has everything a receiver needs," Earl Brown said. "He fakes exceptionally well and knows how to run." He also had a knack for stiff-arming tacklers, which had become somewhat of a lost art. For his first couple seasons, though, Doran would line up on the defensive side of the ball, using his long arms and powerful shoulders to become a pesky pass rusher.

Dibble, a native of Adrian and an All-American at Michigan State, was selected in the third round. Although he would see occasional duty in the secondary, Parker decided that his height, excellent hands, and above-average speed made him a bigger threat on offense than defense. Dibble's 30 receptions and six receiving touchdowns would trail only Hart among all Lions in 1951, while his yardage would top the team. Most impressively, his 20.4 yards per catch was bettered only by the great Elroy "Crazylegs" Hirsch in the entire NFL.

"Parker, Doak Walker, and Bobby Layne had lots of patience with me and taught me several things," Dibble remembered. "Walker worked with me after regular practice sessions, teaching me how to feint and fake. Bobby taught me how to handle all kinds of passes, low, high, slow, and fast. Parker was real patient. He took on the job of making me an offensive end, and I gradually caught on." Dibble's progress helped prompt eight-year pro John Greene to retire and accept a position overseeing the team's scouting.

As a fourth-year quarterback, Layne was still an unfinished work. He had fallen into bad habits playing behind the New York Bulldogs' porous line, frequently pulling out too quickly from center in an attempt to avoid the inevitable avalanche of charging linemen. The result was that he rushed every move he made as a passer and a ball handler and often didn't have full possession of the ball. Layne led the league in fumbles in each of his first two years as a starter, 13 as a Bulldog in 1949 and a dozen as a Lion in 1950. Parker called him "the fumblingest quarterback I'd ever seen." "We worked with Layne a lot and managed to slow him down," Buddy said. "We stressed protection for him and then he stopped 'giving the ball away.'"

The Lions' first preseason under Parker was brutal, with the team playing three games in eight days in the steamy South. One of them was against the Eagles, now coached by Bo McMillan, who wasn't without a job for long. Philadelphia hired him to replace Earle "Greasy" Neale. The match naturally had a certain "Bo vs. Buddy" undertone, but neither man proved the master of the other. The donnybrook in 100-degree heat in Shreveport, Louisiana, ended in a 17–17 tie.

The highlight of the Lions' preseason was their clash with Cleveland at Briggs Stadium on September 4, a game Parker had been desperate to schedule as a way of gauging his team's strength. It was the annual *Detroit Free Press* Fresh Air Fund Game. The event benefited the newspaper's long-time charity, which each summer sent groups of underprivileged kids to a camp in Sylvan Lake. Harder had yet to join the team, and several Detroit regulars, too banged up to play, could have used a week at the lake. Nonetheless, the young and undermanned Lions demonstrated how far desire and preparation could go.

The Tuesday night affair drew 35,165 fans—at the time, the largest preseason crowd ever in Detroit. The game was tied in with the city's yearlong 250th anniversary celebration. Like all of Detroit's sports teams, the Lions would wear a special commemorative patch on their uniforms throughout the season.

Cleveland, masters of the AAFC and now the NFL, seemed invincible. Fielding a lineup chock-full of future Hall-of-Famers, the defending champs had just pummeled the nation's top collegians, 33–0, in the College All-Star Game, then walloped the New York Yanks, 52–0, in their first exhibition. Bookies handling preseason action expected Cleveland to whip Detroit by a dozen points.

Actually, the Browns did slightly better—for a half. They were up, 13–0, as the third quarter began. Then the Lions, who were playing their fourth game in 12 nights, caught their second wind. They stormed back with three touchdowns within a seven-minute span—two on interception returns by Bob Smith and Leon Hart—to turn the game around. The Browns didn't score again until a trick play in the final seconds.

"I told our squad that this was the most important game of the year," Parker said. "They played it right up to the hilt." Paul Brown shrugged off the 21–20 loss, but for the Lions the hard-fought comeback was a turbo boost to their confidence. It also was the first of many examples of Parker's unique hold over his famous sideline rival.

"We saw that we could win, even that first year," Layne said later. "Something tremendous was happening. We had the talent and we had a special sort of closeness, a kind I've never seen before or since. It was a pleasure to play for Buddy. We even looked forward to workouts, and camp was like a vacation. Buddy is one of the few coaches in football who remembers he used to be a player. He makes it enjoyable."

After the Lions beat the New York Yanks in Houston in their final tuneup before the start of the regular season, the team had a party at the upscale Shamrock Hotel. Pop singer Margaret Whiting, a native Detroiter whose father had composed such classics as "Ain't We Got Fun," entertained the boys while Thurman McGraw kept everybody laughing with a rollicking string of old-time railroad chants ("I don't know but I've been told / Susie's got a jelly roll"). Reporters were impressed by the squad's towel-snapping spirit. "I always figured that professional football players were big, rough, mercenary guys," a Texas newspaperman said. "These fellows are horsing around like a high school team."

Parker had the advantage of starting the regular season with five straight home games. Here was the chance to get off to a running start and ignite public interest. The Lions opened September 30 against Washington. Weeks earlier, the Redskins had caught the Lions looking past them to Cleveland and handed Parker his only defeat in six exhibition games. This time Washington held a 17–14 lead in the third quarter when Layne, enjoying one of his finest days, piloted the Lions on three long touchdown drives to pull away to a 35–17 victory. Layne completed 20 of 26 passes for 310 yards. Half of the completions went to veteran end Bill Swiacki, obtained from the New York Giants. Parker had in place what he always called the best backfield he ever saw: Layne at quarterback, Harder at fullback, Hoernschemeyer at right half, and Walker at left half. Between them they ran and passed for 515 yards against the Redskins, with each member of the quartet contributing a touchdown.

The Lions originally were scheduled to travel to New York for a Monday night game with the Yanks. But due to the ongoing Giants-Yankees World Series, the contest was moved to Briggs Stadium. The Lions weren't particularly sharp but still won handily, 37–10, with Walker nabbing two of Layne's three TD pitches and Harder registering a pair of 7-yard scoring runs. The Lions immediately shifted their focus to the following week's opponent, Los Angeles.

The "Hollywood Rams," whose owners included entertainers Bob Hope and Bing Crosby, were the NFL's glamor team. Since moving from Cleveland to Los Angeles in 1946, the Rams had acquired a splashy showbiz persona befitting their sun-blessed surroundings. They were the first pro team to wear a logo on their helmets, the yellow curved ram horns making them appear even more dashing. Quarterback Bob Waterfield was married to "bombshell actress" Jane Russell and halfback Glenn Davis had just tied the knot with "Hollywood's sexy tomboy" Terry Moore. Several Rams worked in the movies. Waterfield was featured in the 1951 Johnny Weissmuller film, *Jungle Manhunt*, while the flashiest Ram of them all, Elroy "Crazylegs" Hirsch, was set to star in *Crazylegs*, an upcoming biopic billed as "a gay love story that all America will cheer!"

Hirsch, the first man to letter in four varsity sports in the same year at the University of Michigan, was on his way to a spectacular season in 1951, setting or tying several receiving records as the Rams pursued a third straight conference crown. "At that time pro football was really opening up," recalled defensive end Andy Robustelli, who broke in with the Rams that year. "The formations right after the war were still variations on the single wing, which is a power way to play football. The Rams started to bring in a lot of variations which were kind of against the grain—man in motion, all of that stuff—and that was the beginning of what pro football is today. The war caused a break in tradition, and people had to face a lot of new things. Everybody wanted new cars, new houses, new everything, and football changed along with everything else."

Waterfield shared duties with another pin-point passer, Norm Van Brocklin. Their chief target was big-footed Tom Fears, who complemented Hirsch at the other end spot. The "Bull Elephant Backfield" of "Deacon Dan" Towler, Dick Hoerner, and Paul "Tank" Younger, each of whom weighed more than most of the linemen blocking for them, trampled the grass and reluctant tacklers. "That is the team we have to be beat if we are to be contenders," Parker said.

On October 14, Los Angeles visited Briggs Stadium and left three hours later with a 27–21 victory. The Rams jumped out to an early 10–0 lead and never trailed. Jack Christiansen provided most of the highlights for the home team, returning punts 69 and 47 yards for touchdowns. Rams coach Joe Stydahar, seeing the ever-dangerous Walker and the untested rookie positioned as twin safeties, had instructed Van Brocklin to "Kick to the tall, skinny kid," meaning Christiansen. "The second time, I thought the odds were on our side," Stydahar said.

Under pressure from Robustelli, making the first start of his Hall-of-Fame career, and the rest of the L.A. defense, Layne had a miserable day, completing just five of 19 flips for a paltry 63 yards. Four of his passes were intercepted. "The Rams were sure fired up for that game," Walker observed in "Doak's Dope," his weekly column for the *Free Press*. "They had just been beaten [by Cleveland] a week before and perhaps were just a little bit 'higher' for the game than we were."

That evening, Carol Layne joined several players' wives for dinner, where they commiserated over the loss. Of Hirsch, who had scorched the Lions for a 70-yard touchdown, Carol said: "He can't possibly be that good. He was just lucky, that's all." To her embarrassment, she discovered Hirsch seated at an adjacent table. She apologized profusely, explaining she was a sore loser, but Hirsch just laughed it off. Sometime later, she received a piece of mail with a clipping inside. The article from the *Los Angeles Times*, regarding a woman with a similar name, was headlined: "Carol Lane Again Arrested for Prostitution." The accompanying note read: "I see you're up to your old tricks—E. H." Hirsch's waggery tickled Bobby, who shared the story in the clubhouse.

The Los Angeles game was a benchmark moment in the history of pro football in Detroit. Officially, 52,907 people clicked through the turnstiles, the largest turnout yet for an NFL contest in the city. It easily surpassed the previous record of 48,118, set eight years earlier against the Bears. Capacity crowds would soon be the norm at Briggs Stadium, spurred by an aggressive season-ticket campaign. Thousands took advantage of packages costing between $15 and $21.60 for six home dates, which worked out to $2.50 to $3.60 per seat per game. In a six-season stretch starting in 1951, the Lions would place second in home attendance every year except 1954, when they led the NFL.

A few years later, with the team now fat with profit, Nick Kerbawy looked back and remembered how vital those early successes were to keeping the franchise afloat in the weeks after Parker took over from McMillan. The payout to Bo had drained the coffers.

"The treasurer's report showed we had no money in the bank," Kerbawy said of a directors meeting in early 1951. "One of my first official acts as business manager was to arrange a loan of $50,000 from a local bank so that we could operate. Then I started our season ticket sale on February 1 instead of March 1 so we could pay off the loan. I guess we had the bank's money for about eight weeks, and we haven't had to borrow since."

Two weeks after their first meeting, the winless Yanks returned to Briggs Stadium. The Lions, looking stale, managed to escape with a 24–24 tie when a New York field-goal attempt from midfield fell just short at the final gun. Not for the first time, fans chanted, "We want Enke!"

As far as Parker was concerned, that was an unreasonable request. The offensive line, which included two rookies—center LaVern Torgeson and right guard Dan Rogas—was too inconsistent and receivers were dropping too many balls to put the blame on the quarterback. "Layne has done a good job of running the team," Parker claimed. "When a quarterback doesn't get any help from the blockers up front, any one of them will have a tendency to look bad."

The deadlock with the punching-bag Yanks, who would finish with a 1-9-2 record, wound up costing the Lions a vital half game in the final standings. Parker had always disliked no-decision games, which were discounted when the NFL calculated winning percentages. Under this formula it was possible for a team with a 7-2-3 record (.778 percentage) to finish ahead of a club with a 9-3 (.750) record despite the latter having two more victories. Like Bert Bell and most coaches, Parker favored playing all games until there was a winner. However, owners endorsed "sudden death" overtime for postseason games only. (It wasn't until 1972 that the league began counting a tie as half a win and half a loss in computing winning percentages, and it was 1974 before overtime finally was approved for regular-season contests.)

The commissioner also wanted to eliminate conversions, arguing that the kick after touchdown was an almost automatic point that added no suspense to the game. During the 1951 season, Bell floated the idea of making all touchdowns worth seven points, but his proposal went nowhere. In retrospect, Detroit would have benefited more than most teams from such a rule change. Between 1950 and 1954 the Lions lost three games by a single point (once to San Francisco and twice to the Bears), each time because of a botched conversion.

A week after tying the Yanks, the Lions hosted the Bears. Following a midweek players-only meeting called by co-captains John Prchlik and Bob Hoernschemeyer, the team was fired up and determined to correct course. The score was tied early in the fourth quarter when Ed Sprinkle broke through and blocked a Bob Smith punt. Bill Wightkin, once a prep star in Detroit, picked up the loose ball and ambled into the end zone for what turned out to be the decisive points in a 28–23 Bears win. It was the Bears' 11th straight victory over the Lions dating back to 1945.

After a quick start, the 2-2-1 Lions were now winless in three games and looking up at four teams in the standings. "I still feel that this club of ours is going to be tough," Parker said. "We can't keep getting all the bad breaks. This three-game road trip we take will tell the tale pretty much."

For the road opener at Green Bay, Parker shifted three defensive starters to the offensive line to improve the blocking. Jim Martin took over the left tackle spot from Floyd Jaszewski, Dick Flanagan replaced Rogas at guard, and Les Bingaman was installed at center. A snowstorm hit Green Bay the night before the game, and equipment manager Roy "Friday" Macklem and trainer Ben Sonne had to traipse around town to find enough long underwear, gloves, and tennis shoes to outfit the team. Deadlocked at a field goal apiece at the half, the Lions finally caught fire on the frozen field with Layne pitching three second-half touchdown strikes. One went to Walker and the other two were circus catches by Leon Hart. Detroit won, 24–17.

Hart was in the midst of his finest overall season, one that would see him named a Pro Bowler and a First Team All-Pro for the only time in his career. After catching a single pass for zero yards in the first three games, he exploded as an offensive force. He collected a dozen touchdown throws, scoring in all but one of the last nine games of the season. The two-way end also used his reach to pluck two enemy passes out of the air.

"He likes nothing better than to jump for a high pass with a couple of the opposition breathing down his neck," one reporter wrote. "Hart usually winds up with the ball and the enemy strewn around the gridiron. Hart's development into a top-flight end doesn't stop with the catching of passes. He is one of the steadiest defensive players on the club—using his great size and speed to bowl over pass protectors and scatter interference on running plays."

Hart would play eight seasons with Detroit. For a good deal of that time he was plagued by hamstring pulls. The problem was especially severe during the 1952 and 1957 seasons. "My muscles would tighten up, especially in cold weather," he said. "We didn't know all about stretching to keep muscles limber. I preferred to stay on the field because if I cooled off, my muscles would cramp up. I played both ways full-time my first three seasons with the Lions. I did it at Notre Dame, so there was no reason not to do it in the pros. At the time, the pros were easier."

Defense or offense, Hart had no preference as to what side of the scrimmage line he was on. "I just liked to play football."

Every bone-crunching ounce of big Leon was needed in the rematch against the first-place Bears at Wrigley Field. It was November 11, Armistice Day, exactly six years since the Lions last beat the Bears. As always, George Halas was looking for any kind of edge. Opponents constantly griped about "Papa Bear" allowing bands to pound drums and blow tubas behind the visitors' bench—the better to drown out telephone conversations between the sideline and the press box. His policy of selling bleacher seats on the field too often led to spectators interfering with play.

"One time there I felt a tap on my shoulder," Parker recalled. "I looked around and it was some guy I'd never seen before. Just one of George's followers trying to get into the act." Another visiting coach complained: "The game would be in progress and this hot dog vendor would be walking out there in front of our bench, leaning over players to make a sale to the fans."

Tubas and hot dogs did not distract the Lions from the job at hand. With Martin, Bingaman, and Lou Creekmur joining Hart as two-way stars, the Lions' defense intercepted three passes, recovered all four Bears fumbles, and forced three Chicago drives to die inside the 25-yard line. Meanwhile, the offense clicked from the get-go, with Layne finding Dibble for a 26-yard touchdown on Detroit's first possession and then tossing a couple of six-pointers to Hart in the second quarter.

Pat Harder had a productive day, scoring two touchdowns and kicking a long field goal. "I didn't gain many yards," he said, "but I blocked hell out of them all day long." Detroit won, 41–28, to pull within a half game of the top spot in the National Conference. The players, impressed with how thoroughly Parker had prepared them, voted him a game ball. It was the first time in Lions history that a coach had been so honored.

The Lions followed up with a 28–10 victory over Philadelphia in a free-swinging affair at Shibe Park. Bo McMillan was no longer coaching the Eagles. In October he'd undergone surgery for stomach cancer, and the prognosis was grim. Wayne Millner took over for McMillan, who managed to leave his sick-bed to watch a quarter of the Lions-Eagles action. It was the last game Bo ever attended. The following March the emaciated coach died of a heart attack. He was 57. He left behind a wife, five children, and the foundation of a winning program in Detroit.

"Even in the pro league, where reputation means little, Bo left his mark," Bob Latshaw eulogized in the *Detroit Free Press*. "He is credited with selling pro football in Michigan and doing the missionary work which opened up Texas as one of the most profitable pro football areas in the country. He drafted the players which moved Detroit into the top bracket. . . . McMillan's oratory enabled him to sell football almost as well as he sold himself. Few who had an opportunity to listen to McMillan went away unimpressed with the little gray-haired man with the soft Texas drawl."

After beating the Eagles, the Lions returned home to pocket another win with a 52–35 throttling of Green Bay on a soggy Thanksgiving. It was the first of 13 consecutive Turkey Day clashes between the Lions and Packers, a series the Lions would dominate. Once again, Hoernschemeyer had a big holiday, peeling off an 85-yard scoring run, and once again it stood up as the longest run of the year in the NFL. Feather-footed Jack Christiansen returned punts 71 and 89 yards for touchdowns, both in the third quarter. This gave him four for the season, a new league mark that has since been equaled by three other players. However, his 21.5 yards per return in 1951 remains the NFL record.

When the Rams and Bears both unexpectedly lost on Sunday, Parker's squad found itself all alone on top of the standings. With three games left, and riding a four-game winning streak, the Lions were now in control. Their 6-2-1 record put them a half game ahead of the 6–3 Rams and Bears. Win out, and Briggs Stadium would be hosting the 1951 title game the Sunday before Christmas.

This was far easier said than done. The Lions had to face San Francisco twice, sandwiched around a game with the Rams. In their season opener, the 49ers had handed Cleveland its only defeat of the regular season, after which coach Buck Shaw's squad sputtered along through October and November. By the time they visited Detroit on December 2, they were break-even with a 4-4-1 record.

That Sunday marked the inaugural Lions Homecoming, an annual alumni event that continues to this day. Parker had been responsible for organizing the association earlier in the year. Briggs Stadium was filled with balding and silver-haired ex-gridders invited as guests of the Lions, as well as some 52,000 others who paid to get in. All watched in miserable weather as the 49ers whipped the Lions in their last home game of the season.

Hoernschemeyer left early with a head injury and spent the next three days in Grace Hospital with what was described as a "mild" concussion. Missing their top ground gainer and his dependable blocking, the Detroit offense sputtered against the rugged 49ers line. Y. A. Tittle, in relief of Frankie Albert, slung a pair of second-half TD passes to account for the final 20–10 verdict. It was a flat performance by the home team, and the fans let them know it.

Layne was happy to leave the boo-birds behind as the Lions embarked on the California trip that would make or break the season. He already had 25 scoring passes, three shy of Sid Luckman's single-season record. Thanks to the sponsorship of Edwin Anderson and the recently completed coaxial cable linking the eastern and western halves of the country, Detroiters could watch both games.

This was a special treat. It marked the first time West Coast football games had been televised exclusively by a Detroit station. Don Wattrick provided the play-by-play simultaneously on WJBK-TV and WJR radio, while a man costumed as the brewery's golden-feathered mascot, Brewster the Goebel Rooster, conspicuously prowled the sidelines, a reminder to viewers of who was responsible for the telecast. Ironically, Anderson was under strict orders not to watch. He had suffered a heart attack on December 4 and was recovering at St. Joseph's Hospital in Pontiac. Doctors were afraid of the stress the games might place on his weakened ticker.

The Rams, who had just beaten the Bears, now held a half-game lead over Detroit. A victory over the Lions on December 9 would knock Detroit out of the race. The Lions hadn't beaten the Rams in their last dozen meetings, dating back to their days in Cleveland. The oddsmakers made the Lions two-touchdown underdogs. The youthfulness of Parker's squad was working against them at times. They were prone to making mistakes at key moments, especially in the secondary, where Christiansen was twice burned in the loss to the 49ers. Elroy Hirsch, L.A.'s "atomic bomb," had scored in every game of the season—14 touchdowns in 10 games, so far—and had already broken the single-season record for receiving yardage.

The Rams-Lions clash at Memorial Coliseum was a classic seesaw affair, with the lead changing hands seven times. The Lions were ahead, 10–9, at halftime, but Los Angeles pulled back in front on Dan Towler's third-quarter scoring run. Later in the period, Doak Walker's 11-yard touchdown on a reverse and the accompanying extra point made it 17–16 in favor of the visitors. In the fourth quarter, Bob Waterfield booted two more field goals—giving him a record-setting five for the day—to make the score Los Angeles 22, Detroit 17.

The Lions got the ball back with four minutes left to play. "Lotsa time," Layne said in his gravelly drawl. "We're gonna win it."

Layne, who completed only six passes for 69 yards all day, accounted for half of his output on the winning drive. Starting from his own 21-yard line, he hit Bill Swiacki for 10 yards, Hoernschemeyer for one, and then Walker for 20 to put the ball on the Los Angeles 47. Layne next peeled off a long run on a bootleg around the left side to give the Lions a fresh set of downs on the 22.

Time was ticking off the clock. Inside the huddle, Layne glanced around at the grimy, sweaty faces. "Now Doak, Leon, the play we talked about," he said. "Make it look good."

On the snap, Layne handed off to Walker on what appeared to be a sweep around right end. But as the Rams rushed up to stop him, the Doaker pulled up, retreated a couple of steps, then zipped a pass to Hart, who had feigned a block before heading downfield. Hart snared the ball at the goal line and stepped into the end zone. The touchdown had thousands of viewers whooping it up inside taverns and living rooms back in Michigan. *Free Press* editor Lyall Smith admitted to dissolving into a "delirious, hilarious, jibbering mass of gooseflesh" whose partisan hollering frightened his Pleasant Ridge neighbors.

Walker's extra point made it Detroit 24, Los Angeles 22, a score that held up as the Lions shut down the Rams for the last two minutes of the game. The defense had played magnificently, with Bob Smith knocking beefy fullback Dick

Hoerner from the game with a crunching shoulder tackle and Don Doll keeping Hirsch out of the end zone for the first time all season. "Any time a team holds the Rams to one touchdown," said Aldo Forte, "they have played themselves a great ball game."

The Lions' first win over the Rams since 1944 put them a half game ahead of the Rams and Bears going into the final Sunday of the regular season. Remarkably, there was a possibility that as many as *four* teams could wind up deadlocked at the top of the conference standings. In the highly unlikely event that the Rams-Packers and Bears-Cardinals games both ended in draws while Detroit lost to San Francisco, the Lions, 49ers, Bears, and Rams would all finish with 7-4-1 records. This would mean an unprecedented tournament of three conference playoff games just to determine Cleveland's opponent in the championship game and would push the title game back two weeks, to the first Sunday in 1952.

Another scenario was San Francisco beating Detroit while the Rams and Bears both lost. This would force the 49ers and Lions to go at it again the following week in a special tiebreaker that would be their third meeting in four weeks. There were other dizzying combinations for the league office in Philadelphia to sort through, but the short of it was this: Detroit was the only team controlling its own destiny. Beat or tie the 49ers, and the Lions and Browns would meet in the title game the following Sunday.

Tickets already were being sold in Detroit. The club stood to gross at least $225,000 from the gate alone. A chunk of the postseason boodle would go toward player shares and contract raises for 1952. Ollie Cline could practically taste the championship money. "We got to win this one," said the former Ohio State standout, aware that even a losing share would dwarf the $594.18 winning payout he'd received three years earlier as a member of the undefeated Browns. "The extra dough will just about pay off the mortgage on the house."

The Lions were unbeaten on the road while the 49ers had never lost the final game of a season. Something had to give. Parker sequestered the squad in Ignacio and held closed sessions at Hamilton Air Force Base, where even coaches and players needed a signed pass to enter the practice facility. Layne continued treatment on his shoulder. After throwing 17 touchdown passes in a five-game span, he'd only had one in the last two games. His misfiring had become a cause for concern. Even some club directors remained unsold on Layne. One in particular was often spotted stomping around the third-deck press box, yelling, "Get that bum out of there! Bring in Fred Enke, for gosh sakes!"

"No one really understood what Layne went through as a player," Parker said years later. "It wasn't publicized but he had bursitis in his throwing arm right on from college. I've seen him on the bench while our defense was on the field when he couldn't raise his arm to his nose . . . if he had had a healthy arm like Waterfield or Van Brocklin, there would have been no one close to him. Layne took more shots than anyone I know. And he took more criticism. I always taught my quarterbacks to throw the ball away when they were in trouble, but to throw under control. Layne would unload and overthrow a man 10 yards. The fans booed him. What they didn't realize was, he was doing what had to be done."

In his most important game yet as a pro, Layne had a poor showing, completing 13 of 33 passes and throwing four interceptions. Nonetheless, the game was gripping entertainment to the end. On the fourth play of the game, Bob Smith recovered a Joe Perry fumble on the San Francisco 24-yard line. When the drive stalled, Harder came in and kicked a 14-yard field goal for a quick 3–0 lead. On the 49ers' next series, the Lions blocked a Gordy Soltau field-goal attempt, allowing Layne to set up shop on the San Francisco 41. Minutes later, Harder capped a 13-play drive with a short plunge. Walker's extra point made it a 10–0 game. The Lions seemed to be in command.

However, the 49ers rallied with a pair of touchdowns in the second quarter, each the result of an interception by Lowell Wagner. Once again, Y. A. Tittle came off the bench to stymie the Lions. Following the first pick, Tittle guided the 49ers to Detroit's 31 before calling on Perry, who surprised the Lions' secondary with a pass to Billy Wilson for the score. After the second interception, Tittle needed just three plays to produce the go-ahead touchdown, this time on a 27-yard pitch to Soltau. In the waning moments of the first half, Layne moved the Lions to San Francisco's 9. On third down, Hart maneuvered into the clear but Layne's pass hit the crossbar—a not unusual occurrence with the goalposts stationed on the goal line. Harder then attempted a field goal, but his kick sailed wide.

In the third quarter, Layne moved the Lions into a 17–14 lead with a 28-yard scoring pass to Hart. There matters stood until the final tense minutes, when the 49ers defense stiffened and forced a punt. Joe Arenas fielded the kick on the dead run on his own 27. The flashy rookie raced past the first wave of Lions and covered more than half the field before finally being pulled down inside the Detroit 20. After Perry picked up four yards on a run, Tittle's second-down pass bounced off the goal post. On third down, Tittle completed a throw to Soltau at the 1-yard line.

The Lions, knowing a tie would still put them in the title game, were desperate to hold San Francisco to a field goal. On first down, Les Bingaman and company smothered a run up the middle. On the next snap, Tittle faked a plunge to Perry, then acted as if he was handing off to halfback John Stryzkalski on a slant. With the linebackers biting on the second fake, Tittle hid the ball on his hip and dashed unmolested into the end zone. Soltau's all-important extra point made it a four-point game, 21–17. The Lions now needed a touchdown to advance to the championship game.

There still were three minutes left to play, plenty of time for Layne to replicate his heroics against the Rams. But not this afternoon. After picking up a quick first down on a pass to Hart, Layne went for broke with a deep throw. Verl Lillywhite picked off the pass, after which San Francisco methodically ran out the clock. The Lions finished the season with a 7-4-1 record, the same as the 49ers.

Three hundred miles south at Memorial Coliseum, Bob Waterfield was in the process of throwing five touchdown passes—three to Crazylegs Hirsch—as the Rams rolled over the Packers, 42–14, to complete an 8–4 season. The Bears had already been upset by the Cardinals in subzero conditions at Wrigley Field, ending their hopes, and now the Lions had been beaten. Cal Whorton of the *Los Angeles Times* reported a scene that put the lie to the old axiom that there's no cheering in the press box: "The scribes themselves gave away the 49er touchdown when every last man in the press section dropped what he was doing and went into a wild emotional dance when it was flashed that Y. A. Tittle had skirted end on a run that was to eliminate Detroit and make the Rams conference champions." The jubilant Los Angeles bench was penalized for delay of game. "We ought to have the 49ers in here with us," cracked one Los Angeles player as the happy Rams assembled for a team photo afterward. Their smiles would grow wider when they beat the Browns, 24–17, in their championship-game rematch one week later on the very same turf.

Back at Kezar Stadium, the mood among the Lions was ugly, defiant. The team had come far, but at the very end what had been theirs for the taking slipped through their soily, battered fingers. "As I walked off the field," Tittle recalled, "Hunchy Hoernschemeyer, the Lions' halfback, said something nasty to me, called me a dirty name. He was boiling mad . . . we had upset Detroit and cost Hunchy and his teammates a lot of playoff money."

It was Parker's birthday, and the team had planned to celebrate with a huge cake at the St. Francis Hotel. "The most fitting thing to do with it now," said Nick Kerbawy, "is throw it at Tittle."

Inside the somber Detroit locker room, players stewed in their disappointment. Harder finally stood on a bench and, waving a towel, reportedly yelled: "We'll be back next year to lick the stuffing out of somebody!"

Ol' Sarge's actual exhortation was more obscene and needed to be cleaned up for publication in the next day's newspapers. But his sentiment was shared by teammates, many of whom harbored a grudge against San Francisco's "robbers." When players from around the league assembled in Los Angeles for the Pro Bowl in January, Bingaman found himself sharing a hotel room with a couple of 49ers, safety Jim Cason and tackle Ray Collins.

"What sort of guys are they?" someone asked Bingaman upon his return to Detroit.

"I didn't even speak to 'em," the grumpy guard said. "They cost me $2,500."

CHAPTER

3

World Beaters

Every son of a bitch on that team was all football.

—Bobby Layne

"**O**ur Lions didn't quite make it," Bob Murphy of the *Detroit Times* wrote the day after Buddy Parker's scrappy squad left their hearts in San Francisco. "But they closed out the 1951 regular pro season with a game fighting finish that definitely has put 'post graduate' football in a most healthy state in Detroit."

After spending most of the last decade wandering in the NFL wilderness, the Lions' near-miss in 1951 provided a welcome boost to the bottom line and gave a taste of greater success to come. The turnstile count at Briggs Stadium jumped from an average of 24,600 per game in 1950 to 36,244 in 1951, helping the club post a net profit of $65,525 for the season.

As nice as those numbers looked in the ledger, they weren't enough to pull the club out of the red. Edwin Anderson pointed out to stockholders that the syndicate still was $156,726 short of offsetting the $222,555 it had lost between 1948 and 1950. Nonetheless, there was a great deal of optimism among owners, coaches, fans, and writers that, with a solid nucleus of veterans and maturing young players, the Lions' fortunes were following the upward trajectory of a Bob Smith punt.

Parker signed another one-year contract to coach the team in 1952. Looking for someone he knew and trusted to handle the defense, he was able to land Garrard "Buster" Ramsey—thanks to some machinations by Nick Kerbawy, the clever publicity director who had just been promoted to general manager.

During an offseason meeting in Chicago, Kerbawy offered halfback Jerry Krall to the Cardinals in exchange for Ramsey, then a player-coach with the Cards, even though Krall was an unsigned free agent who had last played with the Lions in 1950. After the Cardinals agreed to the trade, Kerbawy hurried to Toledo, where Krall was working, signed the surprised back to a predated contract, sent the paperwork to the commissioner's office, and then closed the deal with Chicago. Krall never played another NFL down while Ramsey coached eight seasons in Detroit.

Ramsey had earned All-American honors at William & Mary before becoming a perennial All-League selection at guard for the Cardinals. The burly Tennessee native, only 32 when he came to Detroit, was talkative and intense.

"He liked people to hit," said trainer Millard Kelley, recalling Ramsey's frustration over Doak Walker's reluctance to mix it up with linemen during some blocking drill. "Walker weighed 165 pounds, and he might block somebody if he had the angle on him, but he wasn't about to pit himself against some monster who weighed seventy-five pounds more than he did. Buster would get mad and start yelling, 'Doak, come on. Knock somebody down.' Parker understood, of course, and didn't expect him to do anything of the kind."

Ramsey is too often overlooked when discussing the Lions of the '50s, but as defensive coordinator he deserves a good deal of the credit in turning the Lions from title aspirants into NFL champions. He helped mold an un-fledged group of defensive backs into the best secondary in football. He also popularized the maneuver known as "red dogging"—sending normally stay-at-home linebackers rushing into the opponent's backfield, raising havoc and throwing quarterbacks off their game. No team used this "blitzing" tactic more often and more effectively than the Lions. The addition of Ramsey and a brilliant class of rookies would put the finishing touches on Bo McMillan's original five-year plan.

Another new assistant was Russ Thomas, fresh off a two-year stint on the coaching staff at St. Bonaventure. The former All-Pro tackle for the Lions had

been a two-way starter and team captain under McMillan until a knee injury ended his playing career in 1949. Thomas, holder of a business degree from Ohio State, was eager to move into the ranks of management. In his second go-around in Detroit, he performed a variety of duties that kept him shuffling between the sidelines, film room, press box, and airport. As game scout, he spent Sundays out of town, watching and then preparing an advance report on the following week's opponent. He also scouted collegiate talent and assisted Kerbawy in signing some of the team's draft choices. This was valuable training for the physically imposing Thomas, who would gain a reputation as a tough, tightfisted negotiator during his long and contentious career in the front office.

Pat Summerall was Detroit's fourth-round pick in the 1952 draft. In addition to his strong defensive play, the stout-legged Arkansas end had led all of college football with four field goals his senior year. As laughable as that figure appears today, Summerall's output actually matched or exceeded the number of field goals made by four NFL teams in 1952.

The future broadcaster discovered that when it came to haggling, Thomas already had a few trick plays in his playbook. Before Thomas left for Fayetteville to talk money with Summerall, he implied that the collegian had already made the team and was in line for a healthy contract. "After I heard that," Summerall remembered, "there were several nights of hard partying at our favorite bar, Hog's Heaven, and I put round after round on my tab."

However, when the two later met at Hog's Heaven, Thomas told Summerall that the Lions were only willing to offer him a $5,000 contract with no signing bonus. Thomas explained that all players on the club made the same salary—a sacrifice for the sake of team unity. Furthermore, he said, Detroit didn't give signing bonuses because that would mean raising the salaries of everyone else.

Summerall was incredulous. "I couldn't believe that big-name Lions such as Doak Walker, Bobby Layne, and Leon Hart would have the same salary as a rookie who hadn't played a down yet. Things didn't seem to add up to me, and I let Thomas know it. After a lot of back and forth, he backed down and agreed to increase his offer to $6,000 a year with a $500 signing bonus. When he finally caved, I remember thinking, 'At least it'll pay off my bar tab.'"

Summerall suffered a compound fracture of his forearm during a kick return in the second game of the 1952 season, at Los Angeles. He missed the rest of the season and the following year was sold to the Cardinals. But two other picks, Yale Lary and Jimmy David, moved right into the lineup and stayed several years.

Lary was only a toddler when he was given a football by his father, a Fort Worth shoe salesman, and promptly kicked it through the living room window. Lary's athletic skills had improved considerably since that day. He became a star two-way back at Texas A&M while also being pursued by big-league baseball scouts. The fleet outfielder, who turned down a $20,000 offer from the St. Louis Cardinals following his junior year, would spend his first few Lions off-seasons playing for various teams in the low minors.

While Lary impressed with his intelligence, instincts, and speed, David's most notable trait was his willingness to mix it up with men much bigger than himself. He was only 5-foot-10 and 175 pounds, but Jack Christiansen had played alongside him at Colorado A&M and vouched for the shy rookie's fiery temperament. Based largely on Christiansen's recommendation, Parker made David the Lions' 22nd-round draft choice. Buddy thought a leaky secondary had caused the Lions to miss out on a division title in 1951, and now he was plugging the holes.

The Lions were legitimate title contenders, but their chances took a scary turn on June 13. Doak Walker was attending the National Open at Dallas's Northwood Golf Club when he saw a car blocking his in the parking lot. Unable to locate the driver, he was attempting to push the car out of the way when his right arm slipped and crashed through a window. The broken glass sliced through his triceps muscle. Another centimeter here or there, and the Doaker's career might have been over. He was rushed to Baylor Hospital, where doctors performed emergency surgery on the ugly-looking three-inch gash.

"It was a miracle that the nerves in the arm were undamaged," doctors stated afterward. "Doak had the full use of his fingers. The damaged muscle was repaired in surgery." Doak wore a cast to protect the wound until training camp opened six weeks later. By the start of the regular season he was in his familiar spot in the starting backfield.

The Lions broke camp with 11 newcomers, fully one-third of the squad. Their number included two quarterbacks to replace discarded backup Fred Enke: rookie Tom Dublinski from Utah and veteran Jim Hardy, a carefree Californian who was the latest Cardinal to come to Detroit. The Lions blew through the preseason, winning all six games. "We went all out to win them all," Parker said. "It made sense. Every game we won before the season made the fans just that much more anxious to buy tickets to watch us in the regular season."

The last exhibition, a pasting of the Redskins in Norman, Oklahoma, had its light moments. When Kerbawy had the team stay at an Air Force base in the boondocks while he took a room in Oklahoma City, Hardy organized a protest that culminated with the general manager being hanged in effigy. "The kid was a real nut," said Roy Macklem. Later in the season, after a road game, Hardy missed the team bus to the airport because he wanted to call his wife on the phone. Afraid of being fined $150, he grabbed a cab and got to the airport before the bus arrived. "I hid in the lavatory until we were in the air," Hardy recalled, "and then I used the stewardess's P. A. microphone and I really gave them hell for taking off and leaving me."

The fun-loving Hardy had a gift for keeping teammates loose, always a plus during a pressure-packed race. Throughout the season, players found messages of encouragement addressed to them individually, all signed by a mysterious "Logan." The person writing the notes, of course, was Hardy. (Bill Swiacki also was in on the gag.) In the end, Hardy saw little game action, but he was a vital addition nonetheless.

"It isn't so much what Hardy did," Parker said later. "It's what Hardy could have done that counted. We knew that if Layne got hurt Hardy could step in and call a good game. With a good capable sub like Hardy on the bench, we could take a calculated risk and let Layne run with the ball more than the average well-protected pro quarterback—who seldom does anything except hand off the ball or pass it from the T-formation."

The Lions had a brutal first month, opening on the road against the 49ers and the Rams and then returning home to face their two biggest division rivals in back-to-back rematches. If they weren't careful, the season could be over before trick or treaters hit the sidewalks.

In the September 28 opener at San Francisco, the Lions committed five turn-overs in dropping a 17–3 decision. They appeared more lively in their Friday night game at Los Angeles, with Layne rifling a couple of touchdown passes to Cloyce Box and Walker adding a field goal in a hard-earned 17–14 victory. The game marked Hamp Pool's first as head coach after Joe Stydahar resigned. The defending champs were winless while Detroit came home with a split, an acceptable enough result for Parker. San Francisco was next; beat the 49ers and the teams would be tied for the top spot.

Parker had settled on an eight-point "code" that he believed resulted in a championship team:

1. physical qualifications of players
2. team desire to win
3. team poise
4. a simple offense and defense
5. repetition of drills to achieve perfection
6. the ability to come from behind when losing
7. a minimum of turnovers
8. recognizing that a defeat is not "disastrous," that what was important was how you react after a loss

Parker and Layne, a pair of notoriously poor losers, were sorely tested on that last point when San Francisco visited Briggs Stadium on October 12. The 49ers blew past blockers and hounded Detroit quarterbacks all afternoon, chasing the Lions out of the park, 28–0. In getting shut out for the first time since 1948, "the Lions gave as inept an exhibition as has ever been seen in Briggs Stadium," the *Free Press* reported. The team didn't get its initial first down until midway through the third quarter, and totaled only four for the entire game. Detroit was held to just 65 yards of total offense, including a net 25 passing yards from Layne, Hardy, and Dublinski. To make it even more embarrassing, the debacle took place in front of a record crowd of 56,822, who had been warned beforehand by management to arrive early so as to avoid missing any of the action.

After just three games, the Lions were already two games behind a loaded San Francisco club in the standings. Layne was beside himself. "Bobby just hated to lose," Doak said. "I don't know if he ever learned how to pronounce or spell that word."

That evening at the postgame buffet, Layne waited until the hotel dining room was almost empty before he went berserk, going around the room and smashing chairs. "Kind of silly, but I sure do feel better," he said when he gave Nick Kerbawy a personal check for $200 the next day to cover the damages.

Layne, afraid that his job was in jeopardy, also paid Parker a visit at his Dearborn home that Sunday night. "I'm going to be your quarterback," Layne said, "and this team is going to straighten out in a hurry."

The squad held a closed-door players-only meeting on Tuesday, emerging with renewed resolve. Parker told them they could be back in first place on Thanksgiving. To aid in the motivation, he kept the final score from the San Francisco game up on the stadium scoreboard all week during practice.

It was not far-fetched to feel that, though it was only the third week in October, the Lions' season hinged on their upcoming clash with the Rams. Once again, the team appeared sluggish while falling behind, 13–0. Boos poured out of the stands. Pat Harder, his left leg wrapped from hip to ankle, was clamoring to join the fray.

"I can't sit on the bench any longer, knee or no knee," he told Parker. Harder went in during the second quarter, and from that point on the club seemed to block, run, and even pass better.

Harder booted three extra points and the clinching field goal in the Lions' scrappy 24–16 turnaround victory. The touchdown that put the Lions in front to stay came off a reverse halfback option, with Bob Hoernschemeyer evading three Rams before shooting a pass to Box, who outfought a swarm of defenders to make a diving catch. It was Box's second score of the game; he had earlier split the safeties and taken a long Layne pass 65 yards to the end zone.

"This was as brutal a football game as has been seen in Briggs Stadium in many a day," wrote Bob Latshaw. "Fists, elbows, and feet flew freely throughout the contest. The referee, Ronald Gibbs, held a consultation with both clubs concerning the roughness. But the players paid little attention to his admonishments, and there were several individual boxing matches around the field." John Prchlik was tossed for fighting, but his and Harder's fighting spirit lifted the team and turned the jeers into cheers at Briggs Stadium.

Slow starts by Walker and Leon Hart contributed to the Lions' sputtering offense. Both stars were hobbled by hamstring injuries that caused them to sit out the blowout loss to San Francisco. While Hart's leg woes were chronic, Walker suffered his injury at home the night before the 49ers game. He was squatting in front of the TV, turning the channel knob to watch Sid Caesar and Imogene Coca on *Show of Shows*, when his hamstring popped. This latest freak accident had people wondering if Walker wasn't snake-bit and caused Parker to scramble to replace the league's highest-scoring halfback.

Just having Walker on the field gave the Lions a big advantage. The defense had to devote two men to cover him when he flanked out or was a man in motion, coverage that ordinary backs didn't warrant. In late October, Walker received several days of rest and treatment at Grace Hospital. By season's end, Doak had missed seven games. Meanwhile, Hart was fitted for a leg brace. He was *hors de combat* for just one game, though he often was hurting and running routes at three-quarter speed.

"A torn hamstring, especially in a big man, is almost like breaking a bone," said Hart, who underwent X-ray therapy to promote healing. The cathode rays often burned the back of his legs. "Doak and I had the same problem. I got criticized for trying to play while Doak's dad told him never to play unless he was one-hundred percent."

Parker auditioned a variety of fill-ins while waiting for Doak to heal, including rookie Byron Bailey and Philadelphia castoff Clyde "Smackover" Scott. In July, after Walker's accident at the U.S. Open, he had sent veteran end Ed Berrang and rookie lineman Steve Dowden to Green Bay for Earl "Jug" Girard. The former Wisconsin star quarterback and ex-paratrooper was unhappy playing in the Packers' secondary, so he was tickled to get the news that he'd get a fresh chance at left halfback in the Lions' backfield.

"What made him stand out was, for his size, he was a scrapper," recalled Bob Reynolds, who joined Van Patrick in the broadcast booth that season. "He didn't back down for nobody." Girard had a fine all-around season in 1952, picking up more yards from scrimmage (222 rushing, 316 receiving) than any other Lion except Cloyce Box and Hoernschemeyer. The 175-pound handyman would go on to spend six seasons in Detroit, playing nearly every skill position on offense while also punting, returning kicks, and playing defense.

Box had returned to the lineup after being called back into the Marines and missing the '51 season. With Walker and Hart hurting, he became Layne's favorite target, though he was always utilized more as a bomb threat than a possession receiver. Box lacked finesse and power and, despite his large frame, wasn't much of a blocker. His basic move was straight schoolyard. He would take off at the snap of the ball and run like hell, looking to out-leg defenders as he hauled in another deep throw. At some point during each game, Layne would unlimber his arm and let the ball fly in Box's direction. It worked well enough to make Box one of the most productive receivers of the early 1950s. During his five years in the league, one of every four catches went for a touchdown, and his career average of 20.7 yards per reception has been surpassed by only a few other receivers.

Box had a prolific year in 1952. Most of his output came in the last quarter of the regular season, when he reeled off three straight three-touchdown games. After averaging two receptions in his first nine games, he broke loose for 24 catches and 529 yards in home games against the Packers, Bears, and Texans.

Whereas some quarterbacks were known for pitching "blue darts," Layne threw a softer pass with a three-quarter motion. The ball often fluttered in flight. He had been battling bursitis in his right shoulder off and on since 1949, with speculation that all those innings as a hard-throwing college pitcher had taken their toll. The problem would never go completely away, flaring up for inopportune stretches. "Bobby's passes weren't always very pretty, but he usually got them to where they had to go," Vince Banonis said.

Whatever the condition of his passing and drinking arm, the "Blonde Bomber" lived up to his nickname, on and off the field. By 1952, the Lions were indisputably Layne's team. He turned Mondays into something more than just the traditional off day. While players continued to stop by the Lions' offices on Michigan Avenue to pick up their weekly paycheck, and those who were hurting visited the clubhouse to have their injuries treated, a new ritual took hold.

Every Monday afternoon during the season, players gathered at the Stadium Bar, a saloon across the street from the ballpark's side entrance, to drink, eat, spin stories, talk football, play cards, shoot pool, throw darts, play shuffleboard, and generally hang out for a few hours. The rookies were ordered to attend. Their job was to serve drinks, hang up coats, empty ashtrays, mop up spills, run errands, and keep quiet. The only time a rookie was expected to open his mouth was when he was commanded to chug-a-lug an oversized mug of beer or belt out his school's fight song.

Over the years there was an obstinate rookie or two, but the veterans didn't physically force anybody into anything. "You just give them the silent treatment," Layne explained, "and believe me, that's worse than anything."

The Stadium Bar (later known as the Batter's Box and today the Corktown Tavern) at 1716 Michigan Avenue was run by a man named Hank, who closed the place to outsiders while the team enjoyed its weekly get-together. In the kitchen, an elderly cook prepared a ham or a roast for the day's buffet.

"Doak Walker never drank but he'd always be there," Layne said. "He just wanted to be part of it. We had fun together. The worst thing that can happen to a bunch of players is to have two go one place and talk about two other guys and blame somebody for a loss. We would get together every Monday and if we'd had a loss, hell, by Tuesday we'd be ready to go back to work and think about the next game and not be blamin' somebody."

With Layne serving as activities director, even Bingaman could be persuaded to do a tippy-toe dance to "Theme from Limelight." Naturally, drinking games enlivened the get-togethers. A favorite was "Cardinal Puff," in which participants had to repeat in sequence an elaborate series of actions. A player was required to tap the bottom of his beer mug once, take a sip, touch his right forefinger to the table, stomp his right foot once and then his left foot. The game went clockwise around the table, each player repeating the routine until someone messed up the sequence. At that point everybody would shout, "Drink to Cardinal Puff!" and the offending party would have to down his beer and start the sequence all over again.

After the game successfully made its way around the table, it advanced to Cardinal Puff-Puff, where each step of the routine now had to be done in twos, and then Cardinal Puff-Puff-Puff, and so on. Some players never got the hang of it and were blotto on Pfeiffer's or Stroh's before the afternoon was half over. Unsurprisingly, Layne was a Cardinal Puff champion, even though he usually substituted scotch for beer.

Another favorite drinking game was called "Sevens." Layne explained how it was played. "In 'Sevens,' you just count in order, the same as an army company counting off. But any number with a seven in it, or any multiple of seven such as 14 or 21, was taboo. Instead of saying the taboo numbers, you said, 'Buzz.' When a player says Buzz, it reverses the order of play, so you have to stay alert or you find yourself chug-a-lugging a beer. Sounds like children at play, I know, but you ought to try these games on a dull afternoon. You either stay awake, or you could become an alcoholic." Layne, who bragged that he cut his teeth on Pearl beer, had no such worries. He already was one.

For all his demonstrated gifts as an athlete and a human being, Layne was a flawed and self-destructive individual. As a young celebrity athlete living it up during the 1950s, he gave no more passing thought to his liver and lungs than he did the origins of the Vernor's elf or Goebel's rooster. The many colorful tales that surround Layne's drinking obscure the fact that his incessant boozing, combined with a four-pack-a-day cigarette habit, eventually destroyed his health and led to an early death.

Drinking is an integral part of the Bobby Layne legend, though separating fact from fiction can be difficult. According to Roy Macklem, whom Layne entrusted with his wallet and flask during games and practices, it was not unusual for the quarterback to take a recuperative snort inside the clubhouse—no different, given Layne's constitution, than others downing a hot cup of coffee at halftime to keep the engine running. However, tales of Layne playing a game "hymn-singing drunk" were pure nonsense, insisted teammates. Bobby's passes may have wobbled during

the game, Banonis said, but not Bobby himself. "They're great stories. But being the center, I would've been the first to notice if he'd been out all night."

Dorne Dibble, one of Layne's closest friends, concurred. "I've had fellows come up to me and say, 'I saw Layne Saturday night before the game and he was drunker than a billy goat.' Well, I was with him every Saturday night for six years. He drank during the week. Most of the players did, especially when you're on the road."

For somebody with Layne's habitus, having a few sociable drinks at dinner or a nightcap or two before turning in was not the same thing as going on a full-blown, nightclub-hopping bender lasting until dawn. That kind of cutting loose was reserved for a postgame wind-down or the off day following a game. During the regular season, Layne's routine was to do no serious partying after midnight on Tuesday.

There were exceptions, however, and those typically were games that didn't count in the standings—scrimmages, exhibitions, and Pro Bowls. During the pre-season, Layne and some of his usual running buddies might stay out a little bit later the night before a game. Judging by the team's performance—the Lions lost only six of 36 exhibitions under Parker—any impairment was negligible.

"But we never took advantage of Buddy," Layne said. "He didn't check us and all that stuff. He said just don't plain embarrass me, don't be seen out. Oh, Hunchy, Dib, Jug, Bing, and me, we'd play an exhibition game somewhere and then we'd have a good time after. But mostly it was a real serious group. Damn few of that group took advantage of Buddy."

Parker didn't conduct bed checks or sit in hotel lobbies at midnight. He thought professional athletes should be treated as adults, not college sopho-mores. After a game, Parker might say, "Now, fellas, don't eat too much—or drink too much." Said Layne: "We all went back and had a couple of beers. But if he'd told us point-blank not to drink, the boys might have gone out and stayed late to express their defiance. Buddy does have a few rules to keep the boys in check, but they aren't too tough. Primarily he expects a man to know his limitations and to know how to behave."

Layne's late hours had as much to do with his internal clock as his craving for companionship and action. Even on nights before a game, he only needed five or six hours in the sack to be fully rested. ("I sleep fast," he memorably stated.) He was a sound sleeper and woke up fully recharged and raring to go. Thus going to bed at an "early" hour, such as midnight, meant he might be up at

5 a.m. If it was a game day, he would nervously pace, drinking coffee and smoking cigarettes as he played the entire upcoming game in his head. By kickoff, he was mentally exhausted. Practices during the week only took up three hours of each day, leaving him with many hours to kill.

"I like to be around people and have never been a solitary traveler," he explained. "During the season I get nervous if I don't have company, the same kind of good fellowship that can be enjoyed on the football field. I like to hear the good bands and mix with the gang, something that is hard to do sitting in a hotel room with a television set or a book."

When it came to extracurricular activities, not everybody in the Detroit clubhouse took their lead from Layne. In the early years, there were some holdovers from McMillan's regime who continued to go their own way. Don Doll was so straight-laced he was nicknamed "Coop," after Gary Cooper. "I'm a very dull character compared to Layne and his crew," he once admitted. "They were great on the field . . . I guess they were great off the field, too."

Throughout his tenure in Detroit, if there was friction anywhere on the team, Layne tried to mend it. "Some of the back-biting was terrible," Nick Kerbawy recalled. "And Bobby would always take it upon himself to bring the team together. The situation would always become heated between the players from Notre Dame and Texas. They were always such rivals." On one occasion, Layne rented out a room at Carl's Chop House, where he told the feuding factions to "bury the hatchet, stop the bitching," Kerbawy said. "Then he made sure they got enough to drink."

The Lions, like all pro teams except Pittsburgh, lined up in the traditional T formation, though the Split-T had become popular in college. In the Split-T, the spacing between each offensive lineman was doubled, thus spreading the offensive line from 10 to 16 yards across the field, twice its usual width. This gave the offense more room to maneuver while also forcing defenders to cover more ground. Parker used a variation of the Split-T. All of the backs split, but the line blocking stayed the same. "I've thought a lot about using the full Split T," he said, "but never put it into my system because I feel splitting the line gives the defense an easier shot at the passer."

In putting together a plan for each week's game, Parker and his assistants first decided what kind of offense they wanted to run—heavy on either the pass or run, maybe a balanced attack, perhaps a heavy reliance on traps or screens—depending on the foe and which weapons the Lions expected to have on hand. Daily quarterback meetings helped develop a pattern of attack and a short list of 20 running and 20 passing plays. Those were the ones the team concentrated on in practice, though in a game Layne was free to pull anything out of the playbook depending on the situation.

During the game, assistants spotting a weakness from the press box phoned in suggestions to the bench, but Parker considered it his job to assist, not interfere, in the play-calling. Parker felt proper preparation would result in the quarterback making the right call. Layne spent more time watching game film than anyone except Parker, and that continued right up through the morning of the game.

Parker is credited with being the father of the two-minute offense, a time-management system that took advantage of an opponent's tendency to let down defensively in the final two minutes of each half. "It seemed you could get things done then that you couldn't in the other fifty-six minutes of play," he explained. "So we drilled on it. Every day."

The Lions practiced late-game situations, utilizing sideline throws, button-hook and screen passes, and the occasional run to eat up yardage but not the clock—standard fare today but considered innovative at the time. Parker "would come on the field with a watch and he'd say, 'Okay, you've got a minute and 30 seconds, you've got one time out left, see what you can do,'" Layne recalled. "So we would actually practice this up and down the field. So when it came up in a game you didn't panic."

Of course, the game was already more up-tempo. Prior to the NFL introducing a 45-second play clock in 1988, a team had 30 seconds from the end of the previous play to huddle up, call a play, get to the line of scrimmage, and snap the ball. During Layne's era, the referee kept track of the seconds ticking away on his stopwatch. There were no 30-second or game clocks displaying the official time for the benefit of players, coaches, and fans. Teams were notified when the game clock was down to the final two minutes or so at the end of each half, though the "two-minute warning" of the '50s didn't come with an automatic timeout.

Even in this kinetic environment, Layne stood out as a "fast caller," typically taking only seven or eight seconds to call a play before breaking the huddle. "It may seem insignificant," he said, "but speed in the huddle is really important. The more plays you run, the better chance you have to win. The way I call a play in the huddle makes a difference—the fellows can sense I have confidence the calls will work."

Situational awareness, a businesslike alacrity, and the judicious use of time-outs became a hallmark of the Lions, who could pack in a dozen or more plays during Parker's "two golden minutes." Fast finishes at the end of each half became second nature. "He'd tire you out," one defensive back said of Layne. "He'd put more in three minutes than anybody. And he had a receiver, Cloyce Box, who could run all day. He'd run deep on you five times in a row. . . . they were tough."

Despite his well-deserved reputation as a rounder, Layne always did his homework and worked harder than anybody else out on the practice field. He expected everybody to follow his lead. Somebody who wasn't paying attention in practice was liable to get a ball bounced off his helmet. Someone who blew an assignment during a game could expect a vulgar dressing-down, banishment to the sideline, or worse. The colorful Art Donovan, whose early NFL stops included the '52 Texans, once watched in amazement as Layne screamed at Lou Creekmur while repeatedly kicking him in the shins. Creekmur just stood there like a chastened schoolboy and took the punishment.

"He was a good leader for the team we had," Leon Hart said of Layne, whose generalship he respected despite their sometimes strained off-field relationship. "He was a good quarterback, but he also had the horses around him to be a good quarterback. A back is only as good as the linemen blocking for him. We had some good linemen. The game is won or lost in the trenches. Period."

During the 1950s, the Lions were blessed to have some of the era's finest "pack animals"—tireless offensive linemen who carried out the thankless tasks of opening up holes for runners and protecting the quarterback. In 1952, veteran center Vince Banonis and two young future Hall-of-Famers, Creekmur and guard Dick Stanfel, were part of a formidable line.

Stanfel, the Lions' second pick in the 1951 draft, was a solid 6-foot-2 and 240 pounds and played alongside tackle Gus Cifelli on the right side. "Stanfel does more things naturally than most other guards do after years of practice," Aldo Forte said. Stanfel had torn ligaments in his knee while practicing for the College All-Star Game in Chicago and missed the entire 1951 season. After two operations, the University of San Francisco star seemed to have lost none of his speed or blocking savvy. "When he pulled and cut upfield, we made yardage," Walker said of Stanfel. "Dependable and hard-working, he could pull or block straight ahead, and he'd play hurt."

Creekmur moved seamlessly to left tackle in 1952, with Jim Martin taking over his old guard spot. Creekmur would spend the rest of his career there. Dorne Dibble remembered him as "the best holding tackle in the league," an honor Lou happily acknowledged in retirement. One football writer of the era described him as "an absolute artist in the slick trick of holding an opponent. He could lock a rival's arm under his own, twist, whirl him around and dump him so quickly the poor guy never knew how it happened."

Away from the field, Creekmur was an easygoing lug of a guy. He sold cars at a Pontiac dealership throughout the year and was a favorite speaker at the many sports and scouts banquets around Detroit. He enjoyed hammering opponents as much as he did pounding beer. There was, for example, that afternoon he blew up Packers linebacker Clayton Tonnemaker with one of his atomic elbow blasts.

"Doak Walker had come around end and had just slipped down," he recalled. "Clayton was going to make sure he didn't get up and was just startin' to come down with both knees in the middle of Doak's back. And the timing was just perfect for me. I was on the other side of Doak and I caught it just in time and I let one ride. And at that time they had those big, thick plastic masks—big thick bar—well, I came right through that bar on Clayton. It must have ended up in the upper deck, knocked Clayton cold, gave him a bloody nose, two black eyes, and must have knocked out a couple of teeth. And, boy, did my elbow hurt."

T hanks to another torrid race, Detroiters were pouring into Briggs Stadium in ever greater numbers. In 1952, the Lions established a new home attendance record, with three games drawing more than 50,000 spectators. There was a packed house on November 2, when the Lions hosted Cleveland in what Detroit fans hoped was a preview of an upcoming title match. Looking to calm nerves and minimize distractions, Parker instituted a new policy with the Browns game. Prior to each home game, the team now spent the evening at the Sheraton-Cadillac (née Book-Cadillac) Hotel on Washington Boulevard, a few blocks from Briggs Stadium.

"The night before a game, every player is nervous," Layne explained. "He picks on his wife, his kids or anybody else near him. I venture to say Parker saved many marriages by getting us away from our wives the night before a game. Only another player can tell you of the tension, and, usually, he won't. He wants to make believe it's just another night, but it isn't." On Sunday mornings, Hart, Banonis, and other observant Catholics on the team attended mass at nearby St. Aloysius Church before heading to the park. Layne and other non-Catholics often joined them.

"It was a battle of defenses," Parker said of the first regular-season tilt between the Lions and Browns. "You saw two of the greatest defenses in football out there. That made it hard for any offense to move."

Both lines smashed into each other all day, with Jim Doran drawing special praise for looping around blockers to sack Otto Graham four times. Layne crossed up the Browns with option plays where he'd fake a pass and then run up the middle. Of those passes he did unleash, a 7-yard strike to Hart in the second quarter was the most picturesque. Catching it seemed hopeless—the end later said he thought Layne was deliberately throwing the ball away. But Hart, a few yards deep in the end zone, leaped and gripped the back end of the whizzing ball as it zipped under the crossbar. Hart added a second TD reception that sewed up the 17–6 victory.

"I don't feel bad losing to a team like that," Paul Brown said afterward. "The Lions, at least when we've played them, have been potentially the best team in the National Football League." He called Layne "the outstanding player on the field."

Walker dressed but stayed on the bench against the Browns. For Layne, there was an unforeseen benefit of Doak's prolonged absence: a growing acceptance by Detroit fans. Now in his third year with the Lions, the Pro Bowl quarterback had struggled to win them over. He had led the loop in passing yardage in each of his first two seasons in Detroit, and his total of 42 touchdown passes over the same period easily outdistanced the 31 tossed by runners-up Graham and Norm Van Brocklin. Nonetheless, it had always been Walker who was the chief focus of the offense and the agreeable public face of the team, the man that most fans, writers, and advertisers naturally gravitated to.

"The Layne critics were quick to voice their displeasure over an errant pass or Bobby's earnestness in 'eating the ball' when his blockers failed him," Watson Spoelstra wrote near the end of the '52 season. "Bobby's superb record for arching touchdown passes never got him the acclaim he deserved."

Now, oddly, it was Layne's running that was delighting fans. Parker, reacting to his diminishing corps of ball carriers, had installed a quarterback option play to put some punch into the offense. The play was popular in college ball but, aside from Green Bay, rarely used by pro teams. Layne would take the snap and move laterally down the line, preceded by a pulling guard. Once he got to the defensive end, he had to quickly size up the situation: either keep the ball or pitch it to a trailing back. Disdaining hip, knee, and thigh pads ("They bind me," he explained), and wearing wafer-thin shoulder pads, Layne often took a beating lugging the ball up the field, but he still got up after every tackle. He had a shifty stop-and-go style that allowed him to change direction and avoid too many direct hits.

Parker was roundly criticized for subjecting his star quarterback to possible injury, but he rationalized that Layne's natural ball-carrying instincts and youth would offset the risks. "The chances we took were entirely justified by the results," he said. By season's end, Layne had piled up 411 yards on 94 carries, both career highs and both second-best on the team. In 1952, only eight other players in the league, including Hoernschemeyer (whose 457 yards on 106 rushes led the Lions), gained more yards on the ground.

"If his sinewy legs carry Detroit to the divisional playoff or, perchance, to the championship, Detroit will have to dust off a permanent place for a new favorite," Spoelstra continued. "Layne's passes always were beautiful things to see; his runs have taken him places he never knew before—in the hearts of the cash customers."

Walker finally made it back onto the field on a foggy, drizzly Sunday at Pittsburgh, where he kicked a field goal as the Lions rolled to a 31–6 win to improve to 5–2. Otherwise he was just a spectator as Layne led a pulverizing ground attack that piled up 321 yards, including two scoring runs by Jug Girard. Defensive standouts Bingaman, Prchlik, McGraw, and Doran held the Steelers to –3 yards on the ground. With San Francisco losing its second straight game, the Lions and 49ers were now tied for first place.

One week later, Detroit improved to 6–2, crushing the Dallas Texans, 43–13, at Briggs Stadium. Layne's 69 rushing yards more than doubled that of any other ball carrier on the field. At Chicago the following Sunday, the Lions seemed to have the game won after Jack Christiansen fielded a punt with two minutes to play and raced down the sideline for a 79-yard touchdown and a 23–17 lead. However, George Blanda quickly came back to throw his third touchdown pass of the day, a 2-yard toss to Ed Sprinkle with just nine seconds left. Blanda then kicked the extra point for a 24–23 win. Earlier, a bad snap had caused one of Pat Harder's own conversion tries to be blocked, costing the Lions a tie.

Their first loss in six weeks dropped the Lions into a four-way deadlock for first place with the surging Rams, the slumping 49ers, and the surprising Packers. All had 6–3 records. Nearly 40,000 were on hand on Thanksgiving Day to watch the Lions square off with Green Bay. Tobin Rote hooked up with rookie sensation Billy Howton on three scoring strikes. But Box matched Howton stride for stride, gathering in a pair of touchdown passes from Layne and a third from Hoernschemeyer. The swarming Lions recovered six fumbles and stole two passes as they rolled to a 48–24 victory. Walker ran from scrimmage for the first time in nearly two months, picking up a single yard on a token rush. Once again, Layne easily out-gained all other ball carriers on the field with 63 yards.

The Rams kept pace with the now 7–3 Lions by beating the 49ers for the second week in a row. The following Sunday, both front-runners moved to 8–3 as Los Angeles crushed Green Bay and Detroit whipped the Bears, 45–21, at Briggs Stadium. Layne connected with Box for three touchdowns in the first half against the Bears.

Detroit's running corps was becoming more depleted by the week, with Girard now lost for the season with a knee injury, Hoernschemeyer hobbled by injured ribs, and Walker gingerly working his way back into top form. Parker continued to use Walker sparingly. "If we get to the playoffs," he explained, "we'll need Doak." Christiansen, pressed into emergency service against the Bears, led all rushers with 54 yards, including an 18-yard scoring scamper.

Parker's "interchangeable parts" approach was paying dividends. "When Coach Buddy Parker began putting this year's Lion squad together he insisted that the versatile player would be the one to make the grade," wrote *Free Press* beat writer Bob Latshaw.

"Few of the fans had heard of Bob Miller, a rookie tackle from Virginia. But line coach Aldo Forte will tell you he is one of the best prospects to hit the National Football League in years. Miller has handled virtually every position between the ends. He started as an offensive tackle. He was switched to defense when injuries made that move necessary. Then he was moved into the middle guard spot on defense where he was compared with the stellar Les Bingaman. He wasn't found wanting. . . . Dick Flanagan, who has been an outstanding linebacker, can play that spot, offensive guard or even defensive end. Jim Martin, who has been primarily an offensive guard, can also take over as a linebacker or defensive end. . . . The rest of the squad is about the same. . . . You can take it from Parker—if the Lions win the title this year, it will be because he can take somebody—anybody— off the bench and know he'll do a good job in any position."

The final weekend of the regular season saw the Rams hosting Pittsburgh and the Lions playing Dallas. The woeful Texans, drawing poorly and hemorrhaging money, had been taken over by the league at midseason and were now operating solely as a road team. The Lions crushed Dallas, 41–6, as Box had seven catches for 202 yards and enjoyed his third straight three-touchdown game. Box's final tally of 15 touchdowns (on just 42 catches) was an NFL season high and a team record that would stand nearly three decades. Walker picked up 92 yards rushing and receiving while Christiansen rambled for 94 yards on 13 carries, including a 65-yard scoring run that thrilled the skimpy Saturday afternoon crowd in Detroit.

The next day, a steamy Sunday in Los Angeles, the Rams beat Pittsburgh to finish the regular season at 9–3, the same as the Lions. Bert Bell had previously announced that a deadlock at the top of the National Conference standings would be settled by a special playoff in Detroit on Sunday, December 21. Home-field advantage had been determined by a coin flip. The winner of the tiebreaker would go on to play the Browns, who had claimed their third straight American Conference crown, for the championship the following week in Cleveland.

The experienced Rams would be gunning for their ninth straight win and their fourth consecutive division crown. The upstart Lions, winners of eight of their last nine games, also were riding a wave of momentum. Long lines formed outside Briggs Stadium and the Lions' offices on Michigan Avenue, with 30,000 tickets sold in the first 14 hours. With a sellout seemingly guaranteed, Edwin Anderson successfully petitioned Bell to lift the local television blackout. Bell's decision let Detroiters watch the Lions' first postseason action since the Great Depression in the comfort of their living room or inside the smoky confines of the neighborhood tavern. But it also cut into the gate, with only a few tickets sold after the announcement.

The Rams were necessarily worried about Box, more so after it became apparent that their prize rookie, defensive back Dick "Night Train" Lane, would not recover from the twisted knee he had suffered against Pittsburgh. During the season Lane had intercepted 14 passes, a league record that still stands. Hamp Pool had Elroy Hirsch work out with the secondary in the event his services were needed to shut down the Lions' deep scoring threat. The Rams, with 349 points, and the Lions, with five less, were the top scoring teams in the league.

However, the Lions were fielding the NFL's stingiest defense, having surrendered an average of just 16 points a game. They also led the league in rushing defense. Moreover, they had established a league record with 57 takeaways (32 interceptions and 25 fumble recoveries), nearly five a game. That stifling defense, coupled with the news that Layne, Walker, Hoernschemeyer, and Harder were healthy enough to be playing together in the backfield for the first time since Detroit beat the Rams back on October 19, was enough to make the Lions three-point favorites.

Crazylegs and company flew out from Los Angeles, where temperatures had been hovering around 90 degrees, and arrived to teeth-chattering cold in Detroit. Snow and sleet fell in the days leading up to the game. Both teams ran some of their drills in tennis shoes, in case they were needed on Briggs Stadium's semi-frozen field.

On Sunday, a steady drizzle fell and fog hung over the soggy turf. The park's rooftop lamps, turned on all afternoon, stared unblinking and bleary-eyed in the gloom. "It was 'ceiling zero' and a good part of the time one had to guess what was happening," reported Louis Effrat of the *New York Times*, peering down from his perch in the press box. "However, even through the fog, it was obvious to the naked eye that the Detroit club was superior. The Lions were faster, more certain of their maneuvers and clearly more imaginative."

A damp crowd of 47,645 watched the ghostly Lions take charge from the start. As expected, the Rams double- and triple-teamed Box and also kept two defenders on Walker. This gave Leon Hart room to roam. He caught five passes, including two on the Lions' first scoring drive. That was set up when Norm Van Brocklin, pressured by rookie end Blaine Earon, shanked a 12-yard punt early in the first quarter.

As a passer, Layne wasn't particularly sharp, getting picked off four times. But as a field general, he smartly directed first-half scoring marches of 52 and 80 yards. Each drive took just six plays, and each ended with Harder covering the final distance. On the first, Harder rumbled 12 yards around right end, assisted by a Walker block that took out three Rams. On the second, he blasted over from four yards out. Doak accounted for most of the yardage on the latter drive, grabbing a 51-yard pass from Layne and, two plays later, a 24-yard pass from Hoernschemeyer.

The Rams finally put up some points when Norm Van Brocklin shot a 14-yard scoring pass to Tom Fears late in the second quarter. Detroit led at the half, 14–7. In the third quarter, Walker continued to do everything but score, throwing a 22-yard touchdown pass to Hart. Harder's conversion made it 21–7. Five minutes later, Harder's tired right leg accounted for a 43-yard field goal to make the score Detroit 24, Los Angeles 7.

Midway through the final quarter, the Rams narrowed the gap to 10 points when Dan Towler culminated a drive with a 5-yard touchdown run. On their next possession, the Lions were forced to punt. Bob Smith kicked to V. T. "Vitamin T" Smith, who grabbed the ball on his own 43 and flew down the sideline, a blurry figure in the gloom. Smith's 57-yard touchdown sprint made it 24–21.

The Lions, after dominating the defending champs most of the game, were in danger of a stunning collapse. There was 2:45 left to play when Bob Waterfield, playing his last game for the Rams, started Los Angeles's final drive from his own 12-yard line. He looked for Hirsch, whom the Lions had kept out of the end zone for the fourth consecutive game between the two rivals. Christiansen got a piece of Waterfield's pass and the ball wound up in the hands of linebacker LaVern Torgeson. From there it took only three plays to reach the end zone, Hoernschemeyer covering the final nine yards on a hard run off tackle with 30 seconds left. Harder tacked on the conversion to seal the 31–21 victory.

Harder, slumped on a stool inside the locker room a few minutes later, attributed the win to the team's esprit de corps. "We never worked as a unit before like that since I joined the Lions a couple years ago," said the battered veteran, whose 72 yards on eight carries led all Detroit rushers and whose 19 total points (on two touchdowns, four extra points, and a field goal) were a new postseason record.

In another corner of Briggs Stadium, Hamp Pool admitted his team had been mentally unprepared, something he took full responsibility for. "I knew they weren't ready for such a rugged game this morning at breakfast," he said. He praised his players, who had "fought like demons" after falling behind, and acknowledged their even more tenacious opponents. "What can you say about a team that beats you three times?" he asked.

Perhaps only that they were "a hungry herd of Lions," as one out-of-town sportswriter described the victors. But not *too* hungry as they prepared for the Browns, Harder said. "Sure we'll go light on the turkey Thursday," which was Christmas. "We can eat turkey all winter."

The championship game was set for December 28 at Cleveland's Municipal Stadium. The Browns had never lost a postseason game on their home turf. Counting their four years in the AAFC, it was the Browns' seventh title match in seven seasons, with their loss at Los Angeles in the 1951 championship game the franchise's only postseason failure.

Despite such success, Paul Brown insisted his team deserved to be 15-point underdogs against the talent-rich Lions. "They've got more guns than anything we've ever faced," he said, pointing out that the Browns' own arsenal was sorely depleted. His top two receivers, end Mac Speedie (who had led the league in catches) and halfback Dub Jones, were sidelined with knee injuries, and tackle John Kissell also would miss the game. Lou Groza, the league's top field-goal kicker, would have to play with badly injured ribs that impaired his kicking ability.

"Paul Brown's Browns of 1952 are not to be confused with the slashing Cleveland teams that used to demolish the opposition," Shirley Povich warned in the *Washington Post*. The Browns, who finished with an 8–4 record, were aging. Nine regulars, dubbed the "nine old men," had been with the team since it was formed in 1946. Otto Graham had been uncharacteristically inconsistent all season, leading the loop in touchdown passes *and* interceptions. In Povich's view, the Lions, with their dynamic duo of Layne and Walker and a punishing defensive line, were "packing the wallop that used to belong to the Browns."

Handicappers favored the Lions by three points, but Parker wasn't having any of it. "Anytime a club gets into a championship game seven years straight you can't consider it an underdog," he said. "Brown's crying about injuries, about having an old team, and that the squad will be rusty because it didn't have a game last Sunday."

Brown was right about one thing. He thought the hungry, hardworking Lions "reflected their city." While Cleveland fans appeared largely unmoved by their team's bid for another championship, enthusiasm among Lions fans was sky-high. It had been 17 years since Detroit's last pro grid title. Nick Kerbawy took an empty suitcase to Cleveland and returned with 10,000 reserved tickets, priced at $4 and $5, for Detroit fans. Brown noted that "they're all behind that team. . . . It makes a difference."

It seemed that just everybody in Detroit was talking about the Lions, quite a change from years past. *Detroit News* columnist Edgar "Doc" Greene observed two women discussing the team's chances as each brought in the milk bottles from that morning's delivery.

"Do you think the Lions can beat Cleveland?" Mrs. O'Reilly asked Mrs. Schmaltz.

"I think Cleveland will beat 'em because they've had two weeks' rest," Mrs. O'Reilly replied.

The two neighbors "began fighting happily, with O'Reilly holding a slight edge in more piercing voice tone," Greene wrote. The point being made was that the Lions, "through the graces of television which gets pro football into every garage and bathroom," had now joined baseball and the weather as conversational icebreakers in a way that few other topics could.

The Lions stayed in town for the holidays, working out at Briggs Stadium. Some sad news reached the clubhouse. Michael VanDeKeere, a vice cop who "knew all the Lions personally," had suffered a stroke at the playoff game and died Christmas morning. On December 26, the entire team turned out at the funeral home to pay their respects before heading to Michigan Central Station for the 175-mile train trip to Cleveland. Although DuMont's national telecast was being carried by station WJBK-Channel 2 in Detroit, nearly 8,000 Lions fans traveled by chartered buses and four special trains to watch their heroes in person.

Green-tinted chlorophyll was all over the news then as an additive to toothpaste, chewing gum, and various food products. Chlorophyll's high magnesium content reputedly boosted one's sex drive, causing Parker's players to coin the slogan: "Chlorophyll will put more sock in your jock!" The Lions' wives kept the gag going, making hats out of green-dyed jockstraps and wearing them at the championship game.

There were 50,934 people on hand for the 1:30 kickoff, a larger crowd than expected. It was a bright, clear Sunday, with the temperature slightly below freezing. In the battle of statistics, Cleveland won handily, besting the Lions in total yards (384 to 258) and first downs (22 to 10). Graham had one of his better days against Detroit, completing 20 of 35 throws. But time and again, "Automatic Otto" moved his offensive unit into Detroit territory, only to be thwarted by the Lions' defense.

In the first half, the Browns made three separate forays that reached the Lions' 17-, 31-, and 32-yard lines. Each drive ended with a missed field goal attempt by Groza, who was kicking with tightly taped ribs. In the second half the Browns would squander more opportunities, even as Marion Motley and Harry "Chick" Jagade continued to pile up big yards on the ground. Jagade ran for 104 yards on 15 carries while Motley added 74 more on just a half-dozen rushes. Meanwhile, the Lions spent most of the afternoon bottled up in their own end of the field.

The game was scoreless in the second quarter when a poor punt gave Detroit possession at midfield. Layne marched the team deep into the Browns' backyard. He called Walker's number in the huddle. "Doak, you rested up all year," he said, "you should be ready."

Walker carried to the Browns' 12-yard line. Layne passed to Bill Swiacki at the 3. After an offsides penalty pushed the Lions back to the 8, Walker was given the ball again. He swept the right side and was knocked down at the 2. On the next play, Layne lowered his helmet and plowed into the end zone behind a crunching block by Vince Banonis. Walker's extra point made the score 7–0, a lead Detroit carried into the locker room at halftime.

The second half saw the Lions continue to play conservative, error-free ball. With Cleveland dominating time of possession, they ran only 44 offensive plays all afternoon to Cleveland's 70. Layne threw just nine passes, completing seven for 68 yards, while Walker misfired on his one attempt.

"If they purposely played it carefully, taking no chances and waiting for the big breaks that usually decide a championship game, the strategy worked perfectly," observed the *Cleveland Plain Dealer*'s Harold Sauerbrei. "But the Lions also had one important thing the Browns didn't have. They had a long-short runner, the kind who may be bottled up 99 percent of the time and break your heart with one tremendous effort. That boy was Walker . . . out most of the season with injuries, carried the ball nine times yesterday and was held to 30 yards. But on the 10th time, Doak was sprung through the line like a flash and was gone for the distance."

The Lions had a play called "26 cross buck," where Hoernschemeyer, the right halfback, ran to his left and, following the pulling right guard, Dick Stanfel, cut into the hole between the left guard and tackle. The left halfback, Walker, acted as a decoy on the play, faking a dive into Stanfel's vacated spot. Walker had observed that every time the Lions ran the play, Cleveland's tackle would ignore him and immediately chase Stanfel, leaving a yawning hole in the line. The man wasn't even touching him, Doak told Layne in the huddle. "Give me the ball just once."

The Lions were lined up on their own 33. Layne called "26 cross buck," but this time slipped the ball to Walker. Once again, Cleveland's tackle followed the pulling guard, and Walker bolted through the hole. He shrugged off one tackler and whisked past another. In seconds he was in the clear, sprinting for the end zone. Box ran interference, getting in the way of Warren Lahr, the only Brown with a chance of catching Walker.

"Box was the guy who made Doak Walker's touchdown run possible," said Aldo Forte. Walker remembered: "It was a cross-buck and things just opened up for me. I reversed my field and no one was there, I was too scared to slow down so I kept going. Then I looked up and saw Cloyce Box with me and we just ran into the end zone."

Walker's 67-yard gallop was easily the longest run from scrimmage in his pro career—his next-longest run in six seasons was 51 yards—and the 97 yards he gained on the day was his best rushing output ever as a Lion. More significantly, his six-pointer was the first touchdown he had scored all season. As was his style, the Doaker had saved his best for when it counted most.

"That's pretty much the image you have of Doak," recalled Yale Lary, who had watched Walker perform while growing up in Fort Worth and once played against him in college. Now, here they were teammates in the NFL title game "and whoosh—there he goes for the big score. When he ran, he would just sort of glide down the field. I think the reason he was so hard to tackle is that he was really running harder and faster than you thought he was."

Walker kicked the extra point to make it 14–0. Then there was a shift in momentum. For the next 13 minutes, from the last half of the third quarter until well into the fourth, the Browns clawed back into the game, holding the ball for all but five plays.

Graham responded to Walker's scintillating dash with a methodical 12-play, 68-yard drive, Jagade crashing over tackle from seven yards out for the touchdown. Groza's extra point made it 14–7. After forcing the Lions to punt, the Browns next moved 78 yards in six plays, apparently on their way to the tying touchdown. The biggest chunk was bit off by Motley, who swept left end and rumbled 42 yards before being hauled down by Don Doll at Detroit's 5-yard line.

Once again, Cleveland was banging on the door. But in the pivotal sequence of the game, the Lions stiffened and threw back the Browns. On first down, Motley ran wide right and was dumped for a 5-yard loss. On second down, Graham went back to pass and was snowed under by Thurman McGraw and Jim Doran for a 12-yard loss. On third down, Graham was swarmed but managed to pick up a yard. It was fourth and goal from the 21. Ignoring a field-goal try, the Browns went for all the marbles. But Graham's pass over the middle was knocked down by Dick Flanagan.

There still were nine minutes left to play. After their magnificent stand, the Lions were forced to punt. Bob Smith booted one high down the middle of the field. Ken Carpenter ran up to grab it—and the ball dropped right through his hands. Jim Martin recovered on the Cleveland 23. Carpenter's miscue set up the

clinching points, a Pat Harder field goal from the 36 that made the score Detroit 17, Cleveland 7.

Graham managed to drive the Browns one last time deep into Detroit territory, but an apparent fourth-down touchdown pass to Darrell Brewster with a little over a minute to play was nullified because the ball was first tipped by Ray Renfro. Unlike in college, NFL rules specified that two eligible receivers couldn't touch the ball on the same play.

The Lions took over and ran out the clock. Banonis was getting ready to center the ball when he noticed the umpire futilely trying to fire his gun to signal the end of the game. "He clicked the trigger three times and the darned thing didn't go off," Banonis said. "I saw him reach for his whistle so I just picked up the ball and ran as fast as I could go." Banonis said he wouldn't take $10,000 for the souvenir.

For now, the grinning center, who never made more than $8,500 in an NFL season, didn't need the money. Gross receipts from the title game were a record $314,318, including $100,000 in television and radio rights. After expenses, net proceeds were $248,636, with 70 percent of that divided among players and coaches. Each Lion voted a full winner's share by his teammates received $2,274.77. For the losing Browns, each full share was $1,712.49. Thus, the difference between winning and losing the championship worked out to $562.28 per man—an amount that, even after taxes, was more than enough to cover the cost of a decent used car or a new set of household appliances.

A few hundred fans greeted the returning heroes at the Michigan Central Station. There would be no parade down Woodward Avenue and no diamond-encrusted championship rings to mark the victory, not even a celebratory banquet. Players loaded up their cars, most hoping to enjoy a few days' rest before starting an off-season job or a winter semester at school. To them, the value of being recognized as pro football's champions after a brutal five-month slough was incalculable anyway.

The Lions were indisputably "world beaters." Counting exhibition, regular-season, and postseason games, they had whipped the two entrenched powers of pro football, the Browns and Rams, three times each in a single season. And they did it with an appealing joie de vivre.

"The Lions were more than mechanical football players," observed Harry Salsinger of the *Detroit News*, "they played like men who love to play, with a vim and zest for the game. They had the spirit that makes champions." Citing the team's youth and balance, Cleveland sportswriter Bob Yonkers wrote: "Winners and new champions of the National Football League, the Detroit Lions appear equipped to remain a strong contender in the rugged pay-for-play ranks for several years."

Yonkers was correct; there were more titles and thrills waiting down the road. But as with so many other good things in life, nothing was quite like the first time.

"That game stands out above the rest," said Layne, who drove straight home to Texas after the game. "Nothing was ever as good as that. It's the happiest I've ever been in football, winning the championship."

CHAPTER
4

PRO Football AT ITS Best

> What I remember best of those times was not the games
> we played, but the closeness of everybody on the team.
> There never was a team like the Lions of the 1950s. It was
> just one big happy family—our family against the rest of
> the football world.
>
> —Yale Lary

After Detroit defeated Cleveland in the 1952 title game, a joke made the rounds of Dallas. "Did you know the Dallas Texans won the championship of pro football?"

Recognizing the short-lived franchise as not only a local embarrassment but as one of the biggest failures in NFL history, the typical response was, "How could that be?"

"Sure," the wag would say. "Doak Walker and Bobby Layne."

The Lions' Lone Star contingent continued to grow in 1953 with the addition of Harley Sewell, the club's top draft pick from the University of Texas, Layne's alma mater. Sewell was widely considered to be the finest lineman to come out of the state in many years. "I was glad Detroit drafted me," Sewell said, "because they've got quite a few Texas boys on the club, fellows like Bobby Layne, Doak Walker, and Cloyce Box."

The burly guard with the wispy blond hair had a high tolerance for pain, as evidenced by the punishment he'd absorbed in the Texas-Oklahoma game his senior year. "Early in the game Sewell got his nose smashed," Longhorns trainer Tommy Wilson recalled. "I mean it was crushed. You could see from up in the stands that it was smashed all over his face, but he didn't leave the game. When he finally did come out, I wiped his face. Then he went back in. The next time he came out his right eye was closed. It looked like an eye a boxer might get— swollen shut, a big purple bruise, and bloody."

"Can you get me one of those birdcage things to put over my face?" Sewell asked. Wilson said he'd try. "Only reason I need it," Sewell said, "is I don't want that guy to close my other eye. I know who did it this time and I want to be able to see long enough to get him."

Sewell grew up a hustling, barefooted "hillbilly kid" in the small north Texas town of St. Jo. He was notorious for his grimy face and filthy uniform, as if he hadn't bothered to wash either between games. Paul Pentecost, the Wayne University public relations man who served as Van Patrick's spotter in the broadcast booth, recalled searching for Sewell's No. 66. "After about five minutes," Pentecost said, "it's easier to find him. I just look for the dirtiest shirt and pants around. That's Harley."

In his pseudoscientific way, Sewell attributed his trademark pigpen appearance to "Texas sweat." Texans don't perspire, he explained, they sweat. Sewell sweated a lot, which meant he was always soaking wet. "And then all the dirt on the field seems to stick to me," he said. Which was fine with Sewell, since he felt he played his best when he was hot, sticky, and muddy. "It always comes off in the shower," he pointed out.

Sewell quickly developed into one of the finest pulling guards in the NFL, using his speed and 6-foot-1, 220-pound frame to clear paths for Lions backs on sweeps, traps, and counter plays. He also was an excellent pass blocker and special teams performer. He would play a full decade in Detroit, making four Pro Bowls, before ending his career with a final season in Los Angeles. "You got to be a dawg, a dirty good-for-nothin' dawg people can spit on and walk on," was how Harley once described the thankless job of an offensive lineman.

Sewell was just one of another fine crop of draftees. Seven rookies would wind up making the team, including Ollie Spencer, an easygoing 6-foot-2,

230-pound tackle from Kansas. "When Spencer moves somebody out of there, they stay blocked," said Aldo Forte. Spencer took the place of veteran Gus Cifelli (who was traded to Green Bay for a draft pick) on the right side of the offensive line, alongside Dick Stanfel.

Another addition to the line was Charlie Ane of Southern Cal. The temperamental Hawaiian would spend his seven seasons in Detroit rotating between center and tackle. Other newcomers included Lew Carpenter, a hard-hitting back from Arkansas; Carl Karilivacz, a slender defensive back out of Syracuse; Indiana running back Gene Gedman; and Pitt linebacker Joe Schmidt.

Schmidt, whose hardscrabble upbringing included the loss of two older brothers and his father by the time he was 13, was unhappy about being drafted by the Lions. He had hoped to be playing for his hometown Steelers. The odds of making Detroit's star-packed roster intimidated him and he considered playing in Canada. "Toronto offered me $6,000 and I came close to signing," he recalled. "Russ Thomas told me, 'We have professors who don't make $6,000.' I settled for $5,700. I came home and told my mother. She thought I'd hit the lottery. She worked for five dollars a day."

Gedman and Schmidt drove together from Pittsburgh to Detroit in Gedman's car, with Schmidt expressing doubts en route. The two had met at the Senior Bowl and hit it off. "Gene was a fun-loving guy," Schmidt said. "He pulled a lot of pranks on me. He also was very self-confident. He'd tell me, 'You worry too much, Schmitty.' I'd say, 'Well, you're a second-round draft pick and I'm a seventh-round, so I got a right to worry.'"

Instead of reporting directly to camp, the pair pulled up to the Lions' offices at 1401 Michigan Avenue at Eight Street, a couple blocks from Briggs Stadium. Gedman was an unexpected surprise, as news reports had him seriously considering the Ottawa club in Canada. Nick Kerbawy greeted him enthusiastically. Gedman was slotted to be the number-two fullback behind Pat Harder, and the general manager was eager to get his signature on a contract.

Schmidt sat quietly in the lobby as the two men chatted behind closed doors. Kerbawy asked Gedman who his friend was.

"That's Joe Schmidt," he said. "He's one of your draft choices."

"I thought he was one of your fraternity brothers," Kerbawy said.

Signing Gedman was no easy task. With negotiations looking to drag on for a while, Kerbawy took Schmidt outside and pointed to a fire hydrant across the street, near the stadium. The Michigan Avenue bus to Ypsilanti would be passing by soon, he said, and Schmidt could catch it there.

While Kerbawy took Gedman to a nice restaurant to continue their conversation, Schmidt stood at the bus stop, suitcase in hand, his clothes sticking in the July heat as he breathed in the exhaust from passing traffic. "For years, every time I saw that fucking hydrant I'd think of that day," he said.

A long bus ride and some traipsing through Ypsilanti's unfamiliar streets followed. By early evening, "Schmitty" was settled inside a dormitory at Michigan Normal College. He was nervous and a little bit in awe as, one by one, black-and-white figures from the sports pages appeared in full living color. At one point, Lou Creekmur pulled up and Schmidt and a few others had to unpack his car and lug his suitcases, golf clubs, record player, bowling bag, and other what-have-you up to his room.

Over the coming weeks, Schmidt tried to keep a low profile, especially around Layne, who would always take a bunch of rookies out to drink pitchers of beer after practice. Rookies were astonished at the amount of drinking that went on. It was almost as if they were on an extended Stroh's brewery tour instead of at training camp. Schmidt thought all that drinking was bad for his conditioning. The veterans really didn't pay that much attention to him, and Schmidt was more than okay with that.

Schmidt's low-key arrival was quite a contrast to Jim Hardy's grand entrance. The backup quarterback and morale-building "Logan" of 1952 was torn between reporting or retiring to his lucrative plastics business in Los Angeles. When he finally decided to come to camp, he hired a small plane to circle the practice field. Players watched with amusement as Hardy, hanging from the window, tossed out dozens of jockstraps. Each bore the message: "Have no fear, Logan is here."

But Logan/Hardy didn't stay long. He had a change of heart and retired a few weeks later, leaving Tom Dublinski as the Lions' number-two signal-caller.

The first order of business for the Lions was preparing for the College All-Star Game, the unofficial kickoff to football season in America. Each year since 1934, the defending NFL champions played a select squad of collegians, the bulk of the proceeds going to charity. The game, to be played under the lights on August 14 at Chicago's Soldier Field, was the brainchild of Arch Ward of the *Chicago Tribune*. Ward was the most influential sports editor in the country, having also created baseball's All-Star Game, the Golden Gloves boxing tournament, and the AAFC. Buddy Parker had starred at fullback in the Lions' only previous appearance in the College All-Star Game, a 7–7 tie in 1936.

The Lions were the favorites of oddsmakers, but evidently not the organizers. "The pre-game introduction of the rival squads made the Lions look like they were just invited along for the ride," observed one scribe. "Every member of the collegiate squad was given a personal and spot-lighted introduction to the big crowd. Their coaches, ditto. But the Lions, champions of professional football, were herded out in one big lump and that was that."

The Lions won, 24–10, in front of 93,318 spectators. Hoernschemeyer scored on two short runs and Leon Hart fielded a touchdown pass from Layne. Walker grabbed eight passes while Hart and Cloyce Box combined for a dozen receptions and 214 yards. Whether it was a perceived lack of respect or the swarms of mosquitos that invaded the lakefront stadium, the Lions seemed to be in a prickly mood. They were penalized a record 112 yards as tempers got short and players were sent to the showers. By the end of the evening the Lions had outgained the All-Stars, 473 yards to 187, with Layne hitting on 21 of 31 passes for an All-Star Game record 323 yards.

After rolling through the preseason with four victories and a tie, the Lions dropped their final exhibition, at Philadelphia. "The boys just don't like to lose," Parker said, "even when it doesn't count." As it came time to finalize the 33-man roster, several of "the boys" vanished in a flurry of moves. Dick Flanagan and Pat Summerall were sold, and Don Doll was dealt to Washington for two draft picks.

Doll initially balked at reporting. "I started my pro career here," he said. "I'd like to finish it here." Doll would enjoy another Pro Bowl season with the Redskins in 1953 before concluding his brilliant career with a final year in Los Angeles. When he retired, he was the NFL's all-time leader in interceptions with 41. He remains the only man to record 10 or more interceptions in three different seasons.

Vic Banonis, Vince's younger brother and a center at Georgetown in the late '40s, was tried out at linebacker but didn't make the final cut. Also released was Pete Retzlaff, a big back from South Dakota State. Disappointed, Retzlaff enlisted in the army for two years. The Lions would invite him to camp in 1956, intent on converting him into a receiver to take advantage of his size, good hands, and blocking ability. However, the work-in-progress was sold to Philadelphia for the waiver price of $100. "I had the distinction of being cut twice by the Lions—once as a fullback and once as an end," said Retzlaff, who went on to enjoy a long career with the Eagles as one of the most productive tight ends in the league.

Despite all of his apprehensions, Schmidt not only gained a roster spot but replaced Flanagan as one of the starting corner linebackers. "I went to camp thinking I had no chance to make a championship team," Schmidt said. Before one exhibition, the rookie went into the clubhouse to dress and found a Steelers uniform hanging in his locker. "I thought, 'Great, I've been traded. I'm coming home.'" Clubhouse jester Roy Macklem was responsible for the gag. Instead of suiting up for his long-time favorite team, Schmidt had found a new permanent home in Detroit, where he would play and coach for the next two decades.

The Lions officially opened defense of their title on September 27 with a 38–21 victory over Pittsburgh. It was quite the coming-out party for Detroit's first-year men. Early in the game, Lew Carpenter, filling in at linebacker, electrified the Briggs Stadium crowd by scoring the first time he touched the ball, intercepting a Jim Finks pass and returning it 73 yards. Not to be outdone, Gene Gedman also scored the first time he handled the leather, cracking over from a yard out to give Detroit a 14–7 lead. He later added a second touchdown. Schmidt, anxious to justify the coaches' faith in him, was described as "making tackles all over the field."

Flanagan had joined the Steelers earlier in the week and did his best to foil his old barstool buddies. He wasn't very successful. Layne threw for 364 yards while Walker displayed his usual all-around brilliance, returning a kickoff deep into Pittsburgh territory to set up one touchdown and picking a Hoernschemeyer pass off his shoe-tops to tally another. One official initially ruled Walker had trapped the ball, causing Vince Banonis to yell to umpire Joe Crowley, "You saw it, Crowley, what was it?" Crowley called it a touchdown.

As further proof that it was the Lions' day, Layne mishandled Banonis's snap on the ensuing extra-point try and the ball fell over sideways. It was lying there like a loaf of Silvercup bread when Doak calmly swiped at it anyway and punched it awkwardly through the uprights.

Game two was a Saturday night contest at Baltimore. The city was back in the NFL after the original Colts franchise was dissolved by the league following a dismal 1–11 season in 1950. The new version of the Colts inherited much of the failed Dallas franchise, including more than a dozen of their players, the team's blue and white colors, and even the sideline capes, which now had a Colts patch sewn over the word "Texans."

It was an ornery affair, with plenty of knee-drops and flashing elbows. Detroit opened the scoring with a scintillating 49-yard run by Hoernschemeyer, who absolutely refused to be stopped as he rumbled downfield. "Bob was trapped on two occasions, actually knocked to the ground on another and then made use of a booming stiff-arm to obliterate the last Colt in his way on the trip to the goal line," wrote Bob Latshaw.

The Colts picked off five passes in the first half and harassed Layne and Dublinski all night, holding them to just 74 net passing yards. The Lions went into the locker room at halftime on the wrong end of a 17–10 score, as Fred Enke threw a pair of scoring passes against his former team. But in the third quarter, Yale Lary hauled back a punt 74 yards for a score and Hunchy added a second touchdown run. Meanwhile, the defense blanked the Colts in the second half as the Lions left Maryland with a hard-earned 27–17 win.

The Steelers and Colts were appetizers for the main course: four straight games against the 49ers and Rams, the results of which would go a long way toward determining the division championship. The first game in what was rightfully labeled a "murderous month" was a home date against San Francisco, a team that had won five straight over the Lions dating back to Bo McMillan's final year. Parker had yet to beat the 49ers in four meetings. This was thanks in no small part to Y. A. Tittle, whose slingshot passes and crafty play-making made him a thorn in the Lions' paw throughout his career.

Seven thousand bleacher seats at Briggs Stadium went on sale at noon on Sunday, October 11. After those were quickly snatched up, standing-room-only tickets were sold. By the two o'clock kickoff, a club-record 58,079 frenzied fans had been squeezed into the park to watch the unbeaten rivals go at it. The Lions only needed three offensive plays to draw first blood. On the first play from scrimmage, Layne and Cloyce Box hooked up on a 49-yard catch-and-run. Two plays later, Walker hit Box with a 23-yard scoring pass. On the following series, Les Bingaman blocked a Gordy Soltau field-goal attempt, leading to a Walker field goal that boosted Detroit's lead to 10–0.

On the day, the Lions held the 49ers' vaunted one-two punch of Joe Perry and Hugh McElhenny to a combined 37 yards on 24 carries, while limiting the passing game to a net gain of 59 yards. Nonetheless, the 49ers' offense scored three touchdowns, helped by turnovers and kick returns that allowed Tittle to work with a short field. The first two touchdowns were set up by Layne interceptions. Tittle found Soltau with a scoring pass to make it 10–7, then three minutes later Joe Arenas concluded another short drive with a 10-yard TD run. The Lions took back the lead with a pair of touchdowns. A 4-yard run by Hoernschemeyer late in the first half made it 17–14. Then a 49-yard reception by Leon Hart, who carried a defender the last several yards into the end zone, grew the advantage to 24–14 in the third quarter.

On the kickoff following Hart's touchdown, Arenas sped 66 yards before being stopped deep in Detroit territory. Tittle drove the 49ers to Detroit's 1-yard line, where he called on a favorite play—the bootleg. Tittle scored but paid a heavy price. "Jack Christiansen grabbed my arm as I crossed the goal-line and buggy-whipped me into a circle," he said. "At the end of the whip, my face met Jim David's knee. I could hear the bones crunching in my cheek. It was the worst pain I have ever experienced."

Tittle's touchdown closed the gap to 24–21. That held up as the final score as the Lions shut down defensive back Jimmy Powers, who came in to replace the injured quarterback.

Tittle's right cheekbone was a jigsaw puzzle of shattered bone. He spent the next five days at Detroit Osteopathic Hospital, where the Lions' team doctor, Richard Thompson, performed surgery. An inflated balloon held the reassembled pieces in place. All of the Lions visited Tittle at the hospital. There was no acrimony. The 49ers even sent a thank-you letter to the club, singling out Walker for praise.

Los Angeles was next to invade Briggs Stadium. The Lions, seemingly lulled into lethargy by the balmy October weather, never led, though they did creep to within five points when Layne found Dorne Dibble with a 36-yard scoring pass midway through the third quarter. However, Norm Van Brocklin connected with speedster Bob Boyd on a long pass for the clinching touchdown in a 31–19 Rams victory. Fans booed and chanted "Bobby's got to go!" as Layne was harried all day long by the charged-up Rams.

"We had it coming and we got it . . . got it right between the eyes," one Detroit veteran admitted afterward. The team had become cocky and a bit complacent, he said. Hopefully their poor performance was a wake-up call.

With the loss the Lions fell into a three-way tie for first place with the Rams and 49ers, all now 3–1. They also opened themselves up to renewed charges of dirty football when, for the second week in a row, David knocked a star player out of the game. This time it was Tom Fears, who received two cracked vertebrae, courtesy of another knees-first tackle by David.

"Fears had hit Yale Lary out of bounds on the previous play," David said later, "and I told him he better not come to my side of the field and try that." According to David's version of events, "Fears caught a low pass and fell down. When I saw Carl Karilivacz miss the tackle I kept coming. Fears was still sitting there, but he was trying to get up. The whistle hadn't blown so I came on in and tackled him. Maybe I hit him with my knees. Frankly, I don't know, it was one of those split-second situations where you react automatically."

Elroy Hirsch was among those leveling accusations, though the Rams needed to answer for their own cheap shots. Safety Norb Hecker had kicked Walker in the back after a play was over, forcing Doak to miss much of the game. Several other Detroit starters were hurt in the contest and would see limited action on the West Coast. To shore up the defense, Parker signed end Bob Dove, who had a reputation for nastiness. The eight-year NFL veteran was the latest Chicago Cardinal to rejoin Buddy in Detroit.

The Lions flew to California. On October 18 at Kezar Stadium, the fired-up 49ers enjoyed a statistical romp. They rolled up 25 first downs as Perry punished the Lions with 148 yards on 26 carries and McElhenny collected 130 yards on runs and receptions. Nonetheless, thanks to timely defense, the "outclassed" Lions prevailed with the only numbers that mattered, those on the scoreboard. After spotting San Francisco a 10–0 lead, the Lions repeatedly slapped down the 49ers each time they approached the goal line.

Meanwhile, Layne threw a touchdown pass to Dibble in the second quarter to make it 10–7. In the fourth quarter, he engineered an 80-yard march for the winning score. A gamble kept the comeback drive going. On fourth down with six yards to go, Yale Lary dropped back to punt—then pulled down the ball and ran around left end for a 21-yard gain. The fake punt, called from the sideline by George Wilson, surprised even the offensive unit. It put Detroit in business on the 49ers' 24-yard line. Layne threw incomplete on first down. On the next play, a blitz left Ollie Cline open for a short pass in the middle of the field, and the fullback ran untouched into the end zone. Walker's extra point made it 14–10.

Tittle made his first appearance since being injured two weeks earlier, wearing a shield to protect his splintered cheekbone. He was brought into the game twice in relief of Jimmy Powers. Tittle threw just two passes, and each resulted in an interception that ended a scoring drive. The first time Bob Smith picked off an errant aerial intended for Arenas in the end zone; the second time Christiansen stepped in front of McElhenny and snatched the throw on the Detroit 12. San Francisco fans, already calling for David's scalp, were further incensed when star end Billy Wilson suffered a broken nose near the end of the game. The P.A. announcer credited David with the tackle, even though he was lying on his back several yards away from the play.

Charges of dirty football followed the Lions as they moved on to Los Angeles. Parker bristled. "I want to say for the record that the Lions do not play dirtier football than any other club in the league," he said a few days before the teams clashed at the Coliseum.

David tried to explain himself to Frank Finch of the *Los Angeles Times*. "If I was a dirty player," he insisted, "I'd probably be laughing about them getting hurt. The injuries to Tittle and Fears were just unfortunate coincidences in which I was involved. When you play pro football you have to take your chances. It's no picnic. I'm sincerely sorry they were hurt, but I don't have a guilty conscience."

With his lantern jaw, five o'clock shadow, and a tight smile that was missing several teeth, David made the perfect villain. This was Hollywood, so the hype grew and grew. Swarms of revenge-minded fans turned out on November 1 to see the Rams "get" the pugnacious back.

The throng of 93,751, then a record turnout for an NFL game, remains the largest crowd ever to see the Lions play anywhere. "It was the greatest stimulation of ticket sales I've ever seen," Nick Kerbawy recalled. "It brought the biggest check we ever brought home. It was 'Remember the Alamo' and 'Remember Tom Fears.' The build-up during the week was tremendous—you'd have thought Jimmy was 7-foot-11."

Eight minutes into the game, Detroit had a 10–0 lead. Walker booted a field goal on the opening drive and Christiansen later ran back an interception 92 yards for a touchdown. At halftime it was Detroit 17, Los Angeles 9. In the third quarter, however, the Rams turned the game around. "Skeets" Quinlan peeled off a 74-yard TD run on a sweep. Then, on successive possessions, Woodley Lewis and Jack Dwyer returned Layne interceptions for scores. A Van Brocklin touchdown pass added to the second-half deluge of points as Los Angeles pulled away to a 37–24 victory.

"It was a knockdown, drag-out game," David recalled. "We had a real rivalry with the Rams—nobody liked each other then." Late in the game, with the Rams firmly in control, Bob Boyd took a swing at David, who retaliated and was ejected. David sat out the final minutes on the bench, with fans behind him screaming, "Get No. 25!" George Wilson told Roy Macklem to find David another jersey.

"We gathered in a little circle around him and I whipped out a jersey with a different number and he pulled it on over his No. 25," Macklem said. "When the game ended, a lot of fans came swarming out, yelling, 'Where's No. 25?' But they couldn't find him and he walked out safe and sound."

The loss at Los Angeles dropped the Lions to 4–2 at the midpoint of the season. Detroit and the 49ers were now a game behind the Rams. Parker was unhappy; the 37 points were the most surrendered by his team in three seasons as head coach. There also were rumors of players missing curfew and getting involved in some extracurricular activities. The following Tuesday, the wife of one of the rookies was surprised to run into Blaine Earon on the elevator at the Malvern, the downtown hotel where many young players and their families roomed.

"He should have been at practice," recalled Ann Carpenter. "Without thinking, I said, 'Oh, what are you doing here before lunch?' Then I realized what had happened. He'd been cut that morning. I remember Betty Earon was in her last month of pregnancy. It really was a warning to everybody."

Joe Schmidt remembered that day well, too. He had the locker next to Earon. He recalled the pale, stricken look on the second-year end's face after he was called into the coaches' room and told that he'd been put on waivers to make room for Jim Martin, who was returning from an injury. There was no taxi squad then. Earon slumped on a stool and kept repeating, "I don't know what I'm going to do."

"He was first string," Schmidt said. "No one picked him up, he didn't have any place to go—that was it."

Earon's unexpected release had a salutary effect on the team's performance, as the Lions wouldn't lose another game the rest of the season. It also was an epiphany to Schmidt.

"That just made me realize then that this was not really a sport, but a business and you'd better do a job all the time," he told *Detroit News* sportswriter Jerry Green in his history of the Lions. "Otherwise you'd be facing the same thing. . . . I always labored under that feeling if I didn't do my job someone else was going to take my job or I was going to be released. Even after I'd made All-Pro three or four years in a row, I never had the feeling that I could just walk into training camp and make the team. I never approached the game that way because I always felt it could happen to me, too."

Parker's offense was far less potent in 1953 than it had been the previous year, finishing in the middle of the pack in total yards and scoring. The fall-off in production was due in part to Pat Harder's bad knees, which limited him to five ineffective games; Cloyce Box's bum leg (courtesy of the Rams), which restricted him to only 16 catches and two touchdowns all season; and Layne's throwing arm, which had a "hitch" in it for much of the year. It was left largely to the defense to bail the team out, week after week. By season's end, only Cleveland had surrendered fewer points.

The Lions played the standard 5-2-4 defense of the day. "Of course, there were adjustments," Bobby Layne said, "but basically the five men up front were keyed to stop any inside runnings plays. The two linebackers were responsible for the outside and short passes, while the four men in the backfield played tight to help out with a tackle or be ready for a pass."

As two-platoon football took hold in the postwar years, defense remained almost an afterthought with such coaches as San Francisco's Buck Shaw. "Buck never cared much about defense," Frankie Albert claimed. "He drafted for offense, and all the guys who couldn't run, he put on defense." According to Layne, "the defensive players were often the guys without much speed who couldn't think fast enough to learn the offensive signals." However, by the early 1950s defense had come into its own. In 1951, the wire services named separate offensive and defensive All-Pro teams for the first time.

Even as the game slowly became more specialized, rosters remained small, so some players continued to be two-way performers for at least part of each game. Buddy Parker freely shuffled Leon Hart, Lou Creekmur, Vince Banonis, Jim Martin, Jim Doran, and others between offensive and defensive platoons. At the same time, he was a pioneer in drafting players specifically for defense. Most notably, it was how he built his secondary.

"Buddy was the first coach to put his best players on defense," claimed Yale Lary, who on another NFL team might very well have been a standout running back. Jack Christiansen, who in limited duty as an emergency fill-in during the 1952 season averaged 7.8 yards per rush, also might have shined as a full-time offensive back. Aside from Christiansen's brief sojourn in the backfield, however, both players were used exclusively on defense throughout their pro careers. So was David, who was second in the nation in receptions his senior year of college but never played a single down of offense in Detroit. Parker correctly saw his talents being put to better use preventing catches rather than making them.

"Chris's Crew," the ball-hawking secondary that Parker assembled and Christiansen quarterbacked, was regarded by many as the finest in the league. While veteran Bob Smith was winding down his career with his last full season at right cornerback, the younger core members—Christiansen, Lary, and David—would continue to play together through 1958, except for the two seasons Lary lost to the army. Before the 1953 season opened, Parker permanently shifted Christiansen to left safety, where Don Doll had starred for years, and installed Lary in Christiansen's old spot at right safety. David remained a fixture at left halfback.

"Most of our success lay in good communications," said Lary. "Other than the two years I spent in service we played as a unit and were fairly injury-free." The other long-term member was Carl Karilivacz, who rotated between halfback and safety on the right side during his five seasons with Detroit.

Safeties are the last line of defense, and in Christiansen and Lary the Lions had two of the game's surest open-field tacklers. No less an authority than the great Jimmy Brown called Lary the best he ever faced. Not that taking on a fullback with a full head of steam was an encounter any defensive back craved. "Pass defense was the fun part," Christiansen said. "But every team had a big running back who could just paralyze you. Steve Van Buren, I hit him once and my whole body went numb. Deacon Dan Towler, Tank Younger, Marion Motley . . . he was as close as anyone has ever come to being a human wave."

Christiansen and Lary would collectively pick off 96 passes and return 11 punts, five interceptions, and a fumble for touchdowns before retiring—Christiansen after the 1958 season and Lary six years later. Lary blossomed as a punter upon his return from the army, winning his first of three punting titles in 1959 and compiling an impressive 44.3-yard lifetime average. His booming kicks were known for their hang time, allowing the punt team to get downfield and bottle up the return. Lary also was a master at running out of punt formation. During his career he picked up 153 yards on 10 fake punts, a gaudy 15.3-yard average per carry, and only once failed to pick up the first down.

Christiansen and Lary are members of the Pro Football Hall of Fame, and the argument has been made that David deserves a bust in Canton, too. He was a Pro Bowler in six of his eight seasons, starred on each of Detroit's title teams while never missing a game, intercepted 36 passes, and was one of the most feared cornerbacks of his era. However, electors have so far looked dimly on the idea of enshrining three-quarters of Chris's Crew, no matter how famous—or, in David's case, notorious.

The villainous David acquired a new nickname on the coast: "Hatchet." The press credited him with chopping down three stars in three weeks—Tittle, Fears, and Wilson, an impressive job of lumberjacking. Reviled around the league, he was prized at Briggs Stadium, where cheers went up whenever the public-address announcer named a favorite defender at the end of a play. Detroit was the first NFL city where fans regularly clamored for the defense. Among the rooters was Pete Banonis. Like an unknowable number of others in the "eight-finger city," the punch-press operator had lost his digits one gory day at work. "My dad was from the old country," Vince Banonis said. "He didn't really understand the game. But whenever he'd hear my name on the P.A., he'd say, 'That's my boy!'"

Fred Rice and three of his buddies had season tickets then. The Livonia plumber remembered the delirium all around them as Detroit's defenders out-hustled and out-muscled that week's visiting cast of offensive stars. "One guy in our section was a big gruff guy," Rice said. "He'd always be yelling, 'Get that ball! Get that ball!' He'd say that ten thousand times each game. Finally, he'd get all of us going: *Get that ball! Get that ball!*" The Lions' defense "got that ball" often enough to rack up 53 turnovers in 1953, second only to Baltimore.

There was an organic connection between the spot welder at Dodge Truck losing his voice in the bleachers and the pile of mud-caked, straining bodies smothering Joe Perry six inches short of the goal line. The fan base was overwhelmingly blue collar, and many of those wildly cheering on Sunday would spend Monday grunting through another soul-sucking shift down at the plant. They knew all about putting in a long day with little appreciation. "It was just getting popular, the defense was," Christiansen said. "It became important. The people started to cheer for the defense, to recognize us as a unit."

And make no mistake, it *was* a unit, John Prchlik stressed. "Too often the fan in the stands looks upon defensive play as an individual effort of the man who makes the tackle," the veteran lineman said at the beginning of the season, his last before retiring to accept a full-time position in Ford's industrial relations department. "That's the wrong slant. Defensive play, more than any other phase of the game, is a team effort. Every man has a job to do—and how well you can do yours depends on how effectively the other fellow does his." Such individual statistics as quarterback sacks, blocked kicks, and passes defended were not officially kept then, which suited Detroit's unselfish style. "Our team doesn't care who gets the points or makes the tackles as long as somebody does the job," Parker said.

Each week, Buster Ramsey's crew used the opponent's total yardage to roughly gauge how well they had performed as a unit. "How many yards did they make?" an exhausted Bingaman would ask at game's end. The answer usually was not many, or at least not enough to win.

Bingaman was cognizant of his growing popularity. After being knocked out cold against San Francisco, trainer Grant Foster hustled out onto the field with smelling salts "strong enough to move the stadium two feet off its foundation," recalled Nick Kerbawy. Bingaman lay there, seemingly lifeless, until his eyelids finally began fluttering.

"Bing, Bing, are you all right?" Foster asked.

"Yeah, I'm all right," the woozy guard said, "but how is the crowd taking it?"

The press tried to come up with catchy nicknames for the defense, such as the "Dirty Shirts" and "Detroit Destroyers." One sportswriter labeled the interior line of Prchlik, Bingaman, and Thurman McGraw the "Hunks of Granite." The only moniker that stuck was the alliteratively pleasing Chris's Crew, which broadcaster Van Patrick helped popularize, though the original appellation was a clunkier "Chris's Gang."

Whatever it was called, Detroit's defense was a flinty bunch, known for its crumpling tackles and an enthusiasm that bordered on the criminal. Schmidt, in particular, was impressing observers with his sureness on runs and pass defense. "He also loves to play the game, at times competing despite injuries that would sideline a less sincere player," said an admiring beat writer.

To start the second half of the season, the Lions beat the Colts on a Saturday night in Detroit, 17–7. Layne redeemed himself with fickle hometown fans by hitting Hoernschemeyer and Hart for touchdowns. The Lions next knocked heads with the Packers in Green Bay. In the first quarter, Walker and Layne paired up on an 83-yard pass-run, the longest play of Doak's pro career. Layne threw a second scoring pass, this time to Hart in the final quarter, to open up a two-touchdown lead and provide the eventual margin in a 14–7 victory.

Parker missed the Green Bay game. He was in Texas, having left coaching duties to his assistants. His 70-year-old father had died of a stroke at home on November 13, the Friday before the game. Buddy tried to shake the feeling that the date was a premonition of more bad things to come.

Parker was back on the sidelines for the Lions-Bears game at Wrigley Field the following Sunday, November 22. A chilly rain fell off and on all afternoon. Detroit was down four points in the fourth quarter when Walker attempted a long field goal. It fell short, but Vince Banonis alertly downed the ball at the 1-foot line, forcing Chicago's offense into a deep hole.

George Blanda attempted three straight passes, the last of which was intercepted by Bob Smith and returned to the Bears' 6. Layne fed Gene Gedman the ball three times. On fourth down from the 1-yard line, Walker sprinted wide around the right side for the touchdown that gave the Lions a 20–16 win. Detroit's record was now 7-2. The 49ers were a game back; the slumping Rams a game and a half. The Lions controlled their own destiny. Win the last three games and they would be playing for another championship.

On November 26, Detroiters celebrated Thanksgiving. The Packers were in town, and so was Santa. It was cold and overcast with a dusting of flakes. The largest and grandest Christmas tree in Detroit adorned the facade of J. L. Hudson, the shopping emporium that had long been one of the treasured symbols of a vital metropolis. Hudson's opened in the 1880s, grew in lockstep with the city, and with 12,000 employees and 49 acres of shopping space was now the second-largest department store in the country, behind Macy's in New York. The delicate, blazing branches of the Magic Tree of Lights, nine stories high and containing tens of thousands of hand-screwed bulbs, lit up Woodward Avenue and helped put folks in a festive mood for the traditional Thanksgiving Day parade.

Bundled-up crowds surged along downtown streets that morning to cheer Ol' Saint Nick, played to jolly perfection by the short, roundish radio actor Rube Weiss. The 1953 parade marked the debut of Christmas Carol. The pig-tailed, sweet-singing character was created and portrayed by Maureen Bailey, a precocious 15-year-old from Shrine High School who would graduate to roles on Broadway and television. "It was more than a Santa parade," Louis Cook observed in the following day's *Free Press*. "All of the heroes of childhood passed in review. Pinocchio waved cheerily from a comfortable seat in the epiglottis of a whale with a flail-some tail. Peter, of the Pirates, sailed the bounding main street under hot pink sails, pacing the poop deck in mittens. A shining space ship, mounted on a launching platform aimed at Alpha Centauri, was dragged down Woodward while its pilot blew kisses from inside his plastic bubble. Cinderella was lovely, in her pumpkin coach. A dozen bands whooped it up along the parade route, leaning heavily on 'Jingle Bells' and 'Rudolph the Red-Nosed Reindeer.' Nobody has really lived, however, until he has heard The Kilties play 'Oh, Come All Ye Faithful' on the bagpipes. Santa Claus appeared in good health. He accepted the Key to Detroit from Christmas Carol and vowed to put it up over his fireplace at the North Pole."

The holiday rush traditionally started the day after the game. Hudson's cooks were in the midst of preparing nearly four tons of fruitcake and plum pudding while the store's hundreds of uniformed drivers were bracing themselves for the million or so packages they would deliver over the coming weeks. Kern's, a block south, was decked out in holiday finery, its four-face clock serving as the agreed-upon rendezvous point for generations of Detroiters. Store shelves were stocked with Detroit Lions football outfits for boys (pants, jersey, helmet, and shoulder pads for $9.95) and white-with-brown-stripe Bobby Layne signature footballs at $2.95 each. Although nobody realized it, it was the last time downtown merchants would dominate the Christmas season. The new "atomic age" shopping mall at Northwestern and Eight Mile was in the final stages of construction. By the following year, suburban Northland would be siphoning off shoppers; after 1953, downtown Hudson's would never again post an annual profit. It was the start of a long, slow decline that would one day see the "Grand Old Lady of Woodward" fall to the wrecking ball, a fate unthinkable to the legions of kids wandering wide-eyed through Toyland and the Fantasy Forest.

Among those jammed into the stands at Briggs Stadium that Thanksgiving Day was 12-year-old Mike Cutler, who grew frustrated with the ineptitude he witnessed through the intermittent snow squalls. Vito "Babe" Parilli tossed a pass to ex-Lion Bob Mann for one touchdown, then a short while later legged it into the end zone for another. Fred Cone, who missed both extra points, kicked a long field goal to help the Packers build a 15–7 lead. Meanwhile, the Lions seemed determined to play down to Green Bay's level.

"Detroit was an elite team and Green Bay was basically cannon fodder," recalled Cutler. "But somehow Green Bay had the lead at halftime and the partisan sellout crowd was not amused. They had a kids scrimmage at halftime and many of the disgruntled fans were of the opinion that the kids should suit up for the Lions when play resumed.

"Anyway, the Lions started the third quarter on about their own 20 and promptly gave up a sack, putting the ball on their 3 yard line. The resultant booing was so loud, I swear you could have heard it in Windsor. However, on the next play Bobby Layne dropped back into the end zone and floated a long pass into the outstretched arms of Cloyce Box, who was in full flight and didn't stop until he reached the end zone. This time if Windsor heard anything it was unrestrained cheering, and the Lions went on to avoid what would have been an unforgivable loss." The Lions scored 27 unanswered points and won going away, 34–15. The 97-yard pass play—at the time the longest in club history—turned out to be the last touchdown of Box's career.

In faraway Dallas, a city filled with Lions fans, a 10-year-old schoolboy named Karl Sweetan cheered the record throw. "I saw that Layne-Box pass on television," he recalled in 1966, by which time he was the rookie starting quarterback of the Lions. "I was about yay high and I'll never forget it. It made such an impression on me." Ironically, Sweetan's first NFL touchdown pass was a 99-yarder to Pat Studstill at Baltimore that eclipsed the club record and tied the league mark.

Also on hand at the ballpark was the usual coterie of players' wives, including Fern Box, who missed her husband's historic touchdown while socializing with her regular game-day companions, Carol Layne, Janie Lary, and Norma Walker. The young women shared binoculars and a common Texan heritage, as well as a heightened sense of nerves watching their spouses play. "We don't even eat hot dogs until we've got a lead," Carol said.

Two-thirds of the Lions were married, and every marriage license had a backstory. Jim Martin met his future wife, Gloria, while getting his nose fixed at Detroit Osteopathic Hospital, where she worked as a receptionist. Jimmy David's wife, Shirley, literally picked him up at a Colorado drive-in. "My girlfriend and I recognized him as our big Colorado A&M football star," she said, "so when he and his friend asked if we could give them a lift back to Fort Collins, we did exchanging of secret glances to say, 'Aren't we the lucky girls?' Funny part was that when we reached town, Jim broke down and confessed that he had his own car and would we please drive them back to the drive-in." Charlie and Marilyn Ane (who went by her childhood nickname of "Dolan" because of her passion for Dole pineapple juice) became acquainted as high school students in Honolulu. When the Anes came to Detroit in 1953, they had a year-old-son. Charlie "Kale" Ane would grow up to play seven seasons in the NFL, making him and his dad the league's only father-son combination ever to come out of Hawaii.

Married or single, most players during the season lived in the downtown residential hotels that sprang up between the world wars to accommodate

Detroit's swelling population. Rookies and second-year players stayed at the Malvern and Seward hotels, which stood next to each other on Seward, a block off Woodward. "I roomed with Harley Sewell at the Seward Hotel," Joe Schmidt said. "Neither one of us had a car. We'd go to the bar downstairs, have a few beers, and go to bed."

Lew Carpenter's wife, Ann, remembered their small rented space at the Malvern: a living room with a pull-down Murphy bed and a kitchenette. Sewell, Schmidt, Carl Karilivacz, and other members of the Lions' "bachelor club" regularly dropped by, she said. "They'd play cards and I'd make them bean soup." The homemade soup was a welcome break from the protein-rich diet of steak, ham, and eggs that players were programmed to eat every day in order to "build energy." Having steak dinners every night put a big dent in the budget, so players and their mates were always looking for the name of a good wholesale butcher.

Older and better-paid veterans with families often took an apartment at Lee Plaza, an Art Deco hotel on leafy West Grand Boulevard at Lawton. Appropriately, the exterior of the 17-story building was adorned with dozens of terra cotta lion heads. The Laynes often spent the season there or at the Park Shelton, an upscale hotel on Woodward at Kirby known for its celebrity lodgers. For a time they rented a house in Dearborn to give their toddlers a backyard to play in. Neighborhood kids regularly dropped by to see if the famous Mr. Layne could come out and play, and he usually accommodated them by tossing the ball around.

Once, when the Laynes and the Walkers were spending the season at the same hotel, Doak volunteered to babysit in the Laynes' apartment while Bobby and Carol went out separately for the evening. Carol returned late to find the lights out and Bobby already sleeping in the Murphy bed. Careful not to wake anyone, she changed into her nightgown, crept into the bedroom to check on little Rob, and then quietly slipped into bed alongside Bobby. She was about to give her husband a good-night peck on the cheek when she realized the head on the pillow had dark, not blond, hair. She screamed, waking Doak, who had innocently decided to take a nap after putting the baby to sleep.

The startled pair burst into laughter. When Carol called Norma Walker to tell her what had just happened, Norma laughed and said, "Well, when Bobby comes home, send him on up here."

Harmony at home, as well as in the locker room, was a vital ingredient in helping to make the Lions a success in the '50s. Management understood that a stable home life helped create a happier, more focused player. Edwin Anderson and his wife oversaw an annual preseason shindig for players, coaches, directors, and their spouses where radios, cameras, clothes, luggage, and a new car were given away. Anderson personally paid for the cars. Throughout the season there were postgame parties and team-sponsored gatherings.

"It really was a fun group," Ann Carpenter said. "So many creative people. Somebody would always entertain. Dolan Ane would play the ukulele or Marilyn Gandee would dance. We'd put on skits. Doak played the guitar. The guys would sing Western songs, beer-drinking songs. It was like college. We were a tight-knit group."

The beauty of pro ball is that nobody ever graduates. Before free agency changed everything, players routinely spent several seasons together, and every year they could count on most of the old gang coming back. There was a comforting continuity, for players and fans alike. Harley Sewell wistfully compared it to a family business: "Everybody liked everybody, and you would never be traded."

It was never quite that ideal—just ask Blaine and Betty Earon—but it was still pretty special. "I loved playing for the Lions," Walker said. "It was a fun time for me—the club had some great owners, and they let you know they cared about you. It was an era of loyalty, which I'm not sure you have now—but we almost became like a big family. The club would throw parties for us, and they'd give you a new TV set or something—just something to let you know we were all on the same team. Maybe it's a little hard to understand now, but it was just a different era."

Nobody put on airs, said Carpenter, who remembered visiting the Laynes' apartment shortly after she and Lew settled into their humble lodgings at the Malvern. The team was playing an away game and Carol Layne had invited the wives of the first- and second-year players over.

"I came from a small town in Arkansas," Carpenter said. "I know this sounds silly, but my idea of the big city was all these sophisticated people having parties, dressed up in these wonderful clothes, drinking champagne. It's what you saw in magazines and the movies. I was nervous about making the right impression. I was wondering, 'What do I wear?' I had one Sunday outfit, a nice skirt and a blouse, and I put that on. I got a cab, got to the apartment, and knocked on the door. Carol opens the door. She's wearing pajamas, other women are washing and setting their hair, kids are running around. We all had a great time and I wound up spending the night."

"Hen parties" and dressier group outings were part of being a lady Lion. On Saturday nights, with their husbands either on the road or sequestered in a downtown hotel for a home game, wives often dined out or took in a play together. Sometimes they stayed home, watching *The Jackie Gleason Show* or Ted Mack's *Amateur Hour* and using a ouija board to divine how their spouses would fare on Sunday. "It was a lot of fun," Jug Girard's wife, Joan, told a society writer, "but I don't think any of us are really superstitious." The same couldn't be said of the husbands who refused to get a haircut during a winning streak or prohibited the throwing away of a ratty "good-luck" suit.

The wives attended all home games, sitting in clusters throughout Section 11 in the upper deck. Hearing the crowd cheer for their husbands was wonderful, of course, but it was painful to hear them being booed and heckled.

Once, a fan seated in back of Carol Layne said, "I'd like to sit behind Layne so I could spit on him." Carol's companion turned to the man and asked if he'd accept the quarterback's wife as a substitute. Carol and the chastened critic were introduced and were soon laughing. "Detroit was so much fun," she once reflected. "It was like one big party. We were winning and having a wonderful time."

Amid the laughter and the winning, there was a dark chapter that shook the team. On Wednesday, December 2, as the Lions were preparing for their upcoming game with the Bears, LaVern Torgeson's wife, Mary Lou, was taken to Women's Hospital in Detroit. The perky 24-year-old had been a cheerleader and editor of the humor magazine when she and "Torgy" dated in college. She was several months pregnant and thought to be suffering from a cold. But her condition quickly deteriorated, and she lapsed into a coma. Parker, still smarting from his father's recent death, cut practice short after news reached the team.

LaVern Torgeson was no stranger to tragedy. Three years earlier, he was getting ready for the Washington Cougars' traditional season-ending grudge match with Washington State when he received word that his younger brother, Robert, and two friends had been found unconscious in a car. The trio had driven to Spokane for the big game and decided to sleep overnight in their car with the engine running to keep the heater working. The young men were overcome by carbon monoxide fumes. While his friends survived, Robert did not. Torgeson, captain of the Cougars, missed his final college game as police escorted him and his parents from the stadium to the funeral home where the body of the asphyxiated teenager had been taken.

Now Torgeson was bracing for another heavy blow. His wife was suffering from a severe liver infection and other signs of a syndrome then known as toxemia in pregnancy. She received several blood transfusions but her condition remained critical.

"That was the saddest time," Ann Carpenter said. "She was one of the good people, someone we all had a lot of fun with. I remember going to the hospital. I was young and it was just heartbreaking to see."

On December 4, just a couple of hours after her parents flew in from Tacoma, Mary Lou passed away without ever regaining consciousness. The baby she was carrying died with her. Bobby Layne, always at his best under pressure, took over for the distraught parents. He made arrangements with the airlines and funeral home and helped organize the sad trip home. That Friday night, LaVern and his in-laws accompanied Mary Lou's body back to Washington.

On Sunday, Doak Walker led the team in a locker-room prayer before taking the field at Briggs Stadium. The players dedicated the game to the young woman's memory. "This is a close-knit team, and Mary Lou's death was shocking," Parker said.

With more than 58,000 fans on hand, Layne connected with Dorne Dibble on a scoring pass and Walker contributed two field goals as the Lions turned back the Bears, 13–7. Jim Martin filled in for Torgeson at right linebacker and picked off a pass, one of five George Blanda throws the Lions' defense pulled down. Schmidt took over Torgeson's responsibilities as defensive signal-caller. Later that afternoon, the 49ers crushed the Packers on the West Coast to remain a game back of the Lions with one game to go.

In the midst of grief, life went on. As Mary Lou Torgeson was being buried in Washington, George Wilson's wife gave birth to a healthy baby girl at Oakwood Hospital in Dearborn. The coach, a doting family man, could now "go back to worrying about the team's championship hopes again," the *Free Press* noted.

There certainly was some worrying to do. Layne's arm was so sore he didn't throw all week leading up to the finale with the Giants. With a 9–2 record, the Lions needed at least a tie at the Polo Grounds to clinch a second straight division crown. If they faltered and San Francisco beat Baltimore in their closer, the Lions would be forced into a playoff with the 49ers at Kezar Stadium the following Sunday. The Giants were having a terrible season, but Steve Owen had just announced he was ending his 23-year run as Giants head coach. There were concerns that the Giants would go all out to "win one for Steve."

Torgeson returned to the lineup, saying it was what his late wife would have wanted. He wound up with two of the Lions' five interceptions as Detroit clipped New York, 27–16. The game was closer than the final score indicated. Detroit, paced by a pair of touchdowns by Walker and another by Leon Hart, entered the fourth stanza with a 20–7 lead. But it took a goal-line stand and a pair of clutch interceptions to hold off a furious Giants comeback. The last pick set up Gene Gedman's short touchdown run with one second on the clock.

With its victory, Detroit tied the 1934 team's mark for most wins while its .833 winning percentage was a franchise record that still stands. Most importantly, it meant the Lions would host a rematch with Cleveland for the NFL title on December 27.

"We've beaten Cleveland before and we can do it again," Parker said. "I know they have a good club and I'm not underestimating their ability, but they don't scare us a bit."

Parker's confidence was not misplaced. In a span of four months, September 1952 to January 1953, he had beaten Paul Brown four straight times in head-to-head matchups: once each in the preseason, regular season, and postseason, and then again in the Pro Bowl as coach of the National Conference team. Everybody in football was aware of the phenomenon. Cleveland was the acknowledged powerhouse of postwar football, even after two straight title-game losses had put a bit of a chink in its armor, and Brown was recognized as a trendsetting genius. Yet, as a coach, Brown couldn't beat Parker, no matter what the setting, and as a team the Browns couldn't beat Parker's Lions, no matter what the stakes. The best Cleveland could manage against Parker was a tie in the 1953 preseason.

Much was made of the contrasting personalities involved. It was Buddy, the tolerant players' coach, versus the aloof, autocratic Brown; the swashbuckling Layne versus the programmed, buttoned-down Graham. "Otto was kind of a loner, really," remembered one Browns player. Graham, who lived in upscale Bay Village, was "a master craftsman on the field," but aside from team affairs, "you didn't see Otto. He had his own friends." Graham was the mirror image of his coach, who constantly stressed "execution with perfection," a tagline of sorts for the handful of basic plays the Browns ran over and over.

"I never heard Paul Brown swear, and he never raised his voice," said end Dante Lavelli. "He'd just look at you with his beady eyes, and you knew you were in trouble. . . . He always kept himself separated from you. Brown never took a shower with us in all the years I played for him. He always went to the hotel or home to take a shower. He had a phobia about that. All the assistant coaches took showers, but he didn't."

Perhaps nothing better symbolized the rivals' unlikeness than Brown's insistence on running the offense from the sideline. Prior to 1951, Graham had been his own man in the huddle. But starting that season, the Cleveland coach, always a control freak, decided to call plays through a system of shuttling messenger guards. According to Graham, Brown had become jealous of the growing influence of assistant coach Blanton Collier, with whom the quarterback conferred between possessions. "It didn't make much sense, but I couldn't say much," Graham said. "You had to use the plays."

Of course, Layne would never accept such a bridle. "Bobby Layne was tough, boy," said Ken Konz. The Cleveland cornerback remembered one exhibition game when Parker sent in a play. Layne quickly called time-out and walked over to the sideline.

"Look," Layne told Parker, "you run this ball club, or I run this ball club."

Parker stood there and said nothing.

"If I run this ball club," Layne continued, "I'll call the plays. If you want to run the ball club, you call the plays and send somebody else in there to do 'em." Having made his point, Layne turned around and sauntered back to the huddle.

"If Otto would've said that to Paul Brown," Konz said, "Paul would probably have sent him to the dressing room and told him not to come back."

The Lions feared the Browns less than they did the Rams, 49ers, and Bears, teams they met twice each season and collectively constituted a brutal half of each season's schedule. Detroit considered the Eastern Conference to be less competitive than the Western, an opinion shared by many others around the league. (After three seasons, the two divisions had reverted to their old names in 1953. The National Conference was once again the Western and the American Conference the Eastern.) Each year, Parker almost exclusively scheduled pre-season games against Eastern Conference clubs, in part to get an upfront look at teams he might meet again in December for the title. Under Parker, Detroit compiled a 25-4-2 record in these cross-conference exhibitions. As for games that counted in the standings, Buddy's Lions wouldn't drop a regular-season contest to an Eastern Conference foe until the final game of his fifth season.

Conversely, during Parker's six-year tenure as head coach, the Lions could manage just an even split of their 36 regular-season games against the Rams, 49ers, and Bears. Only the 1952 playoff win over Los Angeles allowed Parker to accrue a slightly better than break-even mark of 19 wins and 18 losses against his chief divisional rivals.

Lions players naturally thought Buddy was the best coach in the NFL, not only for his ability to prepare them well for games but for his broad-mindedness. "Better than Paul Brown," was Bob Hoernschemeyer's assessment. "Brown didn't allow his team to smoke or drink. You gotta be able to relax."

The Lions took "great delight out of Paul's restraints," Lou Groza said, especially Brown's rule of no sex after Wednesday. ("Save yourself for the game," Brown instructed his men.) Groza remembered an exhibition loss in Akron. In a restaurant parking lot after the game, "Detroit's team bus was parked next to ours, and we could see many of their players drinking beer . . . the Lions smiled and mockingly toasted us as we soberly sat in Paul Brown's 'dry' bus."

The Browns were also viewed as being unnecessarily cheap. That impression grew out of a story concerning the previous year's championship splits, when Cleveland players heatedly debated for an hour behind closed doors who should get what. One tightfisted faction argued that all non-playing personnel, including assistant coaches, should receive nothing. Word of the rancorous meeting leaked to the press. Brown, known for his own miserly ways, felt the dissension wasn't newsworthy enough to warrant a comment. By comparison, Detroit players were generous in divvying up the 1952 title-game loot, doling out full shares to the assistant coaches, trainer, equipment manager, and injured rookie Pat Summerall, who had played only two games.

Tickets to see the 1953 championship clash went on sale at 9 a.m. on December 15, twelve days before the game. Upper-deck sideline box seats were priced at $7, while upper- and lower-deck grandstand seats cost $5. Seven thousand bleacher seats were priced at $3. Season ticket holders could purchase the same seat locations for the title game while all other buyers were limited to four tickets apiece.

Wherever they were seated, fans would be watching a juggernaut. Cleveland had reeled off 11 straight victories before a loss to Pittsburgh spoiled its bid for a second undefeated season in five years. As it was, the 11–1 Browns led the league in passing defense and allowed the fewest points. Graham completed 64.7 percent of his aerials (remarkable for the era), topped the league in passing yardage, and was named MVP by the Associated Press. Groza, in addition to his usual fine play at left tackle, had an unprecedented year as a kicker. He booted 23 field goals in 26 tries, a record-shattering output and success rate (88.5 percent) in a season when all other teams averaged just eight field goals and collectively hit on only two of every five attempts.

The 10–2 Lions depended on an opportunistic defense to counter Cleveland's firepower. Chris's Crew picked off 38 passes, including a league-high dozen by Christiansen himself. Bookies installed the Browns as six-point favorites, but analysts talked of the Lions' intangibles of pluck, luck, and team cohesion. Noting the opponents' combined 21–3 record, Bert Bell said, "Here possibly are the two best teams ever to meet for the championship." Of the 66 men who suited up, 16 were future Hall-of-Famers: seven Lions (Layne, Christiansen, Lou Creekmur, Yale Lary, Dick Stanfel, Doak Walker, Joe Schmidt) and nine Browns (Graham, Groza, Marion Motley, Dante Lavelli, Len Ford, Bill Willis, Frank Gatski, Doug Atkins, Chuck Noll). Paul Brown also was a future inductee.

Half of the Lions were first- or second-year players. Several wives were expecting, their contribution to the postwar baby boom that was transforming American society. "There will be a special incentive for both teams on Sunday," Shirley Povich noted in the *Washington Post*. "A victory will be worth $1,000 more per man than their share of the receipts as losers. It's little things like that which can goad the athletes to dedicate themselves to the contest in earnest. Pride in victory is wonderful, but it isn't quite negotiable."

After working out Christmas Day, Parker's squad came into the clubhouse to find a tree trimmed with envelopes, a gift from the Detroit Football Company. Each envelope had a player's name written on it, and inside were $300 in crisp bills.

Most observers were betting on a closely fought contest, perhaps even a classic. "This should be pro football at its best," predicted *New York Times* columnist Arthur Daley. "The Lions don't impress quite as much as the Browns do, but they are tough and resourceful. The Browns will be favored but that doesn't necessarily mean the Lions can't give their hometown Detroit fans a delayed Christmas present, the championship. These are two gifted teams and you can watch them with just a flick of the dial on your television screen."

That flick of the dial had to occur outside a 75-mile radius of Detroit. The game, televised nationally over 137 DuMont outlets—more than double the 63 stations that had carried the '52 title game—was blacked out. Bert Bell said he would permit the blackout to be lifted upon two conditions: the game was a sellout and that the sponsor, the Miller Brewing Company, agreed to refund the ticket price of any buyer who decided to stay home and watch the game on TV instead.

The Milwaukee brewery, which paid $100,000 for the rights, refused. Thus fans without a ticket would have to hit the roads early Sunday and head for the nearest bar or relative's house where an antenna could grab a signal out of the frosty air.

On game day, 54,577 heavily bundled fans spun through the turnstiles as hundreds more milled outside Briggs Stadium, trying to bargain with scalpers asking $20 for a $5 ticket. Thousands of fans paid a buck to park in one of the neighborhood lots; some parked illegally in alleys or wherever else they could find a spot. The temperature was in the low 30s with the sun occasionally breaking through the clouds. The field, soft in some spots and frozen in others, would quickly be stomped into mud.

Both squads were in good shape physically, though Jimmy David had broken his nose against the Giants and was unaccustomedly sporting a face mask. Parker predicted "a whale of a game." Curiously, for the second year in a row, a Lions wife gave birth on the day of the championship. In 1952, it was Betty Dibble delivering a baby girl; this time it was Beryl McGraw, who presented Thurman with their second son.

It was shortly after one o'clock when Layne kicked off, then avoided the usual roll-block from a charging Brown as he followed the kick downfield. From the beginning, Cleveland's passing game went nowhere. Schmidt set the tone on the game's second play, reaching Graham on a blitz and popping the ball loose. Les Bingaman recovered inside Cleveland's 13-yard line. Three plays took the ball to just outside the 3. Disdaining a field goal, Layne kept the drive going with a fourth-down sneak. Detroit then unveiled an unbalanced line for the first time, stacking the right side. After a first-down run to the strong side, Layne crossed up the defense by giving the ball to Walker on a straight dive off the weak side. Doak's touchdown and conversion gave Detroit a 7–0 lead after just four minutes of play.

Graham was handicapped by a badly chafed throwing hand that had bothered him for weeks. His day was made even more miserable by Detroit's crashing ends and red-dogging linebackers. The Browns would have to depend on Chick Jagade's churning legs and Groza's right foot to offset the lack of passing production. Near the end of the opening period, Len Ford recovered Hoernschemeyer's fumble on Detroit's 6. The Lions stacked up two runs. On third down, Graham hit Lavelli with a pass between the goal posts, but Yale Lary broke it up. The Browns settled for a 13-yard Groza field goal.

Late in the second quarter, after Jimmy David returned a Graham pass deep into Cleveland territory, the Lions appeared to pick up another six-pointer. On the Cleveland 20, Layne handed off to Walker, who roamed to his right looking for an open receiver. Finding none, he spotted Layne standing off to the left side, all by himself. Doak floated a pass across the field and Layne grabbed it, slipped a tackler, and outran the Cleveland secondary into the end zone. Officials initially signaled a touchdown, but after a conference it was ruled an illegal forward pass. The Lions were penalized 15 yards and the loss of a down. Walker salvaged the drive with a 23-yard field goal.

The scoreboard at halftime read Detroit 10, Cleveland 3. The Lions' offense, already having trouble advancing across the gooey field, was dealt a blow when Leon Hart was forced to leave the game early after being blocked low on the side of his knee during a kickoff. Parker moved Jim Doran from his regular defensive end position to Hart's spot on the right edge of the line.

Doran, who worked a farm near Boone, Iowa, in the offseason with his brother, was dubbed "Graham Cracker" for his ability to harass Graham. He'd seen limited offensive duty in 1953, catching six passes all season, none for touchdowns. Long-limbed with oversized hands, he was a greater offensive threat than his meager output suggested. Four years earlier at Iowa State, he had set an NCAA single-game record for receiving yardage against Oklahoma. Cornerback Warren Lahr wasn't impressed. Soon he was talking trash to Doran.

In the second half, Cleveland defenders continued to clamp down on the Lions' biggest threats, Walker and Cloyce Box. At the same time, the Browns' running game was grinding along. For the day, the Browns would pick up 182 yards rushing. Jagade nearly duplicated his performance in the previous year's title game, totaling 102 yards on 15 rushes. He was the workhorse in a third-quarter march that culminated with him crashing through the line for a 9-yard touchdown. Groza's point-after knotted the score at 10-all.

Near the end of the period, the Browns launched another drive that reached the Detroit 7. However, Bob Smith broke up a pass to Ray Renfro in the end zone. Once again, the Browns' drive stalled. Forty-four seconds into the final quarter, Groza came on to kick a 15-yard field goal that gave Cleveland its first lead of the game, 13–10.

The Browns' failure to convert opportunities into touchdowns, settling for three-pointers instead, would wind up costing them. For years, Cleveland players groused about Brown's conservative play-calling, especially his tendency to sit on a lead, no matter how narrow the margin or how important the game. But so far their defense had been holding the Lions in check, forcing four turnovers, including two interceptions by All-Pro safety Ken Gorgal. Detroit's only touchdown drive, way back in the opening minutes, had been all of 12 yards. Walker had accounted for all of Detroit's points so far. But he lacked Groza's range, missing badly on two field-goal attempts after his first successful try.

With a little over four minutes remaining, Groza kicked a 43-yard field goal to build Cleveland's lead to 16–10. Following a touchback, the Lions got the ball at their 20. There was 4:10 left on the clock. For much of the afternoon, Doran had been telling Layne that he could get behind Lahr and beat him on a "9-up," a long pass. Layne stored the information for future use.

On first down, Layne shot a pass to Doran on the right sideline for a 17-yard gain. Two incomplete passes followed. There were a little over three minutes to play now. Parker decided that if the Lions didn't convert on third down, they would punt. But Layne fired a button-hook pass that hit Doran square in the numbers for a first down at the Browns' 45-yard line.

With the clock running, Layne next threw to Box for nine yards. On second down, Hoernschemeyer was stopped for no gain. Needing a yard, Layne ran a keeper and picked up three. First down on the Cleveland 33. There was 2:08 left to play. Layne called time-out and walked over to the sideline to talk it over. Coaches thought a screen pass to take advantage of hard-charging Len Ford would work. It was only a suggestion. Layne would call his own play.

Back in the huddle, Layne asked Doran, "Can you still beat that feller?"

"Just throw it," Doran said. "I'll beat him."

Lahr was a hard tackler with average speed. He'd been cussing and wagging his finger, telling Doran that he was going to bust him in the mouth. Doran smiled to himself as he lined up and saw Lahr creeping closer to the line of scrimmage, anticipating another run to his side.

On the snap, Doran shot out of his crouch and headed straight for Lahr, his forearm extended. He faked a block, then cut around the Cleveland defender, leaving him flat-footed. Layne dropped back five steps, watched Doran break into the clear down the right sideline, then lofted a quivering pass to the wide-open end.

"I raced toward the end zone and when I looked up, there was the ball," said Doran, who hauled in the gift package as he was crossing the goal line. There were groans and cuss words up and down the Cleveland sideline while Lions players and coaches yelled and punched the air. Yale Lary always remembered Lahr's helplessness as Layne's pass sailed over his head. "Warren never got over it, bless his heart."

As the last strains of "Gridiron Heroes" faded and fans, still percolating with excitement, settled back into their seats, the teams lined up for the conversion that would break the 16–16 deadlock. If Bert Bell had gotten his way, there would be no need for a kick and the Lions would be ahead by a point. At the league meeting before the season, the commissioner had resurrected a favorite cause, arguing once again that conversions were "automatic" and should be abandoned in favor of seven-point touchdowns. The proposed change went before the rules committee, which again voted it down.

But this was far from an automatic point. Walker had missed twice during the season, and there was always the threat of a botched snap or blocked kick. In fact, the Giants had blocked one of Walker's extra-point tries in the regular-season finale. Detroit was especially worried about Doug Atkins, an agile 6-foot-8 end known for leap-frogging blockers, swatting down passes, and smothering kicks. When the Browns and Lions had last met, in the preseason, the towering rookie blocked Pat Harder's last-second field-goal attempt to salvage a 24–24 tie.

Meanwhile, the man centering the ball tried to drown thoughts of the blown snap that had cost the Lions a one-point loss to the Bears a year earlier. "I made a bad pass," Vince Banonis said of his miscue on the conversion attempt, which wound up being the difference between the Lions winning the division outright and meeting the Rams in a playoff. "The ball dribbled and bounced. Layne couldn't get hold of it in time for the kick. We lost and it was my fault. I wouldn't guess how many times I've passed the ball back for a kick. But I know for sure that was the worst one I ever made—especially when the chips were down. I couldn't forget it."

To add to the drama, Walker was not wearing the special footwear he'd used since breaking into the league. Before every field goal and extra-point try, Doak typically exchanged his low-cut right shoe for a modified high-topped version that gave his ankle greater support. While fully laced like a normal shoe, the kicking shoe was zippered to expedite the changeover. Bell had briefly banned it in October 1951, arguing that it constituted an illegal "detachable object," but a vote of owners allowed Walker to continue using the special footwear.

Now, for whatever reason, Doak was lining up for the most important kick of his pro career wearing his low-cuts. Had his kicking shoe been misplaced or stolen? Was there simply not enough time for him to race to the sideline and make the swap? Nobody today seems to know the answer to this little mystery.

Given all this, sudden-death overtime—something yet to be seen in a title game—was a very real possibility. The unflappable Walker tried to alleviate the tension. Lou Creekmur liked to fool around after practice by attempting a few placekicks. Other linemen like Groza and Jim Martin could do it; why couldn't he? With the title hanging on a successful boot, Doak told Creekmur, "C'mon, Lou, you kick it."

"He scared the hell out of me," Creekmur said years later. "That kick meant the championship. I thought sure Doak would make me kick and I would miss, and Buddy Parker would kill us all."

Atkins positioned himself behind the defensive wall, directly in the kick's expected flight path. As thousands held their breath or peeked through covered eyes, Layne knelt on the 10-yard line and barked out the count. With the precision of watch gears, Banonis flipped the ball, Layne set it down, and Walker swung his right leg—a choreography the unit had performed uncounted times before but never with so much riding on it. The ball flew off Walker's toe and over the blob of shoving bodies and desperately outstretched arms. Atkins, slightly mistiming his leap, hung in the air for a moment before his jack-knifing frame crashed down on the scrum. The ball cleared the crossbar.

"I didn't feel anything until I saw that the kick was good," Walker said. "Then I felt fine."

Detroit 17, Cleveland 16. The Lions kicked off and Ken Carpenter returned the ball to Cleveland's 28. There was one minute and 54 seconds left. Graham needed to move the Browns about 35 or 40 yards to give Groza a shot at a winning field goal. On the first play, Graham was chased out of the pocket and threw badly downfield for Dub Jones. Carl Karilivacz grabbed the ball at Cleveland's 45 and ran down the sideline. It was the first interception of the rookie's career, and it clearly couldn't have come at a better time.

"So we just had to grind it out to kill the clock," Dorne Dibble said. "The first play, wham! This big fist went right into me. It was Doug Atkins. . . . He looked at me and said, 'You guys want that money so bad, you're gonna earn it.' So I came out of the huddle next play and kicked my cleats so the mud flew off right into his face. The ball was snapped and I just took off along the line of scrimmage with him right after me. I ran into Lahr and swung at him. So I got kicked out, but at least Atkins didn't get another shot at me."

A short while later the gun sounded. With that, the Lions trotted off the field with wide smiles and their second straight championship. For the sixth time since early October, they had squeezed out a victory by a margin of seven or fewer points. The Browns trudged into the locker room, the first club in NFL history to lose three straight title games.

"It was the toughest game we've ever lost," Brown said. "I doubt if any team ever lost a tougher one." Asked about the winning pass play, Brown just shook his head.

Once again, Detroit's defense had been superb. It forced four turnovers and recorded three sacks (including one by two-way hero Doran) while holding the Browns to just 11 first downs. Between Graham and George Ratterman, who played one series of downs at the end of the first half, the Browns could muster only three completions in 16 attempts for a net gain of nine passing yards.

Conversely, Detroit's offensive line, featuring two rookies and one second-year man, protected Layne with the muscular zeal of a picket line of striking Teamsters. "Jest give me the time, boys, and I'll get you downfield and back into that All-Star Game at Chicago," Bobby had drawled at the start of the climactic scoring drive. "Jest block." They did, and the man one assistant drolly referred to as "Two-Minute Guy" was as good as his word.

The game, watched or listened to by millions around the country and overseas, and reported on by the 141 sportswriters in attendance, cemented Layne's legend. "As the fans swarmed out of Briggs Stadium in the murky twilight of 1953's final Sunday, they had just seen the Lions indelibly mark themselves with the stamp of football greatness," Lyall Smith wrote. "Quarterback Bobby Layne has been a controversial figure on the pro football scene since he came to the Lions four years ago. Win, lose or tie, he starts arguments when football fans try to pick him apart to see what makes him tick. They saw Sunday what makes him go. Pressure. Gobs of it."

The statistics bore that out. Up until the final scoring drive, Layne had completed only eight of his 19 passes for 102 yards, with two interceptions. But with all of the chips on the table, he coolly hit on four of six throws for 77 yards, capped by the decisive 33-yard pitch to Doran.

Layne was now pro football's top gun, "the new glamor guy of the golden gridiron," warbled one wire service reporter. In a 12-month stretch, from December 1952 to December 1953, he'd led the Lions to three postseason victories over the league's two dominant powers, out-dueling more famous triggermen Otto Graham and Bob Waterfield in the process. He'd won back-to-back titles, something few quarterbacks before or since can claim. He was in his prime, having just turned 27 a week earlier. It wasn't hard to imagine the young and battle-tested champs, with Layne in command, capturing championships into the foreseeable future. Indeed, the Lions would appear in a third straight title game the following December.

However, though Layne still had a full 10 years of pro ball ahead of him, he would never again pass, run, and cajole his team to a victory in the postseason. When the Lions won another championship later in the decade, the injured playmaker would be a spectator in street clothes and an ankle cast, unable to personally influence events on the field.

Layne never cared about individual statistics, which was just as well because his postseason numbers are simply godawful. His overall passer rating of 29.9 in four playoff outings is far below that of such quarterbacks as Bart Starr, Joe Montana, and Tom Brady, all of whom also won multiple championships. (The formula, adopted by the NFL in 1973 and applied retroactively, tops out at a perfect 158.3.) Layne completed less than half of his 97 passes. He threw a dozen interceptions against a single touchdown pass. Yet, characteristically, he made that one scoring pass count.

"Bobby just had a way," Jimmy David said. "He got you there. Say what you want about him and how he lived his life. But he got you there."

Gridiron Heroes

> Ours is a city designed for determined folks, and our stadium
> reflected its surroundings. To be among those throngs of football
> fans clogging its entrances before kickoff on a late fall Sunday
> afternoon, with men in gray and brown hats puffing on pungent
> cigars, the deep and expectant rumble circulating through the
> corridors and aisleways as the mob filtered its way to their seats,
> you felt you belonged, you were part of the home team, familiar
> among what seemed to be the inhabitants of an entire city,
> attired in three sweaters, two coats, two pair of long underwear,
> three pair of socks jammed into what we called galoshes. That
> was the Detroit of another, special era. Our city in another time.
> And as tough as it was, it somehow felt so right.
>
> —Tom DeLisle

When you're a kid, you're always someone else. During the 1950s, whenever Jim Boyle and his older brother, Tom, left their Highland Park home to toss the football around, they immediately slipped into their respective roles. Tom, with the blond hair, was Bobby

Layne. Jim, because he had inherited his father's love for Notre Dame and all things Irish, was Leon Hart. The narrow backyard at 78 Ford Street magically became Briggs Stadium. There the brothers acted out their adolescent fantasies of arching aerials, twisting open-field runs, and last-second, game-winning touchdowns. "It didn't matter what the weather was like," Jim Boyle remembered. "Rain, snow, mud—all of that was even better because then you looked like a real football player."

James Boyle Sr. worked as a tool grinder at the nearby Ex-Cell-O plant. On Sundays in the fall, the ritualized acts of piety never changed: Mass in the morning, football in the afternoon. He sat in the kitchen, listening to Van Patrick describe the action on the radio. Jim Junior remembers the exact date he joined his father as a diehard Lions fan. It was December 27, 1953, the day the title game was played at Briggs Stadium.

"I was eight years old," he said, "and I didn't really understand everything that was going on. But I took my cue from my dad. When he cheered, I cheered, and when he booed, I booed."

The boy could see that his father was getting more nervous as the game went on. The Lions were losing, 16–10. He was pounding on the table, yelling "Throw it to Doran! Throw it to Doran!"

"He kept yelling that," Boyle said. "I think maybe Layne was listening, you know, because that's exactly what he did. He threw it to Jim Doran for the touchdown and we won the championship."

Little Jim took his lead from his cheering father. He jumped up and down and raced around the kitchen, rattling the windows with his screams. From that point on, the youngster was obsessed, collecting game programs and bubblegum cards and clipping articles out of the newspapers. The best moment came a couple of years later, when the 10-year-old received his first football uniform for Christmas. The outfit included a helmet.

"It was blue and white," he said, "so I painted it silver to match the Lions' helmets."

Such little displays of devotion were common among young Detroit fans of the '50s. Tom DeLisle grew up on the city's east side. As an adult he enjoyed a career as a television producer in Detroit and Los Angeles. Along the way, he indulged his nostalgia for the great Detroit teams of his youth. His haul of memorabilia included a pile of bubble-gum cards, a pair of Bob Hoernschemeyer game-worn jerseys, and two footballs autographed by the forgettable 1955 team.

"I knew everything about those guys, lived and died with each game, read everything I could find in the papers and magazines, had all the great football cards, and sent away for the media guides," DeLisle said. "In fact, when I had a fifth-grade public speaking assignment in 1956, I titled my speech 'The Lions Ride a Gridiron Roller Coaster.' I spoke so long and my subject was so boring to the girls and half of the boys in our class that the nun finally had to ask me, after almost thirty minutes of blabbering, to stop. Which annoyed me. I hadn't gotten to the defensive backfield yet, and the birth of Chris's Crew."

As exciting as play-by-play announcers like Van Patrick, Harry Wismer, and Chris Schenkel could make a game sound over the radio or TV, it didn't compare with the experience of actually being at Briggs Stadium. Wayne Walker, who grew up an avid baseball fan in Idaho, knew of Briggs Stadium principally from its association with the Tigers, especially the 1945 World Series and the 1951 All-Star Game. Walker's first visit to the stadium was a Saturday night exhibition game as a rookie linebacker in 1958.

"I remember getting off the bus and going through the tunnel and onto the field," he said. "I never even bothered to look at the locker room. To a kid from Boise, it was like seeing the Seventh Wonder of the World. It was just what a ballpark was supposed to look like." The entire stadium was painted green, from its concrete walls to its wooden seats. The four acres of manicured grass added to its sense of grandeur. The double-decked park was imposing, timeless.

The stadium was the pride and joy of its namesake, Tigers owner Walter O. Briggs Sr. The industrialist was not a football fan, dismissing players as "Sunday afternoon wrestlers."

"He really didn't like what a football game did to the field," said grandson Basil "Mickey" Briggs. "He was extremely proud of his ballpark, all that immaculate green grass, and football really tore it up. He rented it out more from a sense of civic obligation than anything else."

Under Briggs, baseball always received precedence at the corner of Michigan and Trumbull. The Lions moved from their original home at Dinan Field to Briggs Stadium in 1938 but occasionally had to return there when the Tigers were in town. By 1951, the Lions were playing their entire home schedule at Briggs Stadium.

The overlapping baseball and football seasons caused ground crew personnel to hustle to reshape the diamond into a gridiron, and then back again, several times between late August and early October. The pitcher's mound had to be shaved down, the base paths and the keyhole (the path between the mound and home plate) covered with sod, the field chalked, and the goal posts installed.

The transformations weren't without their glitches. It wasn't unheard of for a kicker to miss a field goal because his foot scuffed a slightly elevated part of the mound, or for a ball carrier's feet to suddenly go out from under him after hitting a slippery piece of sod. In a 1954 game against Los Angeles, for example, Bill Stits was on his way to returning an interception for a touchdown when the loose sod covering the infield suddenly turned into a flying carpet.

Some savvy players learned to use it to their advantage. "As an offensive end," said Leon Hart, "you'd try to get a man over that turf. You make a cut, the turf gives away and the defender slips. Of course, everybody had to play on the same field, so it worked both ways."

There were no football-only parks in the NFL in the 1950s. The Lions' home venue (which opened as Navin Field in 1912 and was expanded and renamed Briggs Stadium in 1938) was built specifically for baseball, so accommodating the chalked gridiron resulted in an odd configuration. The gridiron was laid out mostly in the outfield, extending from the first-base line to the wall in left center field parallel with the third-base line.

Depending on the weather, dozens of churning cleats could turn the field into either a dustbowl or a soupy morass. The sight lines weren't as good as those for a baseball game. Spectators in right field and the bleachers were farther from the action than those with seats on the third-base line, making a good set of binoculars and a transistor radio must-have accoutrements for the serious fan. The Lions and visiting team entered and exited the field via the dugouts. The benches for both clubs were on the same sideline in right field, just 50 feet apart, which could lead to some vigorous jaw-boning during games. The goal posts, padded to a height of about five feet, were positioned on the goal line and often employed as an extra blocker or defender.

Average attendance for Lions home games exploded from 24,600 in 1950 to 55,743 in 1957, an increase of more than 31,000 fans per game. "The Lions sold so well they'd have to open up the third deck, the press box area," said long-time public relations executive Elliott Trumbull, then a teenaged fan. "You were way up there, but you had a great view of the whole field."

The less stringent fire codes of the era allowed the game-day sale of standing-room-only tickets, which resulted in the Lions regularly surpassing its official seating capacity of 52,853 by a few thousand. Rows of slatted-wood "cheater" seats were placed in the aisles. On three occasions during the 1950s, more than 58,000 squeezed into the park for a game—a testament to the Lions' hold on Detroit.

Among the regulars at Briggs Stadium during the '50s were John Varisto of Dearborn Heights and his brother-in-law. Both were season ticket-holders. "They were lower-deck seats, in the north end zone," said Varisto, an electrician at Fisher Body. "Mine was Section 3, Row C, Seat 23. It was right on the aisleway. Made it easier to run back and forth to the beer stand. I think a cup of beer cost 35 cents then."

Varisto's section, located directly behind the goal posts, was a prime location for those looking to snag a souvenir. Each season about 600 footballs were lost around the league when extra points and field goals sailed into the stands. This worked out to an average of eight footballs, at $18 apiece, per game. There were no nets like today. Fans were allowed to keep any ball kicked their way. There often were tugs-of-war and fistfights over ownership rights, as well as injuries from exuberant fans leaping over seats.

What happened to all those captured footballs? Most presumably were tossed around the neighborhood for a few years before finally winding up deflated and forgotten in some garage. In one case, however, the lucky fan offered to return the prized pigskin to someone deemed more worthy. Bob Hoernschemeyer's wife, Marybelle, was shopping downtown one day when a stranger approached her.

"He said he had the ball Bob carried on his record 96-yard run on Thanksgiving," she said. "He said they'd used the same ball to kick the extra point and he'd caught it in the seats. I don't know if all that was true, but it was nice that he wanted us to have it."

After a game, the streets around Briggs Stadium were clotted with an exhaust-spewing mix of the chrome and steel gas guzzlers that characterized postwar America: Fords, Chevys, Plymouths, Pontiacs, Hudsons, Packards, Dodges, Kaisers, Buicks, Oldsmobiles, Mercurys, DeSotos, Nashes, and Studebakers. With the Fisher Freeway north of the ballpark still to be built (it wouldn't open until the early 1960s), the creeping postgame traffic literally drove many impatient fans to drink.

"We'd stop at a local bar," Varisto recalled. "We'd say, 'Well, let's wait until the traffic thins out a little.' That was our excuse. We'd get home a few hours later and the wives would say, 'Where you been?'"

Today, older fans pantomime shivering when recalling how cold the concrete-and-steel open-air stadium could get late in the season. This was football in the great outdoors, and it didn't seem to matter how many layers of clothing a person wore, it wasn't enough to ward off the knifing winds, blowing snow, icy rain, or diving temperatures.

"On blustery days there was no way to stay warm," Trumbull said. "You'd huddle under blankets and stamp your feet. You'd go home after the game and it'd take an hour to defrost." Some experienced cold-weather fans brought scrap wood with them to feed barrel bonfires in the center-field bleachers. "How they ever got 55-gallon drums in the bleachers was beyond me," Trumbull said.

Many rooters, of course, brought their own "anti-freeze" in flasks and thermos bottles. Whether one drank hot chocolate or something a bit stronger, the entire experience was intoxicating: the waves of raucous cheering and booing washing across the field . . . the fragrance of cigar smoke and wet wool . . . the disembodied voices of Van Patrick and Bob Reynolds drifting through the stands . . . the communal bonding with ticket-holders Sunday after Sunday, season after season. "Golly, it was wonderful," said long-time fan Fred Rice.

Fans accustomed to today's head-banging, wall-to-wall din would have a hard time imagining Briggs Stadium in the 1950s, a time and a place when there really was a "murmur of the crowd" and the eruptions of partisan uproar needed no electronic cues. Not only was there no piped-in rock or rap music assaulting eardrums, there wasn't even an organist (and wouldn't be until 1966). This left the shouts of vendors, the amplified voice of public address announcer Joe Gentile, and the staticky play-by-play emanating from countless transistor radios to fill in the dead air between downs. "You could actually carry on a conversation," Trumbull said.

When the Lions scored, there were no exploding scoreboards or wailing sirens to celebrate the occasion. For that matter, there were no end-zone histrionics. There were various unwritten rules helping to govern play, and foremost was not showing up an opponent. "All that showboating you see today after a touchdown or a tackle—that didn't exist, in college or the pros," said Wally Triplett. "If I'd started dancing or congratulating myself, my teammates would've crucified me. They would have very quickly reminded me that it's a team game."

Instead, whenever Hunchy or the Doaker hit pay dirt, he simply tossed the ball to the referee, the band burst into a rousing rendition of "Gridiron Heroes," and fans like Rice and his pals beerily sang along to the Lions' official fight song: "Hail the colors Blue and Silver, let them wave / Sing their song and cheer the Gridiron Heroes brave . . . Rah! Rah! Rah!"

Aside from occasional outbursts of the fight song, most of the music on game day was confined to the halftime show. This was a holdover from pro football's earliest days, when marching bands, mascots, and other college-style entertainment were used to help attract fans. The Lions' halftime shows were regarded by many as the finest in the NFL, lauded for their ambition, precision, and pageantry.

This was a tribute to Dr. Graham T. Overgard, the tireless, detail-obsessed head of the music department at Wayne University and a renowned conductor, composer, and educator. Overgard wrote the music and lyrics for "Gridiron Heroes" in 1939 as well as the fight songs for several colleges. He started directing the Lions' halftime performances in 1937 and would continue for another three decades before finally laying down his baton. In addition to his teaching and football duties, for many years he was the impresario of the mammoth State Fair parade on Woodward every summer and director of the music festivals on Bob-lo Island. And "Boy, he could play a mean bagpipe," said his son, Jon.

As much a taskmaster and tactician as any NFL coach, Overgard drew up band formations on chalkboards and oversaw drills from a 24-foot-high scaffold erected at midfield. Remarkably, he created a new program for each game. "You have no idea of the planning and paperwork involved," he said in a 1954 interview. "These shows usually involve 500 people who have to be briefed in advance on exactly what they must do. And we have only one rehearsal."

With all the traffic on the field, things could get a little chaotic. Dick Burman was a trombone player in the Redford Union High School band, which regularly performed at Briggs Stadium.

"One day our band was standing in the end zone getting ready to play the national anthem before the game," Burman recalled. "The Lions were running plays and warming up. Doak Walker went out for a pass, which he caught in the end zone just before slamming into me. I went one way and my trombone went another. Mr. Walker helped me up and said, 'Are you okay, kid?' I told him I was but I didn't know about my trombone. I thought that was a very gentlemanly act on his part. The crowd cheered, we took a bow, and he ran off."

Bands always stood behind the players' bench when they weren't performing, Burman said. He remembered one cheeky incident.

"One time, Yale Lary, with his back to us, dropped his uniform pants in order to adjust himself in his jockstrap. He took his time, too. The girls in the band, as well as I'm sure a lot of the lady fans in the stands, enjoyed that moment."

Like any star performer, Overgard seemed to be at his best in the most important games. In October 1953, columnist Mark Beltaire gushed that "the halftime display at the sensational Detroit Lions-San Francisco 49ers contest was the most colorful show these bloodshot eyes have looked upon in years. Seven bands and over 100 majorettes of all sizes and ages were in the act . . . managed by Wayne University's Dr. Graham Overgard, who should be at least a five-star general. Even if the superb Lions hadn't been there, that performance was, as the hackneyed phrase goes, well worth the price of admission."

Music was Overgard's life, but even he needed an occasional break. When dining out, he always got a table as far from the orchestra as possible. And at home, 14-inch walls separated the conductor's study from the sounds of his children practicing their instruments. "Certainly I love music," he said, "but enough is enough."

On Thanksgiving Day, the ritual was the same for many Detroiters: parade, football game, turkey dinner. When the Lions started their holiday tradition by hosting Bronco Nagurski and the Chicago Bears in 1934, it was just one of three NFL games played that day. From 1945 through 1965, however, the Lions' game was the only NFL contest scheduled for Thanksgiving. The sole exception was in 1952, when the Bears were forced to play a neutral-site game against the Dallas Texans in Akron, Ohio. Beginning in 1951 and continuing through 1963, Green Bay was Detroit's annual opponent.

For many Detroiters, the holiday began with the J. L. Hudson Company's Children's Toy Parade, a Thanksgiving tradition stretching back to 1925. Every year upwards of 200,000 people saw the parade in person, with an unknown number of others watching on television locally (and then, starting in 1952, in dozens of cities nationally). By 4 a.m., people were already assembling to claim the best spots along the parade route, dragging along lawn chairs, ladders, thermoses, flasks, blankets, and sleepy-eyed children.

The extravaganza of floats, bands, and gaily costumed figures in giant papier-mâché heads followed a three-mile route down Second, Vernor, and Woodward. The spectacle was purposely put together from the perspective of a six-year-old, parade organizers said, but even the adults freezing at curbside enjoyed the spaceships, giant animal balloons, and 40-foot Goozie Bug.

Some parade-goers went straight from the parade to Briggs Stadium, just a few blocks away. Because of the local blackout rule, Detroiters without tickets were unable to sit down at home and watch the game on television. Thus more than a few found Thanksgiving the perfect excuse to drop in on relatives in Lansing, Flint, Bay City, or Grand Rapids.

As was always the case at Lions games, especially on Thanksgiving, some fans partied too hard. Twenty minutes after the 1955 Lions-Packers contest ended and Briggs Stadium had emptied, a policeman found Clifford Anderson still in his seat, passed out drunk. Two days later, when the 26-year-old factory worker was brought up on charges of public intoxication, he told the judge that he had nodded off at halftime. "I not only missed the second half," Anderson said, "but I missed my turkey dinner." The judge gave him a suspended sentence and sent him home to his leftovers.

There were various figures on the Briggs Stadium sidelines who were integral parts of the game-day experience, though few spectators ever gave them much thought. There was, for example, the "chain gang" of Ed Howland, Joe Raikovitz, "Moon" Mullins, and Bud Dohring, local officials responsible for handling the chains and down marker at every home game. They labored in the same weather conditions as the players, with the added threats of getting smacked by snow-balls from the stands or being bowled over by a rampaging linebacker.

"Mullins controls the down box," observed a reporter. "Howland and Dohring work the chain. Raikovitz 'spots' the ball by driving a peg into the ground and, even more important, he 'spots' the precise point where each series of downs begins. This becomes an important item whenever Howland or Dohring have to pick up their sticks to get out of the way of a play."

The crew, which Mullins formed shortly after the Lions began playing at Briggs Stadium, stayed together for more than three decades. Although unpaid, they received several benefits, including two season tickets apiece and an all-expenses-paid trip to a Lions road game each year. As for cheating by adding or subtracting an inch to benefit the home team, Mullins insisted, "We've always given them an honest count."

Among the most conspicuous sideline figures were the Lions' two long-time mascots, William "Moon" Baker and his "cub" companion, Blanche Verhougstraete, whose crowd-pleasing antics went into overdrive every time the home team scored. Beginning with the second game of the Lions' inaugural sea-son in 1934, Baker spent Sunday afternoons in the fall dancing and swinging his tail and leading cheers.

Verhougstraete was 10 years old when she joined Baker at Briggs Stadium in 1938. The sunbeamy mascot, all of 53 inches tall, was born in Belgium and came to Detroit when she was very young. Known in local amateur contests and burlesque houses as "The Human Top," the athletic girl could perform up to 10 revolutions spinning on her head, a specialty that earned her a mention in "Ripley's Believe It or Not" and an invitation from the Lions' publicity director. Verhougstraete suited up for 40 seasons, running, jumping, tumbling, and cart-wheeling all over the field while missing just one game because of bronchitis.

All this cavorting in the vicinity of a thunderous herd of 200-pound men could be perilous, such as that afternoon in 1952 when Baker was wiped out by Vince Banonis during a Lions-Bears tussle at Wrigley Field. The banged-up mascot returned to action four days later on Thanksgiving, this time wearing a helmet and using several towels for padding under his costume.

Many who watched Baker and Verhougstraete frolic over the years assumed their roles were being played by a succession of children. That was the one nice thing about being small, Verhougstraete said. "You never grow out of the part."

Not to be overlooked were the team's waterboys, who in those pre-Gatorade days were responsible for providing water to thirsty players and performing other chores under the direction of equipment manager Roy Macklem. Sometimes the club held a contest in conjunction with one of the local newspapers to fill the position, with applicants asked to submit a letter stating why they wanted to be a Lions waterboy.

There were no special qualifications for lugging around a metal pail, packing duffel bags, or peeling tape off floors, though there were countless boys who considered such labor to be a dream job. "Did you ever see a dream running?" Billy Welty, a 12-year-old orphan attending St. Veronica in East Detroit, wrote in his prize-winning essay in 1952. "Well I did. That dream was me running as waterboy for the Detroit Lions. . . . I want to be around a football atmosphere so I can learn more about the game. It will teach me rules and discipline and the fine spirit which makes a fellow a true American."

As in any line of work, it helped to have connections. Peter Whyte was a waterboy in the early '50s. His father was Ray Whyte, a prominent Chevrolet dealer and a club director. "Peter was a little fellow who didn't let his status . . . keep him from doing menial tasks cheerfully for the players and coaches," Bob Latshaw wrote. "He took his job seriously." He even had regulation jerseys for himself and two helpers with the numbers ½, ¼, and ⅛ sewn on. Ray Whyte liked to joke about his conscientious son, who actually owned stock in the club, "running the football team" as "waterboy for the Lions."

Peter reluctantly left his job after the 1953 season, when he was 12 and sent off to school in Connecticut. However, the club's "most loyal fan" continued to follow the team through weekly long-distance phone calls with his dad. On occasion, he'd travel to road games to be close to his heroes. The players liked him, especially Leon Hart, who filled the role of surrogate father.

Peter was an excellent student. In the summer of 1956, he was rewarded with a trip to California, where he stayed with a friend's family. His father encouraged him to remain there until after the July 4th holiday. But Peter was determined to return home to start a new summer job on the day he had promised his employer.

Some Lions players and coaches were uneasy about flying, including Buddy Parker, who superstitiously made sure he was always seated next to sportswriter Bob McClellan. They had a right to be nervous. Air safety in the 1950s was nothing like it is today, even as airliners increasingly replaced passenger trains as the most common mode of long-distance travel.

On the morning of June 30, 1956, the DC-7 carrying Peter home to Detroit was flying parallel to another airliner at 21,000 feet. The planes were beyond the reach of radar, flying under conditions known as "see and be seen." Their possible crash course was the responsibility of the pilots, not air traffic controllers. Passengers were being treated to views of the Grand Canyon when the airliners, skirting the same cloud formation, violently crossed paths.

At the Grosse Pointe restaurant where the Whyte family was waiting to celebrate Peter's homecoming, the shattering news of the midair collision came over the radio. All 128 people aboard the two airliners, including 14 Detroiters, were killed. At the time, it was the deadliest commercial aviation disaster in U.S. history.

"There'll be a big void around the clubhouse next fall," Latshaw wrote just before the Lions opened camp in 1956. "One of the nicest little guys ever to tote a duffle bag for the Lions will be missing." But not forgotten. Family friends funded the building of a new auditorium in his name at St. John Hospital in Grosse Pointe. The disaster was the catalyst for major change, most notably the formation of the Federal Aviation Authority and a severe reining in of the previously uncontrolled skies.

Everybody loves a winner. In the early 1950s, just as the Lions became competitive, various groups of organized rooters sprang to life to offer support for the town's favorite football team. Their ranks included some of biggest boosters—and boozers—in Metro Detroit.

The Crisis Club was an organization of civic-minded do-gooders whose random acts of kindness ranged from giving 50 blind workers Braille wristwatches to outfitting an elderly newspaper vendor in a new topcoat and hat. Started by Wayne County auditor Charley Edgecomb in early 1952, the club's roster featured attorneys, judges, businessmen, municipal employees, and media types. Joe Gentile, a beloved radio personality at CKLW and WJBK and the longtime P.A. announcer at Briggs Stadium, belonged.

Members passed the hat at weekly luncheons at the Hotel Fort Shelby to underwrite their philanthropic deeds. Among their social activities was organizing chartered trips to Lions road games, typically buying 500 to 1,500 tickets each time. Losses didn't put members into too deep a funk. After all, their motto was "Every Day's a Crisis."

Members of the Lions Bleacher Club were more interested in having a bottle than a motto, admitted founding president Fred "Fritz" Wenson. In addition to showing up in force at every home game, "Each year we took one road trip, usually to Chicago or Cleveland," he said. "We'd rent a couple of Scenic Cruisers with a toilet, 'cause we needed a toilet. We'd be half-blind by the time we got to the game. One time we took two buses to Pittsburgh, and we marched into the stadium playing the Lions' fight song. Lyle Fife, one of the owners, came down and got drunk with us. He said, 'I'm gonna take you guys to Los Angeles.' But it was Johnny Walker or Goebel's or whatever he was drinking that was talking."

The Lions Bleacher Club could be a rowdy bunch. During a trip to Cleveland, each member was equipped with a megaphone, which they used to maximum effect. "You could sure hear them," said a Lions assistant. "They made more noise than all the 75,000 others in the park." On another occasion, club members had to practically fight their way out of Wrigley Field. "The Bears fans came down, they didn't like us carrying around a banner at halftime," Wenson said. "There was a rumble on the field."

The Lions Bleacher Club was formed at about the same time as the Crisis Club, right after Wenson came back from army duty in the Korean War. "We had factory workers, merchants, doctors, lawyers, you name it," he said. "There were fan clubs everywhere, but none as classy as we were. We called ourselves a bleacher club because that's where we always sat. We had squatters' rights."

To Wenson, the towering figures in the sports pages were, upon closer inspection, more human-scale, individuals with the same mixed bag of qualities and frailties as the average Joes who were buying the tickets and in effect paying their salaries. "Back in the '50s, players were friends with fans," he said. "They were approachable. You could go drink with them. There was a lot of interaction between players and fans then. You'd see Jug Girard bowling at Crest Lanes or Charlie Ane selling sporting goods."

That was Dan Baker's experience as well. One Sunday after a Lions-Colts game in the late '50s, his dad, mascot Moon Baker, ushered him across the street into the Stadium Bar. Players from both teams commingled easily with fans inside the dank, hazy joint, signing napkins and programs while replenishing their fluids with a few cold ones. Johnny Unitas was there, and so were Artie Donovan and some others, and soon it was time for the visitors to board the team bus for the airport. The teenaged Baker watched the Colts walk out the door and into the cool autumn dusk.

Moments later, Unitas rushed back in. He'd forgotten something. The Baltimore quarterback ordered a half-dozen bottles of beer, shoved the long-necks into the deep pockets of his topcoat, and then ran back out to the bus.

"That's my memory," Baker said. "Johnny Unitas in his crew cut and big overcoat, going out the door with all these bottles clinking. You just don't see things like that anymore."

Bobby Layne had a favorite song, and he sang it at the top of his lungs whenever the mood hit him, which was often: "Ida Red, Ida Red, I'm a plumb fool 'bout Ida Red." The song was one of Layne's trademarks. There are countless variations of "Ida Red," a fiddling song whose roots stretch back to the nineteenth century. In 1955, Chuck Berry adapted its melody for his breakout hit, "Maybellene."

"The guys from Texas were always singing," said Jerry Reichow, who joined the team in 1956. "There was Bobby and 'Ida Red,' and Yale Lary was always singing 'The Yellow Rose of Texas' in the shower." Gil Mains did a mean rendition of "Red River Valley," while Fum McGraw often performed these and other country-western standards at club functions. Joe Schmidt had a fine voice and Harley Sewell certainly wasn't shy about his crooning, either.

Much of the singing was done by harassed rookies—impromptu renditions of William & Mary's "Tribe Fight Song" ("Oh, we will fight fight fight for the Indians") or Texas A&M's "The Aggie War Hymn" ("Hullabaloo, Caneck! Caneck!"). Whether sung inside the dining hall or a saloon, the off-key voices and fumbled lyrics were a dependable source of entertainment for the veterans. Dick Stanfel was known for corralling reluctant "chirpers" at team get-togethers. Nobody was safe. "The wives had to sing, too, and they didn't like that," Schmidt said.

Layne, of course, was the undisputed leader of the band. "Bobby came here in 1950, but there were no hi-jinks under Bo McMillan," said Roy Macklem. "But by 1952, Buddy Parker was here, Bobby was established, and things got progressively worse with rookie hazing. On the first day, Bobby would give the orders to the rookies and Yale Lary would demonstrate, holding his hand over his heart and singing his school song."

Sometimes the rookie couldn't remember the lyrics. "Just hum it, man," Layne would say impatiently. If the rookie still was flustered, he could get by with a rousing rendition of the school cheer. "We heard some great yells," Macklem said. "Thanks to Layne."

During training camp, rookies cleaned ashtrays, polished shoes, and made late-night food and beverage runs. Sometimes they served their masters breakfast in bed. The chores were menial and demeaning, the better to put a highly touted All-American in his place. Alex Karras, a rookie in Layne's last season as a Lion, was ordered to go out and find some flowers to brighten the quarterback's "cheerless" dormitory room.

"Oh, Alex, isn't that sweet!" Layne exclaimed when the big tackle returned, a bouquet squeezed into his meaty paw.

Once, when the team was in Norman, Oklahoma, for an exhibition, Karras was summoned to Sewell's hotel room, where several veterans were drinking beer and playing cards at two in the morning. His mission was to go into town and bring back a sack of hamburgers. After taking everybody's order, Karras asked Layne if he knew of any places that might be open.

"No, goddamn it, find one," he said.

It was a sweltering August night, the air alive with bugs. Karras trudged through the dark in his wool pants, sport coat, and thick glasses, unsure of where he was going. He'd walked about two miles when he finally found a little all-night joint. Soon he was trotting back to the hotel, greasy sack in hand. "Hot as a bitch. Bugs all over me. I'm just dying," he recalled. By now he had been gone almost two hours. He banged on Sewell's door for several minutes before it finally opened.

"What do you want?" Sewell growled.

"I've got all these hamburgers," Karras said.

"We all went to bed," Sewell said. "Goddamn it." Then he slammed the door shut, leaving the sweaty rookie standing alone in the corridor with a dripping bag of burgers.

Sewell was only giving back what he'd endured himself. "When I was a rookie," he liked to say, "I went with Bobby Layne to get some toothpaste. And we didn't come back for three days."

The caste system continued through the regular season, with veterans hazing the handful of rookies who made the final roster. The idea was to teach respect, Layne explained. When he'd been a rookie with the Bears, he was so afraid of grizzled vets like "Bulldog" Turner that he'd hid in closets. "Rookies in those days," he recalled, "we made miserable."

Few were made more miserable than Joe Schmidt, whose crime was replacing the popular Dick Flanagan in the lineup. "You can imagine how we felt about Schmidt," Layne said. "We hardly spoke to him. Back then you were considered a rookie until the first game of the second season, and he had a long way to go."

Finally, one Sunday after the game, Vince Banonis took some pity on the rookie linebacker. He invited him to Kelly's bar, a popular hangout at Dix and Waterman, where the veterans were gathering to unwind. Things didn't go all that well. Schmidt walked up to John Prchlik and, trying to be one of the guys, breezily addressed him by his nickname. "Hi, Jolly John," he said.

Prchlik turned around and gave Schmidt a death-ray stare. "Rookie," he said coolly, "my name is John Prchlik."

"But Joe took it all," Layne remembered. "I never saw a good one who didn't."

Those who caroused with Layne agreed that he could hold his liquor better than most men and that he was impatient with anyone who couldn't keep up. Yale Lary was proud to call himself "a stayer," someone who survived to the end of the festivities while others fell by the wayside. It wasn't unusual for a player trying to maintain appearances to either feign being passed-out drunk or discretely spill or spit out the booze. Doak Walker, Don Doll, Fum McGraw, and Cloyce Box were among those who didn't care for the taste or effects of alcohol, and some refrained completely.

But there were others who could chug-a-lug with the best of them. Sewell enjoyed demonstrating the "proper" way to drink. He would down a pitcher of beer in a single extended gulp, pouring the stream of suds down his throat and into his stomach as easily as filling a bathtub with water.

The most awesome sight was Les Bingaman draining a case of Falstaff in less time than it took a normal man to finish his third beer. "He would suck up his huge gut so that it became part of his chest, his great jowls expanding as he inhaled and emptied one bottle, and another, and another, faster than fluid flows," a fascinated observer wrote. "All around the National Football League, Les Bingaman is remembered for this great talent."

While many rookies dreaded the head-spinning frathouse-style drinking sessions, most in retrospect saw the benefit.

"You had to go there and drink and play the games," one former Lion said of the carousing. "As much as the drinking could be a hazard, in a way it did keep everybody as one unit and on the same page and thinking the same way. You got a feeling out of it that you were part of the team, that they liked you. It's important to feel that you're part of something. And there's a lot of teams that don't have that. The players go off into their little cliques."

According to Jimmy David, "nobody was a stranger for long. That was Bobby's way. Once you were on the team, you were part of the gang. There would be a spirit party of sorts. There was rookie afternoon at some show bar in town. If you didn't show, we'd send a taxi for you. Bobby was the leader and we all followed. He knew the game and he knew people and he knew how to have a good time. There were some nights he'd be throwing $100 bills into a saxophone till all hours and there were other nights when some of us would kinda commandeer a trolley for a while. But when it came time to play, we were ready. They'd tell jokes that when we'd form the huddle you could smell liquor and stuff like that. But that never happened. Not during regular season, anyway."

Even leaving aside all the singing, the Lions were a remarkably harmonious squad. In the early years, at least, players often wore a leather-sleeved varsity-style jacket around town—one with a large Lion logo on the front and a "World Champions" patch on the sleeve—as if they were still college jocks on campus.

"We went to bars together," Doak Walker said. "Wherever we went, we went together. I know the wives used to get upset and say, 'Can't you leave those guys alone one day?' Everyone was proud just to be on the ball club. It was a complete team. Everybody enjoyed being with the other guy."

"It was Bobby that got everybody together," Dorne Dibble said. "No matter what, if you weren't down at the Stadium Bar on Monday, you heard about it. Some of the wives didn't like us going down there, but we went. Well, there was no question, Monday was just a shot day and my wife knew it. I was going down to get my check and then to the Stadium Bar."

Betty Dibble once made the mistake of dropping in unannounced, searching for her husband. She took one look around, turned on her heel, and promptly walked out. She never said a word about it, Dibble recalled with a laugh.

The Stadium Bar was just one venue for fun. The squad often assembled at Kelly's, where they shot pool (Gene Gedman was the champ), listened to owner Jimmy Kelly's stories of playing tailback for the old Detroit Heralds, and got wasted playing Cardinal Puff. Other times they might meet up for a night of bowling at Crest Lanes at Meyers and Grand River, take in a band at the Rouge Lounge downriver, or gather at the Crystal Show Bar on Grand River, where the club's Sports Room "attracted many high sports figures."

Layne followed one of his favorites, jazz vibraphonist Terry Gibbs and his quartet, all around town. "We got very friendly and he was a frequent visitor to any club I played in Detroit," Gibbs recalled. "Everywhere he went, people would mob him for his autograph. He was a millionaire but also an alcoholic. He didn't have any inhibitions at all. Sometimes, if he was really drinking, he'd come up on stage, take a handkerchief, make it look like it was a saxophone, and make believe he was playing jazz while we were playing. When he'd come to the club where we were playing, he'd bring half the team in with him, people like Joe Schmidt, Dorne Dibble, and Hunchy Hoernschemeyer, and they'd make a great audience for us. They were always ready to party."

While Layne, to his eternal regret, never learned to play an instrument, Gibbs admired the quarterback's jazz-like improvisation on the field. "Bobby reminded me of a musician," he said. "A musician doesn't think of a thing until he goes on stage. When we were with Bobby it was all so natural. I never saw a guy who swung so much but then was so strong mentally and alert on the field." And like so many others, Gibbs was amazed by Layne's recuperative powers.

In particular, Gibbs remembered one summer evening when Layne came to see his band in Detroit, then invited everybody to his hotel room to continue the festivities. The party finally broke up at 10 o'clock the next morning, at which point Gibbs wanted nothing more than to go to bed and sleep the rest of the day. But Layne, "juiced out of his bird," insisted Gibbs accompany him to Ypsilanti to watch him in that afternoon's scrimmage. After a $320 cab ride, Layne suited up while Gibbs nursed his hangover.

"He got on the field ten minutes before the scrimmage started," Gibbs recalled, "and he was so sharp I couldn't believe it. I remember a headline the next day in the Detroit paper saying he was going to have his greatest year."

Whatever was playing on the jukebox during the sometimes raucous gatherings at the Stadium Bar, it certainly wasn't "Gridiron Heroes." It was more likely to be Patti Page's "Tennessee Waltz" (known simply as "Bing's song" because Bingaman was always singing it) or Cisco Houston's version of "Sweet Betsy from Pike" (a great singalong ballad for players in their cups) or possibly even "Skid Row Boogie." The latter was a catchy tune written and performed by a local hillbilly swing band, Bob Durham and the Sunset Riders. The guitar-strumming Ford worker died of a heart attack before he could record his follow-up song about flying saucers. But for a time in the early 1950s, "Skid Row Boogie" could be heard in bars up and down Michigan Avenue, the unofficial anthem of this skeevy part of town: "Everybody's talkin' about Skid Row somehow / Well, the bums down there live the life of Riley now."

Everybody *was* talking about Skid Row, or at least they were inside city council chambers and newspaper offices. During the Lions' glory years, the area around Briggs Stadium was grimy, decaying, and crawling with vice, though special efforts were made to police the district for game days. Michigan Avenue between Cass and Sixth, and the adjacent streets, were especially notorious for dive bars, flophouses, liquor stores, pawn shops, greasy spoons, prostitutes, and all-night theaters. A legion of lost souls, many of them mumbling to themselves, leaned against dirty storefronts, urinated on curbs, passed out on lawns, and accosted passersby for loose change. "Bottle gangs" pooled their nickels and dimes to buy a bottle of booze. *Free Press* reporter Bud Lanker observed a motley group of drunks weaving their way down the street. "One staggered up to the side of the Salvation Army Citadel and vomited on the sidewalk in full view of scores of passers by," Lanker wrote.

Detroit's prosperity was to blame for the army of vagrants that descended on the city in the 1940s and '50s. "They are lured here by promises of high wages, but they arrive broke," an official of the Howard Street Mission said in 1953. "If they don't catch on, they seem to go further downhill." The city under Mayor Albert Cobo slowly began condemning and razing properties, but the winos, whores, drifters, and panhandlers didn't magically disappear. They simply scattered, with many moving into another blighted section around First, Second, and Third streets, an area later known as the Lower Cass Corridor.

Layne, who had a lifelong fascination with the low life, was a soft touch for the derelicts who stumbled into the Stadium Bar, stinking of piss and Wild Irish Rose. Where others simply saw a drunk looking for a handout, he saw an old-age pensioner or a down-and-outer temporarily between jobs. "Layne used to set up drinks and a buffet for the bums and many is the buck he handed to them," Joe Schmidt recalled. "They were astonished that anybody like Bobby Layne cared about them."

One of the eyesore buildings targeted for demolition was the Lindell, a forty-room hotel at 1519 Cass, just south of Bagley. The Civil War–era hotel had been operated by Greek immigrant Meleti Butsicaris and his sons, Johnny and Jimmy, since 1949. The hotel was populated by a mix of gamblers, traveling salesmen, transients, prostitutes, and minor underworld types. Athletes and entertainers staying across the street at the Leland Hotel on Bagley gravitated to the cocktail bar on the ground floor of the Lindell. Sonny Eliot, who was just getting his start in local television, remembered that "you could walk in there and see Milton Berle and Billy Martin sharing a drink." Martin, shortstop for the Yankees and Tigers during the 1950s, became close friends with the Butsicaris brothers and suggested they dress up the place by displaying sports memorabilia.

The Lindell Hotel stood opposite the Detroit Times Building, which made the saloon a natural hangout for newspapermen. When employees of the city's dailies struck in 1955, *Detroit Times* photographers built a darkroom for the strike newspaper, the *Detroit Reporter*, in a back room of the bar. The Lindell's bar was christened the "Lindell A. C." by Doc Greene, a regular patron. He explained that the initials stood for "Athletic Club," a dig at the tony seven-story Detroit Athletic Club on Madison where many Lions directors dined, drank, and socialized.

George Puscas once gave *Free Press* readers a descriptive tour of the original Lindell saloon. "Behind the blind screening out the street lights, the bar stretches maybe 30 feet. Along the wall is a row of cocktail tables, and at the rear standing side by side are two pool tables. . . . On its high, dingy walls are lined a mammoth gallery of pictures of sports celebrities, some autographed, some not, and mementoes—balls, hats, helmets, hockey sticks. At the bar, like as not, might be found the hero of the day's contest, sipping his beer, trying to ignore the creep who wandered in. . . . The Lindell is not a place where wives are found, or brought. It is a retreat of the professional athlete."

Some have claimed the Lindell A. C. of the 1950s was the first sports bar in the country. Certainly it was the first in Detroit. In early 1963, with the Lindell Hotel on the verge of being knocked down, the Lindell A. C. moved into a remodeled building on Cass at Michigan. Sometime during the 1950s, while the hotel was still standing, the Butsicaris brothers installed a two-way mirror inside a room on the second floor. A ritual involved pairing up a Lions rookie with a working girl, the player's performance secretly watched and commented on by a snickering audience in the adjacent room. One voyeur laughingly recalled a studly linebacker from a western college "scoring" in just a few seconds, making the embarrassed victim the brunt of locker room abuse the following day.

Alex Karras told author George Plimpton that the "best to watch were the country boys who came in shy and awkward, and huge if they were tackles or guards, not knowing whether to sit on the bed, which was the only piece of furniture in the room, or to stand, and getting one shoe off finally and maybe another, and often forgetting to get out of their shirts and ties."

Wherever athletes went, there were plenty of distractions, from overly perfumed "good-time girls" to back-slapping hangers-on desperate to share the limelight. Vince Banonis remembered with disgust the "front-runners and well-wishers" who crowded into the locker room after games. "Everybody's got their groupies," recalled Toy Ledbetter, a member of Philadelphia's backfield in the early '50s. "They're buying you drinks and inviting you to parties."

The annual two-week West Coast trip always had a certain boys-will-be-boys vibe to it. More than one old-timer fondly remembers "the Bush"—the Bull 'n Bush in Los Angeles—though the entire Sunset Strip was filled with lively nightspots and temptations of all types.

The 1953 trip was especially eventful. One night in San Francisco, Layne, Hoernschemeyer, Bob Smith, and Gene Gedman dropped in at John's Rendezvous for steaks and drinks. Some patrons began heckling them. The locals unwisely agreed to settle matters in the parking lot. Smith flattened one loudmouth while Hunchy grabbed another by the seat of his trousers and tossed him over a wall.

Following the incident in San Francisco, the Lions moved on to Los Angeles, where the "after-dark sightseeing" by some players got so out of hand that Buddy Parker finally clamped down. The threat of a bed check evidently didn't deter Layne. As Edwin Anderson later described it, "Layne was out half the night" before the Rams game. "It showed in his play, and we lost to the Rams. Afterward the players really chewed him out. There's a possible cut of championship money riding on every game, and the players won't stand for one fellow hurting their chances of getting it."

Parker later denied that any of that had happened, that the six players spotted in the hotel lobby at 2 a.m. by club directors was a case of mistaken identity. Whatever the truth behind that particular incident, there was no denying that Parker's club enjoyed a big side dish of fun along with their football.

"On the field, the Lions were a well-organized, well-drilled, and well-coached team," Joe Schmidt told Stuart Leuthner in *Iron Men*. "On their own they were hell-raisers. I came to Detroit thinking those guys were the pinnacle of professional football and I got my eyes opened up in a hurry. I was the kind of kid who kept himself in tip-top shape all the time, practiced hard, and studied the game every chance I got. I wondered how these guys could be drinking beer and running all over the place and still play football? After I had been there for a while, I woke up to the fact that, 'Hey, I guess these guys can do two things at the same time.' They were all good athletes and knew what they could and couldn't do, how far they could go with their off-the-field activities."

While most interactions between players and the public were innocuous—scribbling an autograph, posing for a snapshot, or enduring some long-winded fan's rundown of his own high school career—players were warned to be careful of unsavory characters, especially gamblers, and cautioned about being lured into compromising situations. The admonitions were delivered in person by Bert Bell each August as he made the rounds of training camps.

The commissioner had a right to be concerned. In October 1950, for example, Detroit police broke up a plot by a local hoodlum and two associates to blackmail Lou Creekmur for rape. The scheme was hatched when a woman named Lucille Genoff told her roommate, Jean Kuhn, that the rookie tackle had assaulted her inside a Detroit hotel room. According to Genoff, the alleged rape occurred after a Sunday night of drinking at a party following a Lions game. Kuhn, in turn, told her boyfriend, Charles Robert Jones, and their mutual friend, a small-time career criminal named Dave Mazeroff.

Seeing an opportunity to make some quick hush money, Mazeroff instructed Genoff to contact Creekmur and tell him that if he didn't pay them $10,000, she would go to the police with her story. When Genoff started to express second thoughts, Mazeroff warned her not to mess around, saying, "I'm a hot package. I'm the finger man in the Hooper killing."

Mazeroff was referring to the sensational murder of Warren G. Hooper five years earlier. The state senator had been scheduled to testify before a grand jury about legislative graft when he was gunned down. Although officially unsolved, it was widely believed that Detroit's notorious Purple Gang had orchestrated the hit and that Mazeroff, who had been on the fringe of the Purples' activities since the 1930s, had identified Hooper for the killers.

Genoff, frightened by the mess she found herself in, went to the Wayne County district attorney's office and told of the plot. The conspirators were arrested and stood trial for extortion in 1951. Genoff, who was not charged, was the prosecution's star witness. The attractive 20-year-old brunette described her profession as "dancing instructor." She testified that the sex with Creekmur had been consensual and that she was only joking about the rape. Creekmur did not take the stand but publicly stated that he did not know the woman. In the end, Mazeroff and Jones were found guilty and sent to prison.

Players' wives, more concerned about home-wreckers than hoodlums, were understandably territorial. Once, when a society writer innocently referred to Yale Lary as a bachelor in his column, Janie Lary asked for—and quickly received—a published correction. With the country's divorce rate hovering around 22 percent during the decade, most Lions couples survived the strains that a pro football career placed on their marriage. The Harts, the Larys, Charlie and Dolan Ane, Don and Diana Davies Doll ("My Triple-D Dynamo," he called her), Wally and Leonore Triplett, and Joe and Marilyn Schmidt were just a few of the many couples who believed in "'til death do we part," with several living long enough to celebrate 50, 60, or even more years together.

But there were exceptions, especially after no-fault divorce laws made it easier for couples to go their separate ways. Lois Bingaman, tired of her husband's drinking and fooling around, filed for divorce in 1956 after eight years of marriage, citing mental and physical cruelty. In the settlement, Les gave up the family home on Santa Barbara Street, $417 cash, and $930 in savings bonds. Fern Box, the daughter of a Methodist preacher, tolerated Cloyce's philandering during and after his Lions career for the sake of their four sons before finally calling it quits. It was restlessness, not a roving eye, that caused Doak and Norma Walker to drift apart after he left the game. "No way he cheated on Norma," Dorne Dibble said. "He wouldn't even sit next to a girl."

It wouldn't have mattered if he did. Coaches and reporters reflexively turned a blind eye to any indiscretions they came across. Buddy Parker knew that one of his stars regularly visited an apartment that Lyle Fife and some other directors kept near the Lions' offices. It only became an issue when directors asked Parker why the player was spending so much time there instead of in training. "The sons-a-bitches had given the guy a key to the apartment," Parker said, "and they knew I knew it."

If a player wanted to huddle up with a cocktail waitress in Los Angeles, an airline stewardess in San Francisco, or a "schoolteacher" recommended by a bell-hop in Chicago, that was between him and his confessor. "You didn't step on toes then," said Edgar Hayes, sports editor of the *Detroit Times* in the '50s. "The theory was, you're a guest in the clubhouse, so you didn't repeat what you saw or heard there. Formal interviews were okay, but what happened in the clubhouse stayed there. The same when you saw an athlete around town."

Not only did most scribes refrain from writing about players' escapades, some joined in. "Hell, the writers were on the streets as much as we were," claimed Paul Hornung, a notorious nightcrawler who broke in with the Packers in 1957. "The writers in those days were heavy drinkers, and very few would pass up a free drink." Tex Maule, the lead pro football writer for *Sports Illustrated*, and Doc Greene were among those who enjoyed making the rounds with the players.

One Sunday night after a game, Greene piled into a car with six players, including Schmidt and Layne. Schmidt was at the wheel and Greene had to sit in somebody's lap in the back seat. Layne had heard of a good band playing at some place in Canada, and the entourage drove off to Ontario to find it. They crossed the Detroit River into Windsor and drove around aimlessly, stopping several times to ask for directions.

After more than an hour of this, Greene finally spoke up. "I don't care where we are going," he said, "but let's arrive somewhere." The players got such a kick out of Doc's exasperated plea that from then on they used "Let's arrive somewhere" as their password.

Of course, it could be argued that being complicit in the merrymaking compromised a reporter's objectivity. Once, when Layne was arrested for drunk driving, Greene used his popular "Press Box" column to plead for Layne's right to privacy. "There is an opinion that a fellow in the public view should be more careful than us average citizens, but it doesn't sit well here," he wrote. "Because Layne happens to be some sort of prominent figure with his little football doesn't indicate that he should have to stay at home and hide under a sofa. A saloon keeper has a right to make a living, too, and Bobby has a right to pursue diversion in his own fashion. He is an open, generous, sincere figure of a football player and should be measured precisely by what he does on Sunday afternoons when 54,000 interested have paid for the privilege of judging him."

Layne couldn't have cared less about keeping stories of his nightclubbing out of the papers. He liked to brag that he left a place the same way he entered it—through the front door. "Bobby Layne didn't give a shit," Schmidt said. "He put his priorities before other people's, and if he wanted to go someplace, he went." Most of the stories about Layne were "bullshit," Schmidt added, "but he would never deny anything because he loved the image."

There are some stories Schmidt knows are true because he was there. One time in 1953, he and Gene Gedman accompanied Layne to Charley Costello's Wedgwood Room on East Jefferson at Riopelle. "There was no place to park," Schmidt recalled, "so Layne just pulled the car up on the sidewalk and said, 'Let's go.'"

The players ordered beers. A few minutes later, a policeman walked in and asked who owned the car parked on the sidewalk. Layne said it was his, and he and the cop walked outside to discuss the situation. Twenty minutes later, Layne returned and announced, "Let's get out of here. I promised Bob Howley we'd have a drink with him. One of you guys drive my car."

Schmidt and Gedman walked outside to find Layne sitting inside the police car. As the rookies drove off in Layne's vehicle, the police cruiser followed with its siren wailing and red light flashing. After arriving at their destination, Layne asked the cop to come in and have a drink.

"Listen," the officer said, "I'm eight miles out of my district and if they ever hear about this I'll be fired. If they find me drinking, I'll get the electric chair. Goodbye and have a good time." As Schmidt and a host of others observed, Layne had a way of getting along with people.

The Flame Show Bar, whose fiery yellow and red neon lit up the corner of John R and East Canfield, was one of Layne's favorite haunts, especially on Sunday and Monday nights. According to one rookie who acted as his chauffeur, "the crowds would stand up and yell 'Mr. Layne's here!' and they'd go crazy."

Owner Morris Wasserman advertised the mixed-race nightclub as "The Most Beautiful Black & Tan in the Mid-West." The Flame had the same lifespan as the original Lindell bar, 1949 to 1963, but it attracted a far different clientele, one willing to pay higher prices for the smoky ambience and first-class entertainment: 90 cents for whiskeys and mixed drinks, 65 cents for a bottle of beer. "The place could hold a couple hundred, maybe a little more," recalled Norm Thrasher, a member of the Detroit-based Midnighters during the '50s. "No cover charge. The stage was built right into the bar. You'd have LaVern Baker, Jackie Wilson, Dinah Washington, T-Bone Walker performing. It was a mixed crowd, everybody enjoying themselves. You'd see Layne sitting right up front, and Reverend C. L. Franklin [Aretha Franklin's minister father] would be at the next table."

Yale Lary accompanied Layne one night to see B. B. King at the Flame. His pockets bulging with "catfish" (Bobby-speak for walking-around money), Layne made sure the music, the fun, and the Cutty Sark flowed all night. "They wanted to shut down," Lary said, "but Bobby would wad up a hundred-dollar bill and stick it in the saxophone player's sax. They kept playing as long as Bobby dumped those bills."

The free-spending quarterback always earmarked a large chunk of his football salary for entertainment. He knew most of his teammates couldn't afford big nights out on the town. Layne didn't try to pick up every check, but he picked up far more than his fair share, and if he tipped well it was only because he was served well. In any event, he viewed money as nothing more than a means to an end, that end being the pursuit of good times with teammates, friends, celebrities, and total strangers.

"I would truly like to run out of breath and money at the same time," the eternal party animal said late in life. "If they could put it on a computer right now and tell me when that would happen, I could plan for it. Then we'd really have a fine time."

ONE OF *Those Things*

When the team loses, Buddy has a routine that never varies. He flops on an ottoman in the living room and pulls out a pocketknife he's been carrying for thirty years. He raises the knife to his throat slowly and cuts his tie at the knot. Until I hear the material rip, I'm never sure it's the tie, not his throat, that he's cutting.

—Jane Parker, 1954

I n the fourth annual Pro Bowl, played January 17, 1954 at half-filled Los Angeles Memorial Coliseum, Paul Brown finally defeated a Buddy Parker–coached squad, as the East beat the West, 20–9. Otto Graham, Lou Groza, and Ray Renfro starred for the East, while Bobby Layne had one of his passes picked off and returned for the clinching touchdown. Parker was characteristically sour over the loss, inconsequential as it was.

"Cheer up, Coach!" said 49ers end Gordy Soltau, a member of the West squad. "If you finally had to lose to Brown, this was the one to lose. It won't show up in the league standings."

"Guess you're right," Parker responded. "I don't like to lose any of 'em, though. But Paul was bound to beat me sooner or later. I realize that. I was lucky to hold it off this long."

In an unusual gesture, East players awarded Brown the game ball in recognition of him snapping his well-publicized personal losing streak to his coaching rival. But the Pro Bowl was a throwaway spectacle played with hybrid lineups. In head-to-head competition between Detroit and Cleveland, Parker still owned Brown. By the time the two rivals met in a third straight championship game at the end of 1954, Parker's Lions would have eight wins and a tie in nine contests against Brown's team, including preseason games. "We'd be playing Detroit, and we could be 28 points ahead in the third quarter, and for some reason, we just knew we were going to get beat," Cleveland's Ken Konz said.

How to explain this strange dominance? There's never been a simple, single answer that anybody could point to, then or now. Joe Schmidt said it was a matter of being well-prepared by the coaches. Parker thought it was because the Lions always changed their formations a little to confuse the Browns—a six-man line with the ends dropping off into pass coverage, for example. Graham, who had some of the worst performances of his career against Detroit, admitted the Lions often were either a better or a luckier team than the Browns.

Some suggested there must be a spy in the Cleveland clubhouse passing on insider information about game plans, injuries, and so forth. Ex-Brown Jim Martin was thought to be somehow involved, though this was never really explained. Another theory was that the secret operative was none other than longtime assistant coach Weeb Ewbank, who left Cleveland in early 1954 to become head coach of the Baltimore Colts. However, there's never been any proof that Ewbank or anybody else in Cleveland's organization worked clandestinely for the Lions. Paul Brown had his own suspicions, alleging in one interview that Parker had a hired man spying from a rented house across the street from the Browns' practice field. Parker denied the allegation.

Others grasping to explain the lopsided ledger in Detroit's favor suggested some sort of hoodoo was to blame. "Nowhere in Paul Brown's scientific world of thorough scouting reports, game films, preparation, and execution did hexes or jinxes factor in," wrote Browns historian Andy Piascik, "but even the great coach could no longer wave aside his team's poor record against the Lions. Actually, the notion of a jinx or hex must have had at least some appeal to Brown, for the obvious alternative conclusion was that Parker's team was simply better than his, something that Brown was loath to admit."

Detroit's overall success under Parker was due in part to his ability to continually refresh the team through astute trades, draft picks, and free agent signings. "New blood every year; that's the ticket," he said. "You get a little self-satisfied and fat-headed and your team falls apart on you. Five or six new men every season is about right." Rookies were vital, supplying youth and enthusiasm and pushing veterans out of their complacency.

For all the work that went into scouting and evaluating prospects, Parker knew that the annual college draft was essentially a crapshoot. A case in point were his top two picks in 1954, Rice University tackle Dick Chapman and Michigan State center Jim Neal. Parker had high expectations for both linemen, but each decided to forego the NFL. (See chapter 12.) There also were the usual busts, such as Cal Poly fullback Bob Lawson. One of the first national publications devoted strictly to pro football, *The Football Graphic*, debuted that preseason. In its first issue, readers were offered a tantalizing item about Detroit's ninth-round pick: "Lawson paints one of the toenails on his right foot a bright red with ladies' nail polish. Seems he has been practicing this ritual since his high school days. Of course every man has a right to his own pet hex, and times do change, but we wonder what would have happened in the Bears' locker room if one of the old-time Monsters of the Midway had been discovered painting his tootsies a bright crimson."

Parker got it right about Bill Bowman and Bill Stits, his third- and fourth-round choices. Stits, an outstanding two-way back at UCLA, would be used almost exclusively on defense, playing well enough to earn the only Pro Bowl appearance of his eight-year career. Bowman was a bruising pass-catching back out of William & Mary with the ability to bite off yardage in large chunks. In what turned out to be his only full NFL campaign, he would record the Lions' longest run, reception, and kick return of the season, a statistical trifecta that remains unique in franchise history.

The Lions officially opened camp on Friday, July 23, 1954, in Ypsilanti, though as always there were many early arrivals. Coaches were impressed by the condition of the players as they checked in for their physicals. The previous summer, eight players had been banished to the dining hall's "fat man's table" for being overweight. So far this year, there were none.

Les Bingaman was in a classification of his own, his listed weight often a rough estimate. When Bingaman broke a bench while bending over to tie his cleats, coaches argued over the guard's true weight. Soon a bet of a steak dinner was placed between Buster Ramsey, who said he weighed under 350 pounds, and Parker, who maintained he was over that mark. Roy Macklem hunted down the only available scale, one with a 400-pound maximum, at the Ypsilanti Farm Bureau.

With coaches, reporters, and Edwin Anderson looking on in anticipation, Bingaman stepped on the grain scale. The needle shuddered, then stopped tantalizingly close to the wager's cutoff weight. "Bing checked in at 349½," Macklem recalled. "So Buster won the bet. I found out later that the scale had been set up wrong and he actually was closer to 375."

The day following this bit of frivolity, the first punch-up of the new season occurred at an all-night burger joint in Ann Arbor. Bob Hoernschemeyer and Dorne Dibble were inside the White Spot restaurant on Main Street, chatting up a young lady in the predawn hours, when words were exchanged with a couple of former Ann Arbor High School gridders.

Cops arrived on the scene. According to the *Detroit Times*, one of the young men threw the first punch. In the melee, Hunchy lost a tooth and "accidentally belted a policeman." The entire bunch was arrested and later arraigned in Municipal Court, where the judge accepted their guilty pleas and released each of them on $25 bond. Parker declared Ann Arbor off-limits for the duration of camp.

Several familiar faces were missing as drills began. Three starters—Yale Lary, Gene Gedman, and Ollie Spencer—had been called to active military service, and old hands Pat Harder, Bob Smith, John Prchlik, and Vince Banonis had retired. As always, new faces replaced them. In addition to Bowman and Stits, there was Andy Miketa, an undrafted free agent who had spent the previous two years in the air force after graduating from the University of North Carolina. Miketa caught Dibble's eye while both were stationed at Bolling Field, and Dibble tipped off Parker when he rejoined the team in 1953. Miketa, the son of Hungarian immigrants, surprised some by becoming the everyday center. By far the lightest center in the league at about 205 pounds, the speedy and aggressive lineman would play every game in 1954 and 1955 before quitting his smashmouth profession to pursue a career in dentistry.

Although the word "three-peat" was not yet part of the vernacular, Buddy's squad was well aware it was chasing history. Green Bay had finished on top of the standings in 1929–31, but that was in the old NFL with its single-division format and no official playoff. Since the league split into two divisions in 1933, no club in the so-called modern era had won three titles in a row. In fact, only two other teams—the 1942 Chicago Bears and the 1950 Philadelphia Eagles—had ever been in the position to do so. Both failed.

Now it was Detroit's turn, and not many were betting against them. The squad's average age was 25½ years, with just five players—Martin, Hoernschemeyer, Cloyce Box, Bob Dove, and Les Bingaman—older than 27. Fielding a bevy of stars in their prime and with back-to-back championships under their belt, the Lions were being touted as pro football's newest dynasty. Joe King of the *New York World-Telegram* compared Parker's deep and well-balanced squad to Casey Stengel's New York Yankees, the winner of five consecutive World Series between 1949 and 1953. "Five straight might be within the reach of such a seemingly invulnerable club as the Lions," King wrote. While some maintained that Cleveland had already accomplished this particular feat, that necessarily meant counting the Browns' four AAFC titles—something Bert Bell refused to do. To this day, the NFL does not recognize the AAFC in its official records.

Parker was not a happy camper. For the second August in a row, he had to prepare his team for the College All-Star Game in Chicago. It was bad enough for the superstitious coach that this year's game was scheduled for Friday the 13th. Worse were the conditions the champs would have to play under.

The All-Star Game was governed by college rules, which normally allowed for unlimited free substitution, the same system the pros had adopted in 1949. The postwar rise of offensive and defensive specialists had made both pro and college football more freewheeling and fan-friendly than it was back in the single-platoon days; it had also opened up opportunities for more players. But the NCAA, looking to tamp down the spiraling costs of football programs by reducing the number of players, scholarships, and coaches, took the radical step of reinstating the single-platoon system. Beginning with the 1953 season, a player removed from the game in the first or third quarter could not return to action until the following quarter. A player withdrawn before the last four minutes of either half could return in those last four minutes; however, a player leaving within that time frame would not be allowed to go back in. There was no provision for kickers; they were expected to be all-around players, too.

Parker understandably didn't want to risk his offensive stars, particularly Layne, on defense. He also didn't want to waste three weeks of camp installing an "iron man" system that would be worthless for the NFL season. He argued the game should be played as it had been for years, for the sake of players and fans. Parker had the support of Bert Bell and the Lions, but those parties didn't want to lose their cut of the proceeds either, should the game be canceled. (The Lions stood to make an estimated $35,000.) All sides publicly squabbled through the spring and summer.

There was no love lost between the imperious Arch Ward and Parker, who the year before had suggested that it was the *loser* of the NFL championship game who should be forced to play the All-Stars. Ward seemed particularly offended by Parker's dismissal of his "dream game" as merely another exhibition.

Just as the matter was headed to arbitration, Parker and the Lions capitulated. Buddy put together a backfield consisting of Doak Walker and Jack Christiansen at halfbacks, Lew Carpenter at fullback, and seldom-used Tom Dublinski at quarterback. The offensive line was made up of ends Leon Hart and Dorne Dibble, tackles Lou Creekmur and Charley Ane, guards Dick Stanfel and Harley Sewell, and center LaVern Torgeson. When the Lions were on defense, Stanfel would line up as middle guard and Sewell and Torgeson would play linebacker.

The bitter buildup to the game continued as Ward wrote a column in early August accusing Parker of trying to pay a college coach $500 to spy on the All-Stars. Parker scoffed at the alleged espionage, saying Nick Kerbawy wouldn't approve spending that kind of cash for an informant. Meanwhile, Maryland head coach Jim Tatum, who was drilling the All-Stars at Purdue, promised some surprises from a lineup of brilliant backs and passers that included Rick Casares of Florida and Zeke Bratkowski of Georgia. Observers, noting that the Lions had to deal with an unfamiliar format and that the college squad was one of the strongest ever assembled, expected a close contest. So did oddsmakers, who installed the pros as mere seven-point favorites.

The game was over after 10 minutes. By then Detroit had scored on its first three possessions and held a 17–0 lead. Meanwhile, the All-Stars had yet to register a first down. Just as Parker predicted, what should have been an exciting spectacle turned into an uninspired slough as two-way performers on both sides lost energy in the second half. The All-Stars were in Detroit territory only twice all night—each time the result of a Lions fumble—en route to getting crushed, 31–6.

Many of the 93,470 spectators started leaving Soldier Field in the third quarter. "There wasn't even a bruise on any of the Lions after it was over," noted one sportswriter. Layne didn't take a single snap and earned $1,666.67. The biggest beneficiary was third-year quarterback Dublinski, who seized the opportunity to impress coaches and teammates.

Paul Christman deserved a share of the credit for Dublinski's development. Christman, who had led the Cardinals to their two division titles and was now a salesman in Chicago, had been brought to camp to work exclusively with Layne and Dublinski. During the regular season, Christman flew out to games every weekend to analyze their play, study their mechanics, and offer suggestions. The Lions' first quarterbacks coach was just the latest sign of specialization creeping into the game.

For the Lions, the highlight of the exhibition season was the annual game in Dallas, which this time featured the participants of the last two title matches. Layne and Walker gave the Cotton Bowl crowd exactly what they had come to see, as Texas's favorite sons led the Lions to a 56–31 pasting of the Browns. Walker tallied 20 points on two touchdowns and eight conversions while Layne threw for three touchdowns and ran for another. Cleveland actually led, 31–28, in the fourth quarter, when the dam burst and Detroit posted four unanswered touchdowns. Tempers flared, with Cleveland center Frank Gatksi ejected for fighting with Joe Schmidt. Parker never let up, calling for a successful onside kick in the last couple of minutes after the Lions had just scored to open an 18-point lead. Layne was in there pitching to the end, sending 43,000 Texans home happy with a scoring strike to Walker with two seconds left on the clock.

The Lions went on to overwhelm Pittsburgh to complete an unbeaten preseason. Paul Brown, meanwhile, was in the midst of a major rebuilding program. Eleven players, one-third of the previous year's team, including such long-time stalwarts as Marion Motley and Bill Willis, were gone. Brown especially needed time to revamp his shredded defensive unit. Yet in three weeks Cleveland was scheduled to host the Lions in the second game of the regular season.

Then Brown caught a break. The Cleveland Indians, the main tenants of Municipal Stadium, were running away with the American League pennant. By September it was clear they would be hosting the middle three games of the World Series the first weekend in October. Game 5 was slated for Sunday, October 3, the afternoon of the scheduled Lions-Browns match. As it turned out, the Indians were swept by the New York Giants in four games, making the fifth game moot. Of course, nobody at the time could anticipate that.

To resolve the scheduling conflict, Parker suggested shifting the game to Detroit. "I can guarantee you a sellout crowd," he said, "and an $80,000 cut of the receipts." This was four times the guaranteed minimum for a visiting team. Brown, the thumping in Dallas fresh in his mind, was not interested in fielding his work-in-progress in front of a hostile crowd, no matter how attractive the incentive. Nor was he open to simply moving the game back a day, to Monday, October 4.

"We're not ready to meet you yet," Brown said. He insisted that Bert Bell reschedule the game for December 19, the Sunday following the end of the regular season. "We'll be ready then," he said.

Detroit players shrugged off the scheduling change as little more than a minor inconvenience. They were happy enough for the $300 each received for the extra week of practice. Because of the ominous numerology (October 3 worked out as 10/3, or 13), Parker normally would have been uneasy about playing the game as originally scheduled. But as events would prove, it was bad luck *not* to have played on that date.

"I had a veteran team and it was in excellent condition," he said. "There's no doubt in my mind that we would have whipped Cleveland and virtually knocked the Browns out of championship contention." Instead, with "an extra week of preparation to solidify his forces, Brown's Cleveland team started a comeback climb that was to find it going all the way. I'm confident, and so is almost everybody else, that they couldn't have even won their division title if it hadn't been for this unusual turn in the schedule."

On September 26, the Lions officially began their title defense in grand style, smothering the Bears, 48–23, in the regular-season curtain-raiser at Briggs Stadium. Bill Bowman returned a kickoff 100 yards for a touchdown—the longest play of the year in the NFL—and Bob Hoernschemeyer hit Bowman and Dorne Dibble with short touchdown passes on the halfback option. The game was tied at halftime, but the Lions pulled away as Doak Walker put on a dazzling display. In the fourth quarter alone, he tallied 17 points, kicking three extra points and a field goal and scoring two touchdowns—one on a 70-yard punt return and the other on a three-yard run.

It was the start to another brilliant season by the Doaker. With Lew Carpenter (who led the team with 476 rushing yards) and Bowman taking over most of the ball-carrying chores, Parker began employing him more often as a flanker or a man in motion. Walker finished the 1954 season with as many receptions (32) as he did rushes. When he did handle the ball, he was the most productive player in the league, averaging a career-high and NFL-best 14.4 yards per touch (rushing attempts, receptions, and punt and kickoff returns). He remained a reliable placekicker, converting each of his league-high 43 extra-point tries and trailing only Lou Groza in field-goal percentage. Walker's 106 total points were bested only by Philadelphia's Bobby Walston.

After enjoying the rare bye week created by the rescheduled game with Cleveland, the Lions resumed play on October 10 against Los Angeles. On a muggy, foggy afternoon at Briggs Stadium, the Lions intercepted the pass-happy Rams four times. Tom Dublinski made his first NFL start in place of sore-shouldered Layne and scored on a 1-yard keeper to cap a long first-quarter drive.

Layne entered the fray in the second half and played conservatively, attempting just five passes. With Detroit narrowly ahead, 7–3, early in the third quarter, Stits picked off a Norm Van Brocklin throw and lateraled it to Carl Karilivacz, who raced 30 yards across the slippery turf to complete the unusual scoring play. Carpenter closed out the 21–3 victory with a 60-yard scoring jaunt in the closing moments of the game. The normally explosive Rams were held without a touchdown for the first time in 67 outings.

The following Saturday night, the Lions shut down the visiting Baltimore Colts, 35–0. Dorne Dibble, who would lead the team with a career-best 46 catches in 1954, caught two of Layne's three scoring passes. "It was great, as long as you caught the ball," the easygoing end once said of the six seasons he spent gathering in Layne's throws. "I used to smile at everything I did. If I caught one, I smiled. If I dropped one, I smiled. Then he realized what my personality was."

The Lions, who had not lost a game of any kind in an entire year—a run of 16 regular-season, preseason, and postseason games stretching back to November 1, 1953—then traveled to San Francisco, where the 49ers slapped the smiles off their faces. Nobody gave Parker more fits than San Francisco, the only team to compile a winning record against him during his time in Detroit. San Francisco beat Buddy seven out of 12 outings, and all but one of the 49ers' losses was settled by four or fewer points.

For 1954, an already formidable 49ers team was fortified by the acquisition of fullback John Henry Johnson, who rounded out what the press dubbed the "Million Dollar Backfield": Johnson, Joe Perry, Hugh McElhenny, and Y. A. Tittle. All were future Hall-of-Famers. Based on their collective salaries, the explosive quartet was more like the $65,000 backfield. Whatever they were paid, they were worth every penny. "Y. A. Tittle used to joke about trying to keep us all happy by giving us the ball," McElhenny recalled. "He certainly has his hands full because we all had egos."

The 49ers had three victories and a tie heading into their game with the Lions at Kezar Stadium. In the battle of the unbeatens, the 49ers ran roughshod over what many considered the best defensive line in football, rolling up 270 yards on the ground. McElhenny jump-started San Francisco to a quick 7–0 lead with a 60-yard scamper and Johnson later added a pair of six-pointers. It was 17–0 at the end of the first quarter. By the fourth quarter, the lead had grown to 37–17 and Layne was lost to a concussion after being gang tackled. The Lions roared back behind Dublinski, however, to pull to within six points.

With less than four minutes left to play, Jack Christiansen gambled on a punt return. He fielded the ball on his own 5-yard line in the midst of a horde of 49ers, carrying it across midfield before he was stopped at the San Francisco 46. But the final drive sputtered and the 49ers remained undefeated with a 37–31 victory. Although the comeback had fallen short, Parker was impressed with how his team had responded. "Any club that played the kind of football they did is made of championship caliber," Buddy said. "We were 17 points down and then 20 points down, but they never quit. This squad doesn't know the meaning of the word quit. I still say we'll win the championship again."

The following Sunday, the Lions regained their winning ways, eking out a 27–24 victory at Los Angeles despite Dan Towler and Skeets Quinlan each shredding the Lions' defense for more than 100 yards on the ground. Parker started Dublinski this Halloween afternoon. But it was Layne, stepping in after Detroit fell behind, 14–3, who captained the game-winning drive in the final minutes. The 80-yard march culminated with Hoernschemeyer taking a pitchout and scoring unmolested from five yards out.

The most outlandish play of the game came in the second quarter when Norm Van Brocklin faded back, faked a throw, then handed off to Quinlan. Leon Hart burst into the backfield, wrestled the ball away from Quinlan, then fled to the end zone with what officially was recorded as a 22-yard fumble recovery.

That same day, San Francisco dropped its first game of the season to the Bears. The 49ers lost more than a game; they lost the league's rushing leader when McElhenny suffered a season-ending shoulder separation. Detroit was now tied for first place with the 49ers. The Lions were back to wearing smiles as they prepared to head home—everyone except Buster Ramsey, whose defense had allowed an unacceptable 555 yards rushing in the two games, and Bob Smith, whose scowl had grown deeper during the West Coast swing.

Smith had been lured out of retirement by Ramsey and Parker, who wanted the veteran cornerback and punter as an insurance policy. He joined the club in late September after missing camp and slowly worked himself back into shape. By October, Bill Stits was a fixture in the secondary, Jug Girard was the regular punter, and Smith was growing angry over his lack of playing time. Bored and unbloodied, he wanted to do more than just collect a paycheck.

As the team filed onto their chartered plane after the Rams game, Smith and Ramsey got into a heated argument. Cross words led to some shoving. Players separated the two before any punches were thrown, but Parker had seen enough. "You're through!" he told Smith, ordering Nick Kerbawy to put him on another flight to Detroit. Smith ultimately was let back on the team's plane, where he apologized to the coaches, but the following morning he was put on waivers. With that, Smith's football career reached its sudden, inglorious end.

The entire episode didn't sit right with Lyall Smith. "I think it is a tribute to Bob Smith that he was so incensed about not getting a chance to acquire bumps and bruises that he was ready to fight about it," he wrote in his *Free Press* column. Citing Smith's past contributions and stating that his indiscretion was "no greater than a dozen others which have been made by other members of the team in the last few seasons," the sports editor maintained that the veteran deserved a better fate than being "sent away under a cloud."

Smith went back to his job with the Ford Motor Company, not entirely forgotten. At the Lions' next home game, bleacher fans unfurled a banner demanding his return. Later, Smith's teammates voted him a half share of their playoff loot, even though he had appeared only briefly in two games before being axed.

The Lions next traveled to Baltimore, where they overpowered the Colts, 27–3, in a Saturday night game. This time the defense was an absolute stone wall, limiting the Colts to just 69 total yards and six first downs. During the lopsided loss, Baltimore's Ken Jackson became enraged by the antics of Gil "Wild Hoss" Mains, who was filling in nicely for Thurman McGraw and Gerry Perry, both nursing injuries. The cocky Mains, a second-year defensive tackle out of small Murray State College in Kentucky, had impressed Lions coaches with his size (6-foot-2, 230 pounds) and raw energy. "It isn't unusual to see Gil making tackles from sideline to sideline," said Aldo Forte. "His biggest asset, however, is desire.

He loves to play football." Mains had lasted exactly one play in 1953, dislocating his elbow against San Francisco and missing the season.

Now it was a new season and Mains was anxious to prove himself. His roommate, veteran Bob Dove, had showed him a few tricks, including the old standby of flinging mud into the face of his opponent. This evening, the target of Mains's mud-slinging was an even-tempered rookie guard named Jack Little. "Jackson was playing tackle right next to Little," recalled Art Donovan, "and he was berating him right on the field for taking that shit . . . on the sidelines Jackson told him to watch him, he was going to show him how to take care of a team that throws mud at you."

The Colts punted. Moments after the play was whistled dead, Mains nearly was, too. In "as flagrant a roughing play seen anywhere," reported the *Free Press*, Jackson clobbered Mains, laying him out like a rug and dislocating his jaw. "So help me Christ," Donovan said, "I thought he killed him." Jackson was tossed out of the game, and some in the Colts organization thought he should be cut. "I think what kept him in the league was the fact that Mains was such a dirty player that a lot of people figured he got what was coming to him," Donovan said.

A few years later, Donovan capped his own personal feud with Mains by kicking him in the face in full view of an official. The resulting penalty wound up costing Baltimore the game, but Donovan grew into old age stubbornly unrepentant. "If I had to do it all over again," he claimed in his autobiography, *Fatso*, "I'd still kick that son of a bitch in the chops."

The victory over the Colts put the 5–1 Lions in sole possession of first place when the 49ers dropped their second straight game. The 49ers were now 4-2-1, and facing a crucial rematch with the Lions. Three weeks earlier, Doak Walker had called the 49ers the greatest team the Lions had ever met, but Parker insisted they weren't even as good as last year's club. "We'll murder 'em when they come back to Detroit," he declared.

On November 14, the rivals took the field in front of 58,431 screaming fans. It was the largest football crowd ever squeezed into Briggs Stadium, with thousands more turned away at the gate. Bert Bell rejected all requests to televise the game locally. No matter. It was a crisp autumn day, perfect for raking leaves while listening to Van Patrick on the radio. The tone of the game was set on the opening kickoff when Sonny Gandee jarred the ball loose from Billy Tidwell and Jim Martin recovered. Walker's 33-yard field goal gave Detroit a 3–0 lead just 71 seconds into the game. But that was just the start of the onslaught.

After San Francisco was forced to punt on its next possession, Layne drove the offense 80 yards in eight plays, darting in for the score from 5 yards out. One minute later, a scintillating 47-yard punt return by the Doaker set up a 23-yard touchdown pass from Layne to Jim Doran. A few minutes later, Walker added another field goal. By 13:22 of the opening quarter, Detroit had amassed a 20–0 lead and the 49ers were reeling. At halftime it was 27–0, thanks to another Layne scoring strike, this time to Jug Girard. At the end of three quarters it was 41–0. Hoernschemeyer connected with Walker for a 66-yard touchdown off the option, and Bill Bowman took a Dublinski screen pass the same distance for another six-pointer. The teams exchanged touchdowns in the last quarter to make the final score 48–7, the worst pounding in San Francisco's nine-year history in the AAFC and NFL.

"Parker was as jubilant as a high school sophomore in the Lions' dressing room after the game," Hal Middlesworth wrote. Buddy pronounced it the greatest game the Lions had played under him. "There have been games where our defense might have been greater, and we have had better offensive days," he said. "But never in my four years as head coach have those departments been better at the same time. We just didn't make any mistakes today."

Every other team in the Western Division had at least three losses, putting the 6-1 Lions comfortably in the driver's seat. Clicking on all cylinders, the Lions cruised into Green Bay, where Layne threw for two touchdowns and ran for a third as Detroit hammered out a 21–17 verdict. "The game, rough all the way, ended in a midfield melee as the Lions' Lou Creekmur and the Packers' Stretch Elliott traded punches," the Associated Press reported. "A good share of the 20,767 fans in City Stadium swarmed onto the field, but impending trouble was averted by the officials."

A major casualty of the day's action was Dick Stanfel. The guard suffered what he thought was a hip pointer and gamely hung on until intermission. "It was finally the half and I went into the dressing room to be examined," Stanfel remembered. "The doctor also thought it was a hip pointer, so they decided to give me a shot of Novocain. They shot me once and I told them it didn't take. They shot me again, and I told them it still didn't take. They shot me a third time and I said, 'Just forget about it—I'll play without it.'"

Stanfel lasted only a few plays in the second half before he was forced to watch the rest of the game from the bench, which was right up against the concrete wall of the stadium. "You could literally reach up and touch the fans," he said. Glancing into the stands, he noticed a man wearing a Lions cap. "Hey, buddy," Stanfel said, "you got a cigarette?" The man lit one and handed it to the wounded lineman. "That was one of the things we did in those days . . . have a cigarette on the bench," Stanfel said.

Neither nicotine nor novocaine helped. The next day, Stanfel was so immobilized by pain that roommate Joe Schmidt had to help him get out of bed and to the doctor's office. X-rays revealed three fractured bones in his back. Forced to wear a corset that restricted his movement, Stanfel wound up missing the rest of the season. Stanfel was tough, Schmidt said, adding that "the novocaine syringe was a good friend to all of us."

The ever-ready Jim Martin took over at guard. The big blond was vain about his physique, and he caught some good-natured flak because of it. Players of the '50s, while generally larger and in better physical shape than the average American male, were quite ordinary looking by modern NFL standards. Layne was self-conscious about what he considered to be skinny calves, but a glance at photographs from the period reveals a clubhouse filled with slack biceps, thin shoulders, and doughy stomachs and chests.

Today's heavily muscled, sculpted physiques were largely confined to superhero comics and physical culture magazines. There were no comprehensive weight-training programs, with players having been warned since high school of the dangers of becoming muscle-bound. Detroit weightlifter Norb Schemansky, who won several world titles and Olympic medals during the postwar era, approached the Lions about incorporating strength training into their program, but the club wasn't interested. "We never had weight rooms, mini-camps, any of that stuff," Vince Banonis said. "All we lifted in the off-season were a few beers."

Such pharmaceutical aids as steroids and human growth hormone had yet to enter the sport's mainstream. "We never dispensed any [steroids] because they were supposed to have side effects, but they didn't know what they were," said Lions trainer Millard Kelley. "As far as drugs go, the only problem we had was with amphetamines, and that didn't amount to much." Commonly known as "go pills" or "pep pills," and widely used in the military during World War II, some players popped amphetamines to ward off fatigue and improve performance, especially as they got older. Dexedrine tablets ("dexies") were popular. "I'll throw a couple dexies in me and we'll have us a practice," Layne once casually told a reporter, referring to his strategy for staying alert for an early morning session.

As for recreational drugs, while various surveys show that the vast majority of today's players have used marijuana (often as a substitute for opioids to
relieve pain), few players in the 1950s had any contact with the illegal herb.
Those who did often came from West Coast campuses where its use had grown
more socially acceptable after the war. In Layne's era, the drugs of choice were
overwhelmingly alcohol and nicotine.

The first studies linking smoking to cancer appeared in the early '50s, but
many nicotine addicts were unpersuaded. Most members of the Lions organization smoked, though some players gave it up during the season and many
abandoned the habit later in life. On game day, tired players looking for a quick
pick-me-up smoked cigarettes on the bench while coaches nervously puffed away
on the sidelines. Parker alone went through two packs each game. For heavy
smokers like Layne, the craving for nicotine was always there. "Know what I
think?" he told coaches during a crucial time-out in the final minutes of the '53
championship game. "I think a cigarette sure would taste good about now."

Layne remembered one veteran on the 1950 team, Dante Magnani, who
was constantly sneaking cigarettes despite Bo McMillan's anti-smoking edict.
"Whenever Bo would come in the vicinity," Layne said, "Magnani would palm the
lighted butts and by the end of the year, he had no skin on the palm of either hand."

Marlboros were favored by Layne and many of his teammates, influenced
in part by the cowboy imagery that tobacco giant Philip Morris so master-
fully employed in its "Marlboro Man" advertising. Camels, Lucky Strikes, and
Chesterfields, endorsed by doctors, celebrities, and athletes, were popular.
Tobacco use was prevalent even among those who disliked cigarettes. Leon Hart
was often seen biting on the stem of his pipe, a professorial look that went well
with the bow ties he favored. Good ol' boy Harley Sewell dipped snuff. Harry
Gilmer, who joined the team in 1955, chewed tobacco, leaving a trail of paper
cups filled with vile-looking brown liquid in his wake.

Later in his career, after he had moved on to Pittsburgh, Layne would tout
his favorite brand of cigarettes in a television commercial filmed inside an empty
Detroit ballpark. "You get lots to like with a Marlboro," he said in a raspy voice.

Four days after their battle in Wisconsin, the Lions and Packers met in
a Thanksgiving Day rematch at Briggs Stadium. Detroit won another
squeaker, 28–24, as Jack Christiansen lugged back an interception and
a punt for touchdowns and Layne hooked up with Walker and Lew Carpenter

on scoring aerials. Layne's 18-yard pitch to Walker made him the fourth quarter-back to throw 100 career touchdown passes. More significantly, Detroit's victory put it just one game away from clinching the division.

A national network of 169 stations carried the Thanksgiving telecast. Among those tuned into the game that day was 13-year-old Kent Falb of Elgin, Iowa, whose father had just bought the family's first TV. It was delivered the day before, but it wasn't until Thanksgiving morning that men came to attach the antenna to the barn roof. A long plastic-coated wire ran from the antenna to the back of the set. The appliance was clicked on, and as the tube warmed up, ghostly figures emerged.

"The first people I saw on that television were the Detroit Lions," Falb remembered years later. "Through all that black-and-white interference, there they were." It was an exciting moment, this magical video link connecting the rural Falb family to Briggs Stadium and other heretofore unseen corners of the world.

Thanks to television, the Lions were winning over legions of new fans around the country. Armand Peterson was 12 years old when his Minnesota family got its first set in 1953. "It was a black-and-white Muntz, probably the cheapest TV we could find," recalled the retired engineer. "We were close enough to Minneapolis to get a signal. There was a big antenna on the roof, and whenever a car drove by there'd be all this static. The reception was always kind of snowy, anyway. It was hard to follow the ball. But that's how I became an NFL fan, cheering for the Lions. They were my favorites—Bobby Layne, Doak Walker—even though the weekly telecast in our market usually was a Green Bay game."

The Lions often were the featured game of the week on the DuMont televi-sion and Mutual radio networks. On several occasions between 1952 and 1954, the peak years of the club's dominance, theirs was the only game on the NFL schedule and thus the only one available to impressionable football fans. Among those captive dates were two College All-Star contests, three title games with Cleveland, the 1952 playoff with Los Angeles, the 1954 regular-season finale against the Browns, and the annual Thanksgiving Day games against the Packers. Whenever there was an important or marquee NFL game during this three-season span, the Lions usually were in it. And they nearly always won, adding to their popularity and growing aura of invincibility.

There was a certain mystique about the Lions. If they weren't quite "America's Team"—an appellation attached to the Dallas Cowboys a generation later in recognition of their dominance, national fan base, and frequent TV appearances—the Lions nonetheless were a ubiquitous presence inside living rooms and taverns during the early 1950s. Turnstile counts reflected their popularity. In 1954, for the second straight season, Detroit drew more total fans (home and away) than any other team.

The most recognizable Lions were used as pitchmen in national advertising campaigns. Square-jawed Leon Hart told the world he owed his smooth shave to Gillette: "In my book no other razor can compare with the Gillette Super-Speed Razor. It just can't be matched for shaving ease and convenience." Big Leon also attributed his gridiron success to his favorite cereal. "Quaker Oats Helps Me Win!" he declared.

Wheaties employed the Doaker to extol the benefits of starting each day with a heaping bowlful of the "Breakfast of Champions," though he needed several takes when taping a TV commercial in New York. "He had such a drawl," remembered Norma Walker. "Doak was supposed to do his Wheaties commercial in fifty-three seconds. He finally did it, but it's hard to speed up like that for a Texan."

Walker was everywhere in the 1950s, vouching for such products as Vitalis ("Messy hair oils? Not for me.") and Beech-Nut chewing gum ("Ease the tension with Beech-Nut Gum!"). He endorsed the distinctive taste of Dr. Pepper, the reliability of Prest-O-Lite car batteries, and the quality of Wilson sporting goods. His line of J. C. Higgins autographed footballs ($1.95 to $7.79 each) was sold at Sears stores across the country. "They're great footballs and I personally recommend them for all playing conditions," he proclaimed.

Layne, of course, was no slouch when it came to endorsements. His familiar muffin-like face popped up on the pages of various large-circulation magazines to reassure readers that "With Prestone Anti-Freeze you're set . . . you're safe . . . you're sure" and to plug his own signature line of footballs for Rawlings. Layne also teamed up with Cloyce Box to urge fashionable but budget-minded young men to mix two pairs of $12.95 Haggar slacks with a sport coat. "In clothes and on the gridiron—the right combination always wins."

To the dismay of interior linemen everywhere, advertisers were most interested in football's glory boys, the offensive stars who always dominated the headlines. In the eyes of Madison Avenue, defensive players simply didn't register with consumers. That attitude would change as the NFL grew in popularity, and before too long players like Jack Christiansen, Yale Lary, and Joe Schmidt would be hawking Arrow shirts, Jantzen sweaters, and top-shelf liquor. For now, ad agencies assumed that nobody really cared what Les Bingaman had for breakfast (most fans supposed it must be a dozen eggs and a plate of steaks) or which breath mint Floyd Jaszewski found most refreshing. The "big uglies" of the era could only be found pitching products and services in local shopping circulars and game programs.

An uninspired industrial ad for the Cadillac Asphalt Paving Company, located at Evergreen and Fullerton on the city's west side, was typical. It featured captioned black-and-white photographs of some of its beefy off-season Lions employees in action. The shots included Thurman McGraw ("I Make the Asphalt") at a control panel inside the plant, his cap askew, and a disheveled looking Bingaman ("I Lay the Asphalt") operating a paving machine at some undisclosed job site. The dominant photo was a dreary exterior view of the plant itself, the real star of the ad.

Like a 33-man paving machine, Parker's powerhouse rolled along in the autumn of 1954, flattening all opposition. The country's leading weekly magazines took notice, showering the Lions with more national coverage in a concentrated period than any previous NFL team. *Sports Illustrated* and the *Saturday Evening Post* both ran in-depth profiles of Parker the same week in November. Elsewhere, *Collier's* featured Bingaman (who was labeled "Pro Football's Immovable Object") on its pages and *Look* published a photo essay about Bill Stits. Most impressively, Layne became the first professional football player to grace the cover of *Time*. The unprecedented honor was as good an indication as any that the NFL had entered the American mainstream.

The story in the November 29, 1954, issue of *Time* helped introduce the Lions and pro football to many general readers who previously knew little about either. The takeaway was that Parker's champions were a colorful, rollicking crew marching toward another title. "Of all the pro teams, the best (for the last three seasons) is the Detroit Lions," *Time* observed. "Coach Parker has learned to live with the fact that his team is not composed of unduly sober citizens. If now and then they belt the bottle (or some barroom companions), Buddy will forgive them—as long as they show up sober for practice."

Since that October evening in 1952 when Layne announced to Parker that he was going to be his quarterback and that the team was going to straighten out pronto, the Lions had been virtually unstoppable, compiling a 29–4 record, including three postseason wins. Their pesky West Coast rivals accounted for three of the defeats. The Bears were the only other team to beat the Lions during this stretch, and that was by a single point. It worked out to a sterling .879 winning percentage. If one included College All-Star games and other exhibitions—which Parker, who played all games to win, was wont to do—Detroit's record during this period was 39-5-1, an .886 percentage.

"It's habit-forming, that winning or losing," Layne said. "The Lions have fallen into good habits."

All in all, it was a fine time to be in Detroit. The Motor City was at its postwar zenith. The heavy fighting in Korea was over, and far fewer men were being drafted. Gains won by Walter Reuther's United Auto Workers had helped make the city the exemplar of middle-class prosperity, with average household income and rates of homeownership the envy of the nation. A sense of progress and optimism was in the often sulfurous-smelling air. Shiny new buildings were going up and freeways were being carved out of the earth. Downtown streets and sidewalks were alive, day and night. Hudson's and Kern's dominated the Woodward Avenue district, with plenty of other merchants vying for shoppers' attention. It was possible for one of the Lions' wives to buy a coat at Grayson's, a dress at Eaton's, a pair of shoes at Mary Jane's, and celebrate her new ensemble with a hot fudge sundae at Sanders—all within a span of four storefronts.

There was no better sports town in the country. The Tigers were also-rans. But with young players like Al Kaline and Harvey Kuenn (both of whom would win batting titles in the '50s), they still drew better than many first-division ball teams. In addition to being the acknowledged capital of powerboat racing and professional bowling, Detroit could claim two of the most famous names in prizefighting: the recently retired Joe Louis and the dazzling Sugar Ray Robinson, both of whom had come out of the same east-side gym. Inside cramped, hazy Olympia Stadium, the "Old Red Barn" at Grand River and McGraw, Jack Adams's Red Wings were rolling toward their seventh straight league championship. Featuring goalie Terry Sawchuk and the fabled "Production Line" of Gordie Howe, Ted Lindsay, and Alex Delvecchio, Detroit's other sports dynasty of the '50s would capture its fourth Stanley Cup in six years the following spring.

Meanwhile, the real production lines were humming, with the "Big Three" automakers of General Motors, Ford, and Chrysler dominating the industry. GM alone owned 54 percent of the market in 1954, the high-water mark in its history. On November 23, the behemoth unveiled its 50 millionth vehicle, a Chevrolet

Bel-Air with gold-plated parts. As a promotional tie-in with GM's production mile-stone, 11 Lions players and coaches took delivery of new Buicks from Cloyce Box, who co-owned a dealership with Doak Walker in Denton, Texas. The family-sized cars made for a nice ride when visiting Northland Center. The country's first shop-ping mall, sprawling across 159 acres in suburban Southfield, had just opened with great fanfare. National publications rightfully hailed it as the future of American shopping. Leon Hart worked as an expeditor on the $30 million project, setting up quantities and production schedules for $1 million worth of asphalt.

The 1950s were a transitional decade, and in his work Hart had an up-front view of the changes. Cornfields were being paved over and turned into subdivi-sions and industrial parks, as the flow of families and businesses from the city to the countryside accelerated. Automakers opened 25 new plants between 1945 and 1957, all on land outside the city. The end of the streetcar lines and long suburban commutes meant every family needed at least one car to get around. It was an era of cheap gas and two-car garages. For most people, life was good and getting better. Modern appliances, going out factory doors by the millions, were becoming more affordable by the day, with manufacturers meeting the postwar demand for newer, bigger, better, and more. When Lew and Ann Carpenter came to Detroit from Arkansas, they eagerly joined the ranks of consumers. "We got our first car," Ann recalled. "It was an ugly orange Chevy. Then the next year we got a new Buick. We bought our first TV and got to watch Soupy Sales. It was all such an exciting time and Detroit was such a welcoming place."

T he week after Layne's appearance on *Time*'s cover, the Lions hosted Philadelphia in the last home game of the year. Lions-Eagles matches were always slugfests. After Layne injured his shoulder and had his nose broken, Tom Dublinski came in and guided a comeback. Carpenter's short touchdown burst in the final stanza, followed by Walker's extra point, salvaged a 13–13 tie. The defensive hero was Carl Karilivacz, who ended scoring threats with his first two interceptions of the year. The "frigid mob" at noisy Briggs Stadium celebrated the deadlock. With two games still left in the regular season, the Lions had clinched a third straight division crown.

The players' response was subdued, though their mood perked up when Parker gave them an extra day off. Some took their families to see Santa at the Ford Rotunda in Dearborn. A few days later, the Lions fell to the Bears, 28–24, in a listless performance at Wrigley Field. Dublinski played the entire game for the injured Layne. Chicago took an 18-point lead into the fourth quarter before Dublinski fired three touchdown passes in a rally that fell just short.

Parker was concerned. Instead of the team peaking at the right time, it was now mired in a two-game funk—and scheduled to face the Browns, in Cleveland, each of the next two weeks. The December 19 contest, rescheduled from October 3, was the only one on the calendar, all other teams having finished the season. The game meant nothing in the standings. After a slow start, the Browns had won eight straight to lock up their division. Otto Graham had already announced that he was retiring at the end of the season.

On December 19, as a raging storm turned Cleveland's lakefront ballpark into a giant snow globe, fans across the country settled in front of their TV sets to watch what amounted to a dress rehearsal of the third straight title match between the two titans. Heavy snow whipped around Municipal Stadium and the temperature dropped into the low 20s as the frostbitten foes battled it out in near-whiteout conditions. *New York Times* columnist Arthur Daley was fascinated by the intensity of the hitting. The rivals "whacked away at each other with such frenzied abandon that the television screen trembled under the impact. . . . If these two teams play such murderous football when nothing's at stake, what will they do . . . when the championship is up for grabs? It makes a guy shudder."

The Browns played a conservative ground-and-pound game, rushing for 109 yards but picking up only six first downs. Graham completed just one of six passes for a net gain of four yards. Cleveland's sole touchdown came in the first quarter, when the Browns recovered a fumble deep in Detroit's territory and Graham cashed in on a fourth-down sneak.

The Lions held nothing back in the "nothing game." Layne was in on every offensive down. Doak Walker, filling in for Karilivacz (who was nursing a charley horse that had nagged him all season), played 55 minutes as a two-way back. "We had to snap out of our slump," Parker said. "We had to regain the winning touch. The only way to do that was to play to win." Layne threw 37 times despite the atrocious conditions, hitting Dorne Dibble and Jug Girard for touchdowns. Dibble's touchdown came on a fourth-down play from Cleveland's 26. "Nowadays they change the ball after nearly every play," Parker explained. "The ball doesn't get waterlogged. I knew we could pass."

The climactic drive was vintage Layne. Handed the ball with less than three minutes left and Cleveland clinging to a 10–7 lead, he crisply marched the team 75 yards in eight plays against the elements and the league's top-rated defense.

All but one of the plays were passes. He completed four of the throws to Girard, the last a beautifully executed 11-yard scoring strike with 50 seconds left on the clock. Once again it was Warren Lahr who let a Lions receiver beat him for the game-winner. "That last pass was just a perfect strike, and there was nothing I could do about it," Lahr said. Walker's extra point made it 14–10, a score that stood up as Detroit's defense swarmed Graham in the final seconds.

The Lions, wet, cold, and exhausted, trooped into the locker room with a 9-2-1 record. The similarly spent Browns, who had just lost for the first time in two months, finished 9–3. Walker's conversion enabled Detroit to edge Cleveland by a single point, 337 to 336, to become the league's top-scoring team for the first and only time in franchise history. While players thawed out, Parker pensively wrapped up an interview session with Cleveland reporters. "We'll see you next Sunday," he said. "I wish this was next Sunday."

Layne's payoff pitch to Girard caused the title-game odds to swing six points in favor of the Lions, changing them from 3½-point underdogs to 2½-point favorites. It also caused some to trot out the shopworn Layne-as-gunslinger analogy. "Wyatt Earp, the gun-totin' marshal of Tombstone, could've used him as a sidekick," Lyall Smith gushed in print. "The talented Texan fits the storybook description of all the fabled characters in the two-gun era of the Wild West. He has the swing and the swagger, the soft-spoken drawl, the air of insouciance and the ice water for the hot spot. If you don't agree, then you haven't compared Layne's football tactics with the ones which flood television screens when the boys are riding like mad to cut off the desperadoes at Eagle Pass. They're the same. He is one of those characters who comes up for the big one and carries the rest of the team with him."

The Lions' latest defeat of the Browns proved once again that when it came to a match-up between the two rivals, Detroit always was going to find a way to win. Brown, however, was conceding nothing. "Well," he said sourly, "at least they're going to let us play the game, aren't they?"

As they spent the week before Christmas preparing to defend their title, Lions players were upbeat and confident. "We beat 'em in a snowstorm, 14–10," Schmidt said years later. "So everybody figured, hell, we'll beat these guys again. Not that we were overconfident, but we had trouble getting up for the game."

There was little nervousness. Eighteen Lions were playing in their third title game; another nine were playing in their second. "There are some experts who hold that the Detroit Lions are the greatest of all pro teams," observed Arthur Daley. "It's a difficult estimate to dispute. They are so astonishingly versatile, able to shift men from offensive to defensive platoons and vice versa or able to move men from one position to another. They can play your type of game or their type of game. They can outscore you or out-defense you. It's an amazing team."

On December 24, the Friday before the game, Layne was presented with the President's Trophy by Edwin Anderson. The cup, awarded annually since 1952, went to the club's most valuable player as voted by his teammates. Dick Stanfel had received the honor the previous year and Jim Doran the season before that. Layne always counted the *Time* cover and the President's Trophy among his most meaningful personal accolades. A man so honored owed it to himself, his team, and the public to do everything he could to ensure victory, even if it meant deviating from his usual routine.

On Christmas night, after enjoying a holiday meal with their families, Layne and the rest of the team turned in early. The following morning, as players and coaches assembled in the hotel lobby to board a bus for Municipal Stadium, Nick Kerbawy asked the quarterback how he felt.

"Super," Layne said. "I had just about ten hours in the sack."

Kerbawy walked away, grumbling. "We're in trouble—Bobby had a good night's sleep."

The Lions started this unseasonably warm day after Christmas with the mad energy of kids on a candy-cane sugar buzz, as if they were in a hurry to tear open their present of a third straight championship. On the first snap from scrimmage, a trap play, Bill Bowman took Layne's hand-off and blew through a hole in the line. He ran 50 yards before finally being hauled down on the Cleveland 33. On the next play, however, Lew Carpenter fumbled a pitchout, promptly ending the Lions' threat.

Graham, who worked out of a straight-T formation all afternoon, started badly. His first pass was intercepted by Schmidt, and just like that Detroit was back in business on Cleveland's 36. Layne immediately threw deep to Dorne Dibble, who let a sure touchdown slip through his hands. "You could just kind of see from those plays what was going to happen," Layne said. Walker salvaged the drive with a field goal to give Detroit an early 3–0 lead.

Billy Reynolds's long return on the ensuing kickoff allowed the Browns to set up shop on Detroit's 41, but the Lions once again stymied Graham. On fourth down, Horace Gillom went back to punt from midfield. He got the kick off, but a rushing Lion, Harley Sewell, ran into him.

At that moment, Parker wanted to give himself a healthy boot in the pants. His special-teams strategy was geared to setting up the return, not blocking the kick. He always employed a double safety on returns. Detroit typically rushed only two or three men, with the rest dropping back in a line to form a wedge for the return man. Buddy always maintained that the punt return was "the most beautiful play in football." During his four seasons at the helm, the Lions had become the most dangerous team in the league in running back punts. They'd returned 10 for touchdowns (no other club had more than four) and led in punt-return average in 1951 and 1952 and were edged out by one-tenth of a yard in 1954 by Green Bay. Jack Christiansen, in particular, was such a threat that other teams developed the spread punt formation in an attempt to contain him. "We had a standard rule when we played Detroit," said one Brown. "Don't throw in his area and don't punt to him."

However, Parker outsmarted himself. In previous championship meetings, Gillom's high, booming kicks had been virtually nonreturnable. Only a week earlier, his 10 punts in the snow had consistently pinned the Lions deep in their end of the field. This time around, Parker decided that "since we weren't likely to get sizable returns on Gillom's kicks that we would pull a switch and attempt to put extreme pressure on him by rushing him. For once, I was going to try to block a punt. The nightmare of that decision probably will haunt me the rest of my coaching days."

The roughing call on Sewell gave Cleveland a new set of downs on Detroit's 35. Rookie fullback Mo Bassett lost two yards on a first-down carry. On the next play, left halfback Ray Renfro circled out of the backfield, sped past Bill Stits and gimpy-legged Carl Karilivacz, and took in a Graham throw for a surprisingly easy 37-yard touchdown. Remarkably, it was the first scoring pass Graham had ever thrown against Parker's Lions in regular-season or championship play. Lou Groza's conversion gave Cleveland a 7–3 lead.

Minutes later, Don Paul picked off a Layne pass and ran it back 40 yards, deep into Detroit territory. Darrell Brewster then slipped past Schmidt, took in a short pass from Graham, and barreled over two defenders for a 10-yard touchdown to make it 14–3. Another long Reynolds return—this time a 42-yard runback of a Jug Girard punt—planted the Browns on Detroit's 12-yard line near the end of the opening quarter. On the first play of the second quarter, Graham tallied on a quarterback sneak to grow Cleveland's advantage to 21–3. The frenzied crowd of 43,827 began to sense a rout. However, the Lions then pounded and passed their way from their own 20 to the Cleveland end zone, the big play being Carpenter's 52-yard run. Bowman capped the drive with a 5-yard rush.

The score was still only 21–10 when a sensational play by middle guard Mike McCormack midway through the second quarter basically sealed the Lions' fate. As Layne faded back to pass, the rushing McCormack made a desperate lunge for the ball—and wound up swiping it right out of the quarterback's hand.

McCormack's steal put Cleveland's offense in business on the Detroit 31. The Lions' luck remained bad. Graham threw a wobbly pass that Karilivacz should have intercepted; instead he deflected it into the hands of Renfro at the 7. Moments later, Graham, running a bootleg, eluded Creekmur's attempt at a shoestring tackle and skipped five yards for a touchdown and a 28–10 cushion.

By halftime the score had climbed to 35–10, thanks to Renfro's fingertip grab of a 31-yard touchdown toss from Graham. With all realistic hopes of their championship hat trick circling the drain, Parker put Walker in the secondary and inserted Tom Dublinski at quarterback. After Dublinski couldn't provide a spark, Layne was sent back out. Nothing helped. "From the roughing call on, it was just a stampede," said Schmidt. "Every-thing they did was right and everything we did was wrong . . . it was just one of those days. We were really shocked after the game—not that we lost, but at the margin. It was one of the longest games I've ever been in, just looking at the scoreboard all the time and wondering when it was going to stop . . . and it never did."

By the end of the afternoon the Lions had turned the ball over nine times, six on Layne interceptions, and the Browns had romped to a lopsided 56–10 victory for their first championship since 1950.

Of the Browns' eight touchdowns, Graham personally accounted for six of them—three rushing and three passing. "Time after time, Graham made Detroit's previously great defensive operatives look foolish," Jack Walsh wrote in the *Washington Post*. "It finally seemed to get them down and the proud Lions were a bedraggled outfit long before the game was over. The two-time NFL champs lost their poise completely in the third period when they seemed to prefer a slugging match to football. Even walking off the field when substitutions were made, the lagging Lions looked uninspired, to say the least." Some scribes thought overconfidence was to blame for the thrashing. "One of the natural results of the Lions' success in two National Football League championships was cockiness," Bob McClellan wrote in the *Detroit Times*. "They came around to the idea that nobody could beat them, and not even Buddy Parker or his assistant coaches could dissuade them. It was merely a case of too much success. They trampled everybody in two full years of football and apparently got a little weary of it."

In Paul Brown's view, the walloping was an emotional outburst, a catharsis against a seemingly invincible nemesis. He insisted that, for a single game at least, this squad was the greatest he had ever coached. "A more gratifying triumph never came to a football team," observed the *Chicago Tribune*'s George Strickler. "After four years of frustration . . . the Browns got even for all time, rolling roughshod over what many had come to regard as one of the greatest football machines in history." Graham was charitable. "Detroit has a helluva team," he said, "but they got the breaks in those two other championship games. This time we got them."

For the Lions, it was a humiliating defeat, the second-worst shellacking ever in a pro title game. Layne blamed a change in routine for the ruined bid for history. "Hell, we all went to bed at ten p.m. the night before the game and got the devil beat out of us," he said. "That's not an excuse for losing but I think it shows it takes more than an early bedtime to win a ball game. I know I was awful. I never felt right." Said Parker: "I guess when a kid's been used to having a drink since he was fourteen, you don't want to change his habits."

In the days and weeks and years to come, Parker kept returning to the roughing call that led to Cleveland's first score. "With that lopsided margin you may think I'm stretching a point to feel the attempt to block a punt beat us, but I can't agree," he said. "Big games often hinge on small things. This one did. That was the turning point, and I can't help but think things might have been far different if I had stuck to my long-standing belief of 'Let 'em kick the ball.'"

The night following the game, Parker sat in the paneled basement of his Dearborn home, drinking and brooding, before exploding in frustration. This time the object of his fury was an oil portrait someone had recently painted of him. It was a nice likeness, the coach conceded, but that didn't stop him from taking a penknife to the canvas and slashing it to ribbons.

Amnesia seemed to set in immediately inside the losers' locker room, as players quietly showered and dressed and tried to shove any memory of the debacle out of their minds. Charlie Ane claimed no recollection of what had prompted his fight with Cleveland end Carlton Massey as the score mounted and frustration set in. Both players were tossed out of the game. "Nobody hit me and I don't remember hitting anyone else," said Ane. "It was just one of those things."

To the end of their days, that was how most Lions of the fabulous '50s chose to describe the one blemish on their otherwise perfect postseason record. The '54 title game, you ask?

It was just one of those things.

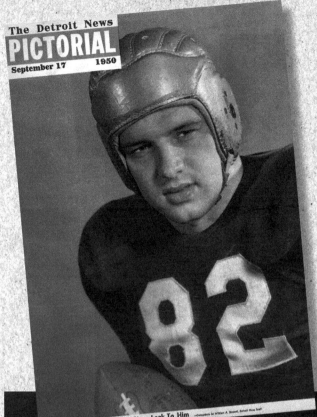

The Detroit News
PICTORIAL
September 17   1950

Leon Hart—Lions Look To Him

Leon Hart won three
national championships
and the Heisman Trophy
at Notre Dame. Drafted
by Detroit in 1950, the
big two-way end helped
the Lions capture four
division titles and three
NFL championships.
(*Detroit News*)

Bobby Layne (No. 22) watches childhood friend Doak Walker
score on a five-yard run against the New York Yanks on
September 29, 1950. (Author's Collection)

Buddy Parker and Bobby Layne discuss strategy on the Detroit sideline. (Walter P. Reuther Library, Archives of Labor and Urban Affairs, Wayne State University)

Doak Walker hurdles tacklers in a 1951 game against Los Angeles. (*Detroit News*)

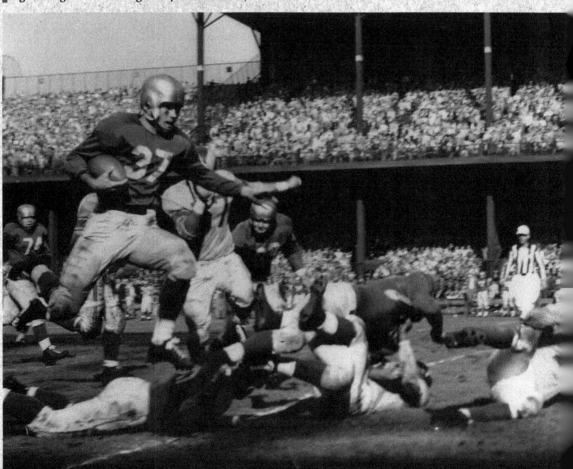

December 28, 1952: The Lions whoop it up after defeating Cleveland, 17-7, for their first championship of the decade. Leon Hart (far left), general manager Nick Kerbawy (with glasses), Buddy Parker, Jimmy David (No. 25), and Lou Creekmur (76) are among the celebrants. (Karpinski Collection)

Roto Magazine

DETROIT FREE PRESS
Sunday, August 22, 1954

On the Inside

Professor Puts His Theory To the Test. See Page 4

Do You Have A Winning Snapshot? See Page 8

They Built Backyard Swimming Pool. See 'Living'

LIVING
Section
PAGE 35

'Big Bing' of the Lions . . . (See Page 6)

Free Press Telephoto by DICK TRIPP

Middle guard Les Bingaman, the biggest man in the NFL at 350 pounds, anchored the Lions' defensive line in the early '50s. (*Detroit Free Press*)

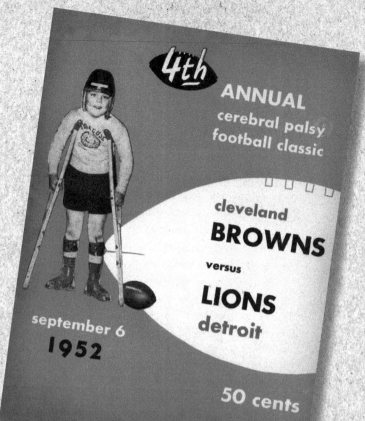

4th ANNUAL
cerebral palsy
football classic

cleveland
BROWNS
versus
LIONS detroit

september 6
1952

50 cents

Many preseason games in the 1950s were played in non-NFL cities with local sponsors donating a share of the receipts to charity. This program is from a Lions-Browns exhibition played in Syracuse, New York, with proceeds benefiting a cerebral palsy fund. (Author's Collection)

Tank Younger

Claude Young

Marion Motley

Put One Cent in Slot.
Push Slide in-then pull
out slowly and receive card
EXHIBIT SUPPLY CO. CARDS

1¢   1¢

A strip of penny arcade cards features three of the growing number of "Negro pro grid stars" of the 1950s. The Lions, who fielded only five blacks during the decade, are the last all-white team to win the NFL championship. (Author's Collection)

Lions' Leading Ground-Gainer Looks for More

Bob "Hunchy" Hoernschemeyer led the Lions in rushing his first four seasons. Many considered him the best third-down back in the league. (*Detroit News*)

Doak Walker models a close-fitting plastic face shield used by some collegiate and pro players in the early '50s. The NFL made face masks mandatory in 1955, though some veterans, including Walker, Bobby Layne, and Bob Hoernschemeyer, were allowed to continue playing without one. (Author's Collection)

The "Ol' Announcer,"
Van Patrick, was the voice
of the Lions during their
glory years. (Author's
Collection)

Guards Dick Stanfel (*left*) and
Jim Martin form a protective
pocket for Bobby Layne. The
white football in Layne's cocked
arm was used for all night
games through the 1955 season.
The Lions were required to paint
their traditional silver helmets
blue for any game played under
the lights. (*Detroit News*)

The Detroit News
Pictorial
MAGAZINE
September 27, 1953   48 Pages

Lions Take Aim on Another Title

Reporting to camp in Ypsilanti in 1953 are (*from left*)
Jim Doran, Doak Walker, Les Bingaman, and Lou
Creekmur. (Ypsilanti Historical Society Archives)

With Bobby Layne holding, Doak Walker kicks the decisive
extra point in the 1953 championship game at Briggs
Stadium. The Lions beat Cleveland, 17-16, for their second
straight title. (Ypsilanti Historical Society Archives)

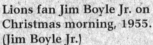

Joe Schmidt stops 49ers fullback John Henry Johnson in mid-flight during a 1956 contest. Schmidt came to the Lions in 1953 and played 13 seasons, establishing himself as a team leader and one of the game's finest middle linebackers. (Walter P. Reuther Library, Archives of Labor and Urban Affairs, Wayne State University)

A 1950 Bowman trading card of Lions halfback Wally Triplett. The sweet-scented bubble gum cards issued by Bowman and Topps helped sell the NFL to the baby boomers who would be essential to growing the game's future. (Topps® and Bowman trading cards used courtesy of The Topps Company, Inc.)

Bill Stits
HALFBACK   DETROIT LIONS

YALE LARY
EF. BACK   DETROIT LIONS

JIM NEAL
DETROIT LIONS

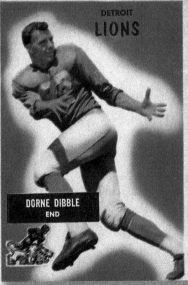

DETROIT
LIONS

DORNE DIBBLE
END

DOAK WALKER
DETROIT LIONS

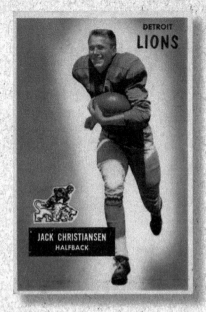

DETROIT
LIONS

JACK CHRISTIANSEN
HALFBACK

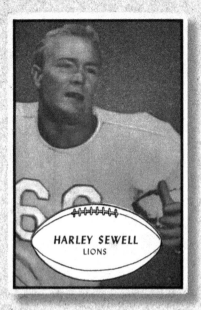

HARLEY SEWELL
LIONS

ROBT. HOERNSCHEMEYER
Detroit Lions

CLOYCE BOX
LIONS

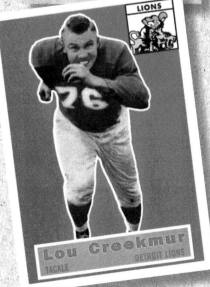

LIONS

Lou Creekmur
TACKLE   DETROIT LIONS

OLLIE CLINE

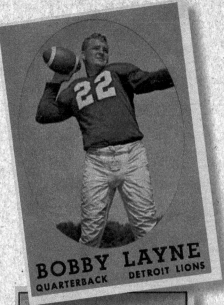

BOBBY LAYNE

QUARTERBACK   DETROIT LIONS

BILL SWIACKI

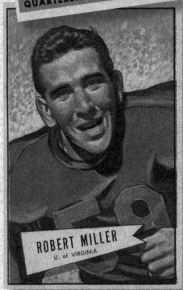

ROBERT MILLER

U. of VIRGINIA

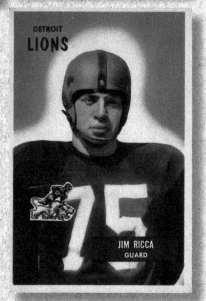

DETROIT LIONS

JIM RICCA

GUARD

JAMES MARTIN

DONALD DOLL

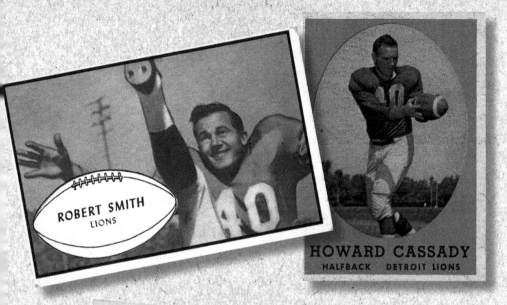

ROBERT SMITH
LIONS

HOWARD CASSADY
HALFBACK   DETROIT LIONS

TERRY BARR
DEF. BACK   DETROIT LIONS

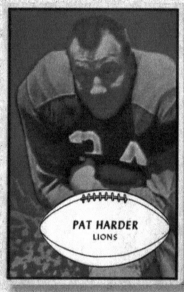

PAT HARDER
LIONS

THURMAN MC GRAW

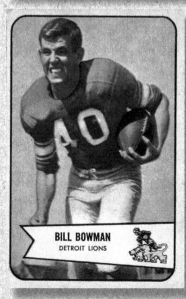

BILL BOWMAN
DETROIT LIONS

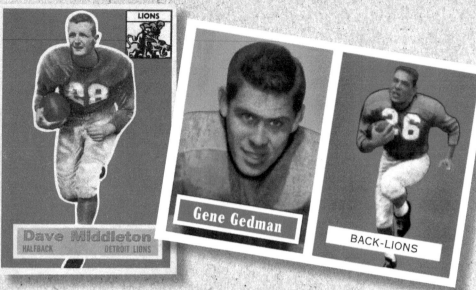

Dave Middleton
HALFBACK   DETROIT LIONS

Gene Gedman

BACK-LIONS

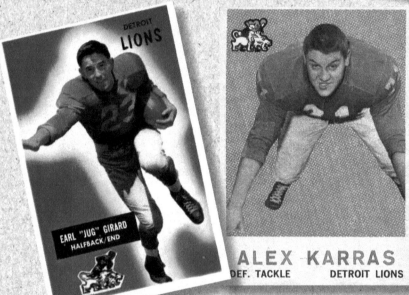

DETROIT LIONS

EARL "JUG" GIRARD
HALFBACK/END

ALEX KARRAS
DEF. TACKLE   DETROIT LIONS

JOHN G. PRCHLIK

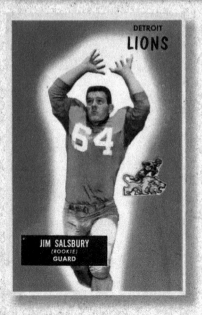

DETROIT LIONS

JIM SALSBURY
(ROOKIE)
GUARD

Veteran stars Tobin Rote, Frank Gatski, and John Henry Johnson were acquired in 1957 and helped Detroit capture its third and final NFL title of the decade.

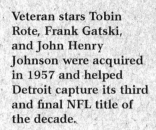

Cleveland halfback (and ex-Lion) Lew Carpenter is swarmed by Roger Zatkoff (No. 57), Joe Schmidt (56), and Ray Krouse (70) during the 1957 title game. (Walter P. Reuther Library, Archives of Labor and Urban Affairs, Wayne State University)

December 29, 1957: Hordes of jubilant fans carry
Joe Schmidt around the field after the Lions' 59-14
title-game rout of the Browns. (Karpinski Collection)

Four figures from
a memorable
decade put their
hats together in
1959. Clockwise
from left: Yale Lary,
Charlie Ane, Howard
"Hopalong" Cassady,
and Tobin Rote.
(Walter P. Reuther
Library, Archives
of Labor and Urban
Affairs, Wayne State
University)

Sorry, Buddy

> Doak was the real All-American Boy. When I was in college,
> I used to read all this "He's so good, he's this and that," and
> I thought, "Nobody's that good." Let me tell you, when I
> became a teammate of his, I found out he was. He was
> probably the most intelligent football player I've ever known.
> Just the nicest person. I can't say enough about the guy. He
> could've been governor.
>
> —Dorne Dibble

C leveland's euphoria over its smashing of Detroit in the 1954 title game
was short-lived, as was Otto Graham's retirement. The following August,
the Browns were upset in the College All-Star Game, the first of five wor-
risome preseason losses for the defending champs. With no quality quarterback
ready to take over, Paul Brown implored his 33-year-old star to return for one last
campaign in 1955. Graham initially wasn't interested, and part of his reasoning
involved the sad comeback of Detroit's beloved "Brown Bomber."

"I wanted to quit on top," Graham said. "I saw Joe Louis. He had been a
great boxer. His name was tops. But they stole his money, and he had to go

out and box when he was over the hill. His name diminished from what it had been. Business-wise, I thought it would be a good decision to quit when I was an outstanding football player instead of just being a half-assed football player." Graham finally relented. His reported $25,000 contract was the highest in the league.

Doak Walker, who also would hang up his cleats after a final go-round in 1955, remained the game's best-compensated non-quarterback. The Doaker's total haul in the latter part of his career was about $24,000 a season when bonuses were added to his base salary. His football income was impressive for the era but hardly obscene. In buying power, it would be equivalent to less than $300,000 in today's dollars. That's pocket change for a perennial All-Pro in the modern NFL, where the biggest stars sign eight- and nine-figure multiyear contracts and the average salary for all players exceeds $2 million per season.

At first, Walker wasn't even sure he would be returning for a sixth pro season. He had joined the Dallas office of the George A. Fuller Company, a prominent New York–based general contracting firm that was grooming him for bigger things. He had other business interests in Texas, including a sporting goods store, a residential construction project, and a Gulf service station where a sign told passing motorists, "If You Can't Stop, Wave." His business ventures, coupled with his commercial endorsements and football earnings, had created a comfortable life for Walker and his young family.

"We've never haggled over my contract terms," he said just before meeting with Nick Kerbawy in the spring of 1955. "They've always given me what I wanted and I'm sure they will again if I decide to play. I've just got to decide whether this is the time for me to quit football and enter business on a full-time basis, or play until I'm 30 and then gamble on my future." Walker felt he was capable of playing another three seasons, if he wanted. "Wouldn't it be terrible if Doak did quit?" Kerbawy mused.

Walker, who leaned heavily on his father's advice in most matters, had always been a nimble negotiator. As a rookie he was instrumental in creating the Lions' annual exhibition at the Cotton Bowl, a charity event sponsored by the Salesmanship Club of Dallas. The organization ran a camp for underprivileged boys, and their share from gate receipts, concessions, and program sales approached $50,000. Walker got a cut of the proceeds, a bonus averaging about $7,000 in each of his first three seasons.

Starting in 1953, his annual bonus was based on the Lions' overall profitability. The Lions paid Walker exactly $23,568.34 in 1953, nearly doubling his $12,500 base salary. For accounting purposes, a player's payouts from championship and College All-Star games were always categorized as bonuses, meaning Walker's profit sharing amounted to about $7,500. The only Lion to make more that season was Bobby Layne, whose total take was $24,690.77, including a $15,000 base salary.

Walker asked for a flat $32,000 to play in 1955. Although he was a genuinely humble person, in his heart he believed he was worth every penny. He had a quiet, fierce pride in himself and his abilities, convinced that nobody in the NFL could do more things as well as he did.

Certainly there was no greater ambassador for the game. A writer for *Sport* magazine followed him around for a feature timed to coincide with his retirement. "Doak's popularity as a pro has extended far beyond the playing fields and locker rooms to the crowds in the ball parks of most National Football League cities," Jack Newcombe wrote. "He is No. 1 in Briggs Stadium. . . . Young Detroiters prize his autograph and stare dreamily at the kid-size Lions uniform with Doak's No. 37 on the jersey in the window of Lippman's Sporting Goods store on Michigan Avenue."

His heroics literally filled volumes, as Norma Walker could attest. At her father-in-law's request, Norma regularly cut out stories about Doak from Detroit's newspapers. She did this for several seasons, regularly mailing envelopes stuffed with clippings to Texas. Many years later, after Doak's dad died, Norma discovered piles of unopened envelopes postmarked Detroit. Ewell Walker Sr. had filled more than a dozen scrapbooks before finally being overwhelmed by the task. Like Les Bingaman, Doak was just too big a hero.

For all the demands placed on his time, Doak remained considerate and approachable. "He would stand on that field for an hour after practice, if he had to, to sign autographs," Joe Schmidt recalled. "He was like the Pied Piper—kids followed him all over the place. He never got upset. He'd say, 'Take your time, kids, I'll get around to everyone.' He'd sign them all."

Even the countless postcards he signed and mailed back always carried a short but appreciative personal note. "Dear Jim," he would write. "Thank you very much for your very nice letter. Doak."

Harley Sewell considered him "one of the finest people I ever met. He's always been the most unselfish, kind, good-hearted person. . . . Doak treated everybody well, rookies included. He was also an amazing athlete who could play just about any position. There wasn't a game or sport that he couldn't pick up and get pretty good at within 30 or 40 minutes. I think he could have been a bull rider if he'd wanted, or anything else."

Walker knew he was overreaching with his salary request. As training camp approached, he finally agreed to a base salary of $20,000. In lieu of profit sharing, he would receive an additional $2,500 annually for the next three years as a special scout in Dallas, making the package worth $27,500 overall. "Just his name is a great asset to this company," Kerbawy said.

While the Detroit Football Company prepared for the day when it would no longer have one of the league's marquee players in uniform, it also contended with poachers from "up north" plucking players off its roster. In the first half of 1955, three veteran Lions defected to the Toronto Argonauts. Two of the "jumpers" would eventually return, but the third became the subject of a two-year court battle that held important ramifications for the NFL.

Canadian football, a hybrid of rugby and American football, has a season that runs from midsummer to late November. At the time, there was no unified entity known as the Canadian Football League (CFL), and there wouldn't be until the country's top circuits organized under that banner in 1958. Instead, there were several provincial and regional leagues, all eligible to compete for the Grey Cup. By 1954, the last of the amateur unions had given up trying to win the cup and the two major professional leagues that would eventually make up the new CFL had emerged dominant. The "Big Four" circuit in the east consisted of Montreal, Ottawa, Toronto, and Hamilton, while the Western Union fielded teams in Regina, Winnipeg, Calgary, Vancouver, and Edmonton. Each club could carry a small, fixed number of Americans on its roster.

Canadian clubs operated on budgets half those of NFL teams. Most benefited from being either wholly or partially owned by the public. It was normal to solicit local boosters for cash donations and off-field jobs to help attract high-quality U.S. talent. Canadian players were poorly paid, with some linemen in the early 1950s making less than $2,000 per season. The standard contract made no provision for paying a player when he was hurt.

This kind of cheeseparing helped make room on the payroll for such expensive imports as Giants halfback Gene "Choo-Choo" Roberts, Cleveland end Mac

Speedie, Los Angeles tackle Dick Huffman, and halfback Billy Vessels, the 1952 Heisman Trophy winner from Oklahoma. In 1954, more than 100 players from the States appeared in at least one game in Canada. Most were college athletes not quite good enough to make a pro roster. However, a score were former NFL players.

For the players being wooed, Canada provided welcomed leverage in contract talks, especially after the collapse of the All-America Football Conference had depressed salaries. Jack Christiansen, Dick Stanfel, Jerry Reichow, Calvin Jones, Gene Gedman, Darris McCord, Jim Doran, Lou Creekmur, Howard Cassady, Bill Glass, Joe Schmidt, and Cloyce Box were just a few of the Lions players and draft picks who contemplated heading north during the 1950s, with some inking contracts.

Box returned from the Marines in 1952 determined to improve on the $5,000 he had last made in 1950. He entered negotiations with Kerbawy with a two-year, $10,000-a-season offer from Winnipeg tucked into his pocket, along with assurances from the Blue Bombers that the club would pay for all of his family's moving expenses to and from Texas and also find him an off-season job paying at least $500 a month.

After a marathon session, Box finally agreed to a one-year Lions deal for $8,500. "I wasn't certain that I wanted to play in the Canadian league," Box explained. "But I was sure that I wanted the kind of money that . . . Winnipeg offered me."

In 1954, after NBC lost the rights to televise NCAA football to rival ABC, the network filled its Saturday afternoons with broadcasts of Canadian football games. The wide-open nature of play made it a fun and slightly exotic sport for U.S. viewers to watch. Canadian football featured a larger field, deeper end zones, restrictions on downfield blocking, three downs instead of four, five-point touchdowns, no fair catches on punt returns, and a 12th man known as a "flying wing."

Many Detroit fans and sportswriters saw nothing wrong with Americans playing on the other side of the Ambassador Bridge. After all, the Red Wings were comprised entirely of Canadian-born players. To the average Detroiter, turnabout was fair play—assuming, of course, that the defectors weren't named Bobby Layne, Doak Walker, or Leon Hart.

Enriched by a $350,000 windfall in NBC broadcast fees, Canadian clubs went on a spending spree, conducting more cross-border raids than ever before. Even retired NFL stars were approached. Frankie Albert, who had gone from being the 49ers' starting quarterback to selling cars, signed with Calgary. The Stampeders "offered me more money than I ever made in the NFL, so I went up there for a year," he said of his 1955 sojourn. "We played two games a week, one on a Saturday, and one on a Monday. That was because the farmers would come to town on the weekends. They'd get drunk, go to the games, and raise hell."

Toronto, which had just hired ex-Lions end Bill Swiacki as head coach, was especially aggressive. The Argonauts pursued a wish list of 10 Detroit players and wound up convincing three of them to switch leagues. In March 1955, the Argonauts signed Tom Dublinski to a two-year, no-cut deal worth $17,500 per season. For "The Dubber," it was a vast improvement over his $7,500 base salary with Detroit. In fact, it was the highest salary in the Canadian leagues that season.

Dublinski's signing was a big blow to the Lions' future plans. He had thrown for 1,073 yards and eight touchdowns in 1954 to rank fourth in NFL passing (which during the 1950s was based strictly on average yards per attempt). Overall, the tall blond had won four of five career starts subbing for Layne. Buddy Parker even used him on kickoffs to take advantage of his sure tackling.

Jim Martin and Gil Mains also were enticed to join the Argonauts. Martin, signed as a player-coach, saw the chance to break into the coaching ranks as Swiacki's top assistant. Mains was swayed by his new employer's pledge to help him establish his pro wrestling career. All three defectors were promised off-season jobs. The offers were so attractive that the Argonauts almost snagged a fourth Lion. But the unnamed player was so critical of Detroit that Toronto officials labeled him a "clubhouse lawyer" and changed their minds. Toronto paid its American imports an average $10,000 in 1955. No Canadian on the roster made more than $6,000.

The Lions couldn't force the jumpers to play in Detroit, but they could seek injunctions preventing them from playing elsewhere. A series of legal actions in American and Canadian courts followed. Monaghan, Hart, and Crawmer, the downtown law firm representing the Lions, argued that the players were contractually bound to Detroit. Kerbawy already had a 1955 contract with Martin's signature on it, while Dublinski and Mains, unsigned for the upcoming season, still belonged to the Lions by virtue of the option clause in their 1954 contracts.

The clause, standard in every NFL contract since 1948, gave a team the exclusive rights to an athlete's services for the following season, his so-called option season. Theoretically, a player could either sit out his option season or play without a new contract while performing under the conditions (including salary) of the old one. After "playing out his option," he then would be a free agent, open to all offers. Realistically, though, anybody who went that route risked being blacklisted by the owners of other NFL clubs, leaving him little choice but to come to terms with his original team.

Jim LoPrete, a young attorney who had just joined Monaghan, Hart, and Crawmer, was tasked with serving a summons on Mains, an unenviable job given the player's ornery reputation. "Mains liked to hang out at the Tuller Hotel," LoPrete remembered. "There was a florist shop in the lobby, and we had somebody there keeping an eye out for him. One day we get a call: 'Mains is here.' So I run from the Buhl Building, where our office was, and catch Mains in the phone booth. I was just a kid, weighed maybe 150 pounds, and he was this big guy. I said, 'Oh, are you Gil Mains?' Then I handed him the summons and turned around and ran like hell. He would've pounded me."

Dublinski insisted the Lions had forced his hand, pursuing a restraining order while he was still weighing offers from both clubs. "I had played for Detroit for three seasons with the idea that my future was there," he explained. "Buddy Parker was a great guy to play for, and Detroit fans treated me well. But I never was able to get an off-season job in Detroit although club officials promised me they would line one up for me when I signed originally."

Dublinski had a wife and two toddlers to consider while trying to make up his mind. Resettling in Toronto was a major decision, one he didn't want to rush into. After a special sit-down with Edwin Anderson, he and the Lions were on the cusp of an agreement. Then came news reports of the Lions' plan to file for an injunction. Before he could be served, Dublinski said goodbye to his family and caught the next flight out of Salt Lake City. "I can't even go back and help them because of that injunction," he moaned to a reporter while holed up inside a Toronto hotel room. "The Lions are at least making it inconvenient for me and my family."

On June 16, 1955, a Toronto court dismissed the Lions' breach-of-contract suit, paving the way for Dublinski to play for the Argonauts. That day, the Lions sent rookie back Bert Zagers, end Bob Trout, and $10,000 cash to Washington for backup quarterback Harry Gilmer. The trade had been on hold for a month, pending the judge's decision.

Toronto, like other Canadian teams wrestling with lawsuits, would soon discover that litigation was expensive and time-consuming. Toronto officials visited the Lions in late August, offering to lay off the team in the future if Detroit would drop all legal actions. The Lions refused. Bert Bell considered the NFL at war with the Canadian leagues, and he viewed the Dublinski affair as a test case for the entire league.

On September 1, a court in Long Beach, California, where Martin lived, ruled that he had violated the terms of his contract and that he belonged to the Lions. Moreover, if he continued playing in Canada, he would be subject to contempt charges once he returned to the States. Martin had recently bruised his ribs in a Canadian exhibition. He now faced the prospect of lawyering up while playing for a team that not only wouldn't pay him if he was hurt but was prepared to cut him loose. Newly married and soon to be a father, Martin reevaluated the financial ramifications of his defection. Mains also began having second thoughts. By mid-September, both jumpers had jumped back to the Lions.

There were no hard feelings. "I'm glad to be back," said Mains, who signed a new Detroit contract with a bump in pay. "I had enough of it up there. They don't play my kind of football. Practically all of the other fellows who went up there from the States feel the same way." Of Dublinski, Mains said: "He doesn't like the brand of ball very much himself. But they got him a good off-season job."

Dublinski tossed 30 touchdown passes in 1955 (along with 34 interceptions, still the Canadian record) while also playing defensive back for the Argos. However, he badly injured his knee the following year and missed the entire 1956 campaign. Toronto had to pay his salary in full while also spending $15,000 on a quality replacement.

Meanwhile, the raiding and the rancor elsewhere subsided, as Bell's strategy to sue the Canadian clubs into submission proved successful. One by one, several teams, some nearly bankrupted by legal fees, settled their cases out of court and agreed to honor all NFL contracts. Their capitulation was accomplished without Bell offering any concessions.

There was a temporary setback in March 1956, when a lawsuit, this time asking for damages arising from Dublinski's signing, was dismissed in a Canadian court. The Lions appealed. On January 19, 1957, the Ontario Court of Appeals in Toronto reversed the lower court's decision. It determined that Dublinski had indeed breached his Lions contract and that Detroit was entitled to damages. It was the first time a Canadian court had sided with an NFL plaintiff.

The landmark ruling, subsequently upheld by Canada's Supreme Court, set an important precedent by recognizing the validity of the NFL's option clause. Dublinski, whose two-year contract with Toronto was set to expire, happened to be in Detroit the day the decision was announced. The Lions made him a flat offer, which he refused. Instead he signed a new one-year deal with Toronto. After a subpar 1957 season, the Argonauts released him, rueing the nearly $80,000 he had cost them in lost salary, legal expenses, and damages.

Dublinski personally was on the hook to the Lions for $6,950 in court-mandated damages. That debt would have been negotiated away if he re-signed with Detroit. But "Dub the Sub," once Bobby Layne's valued understudy and heir apparent, was now a "well-dented" free agent. Detroit was no longer interested. He spent the next five years bouncing around the NFL, CFL, and American Football League, playing sparingly, before finally calling it quits. Dublinski went on to run a successful insurance business in Utah. He died in 2015 on Thanksgiving Day—the U.S. holiday, not the Canadian version.

On August 19, the Lions played their first preseason game of 1955, dropping a 14–8 decision to Philadelphia at the Cotton Bowl. It was billed as Doak Walker's final appearance in "The House That Doak Built," and Dallas fans made sure he didn't go home empty-handed. No other football player in the country had such enduring gate appeal. In 19 previous appearances over three collegiate and five pro seasons, No. 37 had drawn an average of 53,158 paid admissions to the Cotton Bowl. On this evening another packed house gifted him with, among other things, a new air-conditioned Cadillac worth $10,000.

Walker was so beloved by Texans that, in the days leading up to the game, a brief wire-service item mentioning that the squeaky-clean star and several other Lions had recently been put through a "special disciplinary practice" had many fans howling. "They liked to string me up when we went into Dallas," Buddy Parker said.

Parker generally had an 11 p.m. curfew in training camp except Saturdays, when players could stay out an extra hour or two with no consequences. On August 10, a Wednesday, the team had held its first full-scale scrimmage, a grueling affair that left players utterly exhausted. Afterward, Layne, Walker, Gilmer, and a dozen other players piled into cars and drove to a nearby town for what was described as an innocent night of light entertainment: shuffleboard and a few cold pops.

As in years past, some Lions had brought their young sons to camp. Sonny Gandee volunteered to take the boys to a drive-in movie. Buddy Parker's son,

Bobby, was among them. The players missed curfew but might have slipped back into camp undetected, except that Gandee fell asleep and the kids, not wanting to wake him, watched the movie a second time. Meanwhile, Parker went looking for his missing son and found an empty dormitory room. "It's curfew," he grumbled, "and even the damn kids aren't in bed."

Thursday was supposed to be an off day, but Parker ordered all of the curfew violators to report for disciplinary drills. "Bobby Layne, who always was the boss, lined us up the next morning like a drill sergeant and marched us in military cadence over the hill to the field," Walker recalled. "We laughed all the way over. But the coaches saw nothing funny about it. They gave us wind sprints and other tortures until we were almost dead."

The coup de grâce was when the thoroughly spent players were ordered to drop to the ground and roll the length of the field. The notorious "roll drill" was designed to make hungover players throw up. Layne was the only one who managed to make it the full hundred yards.

Layne would need to depend on such grit to carry him through the upcoming season. During a family visit to a riding ranch just before camp opened, he was holding the reins of his son's horse when the animal bolted, violently yanking his right arm. The damaged rotator cuff aggravated his chronic bursitis. After a subpar performance against Philadelphia, he missed the next two exhibitions as doctors treated the shoulder for calcium deposits. Extended rest is essential to rehabilitating injured shoulders, but that kind of time is a luxury during a pro campaign.

Layne would play through the pain and inflammation all season, assisted by massages and cortisone shots. But his passes lacked zip and his accuracy on deep throws suffered. Gilmer, an expert equestrian who during his coaching career was known for hauling his favorite horses around the country with him, took over the reins as needed. For the next two seasons he proved himself a capable stand-in.

In the memories of many older Lions fans, Gilmer is little more than a caricature: a laid-back, tobacco-chewing head coach in cowboy boots and Stetson who hightailed it out of town at the end of the 1966 season amid a volley of snowballs and choruses of "Goodbye, Harry."

Long before his failed two-year stint on Detroit's sidelines, however, Gilmer was a brilliant all-purpose All-American at Alabama, where he started every game during his four years at the university. The single-wing halfback was celebrated for his unorthodox throwing style, which entailed leaping high into the air to fire off a pass. An accomplished runner, passer, punter, and defensive back, Gilmer led the Crimson Tide to three major bowl games and was named Most Valuable Player of the 1946 Rose Bowl. "He was so popular," recalled one teammate, "that people would send fan mail with nothing on the envelope except 'Number 52, University of Alabama' and the post office would get it to him." Curiously, Gilmer and Layne opposed each other in the 1948 Sugar Bowl, with Texas coming out on top and Layne being named the game's MVP.

Washington made Gilmer the number-one overall pick in the '48 NFL draft (two slots ahead of Layne), entertaining hopes that "Jumping Harry" could become the next "Slinging Sammy" Baugh. He didn't, but he proved to be a tough, versatile player who made one Pro Bowl as a quarterback and another as a halfback. He spent another season in the secondary, picking off five passes. If the Redskins didn't always know what to do with him, Parker did. In fact, Parker so respected Gilmer that he kept him on as an assistant when he took over the head-coaching job at Pittsburgh. That was the start of Gilmer's lengthy career as an assistant coach and scout for various clubs, interrupted by his high-profile Lions gig, the only head-coaching position he ever held. "Maybe some of us are better assistants," he admitted many years after leaving Detroit.

Although Gilmer lacked Layne's stature as a field general, the newcomer immediately noticed a certain deference to rank. When he called plays in Washington, he said, players were always talking in the huddle. In Detroit, nobody spoke except the quarterback. Layne had schooled the troops well.

No matter who was calling the signals, he was operating behind some of the smallest interior linemen in the league. While center Andy Miketa struggled to keep his weight above 200 pounds, tireless left guard Harley Sewell constantly fretted that he would be replaced by a heftier draft pick. "He was always looking over the rosters to see who we had drafted, and he would have a few beers and he'd all but cry, 'I'm too small, I'm too small, I know they're going to trade me or cut me,'" recalled a teammate. "As each successive cut in the roster came along, he'd become more tense. He'd go out and get drunk, more drunk as each squad cut passed. One way you always knew when Harley finally was convinced he'd make the team was he'd go out and get stoned out of his mind."

One of the guards in camp in 1955 was rookie George Atkins of Auburn, who at 190 pounds was not only lighter than Miketa and Sewell but 20 pounds lighter than his listed weight. One day a skeptical Buddy Parker told him to come in to be weighed after practice was over. On his way to the scale, Atkins snatched a couple of 10-pound dumbbells and hid them in his sweatshirt, one under each arm.

"I'll be darn," Parker said, "you do weigh 210!" The rookie played just one pro season before returning to Auburn as an assistant coach.

The running game figured to be a problem, even with another Auburn rookie, fleet-footed Dave Middleton, thrown into the mix. Gene Gedman and Bill Bowman were called into the military, and old reliable Bob Hoernschemeyer was past his prime. Lew Carpenter would wind up getting the bulk of the carries. The Lions coveted the Cardinals' Johnny Olszewski, the only NFL player of the 1950s to sport the number "0" on his jersey, but came up with a big fat zero for their efforts. "Detroit would part with almost anyone—except maybe Bobby Layne—for Johnny O," claimed Cardinals coach Ray Richards, "but we're not interested."

Detroit also pursued Alex Webster, a punishing Montreal back and one of Canada's biggest stars, but he eventually signed with the New York Giants. "I went to meet with the Detroit people," Webster said. "About the only thing I remember was getting on the team bus and there was big Les Bingaman sitting with a case of beer."

Bingaman was only 28 when he peeled off his uniform for the last time following the 1954 championship game. In addition to his brewery job, he was now assisting the coaching staff and squeezing into the broadcast booth to provide commentary. While conceding that eventually someone would come along to fill the big man's position, equipment man Roy Macklem said, "But he'll never fit Bingaman's uniform. Looks like we'll just have to keep his old pants and jerseys around here as souvenirs."

Another key member of the defense, Thurman McGraw, joined Bingaman in retirement. The big tackle and team co-captain had missed five games in 1954 because of an injured knee, and an off-season operation to repair torn cartilage didn't heal as hoped. After five pro seasons, McGraw decided to quit to be an assistant coach at his alma mater, where he would retire as the school's athletic director.

In an attempt to fill these two sizable holes in the forward wall, Parker dealt Pro Bowl linebacker LaVern Torgeson and defensive back Jim Hill to Washington for a pair of beefy linemen: middle guard Jim Ricca and end Walt Yowarsky.

Ricca, whom Parker called "our little Les Bingaman," was born blind in his right eye, but his 6-foot-4, 270-pound frame and rough style of play helped compensate for the impairment. Yowarsky was thought to have great potential after having his pro career interrupted by two years in the military. However, neither player panned out. Yowarsky would be released after two games and Ricca cut at midseason.

On September 10, two weeks before the regular-season opener, Otto Graham made his first appearance as Cleveland hosted Detroit in a much-anticipated exhibition. Detroit manhandled Paul Brown's floundering defending champs, 19–3, and made the rusty Graham look like a schoolboy. Parker "used every able-bodied player in getting revenge for last winter's 56–10 humiliation," Bob Latshaw wrote, as the Lions "returned to their role as masters of the Cleveland Browns." It was a small and vaguely dissatisfying triumph. The Lions walked off the field that Saturday evening rueing the fact that they hadn't played nearly as inspired the last time the teams met, back in December with NFL history on the line.

Parker was upbeat about his rebuilt team as the regular season got underway. "This definitely is my best squad," he insisted. "We don't have to take a backseat to anybody in the league. There's no reason right now why we can't win the title again."

Observers were skeptical. They noted all the injuries and missing veterans and downgraded the Lions' chances of winning a fourth consecutive Western Conference crown, something only the Chicago Bears of 1940–43 had ever accomplished. Lowered expectations were okay with Joe Schmidt. "I'm glad they're all picking us to fall apart," he said. "Takes the pressure off."

This time, though, the experts were right. Roy Schairer, who had been following the Lions on the radio for years, bought his first season tickets in 1955, along with three friends. They were among the 36,434 season packages the Lions sold that year, shattering the NFL record of 32,000 set in 1947 by Washington. Ticket manager Maurice Shubot noted that the new subscribers included fans named Frank Sinatra, Robert E. Lee, and David Crockett. "If Lee and Crockett show up for the opener," remarked columnist Mark Beltaire, "we'll have the story of the century."

Schairer had just turned 21 and was starting his career as an accountant in Sebewaing, near Bay City. On autumn Sundays, he and his buddies drove down from the Thumb in his brand-new '55 Plymouth ("red with cream-colored sweeps on the sides") to watch the Lions. Life was good. Unfortunately, his favorite team was not.

"I can remember Y. A. Tittle being chased around in the backfield during the San Francisco game," he said, chuckling. Tittle turned up field and the pursuing Lion fell flat on his face in the mud—a pratfall that could serve as a metaphor for the entire season.

The Lions opened September 25 at Green Bay. It turned out to be a game to remember for the visitors but for all the wrong reasons. The Packers hosted the action at City Stadium having lost 11 straight times to Detroit. The Lions' biggest names were hobbled. A pulled hamstring in his left leg limited Walker to placekicking duties and a single offensive play, while Layne's aching shoulder had him "shot-putting" passes all afternoon. In addition, injuries kept Bob Hoernschemeyer and starting guards Harley Sewell and Dick Stanfel from suiting up.

The Lions, ahead at one point by 11 points, carried a 17–13 lead into the fourth quarter. They squandered a chance to clinch the game in the closing minutes when they came away scoreless after Schmidt recovered a fumble on the Green Bay 5. Tobin Rote then moved the Packers 80 yards on the winning drive, including a desperate third-down 38-yard scamper deep into Lions territory. With the ball on the Detroit 18 and 20 seconds left on the clock, Rote rifled a pass into the mitts of Gary Knafelc, who bulled his way across the goal line with Lions defenders hanging on him. City Stadium exploded.

"It was crazy," the big end recalled. "Everybody from both sides of the stadium came into the end zone, picked me up, and carried me off. There must have been 100 people or more. It was amazing. They picked me up right by the goal post where I scored, and they carried me off the field beyond the sidelines, almost to the bench. The officials made them put me down so they could get the game going. Otherwise, I don't know where they would have taken me."

It took police and ushers five minutes to clear the field so Fred Cone could boot the extra point to make the score 20–17. Jug Girard returned the ensuing kickoff, his desperate zigging and zagging bleeding the last few seconds off the clock. The gun sounded and Packers fans again swarmed the field, carrying Rote and others off in a spasm of pure joy.

If the Lions weren't still in a mild state of shock when they visited Baltimore the following Saturday night, they were when they left. Under Parker, the Lions had never lost back-to-back games before, not even in the preseason. But the tough, frisky Colts, who had never beaten Detroit, won handily, 28–13. "They just beat hell out of us," was Parker's postgame assessment.

Rookie fullback Alan "The Horse" Ameche galloped for 153 yards and two touchdowns for the Colts. The Heisman Trophy winner from Wisconsin, who would go on to win the rushing title in 1955, could have been starring in the Lions' backfield. But in January, Parker had turned down Baltimore's offer to trade Ameche for Leon Hart and a couple of other unnamed starters, thinking the asking price too steep.

Instead, Parker had started working out Hart at fullback prior to the Colts game, looking to use him in certain goal-line situations. "We call him 'The Ox,'" George Wilson said. "Baltimore has the Horse and we have the Ox."

Hart's occasional stints in the backfield during the season would be in addition to his full-time duties on defense. Parker, displeased over the lack of a pass rush from his undersized ends during the exhibition season, had moved him from offensive to defensive end. Told to bulk up, Hart half-heartedly embarked on a muscle-building regime. "I always tried to avoid becoming muscle-bound," he complained, "and now I'm squeezing rubber balls."

As bad as things seemed for the winless Lions, they were going to get much worse. The Lions had to play their next four games against the 49ers and Rams, the results of which would determine the trajectory of their season.

Detroit opened its home schedule on October 9 against Los Angeles. Although Jack Christiansen and several other starters were injured, Detroit was a six-point favorite on the strength of its reputation. The Rams were unbeaten and stayed that way. The Lions piled up plenty of yards on offense but committed six turnovers. Los Angeles moved to a two-touchdown fourth-quarter lead, then weathered a Hoernschemeyer-to-Walker scoring pass to prevail, 17–10.

To heap insult upon injury, Parker's book, *We Play to Win!*, was released a few days later. "I guess the fellows didn't read very well," the embarrassed coach told the press.

Detroit next hosted San Francisco at rain-swept Briggs Stadium. The 49ers, also off to a slow start, represented a last chance for the victory-famished Lions to correct course before the season totally got away from them. "If we could win one, we might get back some of the old fire," Parker said hopefully.

In the first quarter, Hoernschemeyer punched over from a yard out, scoring what turned out to the last touchdown of his career. Later, Dave Middleton rushed for two touchdowns and Walker added a field goal as the Lions built a

24–6 lead. But then Detroit's defense collapsed, allowing three touchdowns in the final quarter as San Francisco rallied to a 27–24 victory.

The decisive score came with less than two minutes to play. Y. A. Tittle fumbled the snap from center, then picked up the muddy ball and lateraled it to Joe Perry, who lugged it five yards into the end zone. Parker was numb. For the Lions, the season was over before it hardly started. "Officially, 51,438 watched the ending of a championship era for the Lions as the light towers blazed through the rain and fog," observed the *Chicago Tribune*'s Edward Prell. "But the big stadium held no more than 35,000 . . . who huddled under umbrellas, blankets, and newspapers."

The skies never really cleared during this suddenly lost season. The team's traditional blunt-force defense obviously was missing stalwarts Bingaman, McGraw, and Torgeson, and key regulars on both sides of the ball were sitting out a game or two at a time with injuries. The Lions flew to California. Harry Gilmer started against Los Angeles in place of Layne, who was hobbled by a bad knee. For the first time all season, bookies made Detroit the underdog. Once again, the Lions blew a fourth-quarter lead in losing, 24–13.

Parker, who had yet to fully recover from the title-game debacle, had to contend with being the coach of a last-place team for the first time in his career. The frustration over the team's tailspin, as well as rumors that management was secretly courting Wisconsin coach Ivy Williamson, caused him to drink more than usual.

"Parker was an extreme introvert, except when he got a little Jack Daniels in him," said Millard Kelley, a Purdue graduate who replaced Grant Foster as trainer that season. "Then he was an extreme extrovert." Sportswriter Tommy Devine described the coach as "a seething hulk of hatred" after a loss. According to Kelley, Parker "never really yelled, but when Buddy said, 'Listen, my boy,' you knew you were in big trouble."

Parker's biting sarcasm proved intolerable to one of his pet projects of 1955. "After every game Buddy would get himself all worked up and pick on somebody," Jim Ricca recalled. "No matter what, that was just his style. I thought it was very degrading and knew if he ever did it to me there was going to be trouble. That Italian background of mine—lots of pride."

After the Lions dropped their sixth straight of the season, losing 38–21 at San Francisco, Parker started in on Ricca during the long flight back to Detroit. Ricca, educated by Jesuit priests at Georgetown, was not about to tolerate the language Parker threw at him. "Don't you dare talk to me like that," he warned.

"I will if I want to," said Parker.

More harsh words were exchanged. Then Parker threatened to fire Ricca, who volleyed with the classic retort: "You don't have to. I quit."

Parker put Ricca on waivers, but Nick Kerbawy called the next morning to say the club had taken his name off the wire. "Do anything you want," Ricca said. "I don't want to play here anymore." Philadelphia, looking to replace injured Frank "Bucko" Kilroy, quickly signed Ricca.

With the team now 0–6 and his one-eyed middle guard gone, Parker shifted Lou Creekmur to the other side of the ball. "I moved to defense because we didn't have anybody to replace Les Bingaman," Creekmur recalled. "This was the year Buddy Parker started experimenting with the man over the middle dropping back and covering in a zone against the pass. I just couldn't do it. I wasn't fast enough moving backwards and laterally."

Fortuitously for the Lions, they had the prototypical middle linebacker—quick, brainy, mobile, equally effective against the run or pass—already on the field. However, it wouldn't be until the following season that Joe Schmidt would permanently make the shift from corner linebacker.

Tthere was a different look to the NFL in 1955. For the first time, most players were wearing some form of face protection—a single bar, a Lucite shield, or a more complex "cage." This was the result of a new rule making face masks mandatory, though players could request a special dispensation to play without one. Not many did.

As Bill Bowman could attest, before there were face masks, there were broken noses. Lots of them. The previous season the fullback, playing with an open-face helmet, had his nose painfully rearranged by Hardy Brown during the Lions' first meeting with San Francisco. When the teams reconvened three weeks later, the 49ers' "man-eating linebacker," notorious for kayoing opponents with a unique shoulder shot to the head, made a follow-up call on Bowman's unprotected proboscis.

"First time I carried the ball," Bowman said, "he busted it again. I told him my nose is pretty big, but that's no reason to camp on it forever."

Up through the early '50s, most players wore open-face helmets. Any player wearing a mask usually did so temporarily, when he was recovering from a broken nose, fractured jaw, shattered teeth, or some other facial injury. These makeshift masks typically were constructed by the equipment manager of wire wrapped with layers of tape and leather.

An innovation that gained popularity at the time was a close-fitting mask designed by Dallas dentist William T. Marietta. His "outer-space" masks were made of clear plastic with sponge padding and allowed full vision. The Doaker was a spokesman for the company, though he personally found any kind of face protection too restrictive. He definitely saw the need for it, however. "More and more players are wearing face guards every year," he said. "In my mind, they're chiefly interested in protecting themselves against dirty football." Marietta's masks were strapped around the head, under the helmet. Customers included 49ers fullback Joe Perry and Texas A&M halfback (and future Lion) Bob Smith, who was dubbed "The Masked Marvel" by the press.

When Otto Graham was knocked out of a game in 1953, he returned for the second half with his battered mouth protected by an improvised face shield: a strip of clear, heavy plastic attached to the sides of his helmet. The crude device became the prototype for the first helmet designed specifically for a mask. Produced by sporting-goods manufacturer Riddell, the helmet had a curved piece of clear Lucite bolted in place. In 1954, Joe Schmidt and Jack Christiansen were among the many NFL players wearing one. However, a heavy hit or freezing weather sometimes caused the plastic to shatter into dangerous shards.

With the Lucite shield proving too brittle (it would be banned in 1957), Brown worked with Riddell to develop a sturdier, safer model. The result was the BT-5 (for "Bar Tubular"), a single bar made of rubber and plastic. It came out in 1955 and quickly was popular at all levels of the game. The royalties made Brown a millionaire.

Headgear also underwent a change. The NFL made helmets mandatory in 1943, but because of a grandfather clause it wasn't until 1948 that the last of the bare-headed iconoclasts had left the scene. By 1955, snug-fitting padded-leather helmets (the "leatherhead" look generally associated with old-time football) had largely been replaced by plastic helmets, which were lighter and provided better shock absorption. The holdouts included Charlie Ane and Lou Creekmur, who tugged on leather headgear through 1959, their final season.

The Doaker wore an open-face helmet his entire career. A humped bridge, the result of at least one broken nose, decorated his leading-man features, but he regarded it as more a badge of honor than a blemish. Several other top Lions of the era, including Hoernschemeyer, Bingaman, Pat Harder, Vince Banonis, and Cloyce Box, played their entire career without a mask.

The most famous renegade, of course, was Layne, who felt that even a single bar hindered his vision on handoffs and pass plays. He reportedly experimented with a Lucite shield in the last game of the 1954 regular season to protect a broken nose but abandoned it for the title game. Interestingly, on those back-to-back Sundays in Cleveland, he had far better success passing with the device than without it. The only other Lion to regularly play with an open-face helmet after the 1955 rule change was rookie halfback Howard Cassady in 1956. Yale Lary would swap helmets with Layne whenever he went in to punt but otherwise wore a single-bar helmet. Layne continued to play bare-faced through his last season in 1962, a dashing relic of the '50s.

The Lions opened up the second half of the schedule by beating the Colts, 24–14, on a Saturday night at Briggs Stadium for their first victory of 1955. Doak Walker's 18-point performance featured a pair of short touchdown runs in the last four minutes of the game, wiping out the Colts' 14–10 advantage. "Ah, Victory! It's Wonderful," the *Free Press* declared in the next day's headline. "Layne, Walker and Defense Rays of Sunshine for Lions."

As the season wore on, Walker continued to demonstrate his versatility. A sure tackler and an adept pass defender, he served as the safety on kickoffs and performed spot duty in the secondary. He filled in for the injured Jack Christiansen early in the season and registered his second career interception. "Look, you can have the same contract, the same everything next year, and all you have to do is play defense," Kerbawy told him. "You could be a great defense man in this league for another six years!" Walker wasn't interested.

Doak was listed in game programs as being 5-foot-10 and 172 pounds, which was a little generous. He admitted to opening one season at 149 pounds. "Most of the time I ran scared," he recalled. "I guess I shouldn't say that, but I knew I wasn't going to hurt anybody if I ran into them."

Parker was careful to conserve his star back, often utilizing him as a decoy and positioning him almost exclusively as a slot back or flanker during his last two seasons. Detroit's offensive philosophy was to spread the ball around to keep defenders from keying on any single player. Consequently, individual Lions seldom finished among the league's leaders in rushing yardage or receptions. That said, it's still surprising, especially in light of today's one-back offenses, how infrequently one of the era's most potent offensive threats actually handled the ball from scrimmage.

Across 71 regular-season and postseason contests, Walker averaged just five rushes and two receptions per game, good for a total of 61 yards from scrimmage each outing. He never had a 100-yard rushing game, though on four occasions he reached the century mark in receiving yardage. Nonetheless, Walker's place-kicking and a knack for timely touchdowns made him a scoring machine. When he retired, his averages of 89 points per season and eight points per game were the highest in league history. According to Layne, the scoreboard factored into Walker's production. "If you were ahead, 28–0, you might as well put him on the bench, because he wouldn't be worth anything. But if it was 7–7, he'd always do something to win the game for you."

The Doaker was widely considered "A Pro's Pro," as *Sports Illustrated* labeled him on the cover of its October 3, 1955, issue. Competitive and uncomplaining, he was a gamecock who could cut the league's hatchet men down to size with a dry remark or a withering look. When Cleveland tackle Don Colo once worked over his face with an elbow after the play was whistled dead, Doak simply said "Nice tackle"—a comment Colo later admitted shamed him.

On another occasion, Baltimore end Gino Marchetti tackled Walker on a sweep, then celebrated by grinding his palm into the downed runner's nose. Marchetti expected Walker to pipe up in his high-pitched Texas twang, but all he got was a long, penetrating stare. "I could see it in his eyes," Marchetti said. "I knew exactly what he was thinking. A big guy like me, with probably eighty pounds and six inches on him, having to resort to a mean, low-down trick like that. That look of disgust reformed me."

After beating the Colts, Parker's squad followed up with a second straight win at Pittsburgh. It wasn't easy. On a balmy 70-degree afternoon, the Lions moved out to a 31–7 lead, thanks to Pittsburgh fumbles, then survived a three-touchdown fourth-quarter flurry by the Steelers to leave Forbes Field with a 31–28 victory. Only Jimmy David's sliding tackle of halfback Sid Watson six inches short of the Detroit end zone in the final seconds prevented a miraculous comeback victory by the Steelers. Bill Stits played both ways at right halfback, tossing a touchdown pass to Walker on the option and later returning an interception seven yards for what proved to be the decisive points.

Playing end for the Steelers that day was a large North Carolinian nicknamed "Country." "On one play I'd handed the ball off to Doak Walker and was watching him travel down the field when all of a sudden somebody smashed into me from behind," Layne recalled. "It was so damned dirty that when I passed a Pittsburgh player I knew pretty well, I asked him: 'What's the matter with that guy?'"

"Damned if I know," the Steeler told Layne. "We don't like him either."

The villain in question was Ed "Country" Meadows. A year later, this time as a member of the Bears, Meadows would put a much more resounding hit on Layne, one that would reverberate for an entire winter.

For now, though, with two straight wins in hand and four games left on the schedule, a modest goal emerged in the Detroit clubhouse: running the table to finish a respectable, if still disappointing, 6–6. However, the downsized dream of a break-even season ended with a 24–14 home loss to the Bears on November 20. In the first quarter, Layne and Walker hooked up on a sideline pass where defensive back Ray Smith "made a dangerous move that let Walker get behind him for an unimpeded dash to the end zone," Watson Spoelstra reported. The catch-and-run went 70 yards. For Layne and Walker, it would turn out to be the last touchdown connection of their six seasons together in Detroit.

Four days later, Detroit and Green Bay clashed in their annual Thanksgiving Day meeting as Harry Wismer and Budd Lynch described the action to holiday viewers on ABC. In the fourth quarter, Lew Carpenter—who earlier had scored on a short pass from Layne—broke off right tackle and sped 49 yards to pay dirt to break a 10–10 deadlock. The teams combined for 13 turnovers, including 10 fumbles. Sonny Gandee returned one of them 46 yards for a touchdown off a botched field-goal attempt to clinch the 24–10 victory. Carpenter picked up 120 yards on the ground. He would finish the season leading all Detroit rushers with 543 yards and tying Middleton with 44 receptions, the third-highest total in the league and the best of any NFL back.

The Lions wrapped up the 1955 campaign with narrow losses to the Bears and the Giants. On December 4 at Wrigley Field, Ed Brown and Harlon Hill combined for the winning touchdown pass with five minutes to play in a 21–20 squeaker. "The shabby luck that rode through the Bears game continued until the last seconds when Doak Walker missed a field goal from the 36," Bob McClellan wrote. "In the pre-game workout Walker tested the strength of the wind blowing at an angle from the right side as he faced the goal. Throughout the game a check was kept. Yet when he made the three-point attempt and allowed for the wind, it had shifted. The distance was adequate but it went off the post a few feet."

The Chicago game was Layne's last of the season under center. In the waning moments of the first half, he was violently sacked by Doug Atkins and linebacker George Connor picked up the loose ball and ran it in for a touch-down. Harry Gilmer played well in the second half and would get the start in the home finale.

All season long, Layne had endured the wrath of Detroit fans, and Parker figured to spare his battered quarterback any more abuse to his sore shoulder and his bruised pride. "It hurts sometimes when you're booed," Layne admitted. "Personally, I know I seem to go a lot better when I hear cheers up there in the stands. I don't respond well to boos. It makes me try too hard to prove what I can do to them." Unable to dependably throw deep, Layne completed enough passes on short routes in 1955 to lead all NFL quarterbacks with a 53 percent completion percentage, though he tossed only 11 touchdown passes, his lowest output yet as a Lion.

Sore shoulder or not, there never was any question in Layne's mind that he would suit up for the last game of the season. December 11 was Doak Walker Day at Briggs Stadium, and if nothing else he would take the snaps for each of his old buddy's placements. The club was retiring Walker's number, an honor previously accorded only one other Lion, Dutch Clark.

The season-long streak of bad luck continued in the run-up to the game. A strike by stereotype operators on December 1 shut down all three of Detroit's daily newspapers for the first time in history, hampering public awareness of Walker's special day and depriving millions of readers of the glowing tributes that ordinarily would have been published by his many admirers in the press. Striking *Free Press* reporter Marshall Dann provided his take on the Doaker's retirement in the small-circulation *Polish Daily News*.

"Detroit will say goodbye—and thanks—tomorrow to Doak Walker," Dann wrote the day before the game. "The little Texan, already one of the all-time favorites of this sports city, will be playing his final football game. . . . The spe-cial festivities, appropriately, will go nationwide via television and radio. There will be proclamations from Gov. Williams . . . a testimonial from Mayor Cobo and the Common Council . . . a special resolution from the Lions Alumni Association as it officially welcomes its newest member. From his teammates will come a solid sterling silver football engraved with their signatures. There also will be a gift from his bosses, the officials of the Detroit Football Club. Many individuals and groups proposed to present gifts, but Walker personally vetoed it. He doesn't need such help, as all fans know. With wide investments in his native Dallas, Doak is in the finest financial position of any player ever to leave the National Football

League. He has earned it all." Noting that there had already been a Doak Walker Day in Dallas in August, Dann concluded: "He's the kind of guy who had two 'Days' coming."

The Lions had played before standing-room-only crowds all season at home. However, the newspaper strike and frigid temperatures combined to produce the smallest turnout at Briggs Stadium since the 1953 opener against Pittsburgh. Veteran journalist Eddie Batchelor considered it more of a coincidence than an omen that his pet parrot, named Doak Walker, died on Doak Walker Day.

The 45,929 spectators on hand were treated to the sight of the bird's namesake scoring the last touchdown of his Lions career. With the game barely a minute old, Gilmer—who set a club single-game record that Sunday by throwing the ball 49 times—hit Walker with a pass on the New York 13. The Doaker slipped past a couple of would-be tacklers and motored into the end zone to complete a 25-yard scoring play. He booted the conversion for a quick 7–0 Detroit lead and later kicked a field goal to account for all of Detroit's first-half points. Meanwhile, the Giants' own golden-boy halfback, Frank Gifford, scored a pair of touchdowns to give the visitors a 21–10 advantage at the half.

At intermission, a caped and helmeted No. 37 was feted on the field. Norma Walker was at her husband's side, clutching a bouquet of long-stemmed roses, radiant as ever. "It was a very exciting day, but it was sad," she reminisced. "It was a wonderful world back then. Detroit was our second home. But I think we both knew it couldn't go on forever."

Doak thanked the governor, the mayor, club officials, and his coaches and teammates. "But most of all," he said, sweeping his arm in the direction of center field, "I want to thank the people out there, the people in the bleachers. They have been wonderful."

There was sustained cheering and applause. The moment couldn't last, and neither would the marriage, but for now everybody's All-American and his pink-cheeked college sweetheart basked in one final display of public adulation, as chilled and wholesome as two freshly poured glasses of Twin Pines milk.

The Giants held on for a 24–19 win. With that, Detroit closed the books on a forgettable season. Buddy Parker's squad finished in the Western cellar with a 3–9 record, the worst mark in the league. There was a bright spot. Even with thousands of unsold tickets for the finale, the Lions had drawn more fans than any last-place team in pro football history: a total of 311,372 paying customers, an average of 51,895 per game.

Los Angeles won the conference title, marking the first time since 1951 that Buddy's boys hadn't been on top of the final standings. Two weeks later, the Rams were stomped by Cleveland, 38–14, in the title game. This time it truly was Otto Graham's swan song. He left having quarterbacked his team into 10 championship games in 10 seasons in the AAFC and NFL while never missing a game.

Bob Hoernschemeyer, whose career in both leagues exactly paralleled Graham's, also was through, though he resisted retirement for several months. A separated right shoulder suffered at Pittsburgh had limited his season to five games, costing him his goal of retiring as the Lions' career rushing leader. As it was, his 2,439 yards made him the Lions' leading rusher of the 1950s and the third most productive runner in the history of the Portsmouth-Detroit franchise at the time, just behind Ace Gutowsky and Dutch Clark.

The oft-injured back was 31 and had lost a step, but he clung to the belief that he could still play, if not for Parker then maybe in Canada. However, Parker refused to either release him or exercise the team's option and invite him to camp. He simply was trying to protect the old pro, who had an alarming history of concussions and was plagued by headaches. "In all, I had eight concussions from playing," Hoernschemeyer recalled. "This is the reason he forced me out. I wanted to sign for '56 but he put the kibosh on me and outlawed me from the league."

During a meeting in Parker's office, Buddy said, "You played long enough. Why don't you quit?" Hunchy shot back: "You're the head coach, you make more money. Why don't you quit?" Parker got a chuckle out of that, Hoernschemeyer said, "but the kibosh held up." For the next several years, the combative back and his good buddy, Jug Girard, would operate the Lions Den at 17441 Mack on Detroit's east side, employing a bartender named Jack Dempsey.

While Hoernschemeyer's intensity would be missed, the greater loss for the Lions was Walker. Statistically, he closed out his career on a high note, piling up 96 points on the strength of seven touchdowns, nine field goals, and 27 extra points to lead the league in scoring for a second time. He retired third on the NFL's all-time scoring list, accumulating 534 points in just six seasons. He trailed only Don Hutson (825 points) and Bob Waterfield (573), both of whom had longer careers. Records didn't interest Walker, who was adamant about leaving the game for good. By season's end Nick Kerbawy had made at least a half-dozen separate offers, all of which he turned down.

Walker also resisted overtures to coach at his college, Southern Methodist. "I have a lot of friends around the country and I want to keep them," he said.

"When you coach, you create enemies." In January, he flew to Hawaii to partic-ipate in the Hula Bowl, then played his "positively final" game in the Pro Bowl the following Sunday. After that he went to work full-time for the George A. Fuller Company.

Walker later explained his decision to walk away from the game in the prime of his career. "I loved football," he said. "I loved it when I was a kid, I loved it when I was a young man playing it, and I didn't retire in 1955 because I had lost the desire. But I had achieved just about everything that I felt I could. I had been All-Pro, I had played on NFL championship teams, I had been treated well, paid well by the standards of the day, and accumulated a lifetime of memories. Football was good to me. But I always knew it was something you couldn't do forever, and I didn't want to be one of those guys who stayed a year too long. I didn't want to leave burned out, or crippled. So, I got out with both my knees, all my teeth, and most of my faculties."

Back home, he purposely avoided reading the sports pages or watching games on television. He concentrated on his new career in construction, which included a move to Colorado to be closer to the missile base the company was building for the federal government. And that was that—for a while.

"He was very restless when he quit football," recalled Norma Walker, insist-ing she wasn't the reason he left the Lions. "He and his dad had decided he should go out while he was at the top. It was his life, not mine. And it was his love. He could've played a few more years. It didn't make any difference to me. We had some problems in our marriage, but he couldn't seem to settle down."

In the summer of 1957, the pull of the gridiron proved too strong. Upending his life, Walker accepted an offer from Parker to come to camp at Cranbrook, the private academy in Bloomfield Hills where the Lions now trained.

His arrival in early August was low-key. The cover story was that the Doaker was visiting old friends and just fooling around out on the practice field. Still fit at 30, he was under no pressure, at least not externally. But despite his growing family and increased business responsibilities—or perhaps because of them—he felt something was missing in his life: competition, camaraderie, acclaim, the familiar spice of leather, liniment, and sweat. After a year and a half out of the game, he thought he might rekindle an old flame.

Walker participated in the first full-scale scrimmage, thinking: "I want to get my ass kicked off so they will send me home." Instead, he was quietly pleased with his performance. Joe Schmidt thought Doak was in fine form, too—but then he "disappeared as fast as he came." On his third night in camp, Walker lay awake in his dormitory bed, rolling things over in his mind. It was two o'clock in the morning when he finally got up, packed his suitcase, and left Cranbrook for the airport.

Norma later said her husband decided he couldn't beat out Howard "Hopalong" Cassady in the starting backfield. Dorne Dibble believed team owners were in a pickle after making the ballyhooed Ohio State back their top choice in the draft. "They were worrying, 'What are we gonna do with Cassady?'" Dibble said. "Who gives a rat's ass? Hoppy couldn't carry Doak's jockstrap."

Walker would only say he left for "personal reasons." The next day, he called Parker from Colorado to apologize.

"Sorry, Buddy," he said. "It just didn't work out."

8

Tackling Jim Crow

> I didn't take nothing from anyone. In a football game . . . I hit
> the black guy as hard as I hit the white guy. I didn't think about
> color when I was playing. On occasion I'd get a little trouble.
> I was called a "nigger" a few times, and all that would do was
> make me play a little harder, hit them harder.
>
> **—John Henry Johnson**

On December 1, 1955, the Lions assembled at Briggs Stadium for what normally was "defense day," Thursdays being the only day during the regular season when Buddy Parker had the entire team practice in full pads. This time, however, Parker devoted the day to tweaking some offensive formations as the team prepared for its upcoming game with the Bears.

That same afternoon, several hundred miles to the south, a serene-looking seamstress named Rosa Parks went ahead with her own version of defense day, protecting her seat and her dignity in a calculated act of defiance that kicked off the modern civil rights movement. The activist was arrested after refusing to surrender her seat to a white man on a segregated city bus in Montgomery,

Alabama. The ensuing Montgomery bus boycott thrust a local Baptist minister, the Rev. Martin Luther King Jr., onto the national stage and highlighted the difficult task of remedying the state-sponsored discrimination that the Supreme Court had just declared unconstitutional. The previous year, in the landmark case of *Brown vs. the Board of Education of Topeka*, Supreme Court justices had decided that the separation of races in the classroom was inherently unequal. A historic precedent had been set, and ultimately discriminatory practices in housing, bank lending, employment, and voting would be struck down as well. This monumental societal shift wouldn't come easy. It would take years of marches, sit-ins, beatings, hosings, bombings, murders, and federal intervention before the web of discriminatory state and local laws, ordinances, and practices—known collectively in the South as Jim Crow—was dismantled.

Detroit, to where Parks and her family moved in 1957, was considered by many southern blacks to be more desirable than the dusty little towns they continued to leave in droves during the postwar years, even as increased automation and consolidation in the auto industry caused the number of unskilled factory jobs to dry up. Upon their arrival in Detroit, transplants discovered to their dismay that in many respects it was still like living in an alien environment. The only difference was that segregation in the North was de facto, the patterns of discrimination ingrained through custom, not law.

Although Detroit's black population would pass 400,000 during the 1950s, until late in the decade there was no black representation on city council, there were no blacks playing for the Detroit Tigers, and policemen patrolled the streets in segregated squad cars. Detroit was the home of the modern labor movement and the membership of the United Auto Workers was one-quarter black, yet there still wasn't a single minority on the UAW's executive board. When a local firebrand named Coleman Young Jr. visited the offices of the *Detroit News*, every reporter, editor, printer, and secretary he encountered was white.

"I did stumble upon a couple of black men mopping the floor in the lobby," the future mayor recalled in his autobiography, "and when I asked how many blacks worked in the building, they said, 'You're looking at 'em.'"

During the 1950s, the dilapidated, overcrowded east-side neighborhood where most blacks lived was in the process of being demolished in the name of urban renewal. (Disaffected citizens called it "urban removal.") The residents being displaced by the Chrysler Freeway and Lafayette Park were not welcome in most areas of the city or the suburbs. Whereas Detroit was roughly one-quarter black by the late 1950s, in its three largest suburbs—Dearborn, Livonia, and Warren—there was, collectively, just one African American resident for every 2,000 whites. In Grosse Pointe, realtors worked with property owners to employ a secret coding system that kept "undesirables" out. Dearborn, where Parker and several other members of the Lions organization lived, was so overtly racist under Mayor Orville Hubbard that a Montgomery newspaper covering the bus boycott featured it in a 1956 story about northern cities whose conditions most closely resembled those found in the Jim Crow South.

Intentionally or not, during the 1950s the Lions were a microcosm of the segregated Motor City. Between 1950 and 1957, there never was more than one black on the roster at any given time. For most of that period, there were none. During a six-season stretch, from 1951 through 1956, the Lions fielded just two black players—defensive linemen Harold Turner and Walter Jenkins—who appeared in a total of five regular-season games between them.

Bill Matney, Russ Cowans, and other members of the black press considered the Lions a historically racist organization. Just how fair that characterization was remains open to debate. It was true that the championship squads of 1952 and 1953 didn't have a single black face in the huddle, making the Lions the last team to win an NFL title with an all-white roster.

But it also was true that, a few years earlier, the entire league had just seven black players—and three of them wore Detroit uniforms. Were the Lions discriminatory, or merely discriminating, when it came to fielding blacks? Buddy Parker insisted it was the latter. "I just hadn't been able to find one I thought good enough to play for me," he said in 1957.

Parker claimed he had tried to make a deal for Joe Perry, who in 1953–54 became the first NFL back ever to rush for 1,000 yards in consecutive seasons, but San Francisco "wouldn't even talk to me about Perry."

However, the 49ers were willing to talk to Parker about Perry's teammate, the intimidating John Henry Johnson, who had spent his first three NFL seasons rattling molars on both sides of the scrimmage line. In the spring of 1957, the 49ers, looking to upgrade their defense, agreed to send Johnson to Detroit for Bill Stits and Bill Bowman. "Johnson is the kind of fullback I've been trying to get for quite a while," Parker said.

Johnson was the only black on the Lions' roster in 1957, but his presence still represented progress, of a sort. For a long spell, no blacks were considered good enough to play in the NFL. A modest number of African Americans had suited up at various times during the league's wild, formative stage between 1920 and 1933. Historians have identified at least thirteen, though none played on the succession of short-lived franchises that operated in Detroit during this period. Then the door slammed shut.

The freeze-out coincided with the ascendancy of George Preston Marshall, who became the sole owner of the Boston Redskins in 1933 and subsequently moved them to Washington, D.C. An innovator who introduced fight songs, halftime shows, marching bands, split divisions, guaranteed gates, and a balanced schedule to the NFL, Marshall's showy broad-mindedness narrowed to an unseemly recalcitrance on matters of race. "We'll start signing Negroes," he famously said, "when the Harlem Globetrotters start signing whites."

For a dozen seasons, 1934 through 1945, not a single black played in the monochromatic NFL. Moreover, no blacks were selected in the league's annual college draft, from its inception in 1936 through 1948, despite there being no shortage of quality players to choose from. Throughout the Great Depression and World War II, club owners, even those moderates who might have considered lifting the unofficial ban on blacks, followed the persuasive Marshall's lead.

World War II saw a steady migration of southerners, black and white, to the industrial North to work in the defense plants. In overcrowded Detroit, America's "arsenal of democracy," it was a combustible mix. There were incidents of white factory workers refusing to work alongside blacks. Violence accompanied attempts to desegregate public housing. Black newcomers experienced the same institutionalized racism they had hoped to leave behind in Alabama, Georgia, and Mississippi. They found some favorite activities, such as an excursion ride on the Bob-lo boats or dancing at the Graystone Ballroom, limited to a single day set aside each week for "colored customers."

In June 1943, the tensions erupted into a full-fledged race riot that remains among the deadliest in the nation's history. Days of rioting claimed the lives of 34 Detroiters. Twenty-five of the victims were black, and most of them had been shot by the nearly all-white police department. Martial law was declared and federal troops were brought in to restore order at bayonet point.

"Younger people don't know how ugly America was in those days," said Wally Triplett, who once had a scholarship rescinded when the university discovered he was black. "It was just a horrible time." Triplett, a Penn State Nittany Lion turned Detroit Lion, remembered fans in some stadiums screaming "Kill that nigger!" during his college and pro careers.

The battles on the home front exposed the hypocrisy of the world's mightiest democracy fighting for freedom in Europe and Asia while tolerating a segregated society at home. In 1946, the same year Jackie Robinson signed a minor-league contract with the Brooklyn Dodgers (he would integrate major league baseball the following season), the NFL began its own process of reintegration.

It was slow and not entirely by choice. The defending champion Rams, who had just relocated from Cleveland to Los Angeles, were pressured by the commissioners of Memorial Coliseum to field black players or lose the right to play home games at the publicly funded stadium. In response, the Rams signed halfback Kenny Washington and end Woody Strode, both of whom had played in the UCLA backfield with Robinson before the war. That same autumn, the All-America Football Conference started play, creating new opportunities. By 1949, the AAFC fielded 20 black players, nearly three times the number who played in the NFL.

No AAFC team benefited more than Paul Brown's Cleveland Browns, whose roster of stars included fullback Marion Motley and linebacker Bill Willis. Acceptance came grudgingly, Motley said. "Of course, the opposing players called us nigger and all kinds of names like that. This went on for about two or three years, until they found out that Willis and I was ballplayers. Then they stopped that shit. They found out that while they were calling us names, I was running by 'em and Willis was knocking the shit out of them. So they stopped calling us names and started trying to catch up with us."

The Lions fielded their first black players in 1948, the year ownership changed hands and Bo McMillan was hired. McMillan's success at Indiana was due in part to his having run an integrated program. According to the *Afro American* newspaper, the 1947 Hoosiers "had more colored gridmen than any large squad in the country."

In April 1948, one of McMillan's "sepia stars" at Indiana, halfback Mel Groomes, became the first black to sign a contract with the Lions. Bob Mann, an end on the University of Michigan's 1947 undefeated national champions, quickly became the second. Both men, passed over in the NFL draft and signed as free agents, played the 1948 and '49 seasons with Detroit. Groomes was hampered by a broken wrist and appeared in a total of nine games before entering the air force. Mann, known for his good hands and precise routes, was a far more productive receiver, setting several team records.

In 1949, the NFL held a historic draft. For the first time, blacks were selected, a consequence of their demonstrated excellence in the rival AAFC. The Lions picked halfback Wally Triplett, characterized by one reporter as "the Negro bundle of power from Penn State," in the 19th round. Triplett became the first black draftee to play in the NFL. (He was not the first black NFL draft choice, however. That honor went to Groomes's former Indiana teammate, back George Taliaferro, who was selected in an earlier round by the Chicago Bears but chose to play with the Los Angeles Dons of the AAFC.)

Over the years, Mann and Triplett offered differing accounts of their reception in the Detroit locker room. On balance, it appears that such clubhouse leaders as "Bullet Bill" Dudley and players from integrated college programs—Michigan's John Greene and Notre Dame's Gus Cifelli and John Panelli—were most open to their new Negro teammates. "I just thought he was here to make our ball club better," Dudley, a courtly Virginian, said of his introduction to Mann. "And I was all for it."

To outsiders, at least, the Lions appeared admirably progressive. There were only seven blacks in the entire NFL in 1949, and three of them—Mann, Groomes, and Triplett—played for Detroit. There almost was a fourth. Richard Boykin, a rangy 220-pound fullback from Ohio coal country with no college experience, was signed to a contract in early 1949. Boykin came to camp but was cut and returned to playing for the semipro Ironton Bengals.

However, during the 1949 preseason the Lions' "colored contingent" learned there was a limit to the club's liberalism. The team was scheduled to play an exhibition game against Philadelphia in New Orleans, a city where mixing races on the athletic field was forbidden. Before the team left Detroit, McMillan called his trio of black players into his office. He explained that the sponsors of the game were leaving it up to him as to whether he wanted to risk the consequences of breaking the local color bar. McMillan ultimately decided that he would not risk tackling Jim Crow on his own home turf. The players could make the trip, but they would be held out of the game. Moreover, they would not be able to stay with the rest of the team at their hotel but would instead be lodged at a black boardinghouse.

Recalling the incident in 2005, a year before his death, Mann angrily said: "Bo told us he didn't think he should be the one to break it. I thought to myself, 'Fine, that's his decision.' Bo could have ended all that. He was supposed to be Mr. Great Liberal. . . . He had a chance to be a hero, step up to the plate, but he didn't do it."

In McMillan's defense, he had a right to be worried. North or south, racial animosities occasionally spilled onto the gridiron. A few weeks after the

Lions' exhibition in New Orleans, a pair of unbeaten downriver Detroit high school teams met in a showdown for the league championship. The host team, Melvindale, fielded an all-white squad. The visiting River Rouge team had seven blacks in its starting lineup (including Howard McCants, who five years later would be one of the few black collegians drafted by Buddy Parker). Epitaphs flew freely and, by game's end, so did fists. A riot involving several hundred fans ensued, resulting in the game being forfeited to River Rouge. Blacks complained to police of being attacked without provocation, with the injured including a middle-aged couple dragged from their car by knife-wielding whites. Four people were seriously hurt, with three of them suffering stab wounds.

Police seemed reluctant to investigate too deeply. They pointed to the teams' long rivalry and maintained the melee was fought along school lines. Local civil rights leaders were unconvinced. Coming just six years after the '43 riot, the violence was the latest reminder that the city was still a vat of racial tensions, bubbling away on slow boil.

"This was not a happy town by any means," Triplett said. "We'd just finished a race riot. Because of restrictive covenants, blacks had to live in certain areas of town. The police department was racist. You couldn't be in certain areas at certain times." However, in many other ways, Detroit "was a beautiful town," Triplett continued. "My dad loved it when he visited from Philadelphia." Triplett fondly recalled Paradise Valley, where he spent probably too much time and money. "Man, the black-and-tans, everybody got along. The speakeasies would come alive at two in the morning. You could walk the street then. You'd put your hat in the back seat of a convertible and at 6 a.m. it'd still be there."

Mann, who liked Detroit so well that he settled there after his playing days were over, experienced the same schizophrenic relationship. "It was an unusual city," he said. "It was bad in one way and great in another. The places that were available were just wonderful."

One such place was the Gotham Hotel, run by local gambling kingpin John White. The twin-towered complex of shops and rooms on Orchestra Place was one of the centers of Detroit's black social life. It hosted Duke Ellington, Lena Horne, Billie Holiday, the Harlem Globetrotters, and other notables who couldn't stay at white hotels. Mann, a fashionably attired man with processed hair and an Errol Flynn pencil mustache, was tipped off by hotel staff whenever an attractive actress or singer checked in. "Segregation was bad," he said wryly, "but it had some good points."

In 1949, Mann enjoyed the best season yet by a black in the NFL. He had 66 catches, second only to Tom Fears of Los Angeles, and led all receivers with 1,014 yards, one more than Fears. A pay raise was a reasonable expectation for the man who had just set franchise records for receptions and receiving yardage. Instead, Edwin Anderson, citing the financial losses the Lions had incurred during the recently concluded war with the AAFC, wanted Mann to take a $1,500 pay cut for the 1950 season. This would have slashed his salary from $7,500 to $6,000. Mann refused to sign a contract.

Complicating negotiations was Mann's off-season sales job with Goebel Brewery, of which Anderson was president. In the summer of 1950, two long-time Goebel employees, both white, were given a distributorship whose delivery area was in a predominantly black section of Detroit. A group called Business Sales Inc. protested that the distributorship should have gone to a Negro and organized a boycott of the beer maker. The boycott collapsed when black bar owners and businessmen, made aware that Goebel employed far more minorities than any other brewery in town, decided not to support the activists.

Anderson believed Mann was somehow involved with Business Sales. On the day players reported to training camp in Ypsilanti, Mann lost his brewery job. Four days later, he was sent to the New York Yanks (formerly the Bulldogs). This completed the transaction that had brought Bobby Layne to Detroit.

Mann later recalled the whole unhappy episode as "just a whole lot of mess." But it was to get worse. He played only three minutes for the Yanks during the entire exhibition season. When he did get on the field, the quarterback was instructed not to throw to him. Mann was told he was "too small" and then waived out of the league—bewildering treatment for one of the NFL's top receivers.

"I must have been blackballed—it just doesn't make sense that I'm suddenly not good enough to make a single team in the league," the out-of-work end said two months into the regular season. When Mann successfully applied for unemployment compensation, Goebel Brewery appealed the decision. "While Bob is just now arriving at the conclusion that he was 'railroaded' out of the league, fans saw through the maneuver when it was made," Russ Cowans wrote at the time. "The word was probably passed along that Mann is a 'bad character' and should be shoved out of the league."

Finally, the lowly Green Bay Packers signed Mann with just one game left on the 1950 schedule. Green Bay was the league's version of Siberia—a frozen outpost filled with white folks who figured to be less than welcoming to the team's first black player. "Green Bay was a little town, but rough," Triplett said. "They let you know how they felt." According to Mann, there were only two other black people in all of Green Bay when he arrived—a hotel porter and a railroad cook—so he got the head coach's permission to regularly drive his Chrysler New Yorker to Chicago and Milwaukee to socialize.

Mann's closest friend on the Packers was tackle Dick Afflis, an exceptionally violent person who demonstrated little patience for those who couldn't see beyond his teammate's skin color. "I was hailing a cab in Baltimore once, but the driver wouldn't let me in," Mann recalled. "Dick opened the passenger door and pulled the guy onto the sidewalk and quickly convinced him to take me."

Mann played for the Packers until he suffered a career-ending knee injury in 1954, the same year Afflis quit the NFL to embark on a full-time wrestling career in the Detroit-Windsor area under the ring name of "Dick the Bruiser."

Many of the top Lions of the 1950s were southern whites, as were several of the coaches. They had grown up in an era of strict segregation, so their attitudes were set early in life and not easily changed. According to Triplett, "the Texans" on the squad were cool to his presence in the locker room, barely acknowledging him, though Doak Walker strived to set the correct tone. Cloyce Box, the proud grandson of a Confederate cavalryman, "was kind of reticent at first," Triplett said. "After he saw how me and Doak got along, things got better." Triplett initially had a small problem with Bobby Layne "saying things out of habit" and dropping the occasional N-bomb in casual conversation, but he considered the quarterback a friend and found him to be an equal-opportunity partier.

During most of his two seasons in Detroit, Triplett lived in a boardinghouse on the near east side. It was a lively and inviting environment for "sports" of all races and tastes. Layne was known to serve as host to visiting black players. San Francisco end Charlie Powell recalled: "We would just get through playing and either the Lions would whip our butts or we would whip their butts, and he would say, 'Charlie, go get dressed. I'll wait for you outside your dressing room.' He would take me to the nicest clubs in Detroit and they would roll out the carpet for him." Layne made the rounds of the Flame Show Bar, the Chesterfield Lounge, the Frolic Show Bar, and other jazz venues, "and everybody in those places knew him, too," Powell said.

Fourteen blacks played in the NFL in 1950, with nine of them suiting up for either Cleveland or Los Angeles. The Browns and Rams met in that year's title game, as well as the next. Such success was not a coincidence, the black press enjoyed pointing out. By 1952, every team except Washington had fielded at least one black since the end of the war, though, collectively, blacks still constituted only a small fraction of the league's players.

Of those who did play, most were stars. In 1954, for example, the league's top five ground-gainers were black. Nonetheless, a racial slur could fly out of the most unexpected mouth, said Triplett, recalling a game against San Francisco. "I hit their quarterback, Frankie Albert, out of bounds and he went into the bench. That precipitated a fight. The coach, Buck Shaw, raised hell to the official and he said, 'Don't worry, Buck, that nigger's out of the game.'"

During the '50s, club owners continued to drag their feet when it came to signing blacks. It's believed most teams had an unspoken quota each felt it could comfortably field without upsetting local fans, sponsors, share-holders, and the perceived harmony of the locker room. During this transitional decade, coaches were guilty of "stacking" blacks at certain positions requiring speed and brute strength, particularly end and back, so that they might elim-inate themselves through competition. This allowed a team to avoid accu-sations of being discriminatory. Meanwhile, other positions were reserved for "brainier" whites.

Pete Waldmeir, then a young, freethinking sportswriter with the *Detroit News*, remembered being tutored in the early '50s about "how things go" in matters of race and sports. He was told by one unnamed baseball executive (presumably with the Tigers) that a team needed to be "smart down the middle." That meant not fielding a black catcher, pitcher, or center fielder. Waldmeir was incredulous. "When I ran that outrageous scenario past a pro football coach," Waldmeir later wrote, "he listened intently, and then agreed. 'Nothing wrong with that,' he said. 'Why do you suppose we don't have blacks at quarterback, center, middle guard, and safety?'"

The Tigers, the second-to-last major league team to desegregate, were widely viewed as a racist organization. Owner Walter O. Briggs was a strong-willed industrialist who made little secret of his distaste for organized labor in his fac-tories and an integrated ball team on his diamond. Edgar Hayes of the *Detroit Times* said old-timers in the press box characterized the Tigers' unofficial policy as "No jiggs with Briggs."

The Lions, closely associated with the Briggs name, were considered in the black community to be just as bigoted. Certainly blacks felt less than welcome at Briggs Stadium, whether they were there to watch the Tigers or the Lions. Black baseball fans were seldom seen in the better seats—the field boxes and the lower-deck reserved seats between first and third base—because employees handling in-person ticket sales quietly steered them to certain "colored sections," particularly the lower-deck bleachers. According to Waldmeir, "when season ticket orders were mailed in, the addresses were checked. And orders that came from 'black neighborhoods' were filled selectively because they didn't want to alienate white customers by seating them next to African Americans."

Throughout the 1950s, the two teams meeting in the title game each December typically were those fielding the most blacks that particular season: Cleveland, Los Angeles, and, later in the decade, Baltimore and the New York Giants. The only consistent exceptions were the Lions, who in four championship games suited up just two black players: Harold Turner in 1954 and John Henry Johnson in 1957.

"I don't think the coaches had anything against signing black players," Joe Schmidt said in Parker's defense. "I think it was more of a case of scouting not being very sophisticated in those days. Hell, they were still drafting some guys out of magazines. Nobody was paying much attention to those small black colleges."

Scouting being what it was back then, scrutinizing the larger out-of-state programs usually involved having a local part-time scout (typically a college coach or former player) bird-dog a particular school or conference and make recommendations. Many picks, white or black, were selected without Parker or any of his coaches once personally setting eyes on the player. For example, Auburn halfback Dave Middleton became Detroit's top choice in the 1955 draft based solely on the recommendation of Louisiana State's head coach. A couple of years earlier, Kansas tackle Ollie Spencer inadvertently caught Parker's eye as the coach slogged through hours of film of that year's East-West Game and Senior Bowl. "So strictly from his performance in those games we drafted him—'from the pictures,'" Parker said.

It's quaint to see the emphasis Parker placed in his 1955 book, *We Play to Win!*: "To demonstrate the importance of the talent-scouting operation, I'd just like to mention that National League teams spend an average of between $20,000 to $35,000 each season on scouting college players." Some of that money went for envelopes and stamps, as every year questionnaires were mailed to several hundred graduating seniors. At the end of the form, each player was asked: "Please name the five best players you have played against during the past season."

"We take these tips and then begin investigating the gridders immediately," Parker noted. With few, if any, of the questionnaires sent to players at historically black colleges, and all of the Lions' scouts being white, it's hardly surprising that most Negro players weren't on the radar.

The Lions' scouting system was upgraded with the hiring of former Michigan halfback Bob Nussbaumer as full-time talent coordinator in 1954. Within a couple of years the Lions were contacting 1,800 players each September, following up with phone calls to the 50 most promising prospects in late November and then telegrams to a select 15 finalists as draft day approached.

A total of 361 collegians were drafted each year by the NFL: a bonus pick selected by lottery, followed by 30 rounds of one pick by each of the 12 teams. The draft was held in January, usually in Philadelphia or New York. From 1956 through 1959, the draft was split into two parts. The first three or four rounds were held just after Thanksgiving in order to give NFL clubs a better chance to sign the top players before Canadian teams got to them. The remaining rounds were then held in January.

The record shows that Parker drafted a handful of blacks, usually in the latter rounds as the pool of talented white prospects dwindled. In 1952, he selected Tennessee end Harold "Bulldog" Turner but lost him to military service. Turner came to camp in 1954 after spending two years in the Marines. He was sold to Cleveland during training camp, released, and subsequently re-signed with the Lions. He got into the final three games of the season, plus the championship game, replacing injured rookie back Dick Kercher on the roster. Turner's teammates voted him a half share of the title-game money.

Ray Dohn Dillon of Prairie View College was Parker's last pick in the '52 draft and the 357th choice overall. "Ray Dillon, the huge fullback . . . has been impressive on occasion but on others looked like an ordinary player," Bob Latshaw wrote not long before Dillon was cut. Recalling his monthlong stint at training camp in Ypsilanti, Dillon later said that one of Parker's coaches dubbed him "Radar" for the aggressive way he shadowed Doak Walker and others on pass defense. "He said, 'Radar, you were supposed to make this team, but it's over my head right now.'"

In 1954, Parker made end Howard McCants, the former River Rouge High School star and the first black player at Washington State, the 49th overall pick.

The 6-foot-8, 230-pound high-jump champion, whose yardage-gobbling strides drew comparisons with the fading and soon-to-be-retired Cloyce Box, signed contracts with Detroit and the Toronto Argonauts.

"I intended to play with Detroit until I saw some things I didn't like," McCants said cryptically, refusing to elaborate on what those things were. That year the Lions also drafted UCLA back Milt Davis, who was called into the army before he could try out for the team.

In 1955, the Lions selected a pair of linemen who impressed coaches and reporters at training camp. Elijah Childers, a "husky Negro tackle" from Prairie View, was described as "a poor man's Les Bingaman." But the 265-pounder was waived a week before the start of the regular season when Gil Mains returned from Canada and took his spot on the roster.

The other lineman was Walter Jenkins, a local star at Miller High and Wayne University. Quick, rugged, and a sure tackler, Jenkins was shifted from tackle to defensive end. In his first game, the 1955 season opener at Green Bay, he slammed into Tobin Rote and caused a fumble, which Mains recovered for a touchdown. Jenkins started his second straight game at Baltimore but two days later was waived. The Lions had acquired Los Angeles end Bob Long, and Jenkins was deemed expendable. A third black, halfback William "Tex" Clark, had been Childers's college teammate. Clark was signed as a free agent but released the same day Childers was cut.

Perhaps the most promising of Detroit's black draftees during Parker's tenure was Calvin Jones, the three-time All-American guard from the University of Iowa. Jones was a two-way marvel and a pioneer. He was the first African American to win the Outland Trophy, awarded annually to the top college lineman, as well as the first black athlete and the first college player to grace the cover of *Sports Illustrated*. Although the Hawkeyes had a poor season in Jones's senior year, the Iowa captain still finished tenth in voting for the Heisman Trophy, a commendable achievement for a lineman of any color.

Today, Jones probably would be a first-round draft choice. In 1956, he had to wait until the ninth round, when Parker made him the 98th overall pick. Jones had already established himself as a man who demanded respect. After committing to play for Woody Hayes at Ohio State, he impulsively joined two black childhood friends in enrolling at Iowa.

"I'll tell you why I came out here," he explained at the time. "They treated me like a white man, and I like it here. I'm going to stay."

The Canadian leagues, which fielded their first black American player in 1946, were an attractive alternative for many black collegiate stars. John Henry Johnson, for example, played his first season out of Arizona State for the Calgary Stampeders before switching to the NFL. Jones, swayed by the higher pay and more hospitable environment many blacks found "up north," snubbed Detroit and instead signed with the Winnipeg Blue Bombers. His career ended tragically when he was killed in an airplane crash after his rookie season.

In the view of Milt Davis, Jones's decision to forego Detroit directly affected his own chances to make that year's Lions squad. Davis, invited to camp after spending two years in the army, was put on waivers after suiting up for the first two regular-season games in 1956, neither of which he appeared in. Davis claimed he was victimized by an unwritten team policy. "We don't have a black teammate for you to go on road trips, therefore you can't stay on our team," he recalled Parker telling him.

"That's one of those slaps in the face," Davis said. "It hurt considerably, but I'd been hurt so many times, that was minor." The following year, he had a successful tryout with Baltimore and signed with the Colts as a free agent. As a 28-year-old rookie, "Pops" Davis picked off 10 passes in 1957, tying Jack Christiansen for the league lead.

Davis retired after just four NFL seasons with Baltimore, having twice led the league in interceptions while helping the Colts win the last two championships of the 1950s. Part of the reason he left the game in his prime was money (he was making less than his white counterparts) and part of it was his desire to finish his degree (he was working on a doctorate in education). The decisive factor was his desire for simple self-respect. The All-Pro cornerback, army veteran, and doctoral candidate was tired of being turned away at whites-only restaurants and theaters, being directed to the "colored taxi stand," and sleeping in rundown boardinghouses in the "Negro section" of whatever city his team happened to be visiting.

In Dallas, the community that so warmly embraced Doak Walker, Bobby Layne, and Parker, black players routinely encountered hostility and humiliation. Seared into Davis's memory was checking into a rundown Dallas boardinghouse, which the manager insisted was air-conditioned. "He goes to this room and opens the door, and he had a fan on a chair in front of the open window," Davis said. "I thought the ceiling was gray; it was all mosquitos up there."

When Buddy Parker moved on to Pittsburgh in 1957, he inherited a team with two black veteran players—defensive back Henry Ford and tackle Willie McClung—and one new black coach, Lowell Perry. By the following season, Ford had been cut, McClung traded to Cleveland, and Perry reassigned as a scout. The shake-up could have been the usual personnel turnover, or it could have been something else.

Ford always maintained that he was cut and subsequently blacklisted because coaches learned he was dating a white woman—a major societal taboo in the '50s. Ford was starting his third NFL season when Parker took over. He was coming off a solid year as a two-way back in 1956 and had just enjoyed a fine preseason effort against the Lions in September 1957, Parker's first game as Pittsburgh's new coach. "I was playing offense and defense and I thought I really had a hell of a day," Ford told Andy Piascik in *Gridiron Gauntlet*.

But when the team returned to practice the following Tuesday, Ford wasn't part of the regular offensive, defensive, or special teams drills. The same thing happened on Wednesday. He figured some rookies were getting a final look-over. "Thursday came, same thing. Friday, same thing. On Saturday I was home looking forward to the game on Sunday, getting myself prepared, getting my clothes packed for the trip and everything, and I get a phone call from the business manager. Not the head coach or even any other coach but the business manager . . . and he says, 'That's it.' I said, 'What do you mean, that's it.' He said, 'They told me to tell you that's it and they'll take care of you when we get back from the game,' and he hung up. And that's how I was cut, right after I had played a hell of a game against the Detroit Lions."

Ford, who suspected the team was listening in on his phone calls, was devastated. Suddenly no club in the NFL was interested in him. The woman he was seeing became his wife of many years, an interracial marriage that survived the expected barrage of ugly comments and snubs, some coming from members of their own families. Although Ford later prospered in the corporate world and as a high school coach, "Being kicked off the team for something that had nothing to do with football or how I played the game caused me a lot of emotional trauma," he said.

In the early '60s, Parker's Steelers included a handful of black players, notably John Henry Johnson, guard John Nisby, tackle Gene "Big Daddy" Lipscomb, and defensive backs Brady Keys and Johnny Sample. Sample was offended by what he saw as Parker's patronizing treatment of an older black man named

Wallace "Bootsy" Lewis. Parker considered Lewis, a craps-shooting handyman he'd first met at Centenary College and later discovered operating a shoe-shine stand in Los Angeles, his "good luck" charm. Parker invited Lewis to sit on the Detroit bench whenever the Lions were playing the Rams. Later he brought Lewis to Pittsburgh to act as his personal valet.

"Bootsy would wake Buddy up in the morning, shine his shoes, get him coffee, and so on, for which he was paid next to nothing and treated like a dog," Sample said. "John Henry Johnson had to drive Bootsy from practice at South Park, about an hour outside of Pittsburgh, to where he stayed in the city, because Parker wouldn't give him a ride. In fact, John Henry bought his lunch because Bootsy never had any money."

It was unavoidable that Sample's brash style would get under Parker's skin. In 1961, they nearly came to blows when the coach brushed aside Sample's demand for a pay raise by saying, "I know you had a great year, Sample. But black athletes just don't deserve that kind of money, and I won't pay it." Parker was hardly alone among old-school NFL types in believing that, on the whole, black players were intellectually inferior to their white counterparts, and thus worth less money.

Buster Ramsey was on Parker's staff in Detroit and Pittsburgh. In retirement, he was asked by sportswriter Dan Daly why Buddy didn't have more blacks on his teams. "I ain't gonna tell you," Ramsey said. "You can figure it out." Given the unenlightened environment of Parker's formative years—Texas in the 1920s and the NFL in the '30s and '40s—perhaps the most charitable characterization of the coach is that he was a product of his times. But those times were changing.

Throughout the 1950s and into the '60s, Jim Crow practices in much of the South continued to restrict the mixing of races in many aspects of everyday life. It was a sign of the times that in August 1957, when John Henry Johnson didn't travel with the Lions to Birmingham, Alabama, for an exhibition game, his treatment elicited no outcry or commentary in Detroit's three daily papers. It was business as usual. That September, President Eisenhower sent the 101st Airborne to Little Rock, Arkansas, to forcibly integrate Central High School. The tense showdown between federal and state authorities played out on television screens across the country and became another landmark victory in the burgeoning civil rights movement. Johnson himself noted some years later that, as bad as race relations were at the time, his predecessors had endured worse. "Some of the guys who came before I did, the problems and discrimination they had to go through, it was rough," he said. "When I started playing, that kind of thing was sort of on its way out. People were starting to accept the fact that we were good football players and we could contribute to the game."

Such contributions were showcased at the 1958 College All-Star Game, when black stars played key roles in the collegians' shocking 35–19 whipping of the reigning NFL champion Lions. Fans saw Michigan halfback Jim Pace break off the game's most electrifying run, Washington cornerback Jim Jones pick off three Bobby Layne passes, and Bobby Mitchell of Illinois spend the evening "making monkeys" out of Detroit's famed secondary.

"Actually both teams were liberally sprinkled with Negro players; and as has been the custom in recent years they were simply taken for granted," Howard Gould wrote in the *Chicago Defender*. To Gould, the prosy reaction to the growing presence of blacks in such a high-profile sporting event was a solid indicator of progress. When the *Chicago Tribune* started the charity game a quarter century earlier, "the state of race relations was such that a Negro student could not play football or basketball at the University of Illinois," he continued.

> Friday night one of the outstanding stars was Bobby Mitchell from that school. Undoubtedly there were fans who noted that Mitchell comes from Arkansas, and who may have commented that he would be denied the right of playing football at Central High in Little Rock. The point of comparison rests in the inevitability of the fact that change will come to Little Rock and similar places, just as it did to Champaign, Illinois. Another comparison may be made of the Detroit Lions of Friday night as against the same team years ago. There was a time when astute fans would have laughed at the idea that a player from a small Negro college might play for the pros, but along with Danny Lewis and Johnson Henry Johnson, Detroit fielded a man from Kentucky State [halfback Henry Herzog]. These comparisons can best be understood by the older adults. Watching a spectacle like the All-Star Game they can think back over the years, and remembering the past from a race relations point of view, recognize the fact that the youngsters of today don't see as many racial barriers as they had to in the past.

While the country was then, and still remains, far from color-blind, 1950s activism set the stage for monumental change, with the Civil Rights Act of 1964 and the Voting Rights Act of 1965 remaking American society. Long before that, it was clear to all but the most delusional obstructionists that black athletes were here to stay.

In 1960, rookie Roger Brown, a huge tackle drafted out of Maryland Eastern Shore, joined the Detroit lineup. That same year the Lions traded for veteran defensive back Dick "Night Train" Lane, a future Hall-of-Famer feared for his necktie tackles, and acquired Willie McClung from Cleveland. With halfback Danny Lewis, who was drafted out of Wisconsin in 1958, this gave the Lions four black players on the roster for the first time. By 1960 a total of 143 African Americans had played in the NFL since the color barrier was permanently breached in 1946, including 10 with Detroit. The league was now roughly 12 percent black, a percentage that would steadily climb over the coming years.

Just as the NFL turned a corner in fielding blacks, the American Football League (AFL) started play in 1960 in eight cities, giving players of all colors another option for their services. College stars often found themselves drafted by both leagues. Many black draft choices—seeking a better opportunity, higher wages, or a more tolerant atmosphere—ignored the established NFL and signed with the AFL, just as others had earlier opted for the Canadian leagues. The Washington Redskins, the last all-white holdout in professional football, were forced to desegregate in 1962 at the risk of losing the right to play in their munic-ipally funded stadium. Meanwhile, the civil rights movement pulled along a new generation unafraid of being militant. In 1965, black players in New Orleans for the AFL All-Star Game forced the league to move the contest to Houston because of the city's blatant discrimination.

The growing number of integrated major college programs meant a deeper pool of talent to choose from on draft day. The Lions enlisted local high school coaching legend Will Robinson to help scout black prospects. Such players as Bobby Thompson, Ernie Clark, Jerry Rush, Mel Farr, Earl McCullouch, Larry Walton, Altie Taylor, and future Hall-of-Famers Lem Barney and Charlie Sanders were signed by Detroit during the 1960s. They were in the vanguard of a remark-able transformation as the NFL and AFL merged into one league in 1970. Within the span of a couple of generations, the complexion of professional football changed from wholly white to majority black on the playing field.

Presently, roughly 70 percent of all NFLers are African American. Although integrating the coaching and management ranks continues at a much slower pace, in 2014 the Lions hired Jim Caldwell as the club's first black head coach, an event that passed with scant commentary about race. Today, Detroit fans cannot imagine a team history that does not include such black standouts as Billy Sims, Al "Bubba" Baker, Barry Sanders, Herman Moore, and Calvin Johnson.

Among the players themselves, little thought is given to the pioneers who took on an intimidating adversary named Jim Crow. "I don't think these young black players in the game today have any idea what we had to go through," John Henry Johnson once reflected. "They might have heard a little bit, but when they came in, we had their beds made for them and it was a lot easier."

Bob Mann returned to Detroit after leaving the NFL, working in real estate and earning a law degree. When the Lions inaugurated their new domed stadium, Ford Field, in 2002, he was invited to serve as honorary captain. One of the team's stars, nose tackle Shaun Rogers, was impressed by the trim and distinguished-looking septuagenarian.

"Man, I'm glad to meet you," Rogers said. "We don't know much about you guys." To which Mann replied: "I know you don't."

CHAPTER

9

Muggings AND *Mayhem*

There's a fine line between being dirty and nasty.
We were nasty.

—Leon Hart

Based strictly on the final NFL standings, the 3–9 Lions were the league's biggest losers of 1955, worse than even such perennial doormats as the Chicago Cardinals and Baltimore Colts. However, the corporate ledgers painted an entirely different picture. Despite a slight dip in attendance and a fall-off in broadcast fees, as well as the absence of postseason revenue for the first time in four years, the Detroit Football Company turned a profit of $105,000 in 1955, allowing Edwin Anderson to declare a 5 percent dividend for each shareholder. This followed the handsome $178,354 the club cleared after expenses in 1954 and was the fifth straight season of profitability.

In a few short years, the once flailing franchise had turned completely around. It now was in the top tier of NFL moneymakers, a dependable draw at home, on the road, and inside living rooms. Briggs Stadium was always filled, to the point of sometimes alarming the fire marshal. The Lions would sell 36,586 season tickets in 1956, extending their NFL record. The financial outlook was bright enough that, in early 1956, directors voted to pursue the purchase of Briggs Stadium.

Presently, the Lions were paying the Detroit Tigers $150,000 a season for rent. Buying the park would make the Lions the only NFL team to own its playing field. The ballpark, along with the Detroit Tigers baseball team, had been put up for sale by trustees of Walter O. Briggs Sr.'s estate after the industrialist's death in 1952. That season, the Tigers became the first professional sports team in history to draw one million fans while finishing last. Despite that demonstration of community support, Monaghan, Hart, and Crawmer, the firm advising the trustees, decided that owning a professional sports franchise was not a prudent investment. "We found that the money the Detroit Baseball Company made from renting the stadium to the Lions and its share of the concessions often was the difference between the Tigers making a profit or a loss for the season," said attorney Jim LoPrete.

For tax purposes, Briggs Stadium was officially assessed a value of $2,031,640. Shortly after Anderson publicly expressed interest, Briggs's heirs decided they would not sell the park and baseball team separately but as a package. There were several prospective buyers for the American League's oldest franchise, including a group of investors who wanted to move it to Canada. "We're not going to sell to just anybody with a lot of money," said Walter O. "Spike" Briggs Jr., the late owner's son and a Lions director. "We want to justify our sale to the people of Detroit."

On April 11, 1956, Anderson proposed the Lions buy the baseball team and the park, then offer shares in the Tigers to the public and sell the stadium to the city. The Detroit City Council voted on Anderson's proposition, splitting 4–4 over the idea of the city becoming a landlord to two pro sports teams.

Bert Bell had a dim view of any team combining football and baseball ownerships. In the recent past, the New York Yankees and Brooklyn Dodgers had tried, and each had failed miserably. In June, NFL owners determined by a 10–1 vote (Los Angeles abstained) that the Lions' purchase of the Tigers would be "detrimental to the league" and thus technically in violation of the league's constitution. "It's time pro football should stand on its own feet," Bell said, adding that the NFL had no objection to one or more Lions shareholders organizing an entirely separate corporation to bid for the Tigers.

With that rebuke, the Lions dropped out of the running. In July, the Tigers and the park were sold for $5.5 million to a syndicate headed by radio executive

Fred Knorr. The Lions would continue renting the stadium until moving into a domed football-only facility in suburban Pontiac two decades later.

As the Lions regrouped for what they hoped would be an unprecedented worst-to-first comeback season in 1956, some players were aware of a salary survey that had appeared in a recent issue of *Sport*. The magazine estimated that among the four major professional team sports, NFL athletes had the lowest average salary: $7,500. This lagged far behind major league baseball, whose players were paid an average of $12,000. The NFL even trailed the National Hockey League ($9,000), a six-team circuit that essentially was a boutique sport, and the floundering National Basketball Association ($8,000).

While *Sport's* figures were estimates, more precise numbers were forthcoming. The following summer, salary figures were introduced into the record of the House Antitrust Subcommittee hearings on pro football. Detroit's $330,375 payroll for 35 players ranked fifth in the league in 1956, while the average Lion's salary of $9,439 was bettered only by the Browns and the Bears. The financials didn't disclose any names, but the range of salaries reported by each club led to some informed speculation. The high figure on Detroit's reported salary scale was $20,000, and that obviously belonged to Bobby Layne. He was matched by Norm Van Brocklin of the Rams and Ollie Matson of the Cardinals. At $20,100, San Francisco's Hugh McElhenny had the highest salary in the league.

The low figure on the Lions' stated salary range was $5,500, and Jerry Reichow, who read *Sport* every month, didn't have to wonder who that unidentified player was. The rookie quarterback from Iowa was signed to that amount by Nick Kerbawy, and he was happy enough for the money.

"In those days, you didn't tell anyone in the locker room what you made because you didn't want someone to know that you were making more or less than he was," Reichow said. "I had a wife and a son while in college and we had a daughter my first year in Detroit. I grew up in a small farming community. My dad was a railroad worker. He said, 'I don't care what you do. Just don't work on the railroad.' Fifty-five hundred wasn't a lot, but other people in other professions were making less. If you were a schoolteacher, you weren't making that kind of money."

Exhibitions were essential to a club's profitability. After Doak Walker's farewell game at the Cotton Bowl, for example, Kerbawy and his Philadelphia counterpart, general manager Vince McNally, "wore $39,500 smiles," the amount each club reportedly received as its share of the receipts. For many teams, the

$100,000 to $200,000 a club made in profits during the exhibition season was the difference between finishing the year in the red or in the black.

Under NFL bylaws, clubs were not obligated to pay players during training camp or for exhibitions, even though the typical six-game preseason slate constituted a full one-third of a team's overall schedule. (The only exception was the College All-Star Game, when the professionals were compensated by the game's sponsors at the rate of one-twelfth their previous year's base salary.) Some teams, however, voluntarily paid players a weekly stipend during the preseason to help cover incidental expenses. The Lions were considered generous in that respect.

"We get more than anybody else," one Detroit rookie bragged in 1956. "I think the Rams get $10. We get $25. That's 2½ times as much as anybody gets. Detroit treats the boys so well. From what I've heard from boys on the other teams, we have a better deal than any other club."

Paying the likes of Bobby Layne and Yale Lary $25 per week seemed a bit stingy even then, but owners countered that players received free room, board, and medical care while in camp. When a player was cut, he got a plane ticket home. Besides, they argued, a player signed his contract for a year, not a season, and that year included as many exhibitions as a team wanted to arrange. Players had to wait until the Monday after the regular season started in late September before they could start drawing their weekly paycheck. In the event of a special postseason playoff to determine the division title—there were five such games during the 1950s, including two involving the Lions—players were paid at just their regular game rate. They did not get a share of the lucrative gate receipts and broadcast revenues. That was only the case in the championship game, when all moneys were pooled and distributed according to a set formula.

While a handful of older, better-paid veterans enjoyed a decent middle-class lifestyle, other players struggled. Many young players in the Motor City either didn't own a car or drove a beater. "It was tough," Reichow said. "That first year, I had to borrow money to make it through." He was able to relax slightly when shares of second-place money were distributed that winter. For finishing runner-up in the conference, each Lion drew $339.09 from the championship game pot, before taxes. "Hey, we were happy to get it," Reichow said.

Each spring, club directors determined the budget for player salaries for the upcoming season. As general manager, Kerbawy was charged with signing players for as little as possible while trying to keep them happy enough to win a championship. There were no agents then. Players negotiated contracts on their own, though Dick Stanfel was known to bring along one of his argumentative and business-savvy brothers, with whom he co-owned a restaurant in San Francisco. "You dealt with old Nick yourself, and he could be a son of a bitch," one Lion recalled. "He acted like he was the guy in the poor house."

Salaries during this era in professional sports typically were based as much on seniority as performance. Working oneself up the ladder was problematic in pro football, though, as the average career lasted only four or five years. Moreover, NFL bylaws permitted a team to slash a player's salary by up to 10 percent from the previous season. (This actually compared favorably with major league baseball's policy, where pay cuts of up to 25 percent were allowed.) Leon Hart saw his salary reduced in steps from $15,000 early in his career to about $12,000 at the end, a financial haircut that embittered him and made him a perennial holdout.

The Lions' policy since a new regime took over in 1948 was to pay a player no less than $5,000 per season, but it still required some effort to pry a decent raise out of management. A man was paid for what he did, not what he promised to do, and for that reason multiyear contracts were an exception.

Some players were better at haggling than others. In 1954, Jack Christiansen was able to leverage the possibility of jumping to Canada into a two-year contract that paid him about $3,000 more annually than the going rate for defensive backs. "The quarterbacks drive the Cadillacs and draw the top salaries," *Sport* noted, "but Chris, an exception among defense men, does well. He drives a new Chevrolet, his wife drives an Olds, and he is paid approximately $10,000 a year."

That same year, Les Bingaman struggled to wrangle a $1,000 raise for his final season. When Kerbawy refused to budge, Bingaman reminded him: "Nick, you and I are the only ones left of the team that Bo McMillan assembled. You came to Detroit as a press agent from Michigan State. I came as a guard from Illinois. Now, look Nick. You're the general manager, and I'm still playing guard." Kerbawy, who would leave the Lions in June 1958 for a $50,000-a-year executive position with the new Detroit Pistons basketball team, relented. He gave the long-time anchor of Detroit's defense the modest pay bump.

Kerbawy was not particularly well liked by either coaches or players. He especially rubbed Buddy Parker the wrong way. Part of it was his flamboyance, part of it was his perceived stinginess. Layne, who never worried much about money when he didn't have any and thought far less about it now that he did, always quickly came to terms with the club. He even volunteered to take a pay cut once, figuring that in his tax situation the loss didn't amount to more than a few hundred dollars anyway.

Layne considered Kerbawy "a tremendous person . . . responsible in a lot of ways for those great teams at Detroit. He put us up in first-class hotels. When we'd go to the West Coast on a two-game trip, the club would slip us a hundred or two hundred dollars for spending money." On those occasions, players couldn't wait to get off the plane in California, Joe Schmidt remembered. "A nice crisp hundred in your pocket—that was big time. The married guys would tell the rookies, 'Don't say anything.' They didn't want to share the hundred with their wives."

According to Layne, "Nick got guys out of financial jams and never said anything about it. And when the team was going through a letdown, I might go to Nick, or our captain might, and say, 'Nick, we need to have a beer party or something.' He'd be all for it, and at the club's expense. He was for the football players. A lot of them didn't think so for a long time, but they finally realized he was for 'em."

The potential for cashing a postseason check was greater with the Lions than with most other teams, a point management wasn't afraid to raise during negotiations. As a rookie, Schmidt earned a base salary of $5,700 in 1953. Bonuses, a bookkeeping classification that included his $2,424 share of title-game loot, boosted his overall take to $8,962. "That '53 title game . . . I had just purchased a new car and I thought, 'If we win it, it'll take me out of the hole,'" he recalled. The few hundred dollars' difference between a winning and a losing share "was a lot of money back then. I was tickled we won because I could pay off that two-door Chevy."

Although Schmidt wasn't around to profit from the 1952 championship, eight members of that team—Layne, Hart, Christiansen, Lou Creekmur, Jimmy David, Bob Miller, Jim Doran, and Jim Martin—collected full shares from all four of Detroit's championship game appearances during the decade. Each man's collective haul was $10,579.91. That alone bought a nice brick bungalow in the 1950s.

An NFL career wasn't the ticket to automatic riches and an early, idle retirement that it is today. "I did substitute teaching, sold real estate, you name it," Wally Triplett said of his experience as a young married player in the early '50s. "I was hustling, trying to do everything to make a dollar. A ballplayer wasn't making more than a guy working at Ford's with overtime."

Players looking to supplement their income were happy to pick up a few extra bucks appearing in a milk ad or speaking at a Scouts banquet. Pro Bowlers like LaVern Torgeson, Charlie Ane, and Creekmur spent their off-seasons selling used cars, hawking sporting goods, moving furniture, tending bar, and working on highway crews. Schmidt worked as a schoolteacher for a couple of years before turning to selling industrial supplies.

Even Heisman Trophy winner Howard "Hopalong" Cassady, who pocketed a five-figure signing bonus and was the league's top-paid rookie in 1956, needed to be a go-getter to provide for his growing family. "I always worked in the off-season as a manufacturer's representative," he said, "because you never had that much money." Most assistant coaches had only six-month contracts, meaning they were left to their own devices every winter and spring.

Despite a wide network of contacts, it wasn't always possible for club directors to line up a suitable off-season job for everyone. It was the principal reason Tom Dublinski left for Canada and coach Earl Brown quit to work as a full-time rep for the American Charcoal Company. "It was always hard to get an off-season job," remembered Lew Carpenter's wife, Ann. "No one wanted to hire you for six months."

In some cases, however, a player was savvy or ambitious enough to grow an opportunity into a lucrative sidelight or post-football career. "At first I didn't work in the off-season," Vince Banonis said. "I figured the money would last forever. Then I woke up. I said to myself, 'I've got to do something.' So, about 1951, I went to work for one of the local auto-supply houses in Detroit. I got into labor relations and got my feet wet in that field. It was a good introduction because it got me into the plant, where I learned how a stamping was made and how anodizing, plating, painting, and so forth are done. Then I went into sales for the same company. I became vice-president of marketing for a company based in Cincinnati that had an office in Detroit, and I retired from that in 1984."

When the Lions nosedived in 1955, there were rumblings that perhaps some players were too distracted by outside business interests. Indeed, several members of that team, including Darris McCord, Bob Miller, and Joe Schmidt, would become wealthy businessmen after leaving the game. "It seems a shame," one sportswriter quipped, "to ask such capitalists to sweat through football."

There may be "do-overs" on playgrounds, but not in the NFL. For the Lions, the 1954 title game rout and the miserable season that followed were etched forever in the record books. The question in the fall of 1956 was whether Buddy Parker's once-powerful locomotive of a team had merely hit a bump on the tracks or been permanently derailed. The '56 Lions answered by rolling out of the station with six straight victories, four of them decided by four or less points. The close wins were reminiscent of the Lions during their title seasons.

Parker installed a more conservative, ball-control offense. The unit got a makeover, starting with the line. Creekmur, a defensive experiment in 1955, returned to being the full-time left tackle; Ollie Spencer, back from the army, assumed his old spot at right tackle; and Ane was moved to center. The reshuffled line, along with Leon Hart now permanently installed at fullback, gave Layne better pass protection than he'd had the year before.

Jim Doran assumed Hart's spot at end. Dorne Dibble, out for much of 1955 with injuries, rebounded with a 32-catch season at the other end position. Dave Middleton moved to flanker and led the team with 39 catches, the second year in a row that he finished in the league's top five in receptions. The backfield also was revamped. Gone were old favorites Doak Walker and Bob Hoernschemeyer, as well as dependable Lew Carpenter, called into the army. The stable of backs now included Hart, returning servicemen Gene Gedman and Bill Bowman, and the team's top two draft choices, Cassady and Don McIlhenny.

Cassady was the Lions' number-one pick in the draft, held just days after the 5-foot-10, 172-pounder helped Ohio State win the Big Ten championship with a 17–0 pasting of Michigan before a record crowd at Ann Arbor. Cassady, the third Heisman Trophy winner to play for the Lions in the '50s, also won the Maxwell Award and was named the Male Athlete of the Year by the Associated Press, adding to his box-office appeal. His speed and size weren't on the same level as McIlhenny, a 6-foot-1, 195-pound blazer from Southern Methodist. But he was quick and shifty, and had a propensity for timely touchdowns. He was a two-way back under Woody Hayes, and it was reported that not a single pass was completed on him in four years.

It was perhaps inevitable that the freckled-face redhead would be nicknamed after Bill "Hopalong" Cassidy, the popular sarsaparilla-swigging cowboy of television's early years. "I only hope I can do half as well as Doak Walker," Cassady said upon signing a two-year pact believed to be worth $14,500 per season, more than most veterans on the team were making. "I know I'm no Doak Walker, but I play football the best way I know how."

Cassady, McIlhenny, and Jerry Reichow traveled together from Chicago to Ypsilanti after playing in the College All-Star Game. That first day in camp,

Layne demanded the rookies join him and a few other veterans for dinner and drinks. "Cutty Sark and water for all the boys," Layne ordered when the group arrived at some downtown restaurant. Reichow was puzzled. "I didn't know what the hell he was talking about because in Iowa all we had was 3.2 beer."

McIlhenny wasn't much of a drinker, and Layne "wiped him out early," Reichow recalled. "Cassady didn't last long and down he went. Then Layne turned to me and said, 'You're my rookie.' At the time I said, 'Oh, boy!' But I wasn't so sure it was a good thing because every night it was, 'Come on rook, we're going out.'"

Like everyone else, Reichow was astonished by Layne's stamina. Perhaps the most memorable part of the experience was Sweet Bobby's blowtorch breath after another long night of Cutty Sark and Marlboros, said Reichow. "He'd show up to eat breakfast and it was like, 'Wow! Whew! Turn the other way, Bobby!'"

Cassady had a harder time fitting in. Dibble recalled one episode at the Stadium Bar. The rookies were all drinking beer, and whenever Layne rang a bell they had to down whiskey shots. "Hoppy disappeared," Dibble said. "Bobby's looking for him. So finally he goes into the women's john. He's looking in the stalls and finally he opens a door and there's Hoppy, standing hunched over on the toilet so his legs wouldn't show."

"Why you little shit, get out here!" Layne roared.

Cassady reluctantly rejoined the merrymaking. "Bobby never really liked him," Dibble said. The feeling was mutual.

The *Sports Illustrated* cover boy further irritated veterans by reminding everyone how things were done at Ohio State. Cassady's squawking caused them to nickname him "Parrot" and to put crackers in his bed. At one point, they decided to teach the voluble college hero a lesson. During a scrimmage they "opened the gates" on him, an old "educational play" where the target's teammates step aside and let enemy tacklers rush in unimpeded.

It was a rough initiation, but to his credit, Cassady took it without complaint. His major gripe during his eight pro seasons, all but one spent in Detroit, was not having his number called more often. "See, in college I was carrying the ball 30 or 40 times a ballgame," he once explained. "In the pros I was more of a receiver, blocking back, and kick returner. I literally carried the ball two and three times, which isn't enough to do anything."

Cassady was the starting left halfback as the Lions launched the 1956 season with a 20–16 road triumph over Green Bay. Layne, injured in the first half, came back to kick a field goal and scored on a sneak to provide the margin of victory. The Packers didn't get their initial first down until midway through the second period. Nonetheless, they kept the game close until a Bob Long interception snuffed out their last chance at a comeback.

The Lions followed up with a 31–14 blasting of the Colts. It was the last of the annual Saturday night games at Baltimore. Layne was in top form, flipping a pair of scoring passes and tallying himself on a bootleg as Detroit built a 21–7 lead at the half. Cassady enjoyed what turned out to be the most productive rushing day of his pro career with 92 yards. Detroit's ballhawks stole four passes, with Jimmy David accounting for three of the thefts.

The game marked the quarterbacking debut of Johnny Unitas, who replaced George Shaw on the Colts' final possession. The gangly rookie with the bowed legs and high-top cleats was playing semipro ball around Pittsburgh for six dollars a game when the Colts decided to gamble on him.

Against the Lions, Unitas took over on the Baltimore 15. His first pass was incomplete. He then took off running for a 21-yard gain, which made him the Colts' leading rusher that evening. His second and last pass was intercepted by David, who returned it to midfield. And that was that. It was an inauspicious beginning to the legendary career of "Johnny U," destined to join Layne and Otto Graham as the only quarterbacks to win back-to-back championships in the '50s.

The Lions next faced four straight games against the Rams and 49ers. For the first time, both West Coast clubs would finish the same season with losing records, helped along by the Lions, who beat each team twice. Detroit topped Los Angeles, 24–21, in the home opener on October 14, stockpiling a 17-point lead and then holding off a fourth-quarter Rams rally.

The Lions' so-called Space Ship Division made its first and only appearance that day. With Aldo Forte and Red Cochran making observations from their vantage point in the press box, Buster Ramsey relayed coded instructions via radio from the bench to No. 56 on the field.

"Couldn't help feeling a little funny every time Ramsey's voice came into my helmet," Joe Schmidt said afterward. "Caught myself looking around a couple of times to see what he was doing out on the field."

Technology was making inroads into the NFL. In the early stages of the 1956 season, several teams, led by rivals Cleveland and Detroit, rolled out an innovative messaging system that was a glimpse of the league's future. For the first time, selected players were "wired for sound"—outfitted with miniature radios that allowed them to receive signals from the bench or the press box.

Paul Brown had been fooling around for years with the idea of using radio signals to more efficiently send in plays. It wasn't until the 1956 preseason, in the second of back-to-back games with the Lions, that he finally field-tested the system against a real opponent. The helmets of quarterbacks George Ratterman and Vito "Babe" Parilli were each outfitted with a receiver about the size of a pocket watch. Brown, who had to obtain a shortwave license to operate the radio, used a four-watt transmitter and microphone to send plays from the bench.

There was no difference in the outcome. A week earlier, the defending champs had lost to Detroit, 17–0, without Brown's gizmo, and on this occasion they were whipped by the same 17-point margin, 31–14, with it.

"There is some speculation that quarterbacks Ratterman and Parilli might have picked up some short-wave police calls, some dance music, or an SOS from a stricken fishing boat off the coast of New Zealand," wrote a bemused Lyall Smith. Actually, Ratterman spent much of the stormy evening in Akron fearing for his life. In addition to the head-hunting Lions targeting the contraption in his helmet, there were the occasional flashes of lightning that threatened to fry his electronic ears.

Buddy Parker was more concerned than amused. With other teams also experimenting, he wasn't about to be left behind. He had Nick Kerbawy explore the cost of putting in a system at Briggs Stadium. The retail price came to $1,161.50, but Kerbawy was able to strike a deal with electronics expert Len Kieban for about $500. Prior to the home opener, the grounds crew installed 2,200 feet of wiring under the sod, criss-crossing nearly the entire playing area. The network allowed a wired helmet to pick up signals extending 30 feet beyond each sideline.

Of course, Bobby Layne wouldn't countenance any play-calling from the sidelines, electronic or otherwise. But Schmidt, the defensive captain, was receptive—literally. A button-sized receiver and an amplifier shaped like a cigarette lighter were fitted into his helmet. The unit weighed a combined four ounces and cost $79.50. "I'm for it solidly," he said. "We can always use a 12th man."

Parker was naturally pleased with the radio-assisted win over the Rams. Ramsey was grateful that, for once, he wasn't hoarse for two days from spending the entire game screaming out formations from the sideline. Afterward, Los Angeles officials complained about not being able to utilize their own gadgetry.

According to Bert Bell, "The Rams said they were told certain equipment was denied them, that they weren't cut into the wire. If the Lions wire the field, I think everyone is entitled to the use of that wire."

The Lions had three additional helmets outfitted, "in case Parker should elect to increase his Space Ship membership for future home games," wrote the *Detroit News*'s pseudonymous Buck Rogers. However, the shortwave revolution was short-lived. Four days later, with the unanimous backing of owners, Bell issued a directive: "All electronic devices, including walkie-talkies, hearing aids of any description used to receive messages, radio equipped helmets or any device of this nature must be eliminated." Although the ban was intended only for the balance of the '56 season, it stayed in place until 1994, when owners officially approved the league-wide use of helmet headsets.

The following Sunday, with Schmidt back to calling signals and pretending not to hear any shouted instructions he didn't agree with, the Lions downed San Francisco, 20–17. Don McIlhenny, who was growing tired of telling people he was not related to Hugh McElhenny, emulated the 49ers back by rushing for 104 yards and tallying his fifth touchdown in four games. However, it was a crucial roughing call on 49ers end Charley Powell that kept the final drive alive and enabled Layne to kick the decisive 17-yard field goal with 17 seconds left.

Lou Creekmur was the man who put the Lions in position to win. He and Powell had been going at each other all afternoon.

"Charley was provoked because just as he was ready to get by and get to Layne, I leg whipped him," Creekmur recalled. "I really used to be able to get those heels around. I'd hit the guy right in the shins. They thought they were gettin' by and all of a sudden they'd end up with their faces in the mud. And, oh man, you talk about gettin' people upset! So by the end of the game they'd really be so mad they'd be ready to fight.

"Well, if I timed it right and I did somethin' on one play, by the next play I knew the guy couldn't stand it any longer and he's gonna really try to take my head off. I'd just nonchalantly walk up to the official and say, 'Mr. Ref, watch Charley Powell, he's been sluggin' me all afternoon.' I'd go back up on the line and say somethin' just before the play. And it never failed—whoever it was would throw a big roundhouse. And here would come the flag and here would be 15 yards."

On this occasion, the frustrated Powell took a swing at Creekmur, who turned the other cheek so as to not draw an offsetting penalty. Moments later, Layne booted the ball through the uprights and the Lions had their fourth straight victory. Powell was disconsolate. "He cried like a baby," Creekmur said.

From there it was on to California for rematches with the Rams and 49ers. At halftime at Memorial Coliseum it was Bobby Layne 13, Los Angeles 0, as the quarterback accounted for all of Detroit's points with a pair of field goals, a short touchdown run, and a conversion. Later, Jim Martin booted a long field goal to make the final score 16–7. The Lions then visited San Francisco, where they bested the 49ers, 17–13.

The win at Kezar Stadium marked the first time Detroit had swept both of its West Coast rivals in the same season. It was as good a sign as any that this was a year of destiny for the Lions. At the halfway point of the season, they stood atop the Western Conference with a 6–0 record, one game ahead of the Bears, who had won five straight after dropping their opener. The teams were scheduled to meet twice in the final three weeks of the schedule. With the field of legitimate contenders narrowing to just Detroit and Chicago, it was becoming apparent that their December encounters would decide the conference winner.

Layne, assisted by regular cortisone shots in his right shoulder, was in the midst of a fine comeback year. Only Green Bay's Tobin Rote would complete more passes and throw for more yards in 1956. Layne would turn 30 in December. Pushed by talk of the younger, bigger Reichow being groomed as his replacement, the old pro "has played with the dash and determination of a college sophomore this season," Tommy Devine wrote in his midseason assessment in the *Free Press*.

Layne was once again running the ball, actually accounting for more touchdowns with his legs (four) than his arm (three) during the first half of the season. Pressed into taking over the placekicking duties after Doak Walker's retirement, Layne would wind up leading the NFL in scoring with 99 points. His range was limited—his longest field goal was only 30 yards—but from close in he was extremely reliable. He converted each extra-point try and was good on 12 of 15 field-goal attempts, an 80 percent success rate that was easily the best in the league. Martin continued to handle kickoffs and long-range field-goal tries.

"You can win a few games with a good quarterback," Parker said. "But to take a championship you must have the great one. Layne was the great one for us when we were taking titles; Sid Luckman was for the Bears when they were on top and Otto Graham during the long reign of the Browns. Layne looks this season like he did when he was steering us to championships."

As field general, Layne continued to dress down the troops as needed. "Bobby had an affinity for chewing your rear end out," Creekmur said. "If you ever missed a block, not only did you know about it, but all the other guys on the offensive team and everybody on the bench knew about it. On top of that, the 50,000 fans up in the stadium all knew about it, too, because he told you right then, out there in front of the whole crowd. And it was so embarrassing that we all made a pact that we would never miss a block that would ever disturb Bobby Layne."

These public humiliations didn't always go over well, with teammates once having to restrain Charlie Ane from going after Layne. During one game in 1956, Layne directed his ire at right guard Jim Salsbury for missing a block. The second-year lineman from UCLA wasn't in the mood for Layne's abuse. "You can't talk to me like that," he said.

Dorne Dibble, standing nearby, relished describing what Layne did next.

"Well, he called a timeout. And he proceeded to tell this guy—here he's looking up at a guy who weighed about 250 pounds—and he just reamed him upside down and crossways—every word you ever heard. And here we were just listening to him, and the crowd and the TV . . . and he just let him know who was boss and to never talk back to him again. Even though he always saved his timeouts, he thought it was worthwhile to call one then."

Salsbury, reportedly suffering from an unspecified injury, missed two starts and was replaced in the lineup by Stan Campbell. The following summer Salsbury was traded to Green Bay—a payback, Dibble believed, for his insubordination.

Layne always protested that stories of him chewing out players were over-blown. "I never yelled at a guy who dropped a pass or fumbled," he said. "Hell, he didn't drop it on purpose."

He wasn't nearly as forgiving about mental errors, however. A receiver running the wrong route or a lineman blowing an assignment was someone who was not doing his job. "When a guy isn't doing his job, you sometimes have to yell a little," he said. "Some guys I never raised my voice at all. It wouldn't work with guys like Walker, Hoernschemeyer, Sewell. Hell, you knew they were going to do their jobs. I used to yell at Creekmur, then one year I stopped. He went to Buddy and asked him to ask me to get after him again. He knew he needed it."

Detroit's balanced, ball-control offense was complemented by a stifling defense spearheaded by Joe Schmidt, who was playing his first season at middle line-backer. In camp the coaches had been impressed by Gil Mains's performance at the position, particularly his quickness and zest in chasing down plays. But it soon became apparent that Schmidt was the ideal man for the new 4–3 defense, which replaced the five-man line that Les Bingaman had once anchored with authority.

Schmidt had played the 4–3 in college and seemed a natural fit, his linebacking skills better suited to the inside than the outside. "I saw all the great middle linebackers of the 1950s," said defensive end Gene Cronin, who made the club as a rookie out of the College of the Pacific and played four seasons in Detroit. "I don't say this because Joe was my roommate, or my teammate, but I never saw a better middle linebacker. Never out of position. No mental mistakes. A leader on and off the field. Never a big head. Wasn't a yeller, wasn't a screamer. Just got the job done."

Schmidt had a size-18 neck and a nose for the ball. In 1955, he was the first defensive player ever to recover eight fumbles in a season. (The record has since been matched, though by players benefiting from expanded schedules.) His teammates voted him that year's President's Cup, an award he would win several more times over the coming seasons.

"Schmidt's was not the flamboyant cock-of-the-walk leadership that typified Bobby Layne's years with the Lions," George Plimpton observed in *Paper Lion*. "But the same competitiveness glowed in him. . . . Off the field he was calm, almost shy. His face was large and wide, with pale eyes, he had thin yellow-blond hair, and . . . his head seemed set immediately on his shoulders, like a stone Aztec head on a wall. Schmidt himself joked about it. He said he had been six feet three inches when he came to the Lions, with a fine neck, not swanlike, but evident enough, and during his playing years of diving and bulling his way through blockers his head had been driven down a few inches into his body, like a cartoon character bopped with a sledgehammer."

As the 4–3 became the standard defense around the league, Schmidt emerged as the game's most respected middle linebacker. Paul Hornung was just one of many contemporaries who considered him to be the best he ever played against.

"He was so quick and he was the surest tackler I've ever seen," Hornung said. "All linebackers are tough meeting you in the hole but when you give a linebacker four or five yards' daylight, you can usually get away from them. But not Schmidt. He put his eyes right on your belt buckle and he stayed with you. I can remember, we'd run a sweep to the right and here was Schmidt, making the tackle."

Schmidt liked to let opponents know that he had their number. "Come on, Horsey," he'd tease, as Alan Ameche settled into his stance in the Baltimore backfield. "Come on, Paul . . . come on, Paul," he'd say as the Green Bay back awaited the snap. "I could hear him waiting, just waiting, like a cat," Hornung said.

Buster Ramsey was pleased with his refortified unit. Yale Lary, back from the army, showed that he hadn't lost any of his old brilliance. He also assumed punting chores, developing into one of the league's best. Ray "Moose" Krouse, a 275-pound tackle acquired from the Giants, strengthened the defensive line. "He's the kind of guy we needed last year," said Aldo Forte. The Moose's acquisition allowed Darris McCord to move to the outside, where he significantly improved the Lions' pass rush. McCord found a permanent home at end, remaining there for the balance of his 13-year Lions career.

Playing alongside Krouse as one of the big guys in the middle was Bob Miller, a 6-foot-3, 250-pound standout from Virginia whose size-8 helmet, the largest on the team now that Les Bingaman had retired, could have doubled as a coal bucket. Miller, playing his fifth season, was a man who always knew his own mind, even as a rookie. Layne "loved to give the younger players a hard time," a teammate said. "He would make the younger players sing their school fight song or something dumb like that. Well, that never went over real big with Bob Miller. Layne could never get him to do what Bob didn't want to do anyway, and you could see it didn't go over real well with Layne. But that's just the way Bob is."

On a team filled with household names, the literally "unsung" Miller crashed pads in steady if unspectacular fashion. In a sense, he was the John Doe of the Lions' glory years. To this day, when his name is mentioned at all, it's often confused with that of Detroit Tigers bonus baby Bob Miller, who pitched four seasons at Briggs Stadium in the mid-1950s. In Schmidt's view, Miller was a very good football player who could have been great except for a bad back.

Bad back or not, Miller was a mainstay. He wound up playing seven seasons in Detroit, 1952 through 1958, and was one of only seven players to appear in each of the Lions' six postseason games during the decade. (The others were Jim Martin, Leon Hart, Jack Christiansen, Jim Doran, Lou Creekmur, and Jim David.) Never a Pro Bowler, Miller had a good enough season in 1956 to be named a first-team starter by *The Sporting News*.

On November 11, the unbeaten Lions visited the Redskins in Washington, a place where they had never won before. After Sam Baker kicked a field goal to make it an 8-point game with three minutes to go, Layne moved the team 80 yards in two plays. A 70-yard completion to Jim Doran was followed by a 10-yard scoring strike to Dave Middleton. But the 'Skins recovered the ensuing onside kick and ran out the clock. Washington won by an eyelash, 18–17, clearly outplaying Detroit in every department. "We had it coming," Parker said of his team's lethargic effort.

The loss dropped the Lions into a first-place tie with Chicago. The Bears continued to roll along, their top-ranked offense propelled by the pinpoint passes of Ed Brown and the bruising runs of fullback Rick Casares. George Halas had stepped aside as head coach, handing the reins to long-time assistant Paddy Driscoll, but few doubted that Papa Bear was still running the show.

The Lions resumed their winning ways with a 27–3 thumping of the Colts at Briggs Stadium. It was a testy affair. The Colts were penalized three times for roughing the passer and "Big Daddy" Lipscomb, a 6-foot-6 product of Detroit's Miller High School, was tossed by the referees for taking a swing at Jim Martin. Late in the game, Jack Christiansen was knocked cold with a perfectly timed elbow by guard Art Spinney.

Detroit was just as physical. The defense suffocated the Colts' potent running attack, holding rookie sensation Lenny Moore, who entered the game averaging a phenomenal 10.6 yards per carry, to – 14 yards on nine carries. The Lions blocked two field-goal attempts, picked off a couple of passes (both by Jimmy David, giving him five interceptions in two games against the Colts), and harassed John Unitas all afternoon. The rookie threw for 314 yards, the season high in the NFL, but couldn't penetrate the end zone. One of those yards came when a pass ricocheted off a charging Ray Krouse and into the surprised quarterback's hands. Unitas was credited with a reception on his own completion.

Schmidt made his presence known. "I went back to pass," Unitas later said, "and I was looking downfield for a receiver when all of a sudden this big guy slammed in on me and knocked the ball right out of my hand. I was lucky enough to recover it, but it was an awful shock. I hadn't even seen him coming. But I think the worst thing was when I picked myself up and he stood there and laughed at me and said, 'You ain't playing for the Bloomfield Rams now, Johnny.' Believe me, I'm not likely to forget it."

The lowly Packers, sporting a 2–6 record, made their annual Turkey Day pilgrimage. Snow covered Briggs Stadium. Detroit seemed in control with a 13–0 lead in the third quarter, but then the momentum shifted. In the fourth quarter Tobin Rote ran for a touchdown and threw for two more—the last a 13-yard strike to Billy Howton in the final minute—as he engineered a 24–20 upset. The loss dropped the Lions' record to 7–2. Three days later in New York, the Bears rallied from a two-touchdown deficit in the fourth quarter to tie the Giants, 17–17, thanks to a miraculous diving grab by Harlon Hill. With a record of 7-1-1, the Bears were now in first place, a half game ahead of the Lions, with the next game a head-to-head match at Briggs Stadium.

More than 57,000 people surged through the gates on December 2 to see the two Western rivals go at each other. Many were still finding their seats when, on the first play of the game, Layne fired a pass that J. C. Caroline snatched right out of the hands of Dave Middleton. The interception was just the first of six turnovers the two teams would combine for in the wild opening quarter.

The game's first points came in the second quarter on Gene Gedman's 1-yard run. By now Gedman had emerged as the Lions' most productive back. After a fast start, Don McIlhenny was hobbled by injuries and missed several games. Cassady, who never was required to catch passes at Ohio State, was still learning that part of the game and didn't score a touchdown all season. Gedman, a solid 195-pounder with enough power and speed to be equally effective on plunges, slants, and sweeps, had the best year of his career in 1956. He rushed for 479 yards and scored eight touchdowns, both team highs.

Later in the quarter, Layne scored, galloping 15 yards untouched through the middle of the Chicago defense on a trap play. It was 14–10, Detroit, at the half. The narrow margin was misleading, however, as the Lions overpowered the Bears on both sides of the scrimmage line. The home team pulled away in the second half, scoring 28 unanswered points as Gedman snagged a TD pass from Layne and Middleton fielded scoring strikes from Layne and Harry Gilmer.

All told, the Lions rolled up 468 yards and 25 first downs. Meanwhile, the Bears' offense, by far the highest-scoring unit in the NFL, was held to just 184 yards and one touchdown, and that came as the result of a questionable pass interference call. Chris's Crew limited Harlon Hill, the league's most explosive receiver, to a single catch.

After the 42–10 romp was over, a drained but happy Parker slumped inside his tiny coach's office, pulling on his ever-present cigarette. "This was like a championship game to us," he drawled, "and the boys couldn't have worked it better."

Inside the visitors' locker room, the Bears were still trying to process what had happened. "They roughed us and we didn't rough back," an assistant said. "I never saw that happen before. Out-rough the Bears? Never." The fact that George Halas was on the sidelines for the first time since the previous season made the display even more embarrassing.

With two games left, Detroit could win the division outright the following Sunday if they beat Pittsburgh and the Bears lost to the Cardinals. The Lions did their part, knocking the Steelers all over the Briggs Stadium turf. Layne started the deluge of points with a 16-yard touchdown pitch to Leon Hart. Later he kicked his 12th field goal, setting a new Lions season record. The score was 38–7 at the half. Jerry Reichow, whose playing time usually was limited to special teams, unlimbered his dormant right arm with a half-dozen passes and also caught a touchdown pitch from Gilmer during the 45–7 rout.

Meanwhile, in a bruising contest played in near-zero temperatures in Chicago, the Bears "out-roughed" the crosstown Cardinals, 10–3, to keep Detroit from clinching the division. That set up the winner-take-all showdown at Wrigley Field. "Tell 'em to keep their guard up," Cardinals end and ex-Lion Pat Summerall advised a Detroit reporter, "and be ready for a slugfest."

The scenario resembled that of exactly five years ago. As in 1951 against the 49ers, the Lions needed a win or a tie in the finale to advance to the title game. Once again, the game was being played on December 16, Parker's birthday.

In the days leading up to it, there was a lot of loose talk coming out of Chicago about "getting Layne," however one wanted to define "getting." Did it simply mean doing a better job of pressuring Layne in hopes of disrupting an offense that had just produced a dozen touchdowns in its last two outings? Or did it indicate something more sinister was afoot?

On Saturday, the Lions took the train to Chicago and checked into the Edgewater Beach Hotel. That evening, Layne uncharacteristically became ill. Parker thought somebody had spiked the star's food or drink. "We all ate together and stayed together the night before the game, and Layne was the only guy who got sick," he said. "He vomited all night. What are you going to think? Somebody at the hotel must have slipped something to him. Layne's never been sick in his life."

Rumors flew that the quarterback actually had been out drinking, possibly at a Bears alumni party held that evening at the Edgewater.

Not so, said Dorne Dibble. "I was with Bobby Saturday night before that game. Everybody says he was out late that night, but I was with him and I don't go out on Saturday nights before a game. We might go out and have a couple of beers or something. But about 9 o'clock, he told me, 'I really feel rotten, let's go back to the hotel.' And he went back to his room and threw up. He had the flu and really was sick. So it was obvious he wasn't going to be sharp the next day anyway."

On game day, Wrigley Field was packed, noisy, and ready for a rumble.

Chicago fans hung banners—"Kill Lions," "We Want Lion Blood"—and booed so lustily that the Lions couldn't hear Layne's signals. Partisans finally took it down a notch when the refs threatened to penalize the home team for delay of game. The showdown was being televised on 120 stations from coast to coast, almost unprecedented coverage for a regular-season game.

The Bears registered the first points on a George Blanda field goal in the opening quarter. It was still 3–0 when Layne walked up behind center a couple of minutes into the second period. The Lions had crossed midfield and were driving. So far, Layne had completed four of seven throws for minimal yardage. He was just getting warmed up on a gloomy, blustery 28-degree day.

The call was for a sweep to the left. Layne took the snap from Charlie Ane, pitched the ball to Gene Gedman, then relaxed as he watched the play unfold. He was standing there, hands dangling at his side, when Bears end Ed Meadows came crashing into him from behind and drove him into the cement-like turf.

"I really don't know what happened," Layne said later. "My back was turned . . . I didn't know anyone was coming . . . and then the lights went out."

Layne was knocked out cold. He was carried off the field and into the locker room, where he was diagnosed with a concussion. No flag was thrown on the play. The referee had been looking downfield at Gedman and missed the hit.

Gilmer came in and piloted the Lions to the go-ahead touchdown, with Bill Bowman gathering in a short pass and bulling his way into the end zone. Jim Martin booted the point-after to put the Lions ahead, 7–3. During the drive, Lou Creekmur switched positions with right tackle Ollie Spencer so he could get in his licks at Meadows.

"I broke his nose and his jaw, gave him two black eyes, the whole works," Creekmur claimed. A few plays after kayoing Layne, Meadows was ejected for kicking at Creekmur and then slugging Bowman as he tried to intervene.

Gilmer did a creditable job in relief, directing the Lions to three touchdowns in what turned out to be his final pro game. It wasn't nearly enough. The Detroit defense, which had performed superbly all season, simply couldn't stop Chicago's backs, who surprised the Lions by running wide all afternoon. Rick Casares, wrapping up the rushing title, ripped through them for 190 yards on 17 carries. On the Bears' first possession after Bowman's score, Casares sprinted around left end and down the sideline for a 68-yard touchdown to give Chicago a lead it never relinquished. Later, J. C. Caroline took a pitchout and tallied from nine yards out to make it 17–7 at intermission.

The Lions crept back to within three points, 17–14, early in the second half, when Leon Hart scored on a short plunge following a Yale Lary interception. But the charged-up Bears scored the next three touchdowns to blow open the game. Fans serenaded Parker: "Happy birthday, dear Buddy." With the outcome no longer in doubt, brawls broke out in the freezing dusk as players began settling scores.

"Knees, elbows and fists flew in all corners of the field," Bob Latshaw reported. "The crowd was on the field three times when players got into fights late in the game." Gil Mains was ejected for taking on what appeared to be half the Bears' team. "I was mad at all of 'em," he said in the locker room, his swollen right hand slathered with ointment. At one point the game was halted for six minutes to disentangle the combatants. "The excitement was running so high no one was sure just which battlers were thumbed out by the officials," Latshaw continued. "Players, fans and police were involved in the melee and at the close of the game hundreds of onlookers swarmed on the field to fight each other and tear down the goal posts."

The final score was Chicago 38, Detroit 21. The Lions had held the lead for all of three plays. Parker and his squad admitted they had been outplayed but insisted the results would have been different if Layne hadn't been deliberately targeted.

"You can't tell me they didn't think: 'Well, if we get him we won't have to worry,'" Dibble said. "And there was just an awful letdown. We felt like we'd lost our leader, and there was no one to tell us what to do."

Meadows gave his version of the incident. "I thought Bobby still had the ball," he said. "You know he stands still after he pitches out and there's no way to tell that he still doesn't have the ball. I hit him and his head hit the ground and that's how he got hurt."

As the Windy City celebrated, Layne spent the night in a hospital bed, unable to remember exactly what happened. Parker decried the Bears' "blackjack tactics" and said it fit a pattern of unsportsmanlike conduct by Halas and dirty play by Meadows. Not for the first or last time in his coaching career, Buddy threatened to quit. Edwin Anderson immediately fired off an impassioned three-page letter to Bert Bell, saying Layne was "deliberately slugged" and calling for the commissioner to throw Meadows out of the league.

Bell was appalled by the rush to judgment. "This is still America and a man still is innocent until he is proved guilty," he declared. "The Lions have no right to crucify this kid, no right to talk of banishing him from the game, unless they have real proof that he was guilty of an illegal act."

Game film showed that Meadows hadn't actually slugged Layne but that he had taken six full steps after Layne got rid of the ball before hitting him. It was a clear case of unnecessary roughness—grounds for a 15-yard penalty, possibly an ejection, but certainly not a permanent ban. Referee Ron Gibbs, who missed the call, described it as a "stiff, hard tackle, but this was professional football and Layne probably has been hit that hard many times before."

As words flew between Detroit and Chicago, other precincts were heard from. Washington's Norb Hecker claimed that when he had been with Los Angeles, the Rams had a pool of money awarded to the player who took out the other team's quarterback, including Layne, an allegation the team vigorously denied. Cardinals assistant coach Charlie Trippi, whose face had to be rebuilt after a vicious hit by John Henry Johnson the previous season, defended Parker, saying that Meadows had tried to do the same to the Cards' quarterback the week before.

After a brief investigation, Bell cleared Meadows and George Halas of any conspiracy to deliberately hurt Layne. Even some Detroit commentators accused Anderson and Parker of being whiners and sore losers. The Bears had outplayed them, Layne still had all of his marbles, and that's all there really was to it, they said.

Meanwhile, Meadows continued down the path of mediocrity. During his six years as an NFL journeyman, he played for four different teams (including two separate stints with the Bears) and wore five different uniform numbers before ending his career with a handful of games in Canada. He was the co-owner of a North Carolina tire store and estranged from his wife when he committed suicide one day in 1974. It was a shabby end for one of the league's top villains of the 1950s.

Meadows's "mugging" of Layne shined an uncomfortable spotlight on the violence in pro football, a subject that was popping up with greater frequency now that television was bringing the game into more homes with every passing week. Although in this particular instance a Lion had been on the receiving end of a questionable hit, Parker's crew had its own unsavory reputation to contend with. "The Lions have two of the biggest thugs, including the dirtiest player in the league," Tom Fears charged in the days following the Meadows incident. "Buddy Parker should clean up his own backyard. Gil Mains is the dirtiest player in the league and Jimmy David is notoriously dirty. The same situation held when Parker was with the Chicago Cardinals."

Decades later, the Lions' reputation for malice was still hard to shake. "The team that I really had problems with was the Detroit Lions," recalled halfback Eddie Macon, who broke in with the Bears in 1952. "They beat me in the face, twisted my legs. When I got in a pile, I tried to come out of that pile because I knew what they were going to try to do." Dom Moselle lined up several times against Detroit while playing for three different teams in the '50s. "When I was with Green Bay, I caught a touchdown pass against them on Thanksgiving Day," he said. "But then I got wiped out on an illegal block on the kickoff and missed the entire second half. They were tough."

Parker was unapologetic about his team's style of play. "We play rough and we teach rough," he said. "And when I say rough I don't mean poking a guy in the eye. I mean gang tackling—right close to piling on." Detroit topped the league in penalty yardage in 1956 and was runner-up in 1952 and 1957. Don McIlhenny defended his teammates' spirited play. "Our boys get enthusiastic, I know. I mean just enthusiastic, good, hard, rough football."

Defensive tackle Dick Modzelewski had several "enthusiastic" encounters with the Lions while a member of the Redskins, Steelers, and Giants. When he started in the league in 1953, he recalled, "all the older guys came up to you and showed you ways to play dirty." The repertoire included a discrete kick or punch away from the play, even an occasional bite in a pileup. "I can remember picking up a handful of snow, or mud, and throwing it in the receiver's eyes," said Jack Christiansen. "They'd holler and bitch, but we'd get away with it."

"It was always a rough, tough battle, all stops were out," Lou Groza said of the typical Browns-Lions meeting. "I remember once I was in a huddle, waiting for the next play to be called. One of their players came off the defensive line and stomped down on my kicking foot."

The foot-stomping felon was Mains, who was schooled by Bob Dove in how to use his cleats to maximum effect. During a 1954 game at Kezar Stadium, Mains zeroed in on an old Lions nemesis, Hardy Brown, nailing him feet-first as he broke up the wedge on a kickoff return. According to *Time*, when Brown was carted off the field, "his groin ripped open by a set of slashing cleats," an observer in the press box was moved to write: "Pro football is getting like atomic war. There are no winners, only survivors."

War, indeed. Pro football showcased all the attributes that a nation filled with millions of citizen soldiers had come to expect in its heroes—toughness, tenacity, sacrifice, brotherhood, courage—but with a brutality that was codified and stopped short of actually killing someone. The sport played at full tilt was fascinating theater, whether watched from the stands or from an easy chair. The emerging lingo was filled with martial references. The gridiron was a battlefield where linebackers blitzed, linemen fought in the trenches, and injured players were casualties. Quarterbacks were field generals who launched aerial attacks, directed ground assaults, and threw the bomb. Overheated commentators called pro football "the hundred-yard war." Some observers saw it all as a natural by-product of the national experience in World War II, when more than 16 million Americans served in uniform and everybody knew of someone—a neighbor, friend, son, brother, uncle, or spouse—who didn't return.

Joe Schmidt, for example, had an older brother, William, who was a platoon commander in the 712th Tank Battalion. The 22-year-old sergeant was killed on his first day of combat, shot through the head by a sniper during the fighting around St. Lô. Too young to enlist, the sturdy teenager soaked up stories of the war from the returning veterans with whom he played on the local VFW-sponsored sandlot team. "We used to ride to the games on buses," Schmidt said, "and they would be talking and I was all ears, growing up just listening to them."

Schmidt's counterpart on the Browns, middle linebacker Walt Michaels, had four older brothers in action, including one lost at Guadalcanal. "I'll never forget when the telegram came: 'Killed in action,'" Michaels said.

"A lot of us grew up in the war, especially those of us who went in when we were eighteen or nineteen," said Philadelphia tackle Mike Jarmoluk, who was in the middle of many a skirmish between the Eagles and Lions in the '50s. "Big Mike" twice was nearly a Lion, having been originally drafted by the club and then reacquired a few years later; each time he was traded before he had a chance to play for Detroit. Prior to all that, Jarmoluk was a young GI caught up in the horror of the Battle of the Bulge. "It made you realize what death really was, and when I got back I was a lot tougher."

Many of the men who played for the Lions in the 1950s, principally in the first half of the decade, were veterans of "the good war," as Studs Terkel famously labeled it. Some had been stationed stateside, typically playing service ball in addition to their regular military duties. Others dodged death in the Pacific and Europe.

Northwestern linebacker Art Murakowski, the first player signed by Buddy Parker upon becoming head coach, was a fireman on a destroyer during the battle of Okinawa. The ship was hit by a kamikaze, killing 19 sailors and leaving Murakowski with survivor's guilt. "I felt a little funny," he said. "I was below handling five-inch ammunition." Howard Brown, who captained Bo McMillan's Indiana squad before playing three seasons at guard for McMillan's Lions, was wounded twice while serving in the infantry. "Jungle Jim" Martin earned his nickname—and a Bronze Star—by swimming through floating mines off Tinian in a dangerous pre-invasion reconnaissance mission. Gus Cifelli, also a Marine, was seriously wounded while serving as a teenaged gunner on the aircraft carrier USS *Intrepid*. Jack Simmons, who centered the ball in Layne's first season in Detroit, earned his Purple Heart as a sailor in Europe. Bill Swiacki survived flak and the Luftwaffe during 30 missions as a navigator on a B-17 "Flying Fortress." As a Marine stationed aboard the USS *Missouri*, Don Doll witnessed the Japanese formally surrender to General MacArthur, ending a war that had murdered upwards of 70 million people. The ungraspable toll included Fred Enke's best friend from childhood, killed in Europe. Enke, who quit college to enlist in the navy during the war, kept the young GI's memory alive at home with a framed photograph of the two as youngsters.

Some sportswriters of the era, who not only reported on professional football but were in effect selling it to the public, owed their cynical worldview to their wartime experiences. Doc Greene's legs were raked by machine gun fire while serving as a Marine lieutenant on Okinawa. Cal Whorton of the *Los Angeles Times* was haunted by the carnage he witnessed commanding a PT boat during the Normandy invasion. One of Whorton's press-box contemporaries, Jack Singer, died in a bombing raid over Germany.

"When was the last time you saw a dead body?" Philadelphia's Bucko Kilroy rhetorically asked an interviewer in retirement. "Most of us never saw one before we got in that war, and then we saw so much, so much of that stink and rot, that when we came back to play football, we play like terrors. We were tough. Everybody used to say, 'What outfit was he in?' That was what you asked a guy, not what school he went to. You'd see somebody really getting into something on the field. 'What outfit was he in?' 'He was a Marine.' 'Ohhhhhhh.' 'Guadalcanal.' 'Ohhhhhhh.' You'd just shake your head."

Contributing to pro football's soiled image were the rules, which were far less restrictive than they are today. Nothing prevented a defender from head-slapping an opposing lineman and then yanking the ball carrier by his face mask to the ground. "Forearms, clotheslines, blind-blocking, it was all part of the game," Jarmoluk said. "It looked to the fans and some of the media like a lousy shot. Not so. It was perfectly legal." There was no specific prohibition against flying kicks like the kind Mains delivered with devastating effect on arch enemies Hardy Brown and the Rams' Les Richter. Instead, it took a personal phone call from Bert Bell before Wild Hoss finally stopped his wild leaps. Quarterbacks were not coddled. "We're not trying to hurt anybody," Bob Miller insisted, "but it's no secret that star pro passers are a bad insurance risk. They get hit even after they get rid of the ball."

The programs that sold for a quarter at Briggs Stadium reflected the game's rather casual barbarity. Nick Kerbawy, not content to recycle the stock illustrations that many teams used, commissioned original art for the cover of each issue of *Lion Gridiron News* (as the publication was called). The gag drawings featured a mischievous cartoon lion whose antics included chasing a Redskin with a tomahawk, bayoneting a New York Yank, branding a 49er with a red-hot iron, and pouring a vat of molten steel on a Steeler. Other opponents were clubbed, sheared, scalped, blown up, or boiled in water. The illustrations were the work of Detroit commercial artist Ted Petok, and many of them would be considered politically incorrect today. But pro football continued to flourish, either despite or because of its uncivilized state.

The NFL's "dead ball" rule was responsible for a good deal of the savagery. Until 1955, a runner was not considered down and the play over until his forward progress was completely stopped. This meant a ball carrier could be knocked off his feet, but as long as he wasn't firmly in the grasp of a defender, he could bounce up or wiggle free and continue his run. (In college, a runner was considered down by contact once his knee touched the ground.) This led to piling on and a flurry of cheap shots. "You'd be down at the bottom of the pile," said Joe Perry, "and this guy is grabbing your crotch and this other guy is trying to twist your leg into a pretzel, just dirty stuff that was done with the sole intent of injuring you." Even going into a "turtle" position didn't ensure survival. As Schmidt recalled, "Everybody waited around for the son of a bitch to so much as raise his head," at which point the real pounding began. "During the 1950s," said Art Donovan, "you used to see guys clawing for that extra yard with tacklers sitting on top of them trying to smash in their skull."

The NFL finally took action after Hugh McElhenny suffered a season-ending injury in a pileup in 1954. The loss of one of the league's most marketable stars caused owners to enact a new rule the following season. Henceforth, "If a player touches the ground with any part of his body, except his hands or feet, while in the grasp of an opponent and irrespective of the grasp being broken, the ball is declared dead immediately." The rule change had a civilizing effect. It eliminated the piling on and close-quarter combat that accounted for most unnecessary injuries, though the cheap shots and paybacks didn't completely go away.

The adoption of another rule intended to protect players, the mandatory wearing of face masks, was a mixed bag. The number of facial injuries plummeted, but players, less fearful of injury, became more aggressive.

"If you go back and look at the old films," Schmidt said, "you don't see guys hunched down like they do today. They used to keep their heads up to protect their faces. The hits weren't so severe because we used our shoulders more." Leon Hart considered it "a cleaner game without masks. Before that your face was vulnerable. Players started using their helmet as a weapon."

While the single-bar (and later double-bar) helmet was favored by players in the skill positions, linemen favored bolting more fearsome looking "cages" and "cowcatchers" onto their headgear. "With those gadgets on, it's possible not only to butt an opponent into unconsciousness, but he can be ripped to bits while he's having his brains scrambled," said one veteran getting fitted for his first mask in 1955. "Now we not only have fists, knees, feet, elbows and a head to butt with, but we've been given a set of brass knuckles to wear on our faces."

Masked or unmasked, most players of the era didn't consider pro football dirty, merely rough, which was not the same thing. They reasoned that many cheap shots were meant to intimidate a player, not necessarily hurt him. It was a way to throw a man off his game, especially if he was having a good day. The controlled violence was the core of the sport's appeal. If the Great Depression and World War II had taught Americans of the "Greatest Generation" anything, it was that life was harsh and one needed to be tough in order to survive. "If you're scared, you have no business in the game," Doak Walker said defiantly. "It has to be rough, and that's the way we want it."

That sentiment was shared by the game's ever-growing number of acolytes. By 1955, the NFL was averaging 35,026 paid admissions per game, an increase of 10,000 in just five years, and attendance would continue to climb. That year, *Sports Illustrated* declared that pro football's coming of age as a major spectator sport "has reached the stage where the passions of its fans . . . seem to reach an ardor equitable only in terms of warfare."

Almost lost in all of the commotion surrounding the Meadows incident was the fact that the Lions had accomplished one of the biggest turnarounds in NFL history, flipping their 3–9 record to 9–3. Parker received the Coach of the Year Award from the Associated Press and a new two-year contract at a reported $30,000 a year, the first multiyear pact approved by club directors since being burned by Bo McMillan's deal.

In the 1956 championship game at Yankee Stadium, the Bears were crushed by the Giants, 47–7, causing the Lions and their followers considerable angst over what might have been. Nobody doubted that a Detroit-New York title game would have been more competitive. Under Parker, the Lions routinely beat the Giants, winning six of seven regular-season and preseason meetings.

While getting stomped by the Bears in the finale was tough to swallow, it was perhaps even harder to choke down the uninspired one-point loss at Washington and the fourth-quarter collapse against Green Bay. A victory in either of those games would have made the regular-season windup meaningless. "Those two games cost us, 'cause they were dog teams," Layne said.

In any discussion of Layne, a stock phrase invariably pops up, a piece of affectionate hyperbole apparently first uttered by Doak Walker sometime in the 1950s. "Bobby never lost a game in his life," the Doaker said. "Time just ran out on him."

After a decade in the NFL, Layne was an authentic folk hero, his performance in 1956 earning him a Pro Bowl invitation, the team's MVP award, and First Team All-Pro honors. Despite the accolades, it was a legitimate question as to just how many passes the two-minute guy of lore had left in his bum right shoulder.

Parker was impressed by Tobin Rote's recent heroics against his club—the last-second spirals that won the 1955 season opener and the '56 Thanksgiving Day game. Parker always praised Layne as the toughest and most competitive quarterback he ever saw. However, that didn't stop him and his top aide, George Wilson, from musing about what it would be like to have someone with Rote's size, grit, experience, and untroubled pitching arm warming up on the Detroit sideline. Just in case.

CHAPTER

10

Pro Bowls
AND ARMY *Legs*

I think the Pro Bowl changed the temper of the game some.
Those were the days when they first started the Pro Bowl
and you were getting to know the other players. Some of the
hostility—the ugliness—went out of it. You couldn't hate a
guy after you got loaded with him.

—**Jack Christiansen**

Ed Meadows's controversial hit on Bobby Layne was still fresh in everybody's minds when Rick Casares checked into the Ambassador Hotel in Los Angeles the Monday prior to the 1957 Pro Bowl. Any apprehension the Chicago fullback may have had about meeting some of the Lions he had tangled with just a month earlier dissipated when Layne, spotting him in the lobby, invited him up to the conference room for a neighborly drink.

Casares arrived to find Layne and several other members of Detroit's Pro Bowl contingent standing around a punch bowl, ladling a creamy-looking concoction into cups.

"What the hell is that?" Casares asked.

"Brandy and milk," Layne said.

"It about gagged me," Casares recalled. "Christ, we got half pie-eyed before I got to my room."

The Pro Bowl, a staple of the NFL postseason for seven decades, has a well-deserved reputation as a weeklong party rudely interrupted by a football game. "I remember the first Pro Bowl game I ever went to, after the '53 season," Art Donovan said. Layne and Doak Walker hosted "a monster party in one of the suites" that "degenerated into an all-night drinking contest. Over in one corner of the suite there were about half a dozen guys just throwing up on the carpet."

Donovan recalled another rambunctious Pro Bowl later in the '50s. One evening, he watched Giants quarterback Charlie Conerly drunkenly dump a mug of beer over Lou Creekmur's head. Moving on to another party, he then saw a jitterbugging 49ers lineman rip the door off a young lady's Volkswagen. Yes, things could sometimes get out of hand. Joe Schmidt spent one night partying with Layne and Jimmy David and somehow wound up on a club stage singing a duet with Buddy Greco.

Despite the off-field rowdiness, the Pro Bowl served a larger purpose as the NFL looked for ways to promote its stars to a wider audience in the postwar era. The league had previously held a postseason Pro All-Star Game between the defending league champion and a squad of players from other teams. The series, which ran from 1939 through 1942 (and which often was confused with the annual College All-Star Game in Chicago), was suspended during World War II because of travel restrictions.

At a league meeting in June 1950, Bert Bell convinced owners to revive the game, only in a different format. This time the contest—rechristened the Pro Bowl—would have outstanding players from the American and National conferences lining up against each other. The game, sponsored by the Los Angeles Publishers Association, would be played each January at 100,000-seat Memorial Coliseum in Los Angeles, a venue that remained unchanged through 1972. The squads were coached by the head coaches of the division-winning teams, though over the years the coach of the second-place team occasionally filled in.

Unlike today, very few players blew off the game. Most NFL teams in the 1950s were located in cold-weather cities. After months of toiling in often freezing, muddy, and snowy conditions, a few days in balmy California was just the tonic for a battered gridder. Beyond that was the personal pride one felt in being officially and publicly recognized for season-long excellence. "In those more innocent times," said Cleveland's Don Paul, "maybe we were naive, but those of us chosen to play in the Pro Bowl considered it an honor. Money wasn't a consideration, which probably was just as well."

In addition to having travel expenses covered, each player on the winning squad received $600 (a figure bumped to $700 later in the decade) while players on the losing side got $500 apiece. The head coaches received $1,000 each. Win or lose, the merrymaking that took place inside hotel rooms, at celebrity get-togethers, and at such places as the Bull n' Bush, the Brown Derby, and the Coconut Grove often ate up most, if not all, of a player's check.

The first Pro Bowl was played on Sunday, January 14, 1951, featuring "the most fabulous array of football talent ever gathered together," Frank Finch reported in that day's *Los Angeles Times*. The 31-man squads were determined by a poll of NFL coaches and Los Angeles sportswriters. Five Lions buckled their chinstraps for the inaugural game: Creekmur, Walker, Don Doll, Thurman McGraw, and Cloyce Box. Along with other all-stars from the National Conference, they were outfitted in red uniforms. Players from the American Conference wore blue.

There was a Hollywood vibe, with the pregame and halftime festivities "studded by a long list of motion-picture stars, radio and TV personalities and cowboy celebrities." Otto Graham, who left his pregnant wife back in Cleveland to hobnob with the likes of Jane Russell and Dinah Shore, scored the last two touchdowns of the game to rally the Americans to a 28–27 victory over the Nationals before 53,676 fans.

Beginning with the 1953 game, the opposing squads were renamed the West (National) and East (American), reflecting conference name changes. As one of the dominant teams in the league, Detroit naturally was well-represented on each year's Pro Bowl roster, with 21 different Lions appearing at least once during the decade and 13 of them playing in multiple games. Creekmur played in the first eight Pro Bowls, a record matched only by Emlen Tunnell of the New York Giants. Creekmur would have participated in an unprecedented ninth straight following the 1958 season, but his boss at the trucking firm he worked at wouldn't give him the time off.

Doll played in the first three, winning the George Halas Trophy as Most Valuable Player in 1953, when the West squad, coached by Buddy Parker, routed Paul Brown's East stars. According to a *Sporting News* correspondent, "The Lion ballhawk intercepted one of Otto Graham's passes, staved off a sure touchdown by bringing down Horace Gillom from behind on the 11-yard line, and generally made a nuisance of himself throughout the game." Pat Harder contributed a pair of field goals and three conversions in the 27–7 thumping. Doll gave no thought to being named the game's MVP, leaving the locker room before he could be officially presented the trophy. "He was dressed," recalled his wife, Diana, "and we were walking up the causeway. They came running up to him and handed it to him, very unceremoniously. He accepted it and went home."

Other noteworthy individual performances by Detroit participants included Jack Christiansen returning the opening kickoff of the 1956 game a record 103 yards for a touchdown, and two interceptions apiece by Joe Schmidt in 1956, Christiansen in 1957, and Yale Lary in 1958 and again in 1959.

It took a while for the Pro Bowl to catch on with the public. The inaugural game wasn't televised, and the first few broadcasts—by NBC in 1952 and 1953 and DuMont in 1954—were seen in a limited number of markets, including Detroit. Reflecting the NFL's wobbly status among advertisers, NBC demanded the game be shifted to Saturday because the network had "other commitments on Sunday afternoon."

Because of a lack of sponsors, the Pro Bowl wasn't televised again until 1958, when NBC broadcast it to the entire country for the first time. A familiar voice, Van Patrick, was at the microphone. Attendance followed a similar growth pattern. Only 19,400 turned out in a driving rainstorm in 1952. Most other years, the game drew crowds in the 40,000 range. By the end of the decade, however, the Pro Bowl was an established showcase capable of holding the interest of 70,000 paying fans and a national TV audience.

During this period the Pro Bowl faced some competition from the Hula Bowl, a game played each January since 1947 between the Hawaii All-Stars and a squad of collegiate players from the mainland. In 1951, Hula Bowl organizers began inviting selected top pros to Honolulu to join the Hawaii All-Stars as "guest players" in an attempt to boost attendance and make the game more competitive. Layne, Walker, Leon Hart, Howard Cassady, and Tobin Rote were among the league's stars who played in the Hula Bowl in the 1950s. By 1957, participants were receiving $700 from the game's sponsors.

The Hula Bowl was played the week before the Pro Bowl. Some players invited to both affairs either were late in reporting for the Pro Bowl or skipped the game altogether, incurring Bert Bell's wrath. The standard NFL contract had language in it that required a player to participate in the Pro Bowl if selected, a clause that went unenforced through most of the decade.

Bell put his foot down in 1959. "A lot of ballplayers want to play in the Pro Bowl game because the money means a lot to them," he said. "But the rich players want to go to the Hula game. They can take their wives with them and it's like a vacation. Ballplayers expect the owners to live up to the contracts, so they should do the same."

At that year's league meeting, owners unanimously approved a measure that specifically banned players from participating in games not authorized by the NFL. The flow of pro gridders to Honolulu stopped, but not before an aloha performance by Layne (now playing with Pittsburgh), who threw five touchdown passes in the 1960 Hula Bowl.

The Pro Bowl helped change the NFL in small, unplanned ways. Players from opposing teams got together under more relaxed circumstances and privately compared salaries and working conditions. Pat Summerall recalled: "The owners always said to us, 'Don't discuss your contract with members of the other teams,' but it was inevitable that we would get around to talking about what the disparity was between the payment for a defensive back on a team such as the Eagles, say, and the Giants. It would often come up while we were all in the bars together, waiting for a meeting to get started, or during a quiet moment in practice: 'How long have you been playing? What are you getting paid?'"

Such informal discussions indirectly helped lead to the formation of the Players Association. It probably was no coincidence that the players most involved in organizing the union were perennial Pro Bowlers. In many respects, said Summerall, "it was like a union meeting disguised as a Pro Bowl."

Some suggested the fraternizing also contributed to a drop in the level of on-field violence. Indeed, from the beginning many purists criticized the buddy-buddy nature of the Pro Bowl. "That wasn't a football game the All-Pros played in Los Angeles Coliseum over the weekend," Shirley Povich scoffed in the *Washington Post* after the "polite" 1953 contest featured unhurried quarterbacks unleashing an avalanche of passes. "It was volleyball in cleats. . . . This was a chance for the boys to pick up a few hundred extra bucks at the end of the league season, and none were in a mood to die for the dear old All-Pro Bowl."

When the West squad lost the following January, Lyall Smith wrote in the *Detroit Free Press*: "If Coach Buddy Parker's All-Stars had spent as much time blocking and knocking down their opponents Sunday as they did picking them up and brushing them off, the score might have been different. Professional football's hard-won popularity didn't come because rival players patted each other on the back during a game. If NFL moguls hope to make the Pro Bowl a true picture of the best in professional football and use it to sell more fans on the pro game, the least they can do is ask the players to act like they are in a regular contest."

Smith need not have fretted. Come the following autumn, when the games once again counted in the standings, camaraderie took a back seat to competitiveness. Christiansen spent one Pro Bowl week hitting the nightspots with his new buddy, Billy Howton. A few months later, in the first Lions-Packers game of the season, the Green Bay end was running a pattern across the middle of the field when Christiansen leveled him with a punishing hit.

As Howton lay on the grass, trying to catch his wind, he looked up and gasped, "Hey, I thought we were friends."

"If you can't deck your friends," Christiansen responded, "who the hell can you deck?"

While players in the '50s looked forward to receiving a Pro Bowl invitation, they dreaded getting another kind of summons—this one a letter from President Truman or Eisenhower beginning with the life-altering salutation: "Greeting: You are hereby ordered for induction into the Armed Forces of the United States."

In midcentury America, the military draft was a fact of life for millions of young men. Even such household names as Willie Mays and Elvis Presley were required to put their well-paying careers on hold for a couple of years as they served their Uncle Sam for a few dollars a month. In all, more than 2.6 million men were inducted into the military during the decade, half of them in the peak years of 1951–53, when the United States was involved in a bloody "police action" on the Korean peninsula.

The deferments later made available to the Vietnam generation were unavailable to most men. In 1954, for example, the Lions lost three starters from their championship team—Ollie Spencer, Yale Lary, and Gene Gedman—as well as several draft choices to the military, a manpower loss that put a crimp in the team's bid to win a third straight NFL title. Coaches had no choice but to work around such disruptions, treating a player's absence as if it were a season-ending injury.

The first NFL player conscripted during the Korean conflict was Wally Triplett, who unhappily saw the army put the brakes on what was shaping up to be a breakout season with the Lions. On October 29, 1950, the second-year halfback hauled back four kickoffs for 294 yards, including a 97-yard touchdown, during Detroit's 65–24 blowout loss at Los Angeles. His return yardage, his 73.50 average per return, and his 331 total yards (rushing, receiving, and returns) were all new single-game NFL records that would last years.

The army was unimpressed. Three days later, Triplett was ordered to immediately report for active duty.

At the time, Triplett was one of only a handful of blacks in the league. At his induction physical, he was examined by a black doctor who happened to be a football fan. He thought he might catch a break. Instead, the doctor stamped "Accepted" on his papers. "I was miserable about it," Triplett recalled. "I was getting ready to sign a new contract. I asked them if they'd wait until the end of the season, just a few weeks, but they wanted me now."

Triplett missed the last five games of the schedule as well as the entire following season, spending much of his hitch playing service ball while assigned to the 594th Field Artillery Battalion at Camp Polk, Louisiana. When he returned in 1952, the Lions traded him to the Chicago Cardinals, where he wrapped up his once promising career with a half-dozen nondescript outings.

As the Cold War heated up, the number of players swapping cleats for combat boots continued to climb. Roughly 260 active players and draft picks had their pro careers interrupted by military service between 1950 and 1959, including more than a score of Lions. Many were key performers. In addition to Lary, Gedman, Spencer, and Triplett, guard Stanley Campbell, ends Dorne Dibble, Cloyce Box, and Bob Cain, and backs Bill Bowman and Lew Carpenter also were called.

Carpenter had led the club in rushing for two straight seasons when he was drafted into the army following the 1955 campaign. "They called Lewis in on Christmas Eve," said his wife, Ann. "The one thing that could have prevented him from being drafted was having children. I found out two weeks later that I was pregnant with our first child, but by then it was too late." Carpenter wound up being sent to Heidelberg, West Germany, where his duties included coaching the base's women's baseball team.

Box, a Marine Corps veteran, was one of 14 NFL players who had served in World War II to be called back to active duty during the Korean War. However, unlike World War II, which claimed the lives of 21 active or former NFL players (including five men who had worn the Detroit uniform), no pro gridders died in hostile action during the 1950s. Indeed, starstruck commanders were widely criticized for coddling the athletes in their units.

Most players remained stateside, typically spending their tour as athletic instructors and playing on service teams. Box, for example, spent his second tour supervising the brig while playing for the base team at Camp Pendleton, California. Jim Hill served his country as a two-way back for the Fort Eustis Wheels in Virginia before moving on to Fort Bragg, North Carolina, as recreation director.

Many players had been members of the Reserve Officers' Training Corps (ROTC) in college and thus owed the government a period of active duty. Lary, who received his ROTC commission while attending Texas A&M, spent his hitch as a second lieutenant at Fort Benning, Georgia. Dibble, who was in the program at Michigan State, was stationed at Bolling Air Base in Washington, D.C. Called to duty after his rookie year, Dibble missed out on the Lions' first championship, but he was able to watch the title game in the officers' club.

Aside from the remote possibility of being sent to a combat zone, players called into service had to contend with relocation headaches, greatly reduced income, family separations, and nagging worries over reclaiming a spot on the roster after their tour of duty was over. One of the biggest fears, said Marv Brown, was developing "army legs"—good for marching, not running.

The speedy back from East Texas State, whose father died in an oil field accident when he was six months old, was motivated to join the ROTC program as much out of financial need as patriotism. Brown spent a hitch in the air force after being selected by Detroit late in the 1953 player draft. At 149 pounds, his size might have kept him from an extended pro career anyway, but three years of military service practically guaranteed that his return to the gridiron in the summer of 1957 would be a difficult one.

"That training camp with Detroit was the toughest thing I'd ever been through," he said. "I wasn't one of those guys who could eat two steaks. At one point I got down to 125 pounds. Bobby Layne told me, 'Marv, if you were 6-foot-1, I'd make you All-Pro. You're so short, I can't see you downfield when I throw.'"

After a frustrating season in which he suited up for just four games before being waived, Brown flew off in a new life direction. He piloted commercial jets for Braniff and Continental and, as a reservist, served a tour in Vietnam.

Robert Lee Smith, known as "Texas Bob" Smith to avoid confusion with veteran Bob Smith (who was dubbed "Tulsa Bob"), never realized his full potential, in part because of military duty. The Texas A&M standout, originally drafted by Cleveland in 1951 before being signed as a free agent by Detroit, was called into the service just as he was hoping to compete with Pat Harder for the starting fullback position.

Smith finally joined the Lions early in the 1953 season after serving two years in the army, including a stint in Korea. However, Texas Bob—who had broken Doak Walker's South West Conference single-season rushing record—never regained his collegiate form. He was gone after two unproductive and injury-plagued campaigns in Detroit.

Joe Schmidt and Gary Lowe made sure they wouldn't lose a chunk of their prime playing days by arranging to enter the Army Reserve before their local draft board got them. The reserves required six months of active duty, followed by five and a half years of monthly meetings and two weeks of training each summer. Lowe, a defensive back, was a local product, having grown up in Trenton before graduating from Michigan State. He was picked up off waivers from Washington during the 1957 season, replacing Marv Brown on the roster.

Schmidt and Lowe reported for duty shortly after playing in the '57 championship game. After boot camp at Fort Leonard Wood in Missouri, Lowe moved on to advanced infantry training in Oregon and Schmidt was sent to Fort Knox, Kentucky. Schmidt was assigned to a tank crew, just like his brother William during World War II. The co-captain of the NFL champions spent his days bouncing around inside a tank and squeezing in and out of hatches. "Everybody up in Detroit was having a good time, and I'm down there busting my ass," he said.

By July, when he was completing his active-duty commitment and getting ready to report to the Lions' training camp, Schmidt was well under his playing weight. "I started eating like I had four assholes. I was trying to bulk up. I was just happy I didn't lose a couple of years to the army." Upon his return, he signed a reported $15,000 contract for the 1958 season, a considerable pay bump from the $78 a month he was making as Private J. P. Schmidt, U.S. Army.

Despite the griping, many players from the era viewed their military experience as being a generally positive one. "I made some good friends," Dibble said. "It was good for me. Everybody should spend at least a year in the service." Schmidt said it broadened his perspective. "You had guys from Texas, Alabama, Jewish guys from Northwestern, guys who couldn't march and chew gum at the same time. So it was kind of neat from that standpoint."

THE *Last*
GREAT *Season*

I just hope next season can be like this season. It couldn't be much better, could it?

—Steve Junker, December 29, 1957

O f the many fans who considered a certain swaggering, pot-bellied quarterback their favorite Detroit Lion, none was more faithful than Harry Mageski, who grew up on a small farm in Huron County. He was 11 years old when the team opened training camp in July 1957. "Bobby Layne was always my idol," he remembered. "My oldest brother was a cop in Detroit, and he'd always tease me. 'I saw Layne coming out of a bar at three in the morning,' he'd tell me. Of course, I didn't want to hear any of the stories. When you're that age, you just know somebody by what he's done on the field."

That was the way it should be, insisted Layne's many protectors in the press.

"Some may be outraged when a sports god romps a bit and say it's bad for the young," *Detroit Times* columnist George Van wrote when Layne was arrested for drunk driving two weeks before the start of the 1957 regular season. "This is so much claptrap. The youngster cares only about touchdowns and home runs and other athletic heroics. Man has his flaws and a sports god can have them, too. And the sooner the youngster knows this the better off he'll be."

By now, many of Layne's hardcore drinking companions from the title teams had retired. Some operated bars. Bob Hoernschemeyer and Jug Girard ran the Lions Den on Mack, while Sonny Gandee had just opened Sonny Gandee's Celebrity House on Biddle Avenue in Wyandotte. Les Bingaman co-owned a cocktail lounge called the Sax Club on West McNichols, near the University of Detroit. There he poured scotch and did his best to console the quarterback after a tough loss. "Slim," he'd say, "if you win them all, nobody will play you."

But Bingaman wasn't always that equanimous, especially with a few drinks under his ample belt. "I remember one time," Layne said, "I had just bought a new car and Bingo and I were off around the town in it. Well, we got to arguing about something. I don't know what it was now, except it was something quite trivial. Anyway, Bingo got mad. He wasn't mad enough to hit me. He was always careful about that because he could hurt you bad by just slapping. So he just got out of the car and kicked the side in." Layne, relating the story to a reporter, could only shake his head and sigh over the thought of his crumpled Cadillac. "A brand new car . . ."

Among the newer, younger Lions, Layne found an enthusiastic bar-hopping buddy in Tom "The Bomb" Tracy. The former Birmingham High standout was an All-Star with the Ottawa Rough Riders in his only season in Canada before signing with the Lions in 1956. Although the fullback with the tree-stump legs and brush-cut hair played sparingly in Detroit, he felt blessed. Not only was he a member of his hometown team, a perennial title contender, he was carousing with the Lion King himself.

Fritz Wenson, president of the Lions Bleacher Club and a part-time musician, recalled the pair making a grand entrance. "Once, we're at a party in Grosse Pointe, it's about 1:30 in the morning, we're playing in the basement, and all of a sudden two guys come downstairs. One of them falls down the steps and his buddy picks him up. The guy who fell was Bobby Layne and Tom Tracy was the guy who picked him up."

Buddy Parker had routinely turned a blind eye to his players' extracurricular activities, figuring it was up to a player to police himself. Once, when asked specifically about Layne's nocturnal larks, Parker responded, "All I asked was that he produce on Sunday. I never knew what he was doing, and I didn't care."

Sober, drunk, or hungover, Parker's Lions were the favorite of many observers to win the Western Division championship that had barely eluded them the previous December. The offense had been fortified by the off-season acquisitions of two backfield stars who had always given Detroit fits.

One was 49ers fullback John Henry Johnson, a powerful runner and blocker. Johnson's mother had named him after the mythical black strongman, John Henry. The Louisiana native was, like his namesake, a "steel-driving man" when he had a football tucked into the crook of his arm, slamming into tacklers and teammates with pile-driver force. San Francisco lineman Bob St. Clair dreaded blocking for Johnson when the team was knocking on an opponent's goal line. "I just hope there will be a hole there, because if there wasn't, John was running up my back," St. Clair said. "I could feel those cleats going up my spine, and into the end zone he'd go."

Johnson had gotten into fracases during San Francisco's last two visits to Briggs Stadium, so for the Lions it was a bit of a relief to get him on their side. His acquisition gave the team its first black star since Wally Triplett was called into the army midway through the 1950 season. Triplett, who had settled in Detroit upon ending his career with the Cardinals in 1953, sportively remembered Johnson as a "happy-go-lucky kind of guy who wrote bad checks at poker games."

The key addition was old nemesis Tobin Rote. Parker swung the deal with Packers coach Lisle Blackbourn prior to the opening of training camp. Green Bay, desperate for linemen and unable to afford Rote's contract, got Ollie Spencer, Norm Masters, and Jim Salsbury, as well as halfback Don McIlhenny, in return.

Rote, 29, was coming off one of the most remarkable individual seasons in NFL history. The tall, rangy Texan was a one-man gang in 1956, personally accounting for 29 of Green Bay's 34 offensive touchdowns. He tossed 18 scoring passes, seven more than anyone else in the league, and ran for 11 touchdowns, a record for quarterbacks that would last two decades. Rote had led Rice University to a pair of South West Conference titles and a Cotton Bowl win his senior year before being selected by Green Bay in the 1950 draft. During his seven seasons with the sad-sack Packers, he never received the acclaim he deserved, and even today he is perhaps the most deserving quarterback not to be in the Pro Football Hall of Fame.

"He was a competitor," said Dom Moselle, Rote's teammate in the early '50s. "He was a tough guy and he could run. There were linemen who weren't as big as Rote." The Lions had firsthand knowledge of Rote's capabilities. He rushed for 131 yards against them in 1951, then five years later threw for 301 yards, both times on Thanksgiving Day.

Parker admitted to being "up in the clouds" over the prospect of having two top-flight signal-callers, something he'd never enjoyed before. "Each of them is a real pro," he said. "Both know you're top dog in this league only as long as you do your job better than some other player who wants the same job. In fact, I figure it ought to make both of them just that much sharper."

Parker announced early in training camp that he would alternate quarterbacks, going with whoever had the hot hand. His loyalty to Layne over the years took a back seat to his commitment to winning. As Buddy liked to say: "Who ever complained about having two good quarterbacks?"

After seven years of training in Ypsilanti, veterans and rookies reported to the team's new training site north of Detroit. The Lions were forced to move when Michigan Normal College—now Eastern Michigan University—announced plans to build a dormitory on the practice fields. The Lions looked at Hillsdale and Adrian colleges before settling on Cranbrook, the private academy in Bloomfield Hills. The scenic grounds had been the original training camp of the Lions when G. A. Richards bought the Portsmouth Spartans and moved the franchise from Ohio to Detroit in 1934.

It figured to take a while to mesh the rookies, newcomers, and veterans into a smoothly operating unit, especially with two number-one quarterbacks in the mix. Old reliables Jim Doran, Lou Creekmur, and Harley Sewell held down the left side of the line. Centering the ball was long-time Cleveland Brown Frank Gatski, who was concluding his Hall-of-Fame career with one final season in Detroit.

Gatski, a man of quiet strength who had worked in the coal mines as a teenager, had been an integral part of all seven of Cleveland's championship teams in the AAFC and NFL. When the 35-year-old veteran held out for a raise, Paul Brown responded by trading the perennial All-Pro to his chief rival for a draft pick. Gatski felt immediately at home at Briggs Stadium. "This club is fabulous," he said. "Why didn't Detroit draft me ten years ago?"

The acquisition of Gatski allowed Charlie Ane to move to right tackle to replace Ollie Spencer. As the season wore on, Ken Russell, drafted out of Bowling Green, would at times take over for the injured Ane. By season's end the entire right side of the offensive line would be manned by rookies: guard John Gordy of Tennessee, Russell, and Steve Junker, a red-headed end from Xavier.

The defense remained Detroit's bedrock. "In blond, strong Joe Schmidt, Detroit possesses, by a good margin, the best middle linebacker in the league,"

Tex Maule wrote in *Sports Illustrated*. "And the four Lion secondary pass defenders, headed by veteran Jack Christiansen, comprise the most polished and effective unit of its kind in pro football."

Christensen, Yale Lary, Jimmy David, and Darris McCord would join Schmidt in the Pro Bowl at season's end. Jim Martin moved to the left linebacker spot to make room for Hamtramck native and former Michigan star Roger Zatkoff. The three-time Pro Bowler in Green Bay had initially been traded to Cleveland, but he refused to report because he was tired of living apart from his family and flourishing business. Zatkoff also nixed a trade to Los Angeles. The Packers finally dealt him to the Lions for returning serviceman Lew Carpenter.

Early in the evening of August 12, 1957, Parker arrived at Detroit's downtown Statler Hotel for the team's eighth annual "Meet the Lions" banquet. The $10-a-plate event was a chance for boosters to get their first good look at the team just before the start of the exhibition season.

The banquet was supposed to be a lighthearted affair. But Parker was hardly feeling buoyant this Monday night. As he got off the elevator at the banquet level, he was told that Lyle Fife wanted to see him on the 10th floor.

"Fife had a suite," Parker recalled. "So I went up. And who is the first person I see but the quarterback I traded three players to get, Tobin Rote. He is having a drink. The next night we have to play our first exhibition game."

Years later, Rote explained what happened that night. "We went to the Statler from training camp at Cranbrook by bus. Buddy Parker told us, 'I don't want you going to a hospitality room with the owners. Go right to your tables. When it is over, go right to the bus.'"

Instead, as the players walked through the hotel lobby, Fife pulled aside a few players and invited them upstairs for a drink or three prior to the start of the banquet. "He was grabbing you by the arm," Rote said. "Bobby. Me. You can't say no to an owner. Buddy left. He went to the bar and had a couple of shots."

Soon it came time for Parker to step up to the podium and speak. Instead of the usual bland comments regarding the team's chances for the upcoming season, he let his frustration fly. "I have a situation here I cannot handle any more," he said. "These ballplayers have gotten too big for me, or something. I'm getting out."

Nobody in the audience of 600 fans, players, and reporters quite knew how to react. Some laughed.

"So tonight I'm getting out," Parker repeated. "So long."

The rookies were bewildered. "We didn't know what the hell was going on," said Marv Brown. Some of the veteran Lions mumbled, "There he goes again." They knew Parker could be compulsive, irrational, and overly dramatic, especially when drinking. More than once the mercurial coach had told players or management that he was through, only to settle down and return to his job. But this time it was more than just Buddy being Buddy. It was Buddy saying goodbye and meaning it.

"Buddy, you're just kidding, right?" asked emcee Bob Reynolds as Parker left the podium.

George Wilson took the microphone. "All kidding aside, this is serious," the assistant coach said. "I've been with Buddy since 1951. We won a lot of championships. His life is football. Buddy is a little upset. I hope Buddy stays and we win the championship this year." The crowd broke into applause but by then Parker had left the room.

Reporters chased down and cornered Parker, who elaborated on the reasons behind his abrupt resignation. "I can't handle this team anymore," he said. "It is the worst team I've ever seen in training camp. They have no life, no go. Just a completely dead team."

The next morning, Layne and Joe Schmidt visited Parker as he was packing his suitcase. The co-captains tried their mightiest to talk him out of his decision, but their efforts were in vain. Parker shared with them what he described as his real reason for quitting, though he wanted it kept from the press. He was tired of being used as a pawn in the ongoing conflict between Fife and Edwin Anderson. "He said, 'I've been here long enough,' and he said it was time to go and there were too many people meddling with it'," Layne recalled.

According to Layne, Parker was upset when some of the directors had taken Leon Hart's side when Hart held out for more money and missed the start of camp. "And then another thing, Buddy wanted to draft a fullback when Hunchy quit. He went to the draft meeting ready to draft Joe Childress from Auburn. We needed a fullback. And certain people told him to draft Hopalong Cassady. That was the story of it right there—when they started runnin' it. And Buddy told us that. He said, 'I can't run it anymore, so it's time to leave. It has nothin' to do with tonight.' Buddy was this type of person. Things would build up inside of him and he couldn't stand to get beat. Things kept buildin' up and he finally couldn't take it anymore."

The day after Parker shook up the football world by quitting the Lions,

Edwin Anderson visited Cranbrook and announced that George Wilson would take over as head coach. The assembled players gave Wilson a rousing reception.

Continuity was essential, making the 43-year-old Wilson, starting his ninth year with the Lions, the obvious choice to replace Parker. The Chicago native had spent 13 seasons as a player and assistant coach with George Halas before joining Bo McMillan's staff in 1949. He was as responsible as anyone for convincing McMillan to bring Layne to Detroit.

As Parker's assistant in charge of working with backs and receivers, Wilson was known as a taskmaster, not as a great football mind. Under Parker he rarely worked late hours, preferring to spend time on the links or with his family. More naturally inclined to be a superintendent than a tactician, the new head coach of the Lions wisely delegated authority to his assistants. Gil Mains figured there would be little real change with Wilson at the helm. "I think we have the material to win," the veteran tackle said. "Front office stuff seldom bothers this squad."

The players liked Wilson, a pleasant and even-tempered man who had often served as an intermediary between Parker and the team. However, unlike Parker, Wilson was an old-school disciplinarian. He immediately established an 11 p.m. curfew for the rest of training camp and personally conducted the bed checks. Offenders would be fined $50 for each hour they were out past curfew. Layne paid it no mind. As always, he set his own hours.

Rookies were in awe of the power No. 22 yielded. "You didn't talk to Bobby a lot," Ken Russell recalled. "He talked to you." The impressionable prospect admired Layne's style. "I learned to drink scotch because that's what Bobby drank," he said. Russell also liked the quarterback's taste in personal transportation, which typically ran to high-powered late-model sedans. "I came up to camp in a '51 Hudson Hornet," he said. "When I made the team, I bought a brand-new '57 Olds Super 88. Had more chrome on it than paint. What a car!"

It was perhaps inevitable that a knowledgeable music lover such as Layne, an aficionado who often bought several copies of a new album so he could share them with friends, would pick John Gordy as one of "his" rookies for the '57 season. The lineman's father was ragtime pianist "Poppa John" Gordy. "Breaking into professional football with Bobby Layne was quite a learning experience," said Gordy, who was nicknamed "Bear" because of his remarkably hairy body.

"The veterans would make us chug-a-lug our beer. Our glasses were about three times the size of theirs. I got very inebriated when I was around Bobby. And he wanted me around him a lot. And I appreciated it. But I got sick and threw up a lot. On the field, Bobby was on me incessantly, and I'm sure it made me a better player. I was used to coaches being tough. The off-the-field trips I had to take with him sometimes got me in a bit of trouble. There were parties and Bobby paid for everything. He decided not to come home after the Pittsburgh and Green Bay games that season. That didn't help my relationship with my family. He flew a couple of us home on a private plane, paid our fines. But he wouldn't talk to my wife. I had to do that myself."

On the evening of September 16, five weeks after Parker's resignation, Layne and Tom Tracy went out looking for a little action. They started off at the Flame Show Bar, then dropped by Les Bingaman's Sax Club for a few drinks. The socializing stretched into the early hours of Tuesday, when Layne and several companions decided to see if a favorite pizza restaurant was open.

At about 2 a.m., Detroit patrolmen Lemmie Pratt and Don Osborn were in their squad car when they noticed a vehicle with Texas license plates driving erratically with its headlights off and on the wrong side of the center lane. The officers followed the car for a couple of blocks before pulling it over on Grand River near Linsdale.

Layne was at the wheel. Also in the car were Tracy, a 36-year-old manufacturer's rep from Birmingham named Jack Nancarrow, and three unidentified women they had picked up somewhere along the way. Layne nonchalantly got out, stating his name and saying, "I play football. What did I do? Why did you stop me?"

Layne had stopped the car six feet away from the curb. According to Pratt, Layne left it in gear, causing the patrolman to pull him out of the way as the vehicle slowly slid back into the police car, causing no damage.

Pratt asked for identification. Layne said he had left his wallet and Texas driver's license in his room at the Tuller, the downtown hotel the team had moved into after Cranbrook opened for fall classes. When the officer asked for his Michigan permit, Layne dropped the name of the former police inspector: "I'll have you know Inspector O'Brien gave it to me."

All the while, Layne kept jabbing Pratt in the shoulder with his finger, emphasizing his words as if he were dealing with a rookie lineman who had just blown a blocking assignment. "After a little of that the pokes got a bit painful and I told him to stop," Pratt said. "I said, 'That's all I can take, my friend,' and I told him we were going to the station."

At the station, Tracy was loud and belligerent, telling Pratt, "I know what I'd like to do to you." It was no surprise that Tracy was agitated. With a wife and an infant daughter at home in Royal Oak, he had some explaining to do once news hit the papers. So did Layne, whose wife and kids were back in Texas. Nancarrow, the only one of the three men who appeared sober, convinced Layne not to blow into a device known as a drunk-o-meter.

"You're a big man today," Layne told Pratt at one point. "You're king, but I'll be king tomorrow. I know some people."

Layne was taken to police headquarters and locked up until Jack Christiansen arrived at 4 a.m. to post the $150 bond. Meanwhile, the women the group had been partying with were quietly sent on their way without giving a statement. The prosecutor's office later tried to track them down, with no luck.

Tracy gave a reporter his side of events. After spending most of the evening at the Flame Bar and then the Sax Club, he said, he and Layne went to a pizza shop near Olympia Arena.

"We parked and walked around to the place and it was closed. We were on Grand River and there were lights up and down the street. It was like daylight. We got into the car, turned the corner and had been no more than a block when we were stopped. Policemen got on both sides of the car and told us to get out. They realized who Bobby was and said he was drunk, talking funny. He told them, no, that was the way he talked all the time. The reason they'd stopped us was that, because it was so light, Bobby had forgotten to turn the lights on, on the car. They took him in and told me to drive. That was crazy. I was in worse shape than he was."

Tracy also maintained that Layne hadn't backed into the police car. "No, the officers forgot to put their car in park and rammed into us."

While the team worked out that day, Layne was arraigned in traffic court. He was accompanied by Nick Kerbawy and represented by Joseph W. Louisell, one of Detroit's top criminal attorneys. Layne pleaded innocent to a charge of drunk driving. A trial date was set.

Layne was deeply embarrassed by the incident, which was page-one news around the country. He admitted to having had a half-dozen drinks but continued to insist he was not drunk. He offered to quit and go back to Texas, but Wilson wouldn't hear of it. The club believed Layne and publicly stood behind him. The curfew violation was a team matter and would be handled internally.

"I think Layne has been crucified enough," Wilson said.

Despite his protestations to the press that he wanted to sit out the season, Buddy Parker landed the head coaching job in Pittsburgh just two weeks after walking out on the Lions. "I've got the itch," he admitted. "I can't stay away from football for a year."

There were suspicions that Parker had engineered his exit from Detroit after secretly agreeing to a pact with Steelers owner Art Rooney, an old friend and racetrack companion. In Pittsburgh, Parker would enjoy non-meddling owners and a five-year contract, both of which had eluded him in Detroit.

Years later, Parker maintained that he had rejected as "devious" an offer by Baltimore owner Carroll Rosenbloom to collect $35,000 while sitting out the 1957 season, after which he would be hired to replace Weeb Ewbank as the Colts' head coach in 1958. According to Parker, his real impetus for signing with Pittsburgh was an unkept promise by George Halas.

"I know Halas will deny this, but I never would have gone to Pittsburgh any other way," Parker said. "I knew what the Steelers had and how they had no money. I went to Chicago and had lunch with Halas and Art Rooney, who owned the Steelers. The deal was I would coach the Steelers for two years and Halas would bring me over to the Bears. That's why I traded so many draft choices away at Pittsburgh. I wasn't building for the future—I had to win right then."

Instead of stepping aside, Halas coached the Bears through the 1967 season, by which time he was 72 years old and Parker had been retired from coaching for three years.

Ironically, Parker's first game as Steelers coach was a preseason contest against the Lions at Buffalo's Civic Stadium on September 8. There didn't seem to be any bad blood as the coaches and their teams took the field. Parker and Wilson chatted briefly, agreeing to talk soon about possible trades, and most of the Detroit veterans came up to say hello to their old coach. Then it was back to business, with Parker overseeing the Steelers' 20–14 victory.

The Lions had won their first three exhibitions under Wilson, but the loss seemed to put them into a downward spiral. They looked bad dropping their next two exhibitions, then looked even worse in the regular-season curtain-raiser on September 29 at Baltimore.

The Colts were an up-and-coming team filled with young stars. One of them, Johnny Unitas, was nearly decapitated with a necktie tackle by Roger Zatkoff, but the brilliant third-year quarterback kept his head and coolly tossed four touchdown passes to guide the Colts to a lopsided 34–14 victory. Wilson's two-quarterback attack fizzled. Layne started, but neither he nor Rote was able to get the offense untracked. The game was well out of hand when Rote found Jerry Reichow for a fourth-quarter touchdown, his first scoring pass as a Lion.

The following week, Wilson got his first regular-season victory as a head coach when Rote returned to familiar haunts in Green Bay. Rote and Gene Gedman ran for touchdowns and John Henry Johnson rushed for 109 yards to produce the 24–14 win.

The next Sunday, in the Lions' home opener against Los Angeles, Rote threw a touchdown pass to Reichow, Layne booted a field goal, and the Detroit defense was responsible for squeezing out a 10–7 victory. The Lions picked off six passes, one more than Norm Van Brocklin was able to complete to his own receivers. The Rams might have pulled out the win, but Elroy Hirsch let a sure touchdown slip through his fingers late in the game. Gedman had another solid all-around game, which astonished Rams first-year tackle Bob Houser.

The night before, several Rams veterans had taken Houser to the Brass Rail on West Adams for dinner and some swinging music by the Al Horvay Trio. Inside a private room, closed off by a folding door, several Lions were also having a good time. Later, as they left the restaurant, the Detroit players acknowledged their opponents with grins and some comments along the line of "We'll see you guys tomorrow." The last of the Lions to leave was so wasted he had to be carried out by a couple teammates, and Houser asked a waiter who he was.

Houser's next view of Gedman was of him leaning against the goal post on Sunday afternoon, vomiting into the end zone as the Rams prepared to kick off. But moments later, Gedman seemed no worse for wear, reeling off a nice return to midfield. "We should see what kind of booze that guy was drinking," Houser told a teammate.

Game four for the Lions was a rematch on October 20 with the unbeaten, high-scoring Colts. Once again, Unitas threw four touchdown passes as Baltimore amassed a 27–3 lead. The gray sky matched the mood of the 55,764 faithful shoehorned into Briggs Stadium. Late in the third quarter, Rote replaced Layne and hooked up with Steve Junker on a 14-yard scoring pass to tighten the score to 27–10. But Rote couldn't make further headway against the Colts. With eight minutes left to play, Layne reentered the fray.

This was Howard Cassady's moment to shine. "Hoppy" was popular with fans and respected as a competitor by his teammates. "He wasn't a very big guy for the time, but he backed down from nobody," Joe Schmidt said. "He had some difficulty adjusting to pro football, but boy, he made some big plays for us and you could count on the guy." Through perseverance the little back had made himself into a reliable receiver whose head-faking ability was second to none in the league. "When he waves his head like that," said one observer, "it seems even his ears wiggle."

In short order Layne hit Cassady with a 26-yard touchdown pass, slicing the lead to 10 points. Then, with two minutes to go, Layne heaved a long pass down the left sideline that Cassady made a sensational play on just shy of the end zone. John Henry Johnson carried the ball over on the next play. With 85 seconds left to play, it was now 27–24. The crowd was in an uproar. Press-box elevator operator Arthur Billingsley literally felt the earth move. "I knew something was happening out there near the end," said Billingsley, whose duties kept him from seeing a single play. "This old stadium was just a-rocking. I could feel it way back here in my little cage."

After the ensuing kickoff, the Colts tried to run out the clock. On third down, Lenny Moore was stripped of the ball, and Yale Lary pounced on it before it rolled out of bounds. Layne set up shop at the Baltimore 29 with 46 seconds left. He didn't waste any time. He arched a long pass downfield, and once again it was Cassady on the receiving end. Touchdown, Lions! Wilson's squad had pulled out a heart-stopping 31–27 victory, eliminating a 24-point deficit in less than 20 minutes.

"It was the greatest comeback I'd ever been in, including college and high school," Junker said. "It's fun being in games like that." The hollering contin- ued in the corridors and inside the Detroit locker room well after the game had ended. Doc Greene, who had seen his share of drama over the years, asked, "I wonder what they've got for an encore?"

So far, the two-quarterback system appeared to be working, though there didn't seem to be much rhyme or reason to how it was implemented. "I play 'em by feeling," Wilson explained. "There isn't any rule. I just play 'em on how I feel they're going to do. On a day like today I'm a great coach. Some other day I'm a bum."

The Lions next traveled to the West Coast, where they lost to the Rams and the 49ers on successive Sundays. The Rams throttled them, 35–17, but the loss at San Francisco was particularly heartbreaking. With the Lions trailing 28–10 in the final quarter, Rote relieved Layne. He ignited a furious rally, throwing three touchdown passes in a span of nine and a half minutes. The last, an 8-yarder to

Jim Doran after Jim Martin recovered a Hugh McElhenny fumble deep in the 49ers' end, gave Detroit a 31–28 lead.

But the 49ers were coming off an emotional comeback win over the Bears, during which popular owner Tony Morabito had died of a heart attack. There was the expected talk about "Winning one for Tony" prior to the Lions game, and now the 49ers were about to do just that. There were ten seconds showing on the clock when Y. A. Tittle and R. C. Owens—a rookie end and former collegiate basketball star with speed, sure fingers, and a kangaroo-like leaping ability—pulled off a gimmick play they called the "Alley-Oop."

From the Lions' 41, Tittle took the snap, nimbly evaded the rush, and waited as Owens and Jim David raced shoulder-to-shoulder down the sideline. "Finally, I could wait no longer," Tittle said. "I let fly. I threw the ball higher and farther than I ever had before—or since. As the ball climbed up there, I got knocked flat. I watched the rest of the play on the seat of my pants. Owens had gotten down to the 1-yard line. He was just standing there. Jim David was standing next to him. Jack Christiansen, who had come over to help David, was standing there. Carl Karilivacz was there."

Outnumbered and surrounded, Owens climbed some invisible ladder, snatched the ball as it fell out of the sky, and with defenders hacking at him all the way down fell back to earth with the winning touchdown in a wild 35–31 San Francisco victory. Bob Brachman reported the scene in the next day's *San Francisco Examiner*: "Fans collapsed everywhere and immediately the siren on the stadium ambulance let go with a blast and headed in the direction of the press box. A fan had died, overcome by emotion. Hundreds of fans ran onto the field. Even the mounted policemen urged their horses through the milling mob to bring some kind of order from this hysteria."

The loss all but crushed the Lions' title hopes. Instead of being tied for first with San Francisco at 4–2, they were now 3–3, two full games behind the 49ers, and the season was half over. Detroit's defense was a sieve, having given up more points than any team except the pitiful Packers. "We're not out of it," Wilson said bravely. "Anything can happen."

As if to prove Wilson a sage, the 49ers lost their next three games while the Colts won three straight. Meanwhile, the Lions rebounded, beating the Eagles in Philadelphia, 27–16, and whipping San Francisco, 31–10, in a rematch before a standing-room-only crowd at Briggs Stadium. Several Detroit starters almost missed the 49ers game. They were trapped in a stalled elevator at the Sheraton-Cadillac

Hotel until finally clambering through a narrow hatch and making it to the park a half hour before kickoff. "I'm through with elevators," said Frank Gatski, one of the players who'd been stuck. "Next time, I'm going to throw a rope out the window."

Just as it seemed the team was rolling, the Bears came to town and pounded out an easy 27–7 victory. Layne was rushed hard all afternoon. At one point he was flattened by Bears tackle Fred Williams. As he lay on the turf, trying to regain his senses, he looked over and spotted Rote on the sidelines. "Let's go, Bobby," Layne said to himself, "there is Rote waiting to take away your bread and butter." Rote didn't fare any better, fumbling twice and throwing an interception.

Both quarterbacks hated the revolving-door approach to quarterbacking.

"A quarterback has to be in charge," Layne said years later. "We just never knew. One game it was him. The other it would be me. The coach, George Wilson, violated just about everything I believed in. He two-platooned me with Rote and neither of us could do anything right. I played a quarter. Then he played a quarter. That can't work. Look, I can be cold as hell for a quarter, but all the time I'm building. I set up decoys, testing pass patterns, then bingo. I pull off the plays I've been working up to and we get a couple of quick touchdowns. If I'm in there for only one quarter I have to go for broke right away. Two-platooning can throw a whole team off balance."

With three games left, Baltimore was 6–3, a game better than Detroit and San Francisco at 5–4. Playing in a steady downpour on Thanksgiving Day against the Packers, the Lions stumbled and bumbled their way through the first half. Wilson read the team the riot act in the dressing room. "It was the maddest I've been all year," he said afterward. "They were fumbling away the championship and it really burned me."

Down by a field goal to open the second half, John Henry Johnson's 62-yard touchdown run early in the third quarter keyed an 18–6 comeback victory in the mud. But on Sunday the Colts and 49ers also won. The teams' order in the standings remained unchanged.

The first four rounds of the NFL draft and the annual owners meeting were held that weekend in Philadelphia. On Sunday evening, inside the tony Vesper Club, Wilson and Bob Nussbaumer were accosted by a bitter and inebriated Buddy Parker, whose Steelers team had just dropped a one-point decision to the Eagles. "You're no coach," said Parker. "I helped the Bears and Colts beat you. I'll help other clubs beat you, too." Parker evidently was referring to sharing game films, which was becoming an increasingly common practice among NFL coaches when preparing for an upcoming game. But the insinuation was that he had also volunteered insider information to Detroit's opponents.

Wilson was enraged but managed to keep his cool. There were more pressing matters on his mind, notably the upcoming trial of another prominent football figure brought low by alcohol.

On the afternoon of Friday, December 6, two days before the Lions' last home game of the regular season, some two hundred people, including several Lions players, squeezed into the courtroom of Judge John D. Watts to watch a jury comprised of 11 women and one man render judgment on Bobby Layne.

The five-hour trial stretched into the early evening, with Les Bingaman testifying that he had served Layne six or seven highballs over a span of several hours and Layne telling the court that whatever amount he drank wasn't enough to impair his driving. The arresting officers testified that Layne had a flushed face and slurred his words.

Defense attorney Joseph W. Louisell asked the patrolmen if they were familiar with a "Texas accent," explaining that it could easily be confused with the slurred speech of somebody who was intoxicated.

It was a crafty yet plausible defense. Layne's heavy drawl often left people slightly perplexed, particularly those unaccustomed to the speech patterns of the South. Although they didn't testify, Wally Triplett and Steve Junker, both midwesterners, could separately attest to doing some helmet-scratching in the huddle when Layne called plays. "It could be hard sometimes," said Triplett, remembering Layne's first season in Detroit. "Bobby and I had a couple of misunderstandings because of the way he talked."

The occasional miscommunication continued even after eight seasons. During the comeback win over Baltimore a few weeks earlier, Junker had strained to decipher Layne's calls.

"Layne had this gravelly, Texas, whiskey drawl," Junker recalled, "and I heard him call my pattern '8 right,' so I cut to the right. But Bobby had actually said '8 drag' where you go down the sideline. Layne threw it for an interception, and goddamn he was mad. He chewed my ass from the huddle to the sideline. He told Wilson, 'Get that goddamn fucking rookie out of here.' I thought, 'Son of a bitch, this is the end for me.' I got back into the game, though, but from then on I looked at his lips in the huddle."

Louisell argued that if the officers didn't know what Layne sounded like when he was sober, "How could they know how he talked when he was drunk?" Officer Pratt responded: "I'm familiar with a Texas drawl, but that wasn't what was slurring Layne's speech that night." The prosecutor, pointing out that Layne admitted to having had several drinks, asked, "How many more did he have that we don't know about?"

There may have been a sly subtext to the prosecutor's question. He probably knew, as Louisell and the Lions' legal counsel did, that at some point after Layne was arrested and freed on bond, he had again been spotted driving drunk. This time, however, the quarterback managed to slip off the hook.

"This was during the regular season, while he was still awaiting trial," said attorney Jim LoPrete. "A bunch of players lived in the Six Mile and Grand River area. Layne was with Tobin Rote in the front seat, and I forget who was in the back. One or two other players. They were all coming back from the Lindell or some place, and Layne was drunk as a skunk.

"The police spotted their car weaving around on Grand River, so they did a U-turn to check it out. Layne was at the wheel, but by the time the officers got out and approached the car, Layne and Rote had changed seats. Apparently Rote was fine. They didn't issue a ticket, and they sent them on their way."

LoPrete laughed. "The old bait and switch."

The public never learned of the incident, and in any event the jurors were confined to the one specific case in front of them. There was no question that Layne had been drinking, Judge Watts said in his charge to the jury. "The question is whether, and how much, he was influenced by what he had been drinking."

Jurors needed only 16 minutes and two ballots to answer that question. The first ballot was 8–4 in favor of acquittal; the second was unanimous. A loud cheer erupted in the courtroom when the verdict of "Not guilty" was read. Bailiffs had to push back several well-wishers trying to congratulate the visibly relieved defendant.

"I voted for acquittal both times," said juror Josephine Kopcz. "Layne stuttered on the stand and had a flushed face. That seems to be his natural appearance."

Layne was hugged by Nick Kerbawy and hastily left the courtroom, causing another juror, an attractive redhead, to pout: "The least he could have done was given us girls a kiss."

Layne and his supporters celebrated by going out to have a few drinks. When players entered the clubhouse the next day, they were greeted by a giant sign put up by Roy Macklem: "Ah All Ain't Drunk, Ah'm from Texas."

On Sunday, the freshly vindicated Texan was behind center as the Lions hosted Cleveland. The Browns had seen their unprecedented string of divisional titles snapped in 1956, but with a stifling defense and an offense centered around rookie fullback Jimmy Brown, Paul Brown's squad was back in charge, posting just one loss and a tie in the first 10 games en route to recapturing the Eastern Conference crown.

Because of the mud, the Lions were wearing extra-long cleats. The tweaked footwear would cost Layne the rest of the season. In the second quarter, with Detroit nursing a 3–0 lead, Layne went back to pass and was gang tackled. As he went down, his cleats stuck in the turf. Layne lay on the ground, clearly in pain. Officials stopped the game.

Layne was examined by team physician Richard Thompson, who told the grimacing quarterback that he would have to go to the hospital. The fibula in his right leg was broken and his right ankle was dislocated. Layne's season was over. A stretcher was brought out. Browns tackle Don Colo, standing nearby, was unsympathetic to the victim's plight. "You son of a bitch," he said, "you'd be better off in jail."

Colo's jibe, which Lou Creekmur overheard and passed on to Wilson, helped fire up the Lions. At halftime, Wilson asked the team to "win one for Bobby. He's won plenty for you."

If Wilson was trying to channel Pat O'Brien in *Knute Rockne, All American*, his version of "Win one for the Gipper" did the job. After intermission, Rote hit Dave Middleton with a scoring strike and John Henry Johnson added a short touchdown burst as the Lions continued their dominance over the Browns, 20–7.

Meanwhile, San Francisco was playing Baltimore on the coast. Gene Cronin visited Layne at Detroit Osteopathic Hospital and found him stretched out on the bed, still in his game pants. There was an ice pack on his ankle and a Marlboro dangling on his lip. The television was turned to the 49ers game.

"They wanted to operate," Cronin said, "but Bobby kept yelling at the doctor to get out of the room so he could watch the game." San Francisco upset the Colts on a last-second touchdown pass from rookie John Brodie to Hugh McElhenny, creating a logjam at the top of the standings between the Lions, 49ers, and Colts.

With one game left on the schedule and three teams knotted at 7–4, the league was forced to address the possibility of the first triple tie in its history—a nightmarish complication that would require a double-round of divisional play-offs and push the championship game back two weeks to January 5, 1958.

As Wilson got his team ready for the regular-season finale against the Bears at Wrigley Field, Bert Bell sorted out the various scenarios for the press. In the event of a three-way tie, the 49ers would play at Detroit on December 22 with the winner moving on to play the Colts in Baltimore the following Sunday. A two-way tie between Detroit and either San Francisco or Baltimore would require the Lions to play on the road.

The Lions were keeping their fingers crossed for no playoff. Just beat the Bears and hope the 49ers and Colts both lost.

This was the sixth time in seven years that the Lions entered the final game of the regular season with the conference title either clinched or on the line, and they were three-point underdogs. It also was a return to the scene of last year's controversial mugging by Ed Meadows. This time around, Meadows wasn't a factor, but Rote's tendency for slow starts was.

Rote had looked horrible two weeks earlier against Chicago. Now, playing a truly important late-season game for the first time in his eight-year pro career, he appeared tight. He threw three interceptions in the first half, and the entire ground game could only muster 13 yards. With the Chicago offense unexpectedly operating out of a spread formation—what today is known as the shotgun—Ed Brown threw a long touchdown pass to Bobby Watkins and George Blanda kicked a field goal as the Bears took a 10–0 lead into halftime.

Wilson was livid. He tore into the team, called them quitters, then calmed down a bit on the sidelines as Rote led the offense to touchdowns on the Lions' first two drives of the third quarter. Howard Cassady scored on a short run to narrow the score to 10–7, and minutes later Dave Middleton grabbed a 9-yard pass from Rote to give the Lions their first lead of the afternoon, 14–10. A Blanda field goal made it a one-point game early in the fourth quarter.

With a little over three minutes left to play, Chicago scored what appeared to be the go-ahead touchdown on a Blanda-to-Jim Dooley pass. But an illegal-motion call, the Bears' only penalty of the afternoon, nullified it. On the next play, Jack Christiansen picked off Blanda and returned the ball deep into Chicago territory. Rote smartly chewed up time and yards, with John Henry Johnson blasting into the end zone with just 24 seconds left to make the final score Lions 21, Bears 13. The victory felt a little strange. As Yale Lary pointed out, it was the first time in eight years the Lions had won a game without Layne in the lineup.

The Lions, having finished the regular season at 8–4, waited for the scores from the West Coast to determine whom they would be playing next. In San

Francisco, the 49ers rallied to beat Green Bay to also finish at 8–4. Meanwhile, in Los Angeles, the Rams upset the Colts. The day's results eliminated Baltimore and set up a tiebreaker between the Lions and 49ers at Kezar Stadium the following Sunday.

The Lions flew out immediately to the coast, looking to soak their battered and swollen bodies in the therapeutic warmth of the California sun. Two rookies nearly missed the flight when Steve Junker picked up John Gordy in his beat-up Ford and the machine started misbehaving.

"I couldn't get it out of low gear," Junker said. "We drove from the Town House apartments downtown to Willow Run airport in Ypsilanti. How fast can you go—maybe 20 miles an hour? The engine was racing and smoking and we thought they were going to take off without us." To the panicky players' relief, the team delayed departure until Junker's clunker, belching smoke, finally made it to the gate.

The team checked into an upscale hotel in Palo Alto and held practices at Stanford University. The 49ers, who had lost at home to the Lions only once in eight years, were installed as three-point favorites. Win or lose, a full house at Kezar and a national broadcast guaranteed the owners of both clubs a lucrative Sunday.

As usual, players wouldn't share in the revenues beyond receiving an extra week's pay equal to one-twelfth of their regular-season salary. For Joe Schmidt, that amounted to $808.33. Given Schmidt's quiet competitiveness, it's tempting to say he would have played for nothing, but the perennial All-Pro was already toiling for a base salary of $9,700 a year. He was unhappy with his contract, which he thought belonged in the bargain bin at Kern's.

The 49ers were sky-high and brimming with confidence. They seemed a team of destiny. They had pulled out several games in dramatic fashion, giving everyone in San Francisco the feeling that this was the year the perennial contender would finally win the championship. "We'll whip 'em," coach Frankie Albert responded when asked about the Lions, though he went on to admit that he would have rather faced Baltimore than Detroit because "I think our boys respect the Lions a little more."

For the first 30 minutes of play, the capacity crowd of 60,000 sat in the early afternoon sunshine and ate up the spectacle on the grass below. Three Y. A. Tittle touchdown passes, including a 34-yard Alley-Oop to R. C. Owens to open the scoring, and a Gordy Soltau field goal allowed the 49ers to file happily into the dressing room with a commanding 24–7 lead at the half. Rote accounted for the Lions' lone tally with a 4-yard pitch to Junker.

Overall, the Detroit offense was in a funk. Jerry Reichow, moved from receiver to backup quarterback after Layne's injury, was Rote's roommate in San Francisco. He remembered Rote being up all night, smoking cigarette after cigarette as he studied the playbook. "He was a nervous wreck, getting ready for this game. And it showed in the first half. We couldn't get going. But we did have a good defense that kept us in a lot of games."

The atmosphere at Kezar was festive. Christmas had come three days early. "Tickets are now on sale for next week's game with the Browns," the public address announcer told the crowd, and thousands of fans stood in line to buy them.

Wilson was out of halftime speeches. One wasn't needed. A wall made of two-by-fours and drywall was all that separated glee from gloom in the adjoining clubhouses. Roger Zatkoff recalled the sounds of celebration carrying through the paper-thin walls and connecting ductwork. "You could hear the guy buying his wife a fur coat, another one buying a car, another one had to get his championship tickets. The game was over as far as they were concerned."

Some 49ers banged on the wall and shouted obscenities as Detroit players sat on their stools and seethed. "We were like a bunch of church mice," Rote remembered. Pride was at stake, of course. But Lou Creekmur told newsmen after the game that the thought of losing thousands of dollars in championship game money was the prime motivator. "When we were down 24–7 at the half we began to see that money going right down the drain. And we knew right then it was a matter of life and death. So we had to start clawing."

The Lions regrouped in the second half, but not before first surviving a scare that threatened to put the game permanently out of reach. On the first offensive play after halftime, McElhenny took a pitchout and broke off a long, weaving run that didn't end until he was finally hauled down at the Lions' 9. After McElhenny's 71-yard romp, the only question in the minds of San Francisco partisans was just how great of a blowout the game was going to be.

Backed into a wall of noise, Schmidt implored his teammates to hold, and they did. On fourth down from the 3, Soltau kicked an easy field goal, increasing San Francisco's advantage to 27–7. But the momentum had shifted. "I remember Buster Ramsey saying, 'We're gonna blitz the shit out of this guy. We're going after him,'" Schmidt said. "We were down by such a large margin, we had nothing to lose."

With the Lions emptying the bag defensively, the 49ers wouldn't score another point the rest of the afternoon. "They pushed us all over the field in the second half," Tittle said later. "We lost our poise and our drive and they forced us into errors of commission and omission."

There were six minutes left in the third quarter when Bob Long recovered a Tittle fumble at the 49ers' 27. By now Wilson had inserted seldom-used Tom Tracy at fullback to replace John Henry Johnson, who was hampered by an injured leg. Nine plays later, Tracy muscled in from the 1-yard line for the score that cut San Francisco's lead to 27–14.

Nineteen minutes remained in the game. Detroit's defense forced the 49ers to punt. Yale Lary signaled for a fair catch at the Lions' 42. On the very next play, Rote faked a pitchout to Gene Gedman and handed off to Tracy. Harley Sewell trapped the end, Tracy ran to his right, then cut back. Chunky legs churning, Tracy broke into the San Francisco secondary and, with Gedman running interference, raced 58 yards to the end zone while teammates on the sidelines roared themselves hoarse and everybody else in Kezar Stadium looked on in disbelief. The visitors had scored two touchdowns in just 89 seconds, and suddenly it was 27–21. And it was still only the third quarter.

The Lions kicked off. Once again the swarming Detroit defense forced San Francisco to punt, and once again the Lions marched downfield for a score. This time it took five plays to go 54 yards, the drive culminating with Gedman plowing into the end zone from two yards out. There were just 44 seconds gone in the final quarter when Jim Martin's extra point gave Detroit the lead for the first time, 28–27. The Lions had scored three touchdowns in four and a half minutes.

Wilson gathered the defense around him. "It's not over," he warned. "You've got to stop Tittle." There still were 14 minutes left on the clock, plenty of time for Tittle to regain his touch.

But the Lions proved equal to the task. Time and again they took the ball away from the 49ers. The costliest San Francisco miscue was the second of the three interceptions Tittle threw in the fourth quarter.

"I had been warned that Tittle liked to roll out and throw a little screen to McElhenny, so I was looking for it, and sure enough, here it comes," Schmidt said. "Tittle sort of lobbed it. I cut in front of McElhenny, caught it, thought I would score, but I was tackled at the 2." The San Francisco defense stiffened, but Martin kicked a 13-yard field goal to pad the Lions' lead to 31–27 with under three minutes to play.

Tittle moved the 49ers offense one last time. With just over a minute left, they lined up on the Detroit 49. The Lions braced themselves; they remembered too well what had happened the last time they'd visited Kezar. Tittle went back to pass, but before anyone could say "Alley-Oop," Darris McCord burst through and buried him for an 11-yard loss.

On the next play Tittle went back to pass again, and this time he was hit by Gil Mains just as he got off the throw. The wobbly ball was intercepted by Zatkoff. Rote ran out the remaining seconds with quarterback sneaks, and the Lions were improbably headed to the championship game.

Layne, on crutches, watched the whole scene unfold on the sidelines. Standing next to him was a myopic Iowa tackle that the club had just signed to a contract for the 1958 season. "I don't believe it," Alex Karras repeated. "You better," Layne said. "You better believe it."

There were heroes aplenty. Tracy, who had not carried the ball once in the previous four games, led all ground gainers with 86 yards on 11 rushes. His two touchdowns were the first of his NFL career. Junker caught nearly every ball thrown his way and wound up with eight receptions, the most he would ever have in a game. Gedman, who had missed the Chicago game and the first half of the playoff because of a separated shoulder, took a shot of novocaine and helped ignite the offense in the second half. Both lines wore down the 49ers.

Wilson called his spirited squad the finest comeback team he'd ever seen. On that point, the record guides officially agreed. The Lions' victory would remain the NFL's greatest postseason comeback for nearly four decades, until the Buffalo Bills erased a 35-point deficit to the Houston Oilers in the 1993 play-offs. Beyond that, it simply was "a hell of a game," Schmidt reflected, one that thrilled millions of viewers around the country and still ranks among the greatest in Lions and NFL history. Today, the defensive stalwart considers it the best game of his career, and the most memorable.

Inside the tomblike San Francisco locker room, Joe Perry pondered his swollen cheeks. "I think they broke my jaw," he said. "I can't open it." Buddy Parker, reached in Pittsburgh, was asked his opinion of the squad he had called the worst team he'd ever seen in training camp. Like Perry, he found it hard to speak.

"No comment," he said brusquely. "I got my own business to take care of."

On December 29, 1957, at Briggs Stadium, Detroit and Cleveland squared off to decide the NFL championship. It was the fourth title-game tussle between the rivals in six seasons. The clubs had traveled different paths to reach this point. While the Lions navigated a storm-tossed course, Cleveland had been on a comparative cruise. The Browns had clinched their division the day before their December 8 contest with Detroit, the result of Parker's Steelers upsetting the New York Giants in a mud bath at Pittsburgh. The Browns, despite losing to the Lions just three weeks earlier and having to play at a venue where they had never won, were three-point favorites to claim their third NFL title in four years.

As always, Paul Brown downplayed the Browns' chances. He was worried that his team had grown complacent while Detroit's competitiveness had been whetted to a razor's edge by playing one must-win game after another. He also was concerned that for the first time he would be coaching a championship game without Otto Graham at quarterback. The men who had replaced him, little Tommy O'Connell and Penn State rookie Milt Plum, were hardly Graham's equals when healthy. But now O'Connell was secretly nursing a fractured ankle and Plum was hampered by a pulled leg muscle. Neither hobbled quarterback would gain much traction against the fired-up Lions.

Enthusiasm in Detroit was off the charts. The Lions had extended their league record by selling 39,844 season tickets in 1957, in the process becoming the first NFL team ever to earn $1 million at the gate. These devotees were given first crack at buying seats for the championship game. Admission prices were the highest ever charged for a title game: $10 for box seats, $7.50 for reserved, $5 for standing room, and $4 for bleachers.

The prices didn't deter bundled-up Detroiters from lining the sidewalks for three blocks in frigid temperatures while waiting their turn at the box-office window. The record gross receipts of $593,967 included $200,000 from NBC for television and radio rights. When everything was tallied and divided, the winning shares would work out to a record $4,295.11 per man. This was $65 more than the average American worker made in an entire year in 1957—a spectacular payout for a single afternoon's labor.

Although the game was a sellout, Bert Bell stated that the league's long-standing TV blackout rule would remain in effect. As far as the league was concerned, the only people within a 75-mile radius of Detroit who could legally see the game were the 55,263 who had bought tickets to it. The blowback was immediate, with everybody from discombobulated cab drivers to opportunistic politicians making their outrage known to the media.

"I have to protect the working football player and his family," the commissioner explained. "Then, too, it would be unfair to the fans, who paid amounts ranging from $10 to $4, to see a game they could see free of charge."

Interest in the game was so high that Michigan's powerful governor, G. Mennen "Soapy" Williams, made a Christmas Eve plea to Bell to lift the blackout. Bell remained firm. He also grew exasperated, saying he was being criticized for being honest. At a press conference the day before the game, Stanley Akers, the owner of a local closed-circuit TV network, made a last-ditch proposal to have the telecast piped into theaters around town. The entrepreneur estimated he could get 20,000 fans to pay $2.50 each, a nice revenue maker for everybody involved.

"No, no, a thousand times no," Bell responded, amusing reporters by breaking into a song from an old Betty Boop melodrama. "That's the first verse, the middle verse, and the last verse. Shall I sing it again for you?"

"Don't bother," Akers said. Instead he arranged to have an antenna placed on top of a 55-foot crane next to his office, where he planned on watching a pirated broadcast with a large group of invited guests.

According to a survey conducted by the *Free Press*, at least 55 bars and restaurants claimed the ability to pluck a signal out of the sky. On game day, more than 300 fans gathered outside the door of one tavern, waiting for the place to open before the 2 p.m. kickoff.

Some fans took matters into their own hands. On Detroit's east side, Pete Evangelista climbed onto the roof of his house on Raven Street and rigged an antenna booster out of a 20-foot-high pipe. "We were able to get Channel 6 out of Lansing," remembered Evangelista's nephew, Mike Dalessandro, who was 15 at the time. "All my cousins and uncles and friends, maybe 50 guys in all, were in Uncle Pete's basement rec room, watching the game."

Mike's kid brother, Tony, also was there. "It was, I guess, my first Super Bowl party," he said. "I remember that day like it was just yesterday."

An ever-dwindling number of aging Detroiters also remember it with exceptional clarity, principally because it remains, as of this writing, the team's last championship, the capstone to a wild and unpredictable season.

It was cold and sunny when Jim Martin, who had taken over all placekicking duties after Layne was hurt, boomed the opening kickoff through the Cleveland end zone. For the next two and a half hours, the Lions outmuscled their opponents on both sides of the ball, giving Martin's right leg a workout as he kicked extra point after extra point—a record-tying eight in all.

"The crippled Lions battered the healthy, rested Browns into a state of shock in the first quarter and kept them there for the next three," *Sports Illustrated*'s Tex Maule would report after the game. "They played with the tough insouciance which is a trademark of this team, and they destroyed the poise of an opponent which had played the whole season with such calm efficiency." Joe Schmidt's postgame evaluation was more succinct: "Cleveland isn't a hard team anymore."

The heart and soul of the Lions' defense almost wasn't around to deliver the comment. In an untold story of that day, Schmidt impulsively went on strike, refusing to suit up if he wasn't given the $3,000 bonus Edwin Anderson had earlier promised him if the Lions made it to the championship game. The league's premier middle linebacker, who had just played the game of his life in San Francisco, was steamed. He didn't have the check. But with game time approaching, he damn well had the leverage.

"I was sitting there in my pants and shoes, guys getting dressed, and I told George Wilson, 'I ain't playing,'" Schmidt recalled. "He said, 'What do you mean?' I told him Andy promised me a three-grand bonus and I went to get it the other day and he wouldn't give it to me."

Wilson counseled patience. A short while later, Anderson appeared in the locker room. He quietly took Schmidt aside. "You got your three," he said. "Don't worry about it."

Satisfied, Schmidt dressed for the game. "So, I made seven thousand bucks that day," he said, tacking the bonus onto his title-game share.

The championship game was seven minutes old when Martin started a deluge of points by kicking a 31-yard field goal. On the Browns' next possession, Bob Long picked off Tommy O'Connell and lugged the ball to the Cleveland 19. Rote faked a pass, then pulled down the ball and ran 18 yards to the Cleveland 1-yard line. Moments later, Rote lowered his helmet and slipped through a hole opened by Lou Creekmur for the touchdown. Martin's extra point made it 10–0.

After the ensuing kickoff, the Browns' offense again coughed up the ball, this time Milt Campbell fumbling it away at the Cleveland 15. Rote quickly moved the Lions into the end zone, with Gene Gedman slicing over from a yard out to build the home team's lead to 17–0. It was only the first quarter, and already the Lions had matched their highest point total in three previous title-game tilts with the Browns.

Cleveland finally settled down. On the first play of the second quarter, Jimmy Brown powered over the right side of the Lions' line, shrugging off two tacklers as he sped 29 yards to the end zone. The scoreboard now read Detroit 17, Cleveland 7. It was still very much a ballgame.

On the Lions' first possession after Brown's score, Rote's passes took them into Cleveland territory. The drive stalled at the Cleveland 26. On fourth down with 11 yards to go, Wilson motioned with a kick of his leg that he wanted Martin to attempt a field goal. As Martin trotted onto the field, Rote, the holder, decided to disobey orders.

"We'd been working on a fake field goal all week in practice," Ken Russell recalled. "So in the huddle, Rote says, 'Damn it, this is our money and we can play with it if we want.' So he called for the fake."

It was a gutsy call. If it didn't work, Cleveland would regain possession and momentum and still be down only 10 points.

But the play did work. As the kneeling Rote took the snap from center, Steve Junker pretended to block down on the linebacker before running an out pattern past Ken Konz. Rote sprang up, whirled to his right, and zipped the ball just past the outstretched fingers of Konz into Junker's waiting hands. "God, don't drop it," Junker said to himself as he hauled in the pass and legged it across the goal stripe.

The Rote-to-Junker hook-up increased Detroit's lead to 24–7 and put the place in an uproar. The din grew even louder when Terry Barr, a rookie defensive back out of Michigan, intercepted an O'Connell pass on the Browns' next possession and returned it 19 yards for a touchdown. Just like that, the game had turned into a 31–7 rout, and there still was more than half a game to play.

Russell, the rookie from Bowling Green, Ohio, remembered that when he was growing up he used to watch the Browns work out in training camp. "I thought those guys were monsters," he said. "Four or five years later, here I am playing against them. Either I got bigger or they got smaller, because they weren't nearly as tough and mean as I remembered them from when I was a young high school kid."

At intermission, Wilson warned his team about the dangers of easing their foot off the gas pedal. "Remember last Sunday when you were behind 27–7 and won," he said. "The Browns can do the same thing."

Sure enough, the Browns managed to narrow the gap to 31–14 midway through the third quarter when ex-Lion Lew Carpenter capped an 80-yard scoring drive with a 5-yard sweep. But any illusions of an otherworldly Cleveland comeback evaporated when Rote immediately answered with a long peg to Jim Doran, who streaked past Konz and raced 78 yards to make it 38–14. That, most Browns agreed, was the backbreaker. Less than four minutes later, Rote hooked up with Junker on a 23-yard scoring strike to run the score to 45–14. It was still the third quarter. The Browns were shell-shocked.

Earlier in the week, on Christmas Day, one of the Detroit coaches had scrawled "Remember 1954!" on the blackboard in the dressing room, a message players filing in from a two-hour workout dismissed as needless, almost hokey, motivation. The prospect of a record playoff share seemed incentive enough, especially to those players—fully half of the squad—who hadn't even been on the field in Cleveland three years earlier.

Now, though, with the score mounting and the championship in the bag, the spirit of revenge took hold. "Sure, we talked about trying to top that 56–10 score," Lou Creekmur admitted. "We talked about it on the sidelines, we talked about it in the huddles—we kept saying, 'C'mon, let's get one more, one more.'"

Seven seconds into the fourth quarter, Rote hit Dave Middleton with a 32-yard touchdown pass. That made it 52–14. Briggs Stadium rocked with the chant: "More . . . more . . . more." Chuck Heaton of the *Cleveland Plain Dealer* reported that "Detroit partisans, recalling the [1954] debacle, were screaming today for their heroes to 'pour it on' at the finish." The din interfered with the Browns' signal-calling, Paul Brown said after the game. "We couldn't hear our own signals. That crowd noise was terrific. There's something about this ball park that makes the crowd noise drown our signals. Finally we just gave up trying to defeat the confusion."

Rote, having wrapped up his greatest performance as a pro, gave way to Jerry Reichow. In addition to his scoring run, Rote had completed 12 of 19 tosses for 280 yards and four touchdowns against the league's top-ranked pass and scoring defense. Meanwhile, the Lions' defense forced seven turnovers and held Jim Brown, the league's top ground gainer, to 69 yards rushing.

As the game clock ticked down, the chanting, cheering, and merrymaking reached a crescendo. "It was euphoria," remembered season-ticket holder Roy Schairer, who was seated in the south end zone. "It was real pandemonium." A couple of bare-chested fans danced in the bleachers, a now common sight that in 1957 still was enough of a spectacle to be mentioned by the press.

"Here's a time-capsule scene for you," said Tom DeLisle, who had dipped into his carefully hoarded confirmation money to buy bleacher seats for himself and his dad. "At one point late in the game, some drunk in our area of the bleachers jumped up and yelled something like, 'We're beating the shit out of these guys!' And with that, about four or five men, including my father, turned on the guy angrily, with one man rising to say that there were kids and women within earshot, and that kind of language wasn't welcome. Shamed, the guy sat down, muttering apologies. Imagine that today?"

DeLisle's favorite memory was when Jim Martin booted the extra point following the Lions' last touchdown, a 16-yard pass from Reichow to Howard Cassady off a fake run with just a couple of minutes left to play. Curiously, it was the only touchdown pass the quarterback from Iowa would ever throw during his eight seasons as a pro, which would include a second championship in 1960 with Philadelphia. Don Colo, who had sneered when Layne was injured on the same field just three weeks earlier, took offense at the way the Lions were piling it on.

"He must have had two or three personal foul penalties on him," Reichow recalled. "I don't blame him. It just happened, and I hadn't played much, so it was my chance. I told him that, too. I said, 'Hey, I don't care what you say, I'm firing and you can do what you want.' And he did. He knocked the daylights out of me a couple times a little later than he probably should have."

By now the end zone was flooded with empty beer cans. After Martin's kick flew through the uprights, accounting for the final point in the 59–14 wipeout, "a drunk crawled out of the stands, weaved through the beer cans into the end zone, and though staggering wildly, was able to corral the bouncing ball," DeLisle said. "He clutched it, weaved back through the cans, and was pulled back into the seats by his buddies, to wild cheering. A great moment, made in Detroit."

Cardboard Lions

An easy-going guy off the football field, Gene becomes a terror
when he steps on the gridiron. Opposing passers get a solid
thumping all afternoon, thanks to his pass-rushing tactics.

—From the back of Gene Cronin's 1959 football card

For Tom DeLisle, a second-grade student at Our Lady of Good Counsel,
there were holy cards—and then there were *holy* cards. It was the
autumn of 1954, and the seven-year-old had just discovered the wonderful world of bubble-gum picture cards. It was more than a temporary schoolboy craze; it was a religious experience on par with his upcoming First Holy
Communion. The sweetly perfumed football cards issued by the Bowman Gum
Company that fall were the gateway to what became DeLisle's lifelong love
affair with all of Detroit's sports teams, but in particular the Lions of the 1950s.

"The 1954 Bowman NFL cards were my all-time favorites—brightly produced color pictures of our favorite players featured over gorgeous green grass,"
he said. "Bobby Layne—always the most in-demand Lions card—was shown flipping a lateral on the memorable emerald pitch at Briggs Stadium. But the highlight for me was the shining card of my all-time hero, Doak Walker, who was

depicted reaching for a white football in his iconic No. 37 Lions Honolulu blue jersey. I stared at that card for weeks, months, years. Decades."

One day at school, DeLisle carefully spread out all of his Lions picture cards on his desk. He sat there, admiring the air-brushed visages and valorous poses, until his home-room nun threatened to confiscate the entire caboodle if he didn't immediately put them away.

"But Sister," he pleaded, "aren't they beautiful?"

They *were* beautiful, and they remain a delight to this day—colorful morsels of Americana that are instant triggers of frothy *Happy Days*–style nostalgia. Kids ate them up, more so than the pink slab of stale gum that came with them. The cards could be traded, flipped, gazed at, or even talked to. There was Hunchy and Hoppy and the Doaker. And Ollie and Bingo and Jug. And lots of Jims, Johns, Joes, Dicks, and Bobs, and one Buddy. And some others who never stepped foot in Briggs Stadium yet for some reason still got a card. To smitten young Lions fans like DeLisle, it was all good.

For all the joy bubble-gum cards engendered, it was a cutthroat business in the 1950s, with Philadelphia-based Bowman battling the Topps Chewing Gum Company of Brooklyn, New York, for supremacy in the sports cards market. The smart money was on Bowman because of its founder and chief driving force, J. Warren Bowman. Burly, lusty, and flamboyant, Bowman was the industry's "King Bub," marrying five times and making a fortune during a colorful and adventurous life.

Among Bowman's many false starts was trying to sell his own line of gum in Detroit in the 1920s. That lesson in futility caused him to leave the Motor City with $25 in his pocket and set up a factory in his native Pennsylvania.

In 1928, Philadelphia's Fleer Chewing Gum Company came out with a new fun product called Dubble Bubble gum. Bubble gum, a more elastic version of regular chewing gum, allowed kids to blow enormous pink bubbles. The formula was never patented, and soon Bowman and Fleer were competing for the pennies of America's youth. Within a few short years, Bowman controlled the biggest share of the market, due to savvy promoting that included the packaging of a picture card with each penny piece.

Picture cards of all sorts, including those with non-sporting themes, had been part of the American advertising landscape since the 1800s. In the 1930s, baseball cards were paired with bubble gum for the first time. Previously, baseball cards had been included as premiums only with tobacco and such candy products as

Cracker Jack. After World War II, with Americans buying 2.5 billion pieces of gum annually, Bowman emerged as the leader in baseball and football trading cards.

Bowman issued the first major national sets of the postwar era. In addition to baseball cards, it produced its first pro football set in 1948. After skipping 1949, it released NFL sets every season from 1950 through 1955, its monopoly protected by an exclusive agreement with the league.

Bowman's 1950 cards have been described as miniature oil portraits, with artists hand-painting color replicas of stock black-and-white photographs. The card fronts contained no text, not even the player's name (which was on the back, along with a block of biographical copy). In 1951, Bowman enlarged its cards and began placing the player's name and team logo on the front. The 1950 and 1951 sets both numbered 144 cards; each featured a dozen different Lions.

As the first waves of baby boomers began to make their mark on pop culture in the early 1950s, football cards, like their baseball counterparts, became a seasonal ritual. The boxes of wax packs started appearing on the shelves and countertops of dime stores, drugstores, grocery markets, sporting goods shops, and other venues in September, just as the baseball season was beginning to wind down and the football season was starting. They were sold through the fall and winter, a new series of 24 or 32 numbered cards released every few weeks until the entire run had been shipped from the plant.

At the time, a single card and a stick of gum could be had for just a penny, but Bowman's cards also came in nickel packs, where the buyer got six cards and two sticks of gum. The gum itself was a problem. Its sticky pink dust often inflicted an irreparable stain on a card's varnish, ruining its looks and its value. Within the span of another generation, bubble-gum cards would actually start being sold without the bubble gum.

In 1952, with the Bowman Gum Company at the height of its profitability, Warren Bowman cashed out. He sold his thriving business to Philadelphia-based Haelen Laboratories just as Topps aggressively moved into the market. The upstart maker of Bazooka bubble gum came out with a giant, groundbreaking baseball card set that summer featuring 407 players, many of them already under exclusive contract with Bowman.

Seymour "Sy" Berger, widely acknowledged as "the father of the modern baseball card," was responsible for the new look, which featured striking portraits and for the first time included a line of statistics on the back. The 1952

Topps baseball set—the most famous set ever produced in any sport—established a new standard for bubble-gum picture cards, especially its larger size: 2½ by 3¾ inches. As more than one collector has since noted, from 1952 on it was clear that Topps was marketing cards while Bowman was still most interested in selling bubble gum.

Bowman was caught flat-footed by Topps's success in the summer of 1952. In response, that fall the company produced two different versions of its 1952 football cards. The "small" Bowmans had the same dimensions as previous sets, while the "large" Bowmans, issued later in the season, were printed in the new card size. Other than size, the two 144-card sets—which included 10 Lions—were identical in every way.

Haelen Labs sued Topps for violating Bowman's contractual rights. Haelen eventually won a partial victory in court, with many of its exclusive contracts with players being upheld. But the high cost of litigation caused Haelen to pull back. The 1953 football Bowmans numbered just 96 cards, with nine Lions surviving the downsizing.

From one year to the next, it was a mystery to collectors why some players got a card while others didn't. What, for example, were Lions fans to make of the 1954 set? That year, Bowman produced cards for Buddy Parker's top four draft choices: Dick Chapman, Jim Neal, Bill Bowman, and Bill Stits. The company, confident that all four players would make the final roster, airbrushed their collegiate uniforms in the Lions' colors. The gum maker was right about Stits and Bowman. But to the dismay of the kids who were stuck with their cards, Chapman and Neal never played a single down of professional ball.

Chapman, a highly regarded tackle at Rice and co-MVP of the 1954 Cotton Bowl, had also been drafted by the Toronto Argonauts. He was open to pulling on a jersey on either side of the U.S.-Canada border, but neither club was able to come up with a solution that would allow the Academic All-American to play while continuing his education in nuclear physics. Thus, while other Lions rookies were scrutinizing playbooks and bar napkins, Chapman remained at Rice, studying the reactions of neutrons produced by proton bombardment of atomic nuclei. He went on to earn his doctorate and author 32 scientific patents, never regretting his decision to stay in Texas.

Neal, the center on Michigan State's Rose Bowl championship team, actually signed a contract with the Lions for $6,250. Parker envisioned him replacing Vince Banonis. However, Neal, who had just married a deeply devout churchgoing girl, later admitted that he had signed just "to get them off my back. I was a new Christian, and I didn't want to play on Sunday."

Following a long career in forestry, Neal and his wife took dozens of evangelistic missions to remote and dangerous parts of South and Central America. "You always wonder if you could have made it," he mused in old age about his missed NFL opportunity. "But why wonder about that? The Lord has blessed me."

In order to use a player's likeness on a card, a gum company had to have a signed agreement granting it permission to do so. The standard licensing contract paid a veteran player $100 for that season's rights. Some players inked multiyear contracts, giving them a bigger check upfront. A rookie was given $10 upon signing a contract; the $90 balance would be paid if he stayed on the team for at least a month. By the end of the decade the going rate was $125 per player per season.

Unlike their baseball counterparts, there were no instances of football players signing "exclusive" contracts with multiple gum companies, and thus no possibility of competing sets of pro football cards. That's because the standard NFL player contract stipulated that every outside source of income, be it a commercial endorsement, ghosted magazine article, or trading card, had to be cleared by the commissioner's office.

Detroit's three most recognizable players, Bobby Layne, Doak Walker, and Leon Hart, were the only Lions to grace a bubble-gum card every fall. Bob Hoernschemeyer, Lou Creekmur, and Jack Christiansen only missed a year here and there. Conversely, Les Bingaman didn't get his first card until 1954, his final season, and Joe Schmidt's fans had to wait until 1956, his fourth year as a starter, before getting what collectors today consider his "rookie" card. And then the Pro Bowl linebacker was misidentified as a halfback!

If a kid happened to be a big fan of Carl Karilivacz or LaVern Torgeson, it didn't matter how much loose change he pushed across the counter at the corner Kinsel's, he never was going to be able to get a card bearing their likeness in a Detroit uniform. Indeed, only about one-third of the 135 men who suited up for Detroit between 1950 and 1959 ever appeared on a Lions picture card during the decade.

Of the many "un-carded" Lions of the '50s, a handful were issued cards while playing for other teams. Frank Gatski, for example, appeared as a Cleveland Brown, and Earl Morrall and Tom Tracy as Pittsburgh Steelers. Don McIlhenny, Ollie Spencer, Roger Zatkoff, and Lew Carpenter received cards as Packers, and Harry Gilmer got his as a Redskin. A few other '50s Lions—Darris McCord, Jim Gibbons,

Danny Lewis, Nick Pietrosante, Jerry Reichow, Wayne Walker, Dick LeBeau, and Gil Mains—didn't get carded until the 1960s. Some Lions, such as Sonny Gandee and Steve Junker, never received a card at any point during their NFL career.

Mains actually made his sports card debut in 1955 as a wrestler, five years before Topps produced his first and only football card. The colorful tackle was featured in the 1955–56 set of wrestling cards manufactured by Parkhurst Products, a Toronto-based confectionary company. In Mains's latter years, he carried around both of his cards, pulling them out for fans, collectors, and reporters. He was proud of those little rectangles encased in plastic. After all, it wasn't every old-timer signing items at a memorabilia show who could claim to have once shared wax packs with such disparate characters as Frank Gifford and Bo-Bo Brazil.

The case of Tom Dublinski was unique. Dublinski tugged on a jersey with the Lions and Giants during the '50s, but his only NFL card, a 1953 Bowman, shows him pitching a pass for a team he never played for. That year Dublinski, then starting his second season as Layne's backup, appeared as a member of the Baltimore Colts. The botched card wasn't a case of mistaken identity but of simply poor timing. In the spring of 1953, Dublinski was traded to the Colts for fullback Dick Hoerner. Bowman issued a card using a publicity photo of him in his Lions uniform with the Colts' colors painted in. However, Hoerner decided to retire rather than report to the Lions. The trade was rescinded, but by then it was too late for the gum company to correct the error.

The last Bowman set was issued in 1955. That year the company assigned Doak Walker the No. 1 card, just as it had in his rookie season. This was a nice little honor that adversely affected future value. That's because many kids organized their cards numerically—lowest number on the top, highest number on the bottom—before wrapping the entire stack with a rubber band. Thus the No. 1 card in any set has typically come down through the years with more condition problems—scuffs, dents, bent edges, and crusty residue when the bands dried up—than others in the middle of the stack. The same holds true for the last number in a set. Some collectors call it "rubber band-itis."

Of course, kids in the '50s weren't eyeing their cards as future investments, though some young connoisseurs treated them with the utmost care and respect. DeLisle's sensibilities were offended by one particularly egregious incident when "some dumb-ass kid from a nearby neighborhood came driving up to our corner on his bike one fall day, and he had a baseball card clipped onto the spokes of his bike to give it kind of a dopey engine sound . . . and we saw that the card was actually a new football card . . . and I looked and it was Bill Bowman, the rookie of the LIONS! Bent up on that kid's bike tire!" DeLisle carefully removed the card from the spokes, gave the kid a Pete Pihos or Andy Robustelli card to replace it, "and after a verbal tirade we sent him on his way. What a dope! The guy had to be nuts."

By 1955, Topps had blown past Bowman to become the leader in baseball card sales. Bowman was hanging on in the sports card market principally because of its football card sales, which remained strong. But its dominance in that field was about to come to an end, too. That year, Topps released its All-American set of 100 collegiate greats (including Bo McMillan) in direct competition with Bowman's NFL set.

Topps had previously released non-NFL football sets, all of which flopped. But this time it had a winner with its new series, which gave buyers a whopping nine cards for a nickel. According to Dean Hanley, author of *The Bubble Gum Card War*, "Topps took what appeared to be a major disadvantage, not being able to issue cards with the images of current NFL players, and turned it into a positive to create a historic set. Collectors responded well to the set of cards that featured the stars from football's past. The All-American card set accomplished its intended purpose and cut into Bowman's badly needed football card sales."

Bowman, its profitability eroded by sagging sales, rising production costs, and years of litigation, finally threw in the towel. In early 1956, its parent company sold the entire sports card business to Topps for the bargain-basement price of $200,000. Soon afterward, Sy Berger visited Bert Bell to negotiate terms for the upcoming NFL season.

"I don't need money," the commissioner said. "I need publicity! I have to show my owners that these cards are doing right for our league."

Bell understood the real value of bubble-gum cards was in their appeal to children, the preteens who would help grow pro football's future. Despite his protestations about money, Bell instantly accepted Berger's suggestion that the nearly $17,000 Topps offered for that season's rights go directly into a fund for players. "We'll have a thing just like the baseball people have," Bell said. That was the start of the Bert Bell Benefit Fund, a first step in official NFL benevolence.

Topps's initial pro football set, released in 1956, had 120 cards. The '59 set grew to 176 cards, the largest yet offered. Eight-year-olds relished the excitement over unwrapping the next fresh pack. Would there be a Hopalong Cassady inside to display on the dresser top in all of his glossy and implacable cardboard glory? The anticipation was heightened by a certain Christmas-morning sense of wonder over how it all came about.

However, it probably was best that curious youngsters never got the chance to visit Topps's version of Santa's workshop, for they surely would've been disappointed to find cigar-chomping designers, copywriters, and printers in green visors cranking out Dorne Dibbles and Yale Larys in the same poky fashion that their dads bolted together Chevy Bel-Airs and Kelvinator refrigerators every day at work. "Contrary to what children at the time might have imagined," Dave Jamieson wrote in *Mint Condition*, a quirky history of card collecting, "the Topps offices weren't exactly a place where elfin men chewed bubble gum and cheerfully designed next season's . . . cards. Instead, picture a batch of poorly dressed artistic cranks toiling away in a dilapidated plant in an industrialized part of Brooklyn."

At that, the company was tremendously successful. The decade ended with Topps positioned to monopolize the sports card market for many years to come. Left behind was the golden age of pro football picture cards.

Taken as a whole, vintage football cards today don't command the same prices that baseball cards from the same era do. However, to aging baby boomers with lingering memories of Ollie Cline and Ray "The Moose" Krouse, their true worth has always transcended dollars and cents.

"The best part of the Lions cards in those early days was the terrific team logo that was prominently displayed on the front," DeLisle reminisced. "Our eyes lit up when we beheld that logo in the middle of a five-cent pack of cards. A Lion!"

13

Goodbye, TWO-MINUTE *Guy*

In football you can't stay at one place for a long time.
It's kind of like a car dealer being in town for a long time—
sooner or later he's a son of a bitch.

—Bobby Layne

Despite Detroit's run of four division titles in six years and a core group of old reliables, not many preseason observers had the "man-eating Lions" repeating as champions in 1958. The Baltimore Colts were ascendant, while it was thought that Detroit's roster had not been adequately replenished with fresh blood over the previous couple of seasons. "I think we can do just as well as we did last year," Harley Sewell told a Texas reporter before leaving for camp, "if we have the same kind of luck."

Of course, it's impossible to plan on the breaks all falling a certain way. "Our best football team was 1956, not '57," Jerry Reichow said. "A lot of good things happened to us in '57. Then all of a sudden a lot of not-so-good things happened to us, and it was all downhill from there."

The first pebbles of the Lions' downhill slide shook loose on August 15, 1958, at Chicago's Soldier Field. In front of 70,000 spectators and a prime-time television audience, the reigning NFL champions were upset by the College All-Stars, 35–19, despite holding them to three yards rushing and piling up 22 first downs to their 11. Michigan State's Jim Ninowski, a former Detroit prep star drafted by the Browns, hit on 14 of 20 passes for 243 yards and two touchdowns. Both scoring strikes went to Illinois star Bobby Mitchell and were part of a 20-point splurge in the second quarter that wiped out the Lions' 7–0 lead. Detroit's vaunted secondary was shredded, leading to the most points yet scored by the collegians in the series' history.

Layne never looked comfortable, getting picked off five times and missing two extra-point attempts. Admittedly, it was his first competition since injuring his right leg eight months earlier. But the sorry exhibition may have started his exit from Detroit. Otto Graham, coaching the All-Stars, relished Detroit's defeat, something he had rarely experienced as a player.

Alex Karras, the 10th overall pick in the draft, played for the All-Stars (sacking Tobin Rote for a safety) before joining the Lions at camp. The 6-foot-2, 248-pound tackle with the horn-rimmed glasses, the son of a Greek immigrant, had won the Outland Trophy as the country's top lineman, finished second in Heisman voting, and already made $25,000 wrestling professionally since the end of his senior season. He rolled into Cranbrook on a sultry, mosquito-filled night. He hadn't gotten along with Graham, and he was afraid word might have already reached Wilson about his supposed bad attitude. He was unpacking in his dorm room when Wilson suddenly appeared in the doorway.

"I have a report from Otto Graham about you," the coach said. "It's awful. As a matter of fact, he thinks you're not going to make it here. What do you have to say for yourself?"

Karras said he hoped Wilson would just give him a chance.

"Well, Alex," Wilson said, "I want to tell you exactly how I feel. If Otto Graham says that about you—you must be one great sonofabitch. I'm glad to have you here."

NFL rosters had been expanded to 35 players in 1957, making room for more specialists. Although colleges continued to play single-platoon football (Karras had also played offensive tackle at Iowa, albeit half-heartedly), the era of the two-way players that had characterized Detroit's teams earlier in the decade had all but passed. In fact, in 1960, when injuries caused Philadelphia's Chuck Bednarik to play both center and middle linebacker, he was widely hailed as a heroic anachronism, "the last of the 60-minute men."

One-quarter of the Lions' final roster in 1958 were first-year men. Among the nine rookies making the team was Wayne Walker, who centered the ball at Idaho but was more impressive at linebacker, the position the Lions drafted him for. Walker drove in with Karras from Chicago, the stories about the Lions' famous hazing fresh in their heads. The two shared a room in camp. Both were fearful of being made the focus of abuse.

"You respected these guys so much, you had heard so much about them," Walker said. Being singled out and embarrassed "was really hard to take. You never knew when they'd have you singing, chasing things down for them, shining shoes, bringing them coffee, running errands. The best thing you could do as a rookie was stay by yourself. That's not a very good existence or atmosphere to have on a ball club. Even after you made the team and proved yourself, you were accepted a little more, but that thing still continued."

Layne immediately claimed Karras as his own. "Rookie," he said one day, "from now on you just follow me around like a puppy." Layne dubbed him "Puppy," then "Tippy" because of the "tippy-toe" way Karras ran. Layne had Karras chauffeur him around in his high-powered Pontiac, hitting any number of show bars and barbecue joints in and around Detroit.

One memorable night Karras was too sick from drinking to drive. He sat in the passenger seat, his spinning head in his hands, while Layne took over the wheel.

"He was happy," Karras said. "He was singing 'Ida Red.' That was his favorite song, though he only knew two or three phrases from it, which he'd sing over and over. I looked across at him and when my head cleared I could see that he had his right foot up on the dashboard, and his left leg out the window. He had something jammed in the accelerator which held it right to the floor, because we were doing about one hundred miles per hour, the car just shaking itself to pieces, down the expressway."

Karras sobered up in a hurry, and from then on he made sure he drove, no matter how much Cutty Sark and water he had in him. "Sometimes I rested my chin on the steering wheel and drove four miles an hour," he said. "He didn't seem to mind."

Layne and Rote went into camp unhappy about sharing quarterbacking duties. With a championship under his belt, Wilson had no real incentive to change the system. Although Layne and Wilson both denied any friction, there seemed to be subtle tension between the two strong-willed individuals.

Dorne Dibble, one of Layne's biggest supporters, always thought Wilson was jealous of the quarterback's "power," by which he meant influence. The keenly observant Karras also picked up on a certain vibe between Layne and some of the staff.

"The coaches never liked Layne much," Karras claimed. "He trampled on their authority. When he was on the field, it was his field, not theirs. The coaches would work these plays out on the blackboard, precise diagrams which they'd copy into the playbooks for the players to study and learn, and then down on the practice field Layne would give a little yawn and say, 'Hey, George, tell that boy over theah when he makes that outside cut, to make it about fahv more feet deep. Heah?' The coaches didn't like that sort of thing. It made them look like fools. But they went along with it, because they know that nobody knew quarterbacking like Layne."

Despite the Lions' mythologized camaraderie, it had been a while since Layne could count on a full house every Monday afternoon at the Stadium Bar. The ringleader was now 31 and starting his ninth season in Detroit. Not everyone bought into the legend. Walker spoke for more than a few harassed rookies when he said, "I could have cared less about Bobby Layne," but even some veterans, such as Howard Cassady and Leon Hart, had little use for him off the field. Respected long-time clubhouse employee Charles "Rip" Collins, who as a boy was Hank Greenberg's favorite and as a Marine pilot flew jets with Ted Williams in Korea, was put off by some of Layne's unreported exploits. "He wasn't a gentleman," said Collins, who knew a few things.

The merrymaking that marked the championship squad of the early 1950s was fading, replaced by a kind of perfunctory conviviality that some veterans—those with growing families and businesses and other outside interests to attend to—quietly did their best to avoid. "After 1953 I saw this spirit start dwindling away," Layne said later, blaming the change on money. "When I was playing at Detroit in those early years, no ballplayer ever heard of the goddamn stock market, and they didn't have any money to put into it anyway. But now you see guys sit down on the edge of a secretary's desk and pick up her phone and say, 'What's General Motors doing today?'"

General Motors, with half of the market, was doing fine. The Lions, not so much. On September 28, Detroit opened the regular season against Johnny Unitas and the Colts. The Lions were coming off of an uncharacteristically poor preseason, dropping their final three exhibitions. The last was a 41–7 shellacking at the hands of the Browns, which should have set off warning bells.

"Do the Lions still have it?" George Puscas wondered in print. "The Lions are aware that there are teams with better all-around personnel than theirs. Baltimore, in some quarters, is given a clear vote as the most talent-rich team of all. Yet, the same was true a year ago. And still the Lions won the championship. Resourcefulness, poise, and muscle did the job in 1957."

At Baltimore, Layne and Rote both threw scoring passes to Cassady as Detroit clung to a narrow 15–14 lead in the fourth quarter. It was a typical Lions-Colts tussle. At one point, defensive back Carl Taseff gave John Henry Johnson a mighty kick in the ribs as the fullback lay sprawled on the sideline. Later, Johnson smacked linebacker Bill Pellington in the face. The penalty led to Baltimore's go-ahead score, a short touchdown pass from Johnny Unitas to Raymond Berry. The Colts added another six-pointer to account for their 28–15 victory.

There was no need for panic. The Lions had played well, and it was recalled that the '57 team had split its first six games before settling down and winning the championship. Still, the next game at Green Bay was crucial. By Thanksgiving the Western Conference would undoubtedly be tightly bunched, as it always seemed to be. If the Lions were true title contenders, they needed to beat up on the league's little cousins.

Rote started and played the entire first half. He and Jim Doran connected on a 65-yard scoring pass, the Lions' only points as the Packers took a 13–6 lead into intermission. Layne, who had blown an extra point against the Colts, missed again after Doran's touchdown. Rote, the holder, came to Layne's defense. "It wasn't Bobby's fault," he said. "I got a high, wobbly pass from center and couldn't get the ball down in time. When Bobby kicked, our timing was off." The missed extra point would turn out to be crucial.

Layne started the second half and led a drive that ended with a short touchdown run by Ken Webb, a rookie back out of Presbyterian College. Layne converted to knot the score at 13-all. But in the fourth quarter, the Lions squandered four chances to break the deadlock. Webb fumbled away one opportunity on the Packers' 10-yard line and another drive died when Layne was intercepted on the Green Bay 11. Rote came back in and guided a foray that stalled at Green Bay's 10, after which Jim Martin missed a short field-goal attempt.

Then, with two minutes to go, Gil Mains recovered a fumble on the Packers'

16. Layne brought the offense back onto the field. Webb gained two yards on a run, then Layne overshot a receiver. On third down, Layne called for a pitchout to Gene Gedman. His toss to the halfback was off the mark. Gedman desperately reached for the ball, but he couldn't corral it. Green Bay recovered and the game ended in a 13–13 tie.

It was a brutal performance against an inferior opponent (Green Bay would finish 1-10-1), and Layne got much of the blame. "Bobby Layne is a bundle of nerves and the Detroit Lions, flopping in the defense of their championship, miss the calm leadership they used to get from one of professional football's great quarterbacks," Watson Spoelstra wrote in Monday's *Detroit News*. "Before it is valid to ask what's wrong with the Lions, one must figure out what's wrong with Layne."

Layne was miserable. He couldn't find his rhythm splitting chores with Rote, and even point-afters had become an adventure. He seemed to have lost his composure, reverting to the fumbling ways of his early years and screaming at an offense that was stuck in low gear. During the Packers game, he gave Doran and guard Stanley Campbell each a going-over in plain sight of the delighted Green Bay crowd, once wasting a time-out in order to deliver his rant.

Layne was getting beat up by the press and unhappy fans. And in a few days, those critics would be out in force for the home opener against Los Angeles. The depressed quarterback thought of going home to Texas. When he called his wife, she told him to stay put. She would come up to Detroit.

On Monday, October 6, Wilson spoke at the weekly Lions Fan Club luncheon at the Statler. He blasted the team, something he had rarely done in the past. He especially fumed over the lack of production from his backs. "I've got four girls and a boy at home," he said. "We can get more yardage than that—and you can print that. You want the names of the girls?"

Wilson also criticized Layne's judgment on the final drive, questioning why he hadn't kept the ball in the middle of the field to line up the potential game-winning field goal instead of pitching the ball wide to Gedman. There was a sense in the room that something was afoot.

There was. Earlier that morning, Wilson had called Buddy Parker in Pittsburgh. Would he be interested in Layne? Wilson had been mulling the idea of trading the quarterback since training camp. After the events of the weekend, he was ready to pull the trigger.

On the evening before the Green Bay game, Wilson had unexpectedly called a 10 p.m. meeting. Veterans grumbled over the unusual Saturday night session.

Some showed up having had a few drinks. Wilson was steamed over Layne's condition and was in the mood to fine him, though he later downplayed the incident when reports of an acrimonious meeting and a "smoldering feud" between him and Layne appeared a couple of days later in the press.

"Layne probably had a couple of cocktails," Wilson admitted. "Sure, and some of the other players probably had a couple of drinks or a beer or two. But that's not unusual. Layne was not drunk, and neither was anybody else. And nobody had any cross words." On the plane ride home from Green Bay on Sunday night, the drinking and the bitching resumed, as Layne was openly critical of how the team was being run.

On Monday, Wilson and Parker went back and forth a little before settling on a price for Layne: a promising young quarterback named Earl Morrall and two future draft picks. Morrall was a local hero, the Muskegon native having led Michigan State to a Rose Bowl win in his final college game. He was the second player chosen in the 1956 draft, with the 49ers intending to groom him as Y. A. Tittle's eventual replacement. However, after Morrall's rookie season he was traded to Pittsburgh for two first-round draft picks and Pro Bowl linebacker Marv Matuszak. Morrall floundered as a starter in Pittsburgh. He needed seasoning, but Parker was impatient. He wanted to win now.

There was little pushback as Wilson rounded up approval for the trade. Nick Kerbawy, a Layne ally, had left the club in the spring for his new executive position with the Detroit Pistons. Edwin Anderson was now general manager as well as club president, having resigned his position at Goebel to take on both Lions jobs for a handsome salary of $50,000. Anderson backed Wilson. So did the directors, some of whom may have simply grown tired of Layne. One prominent director had enlisted his son, a recent college graduate, to surreptitiously keep tabs on Layne's off-field activities, though it's unknown what he reported back.

The trade for one of the NFL's biggest names, announced Monday afternoon, caught everybody by surprise. Wilson intended to inform the quarterback personally when he stopped by the Lions' offices to collect his weekly check. But Layne was at the airport, picking up his wife. When Layne was paged over the P.A. system, his first reaction was, "I'll bet they have traded me." He admitted to being shocked and depressed after talking with Wilson on the phone.

Teammates were naturally taken aback by the news. "Bobby is still a good leader and we think he's a fine quarterback," said Lou Creekmur, now the senior member of the team. "I guess we all know how we stand. You never know where you'll be tomorrow." Doc Greene was present when Bobby and Carol paid a quick goodbye visit at the Stadium Bar. The cook lady started crying, and soon the Laynes were blubbering, too. "Great quarterbacks will come again to town; great roisterers too, perhaps," Greene wrote. "But there'll not be another like this one."

Viewing the trade from the perspective of many years, Joe Schmidt said: "I couldn't figure it out. I couldn't understand why. Not that Tobin wasn't a good guy or a fine quarterback. I just thought that would never happen because Layne did so much for Detroit. It was like the Yankees trading Joe DiMaggio or Mickey Mantle—you just don't do it. I always thought there was an underlying reason."

Stunned Layne fans also tried to figure out the *real* reason behind the unexpected departure of one of the town's favorite athletes. There had to have been some ulterior motive. Surely the move couldn't have been entirely performance-based. There were all kinds of rumors. To this day, a former groundskeeper insists he witnessed a fight outside the Stadium Bar between Layne and Rote, a dust-up evidently nobody else saw or heard about.

Anderson suggested a simmering rivalry had backs and ends quietly choosing sides. "Openly they got along fine," he told the press. "But they must have had some resentment of each other. Each thought he should start every game. How wide the breach was no one knows because they never discussed it."

Players, then and now, insisted there was no apparent personal feud, just a naturally competitive rivalry in a system that neither man liked. "They were two different kinds of quarterbacks," recalled Ken Russell. "Tobin was a bit more polished at ball handling and threw a better pass, and Bobby would get in your face more. But there wasn't anything between them that I ever noticed. Both of them were winners, and they both wanted to play."

More sinister were the stories that later came out—that Layne had placed large bets on games, including those in which he played, and that his poor performances were attempts to cover the point spread. In this scenario, management had no choice but to get rid of him. On the surface, the rumors seemed plausible. Layne regularly wagered on just about anything, and the country was periodically rocked by sports-betting scandals. But even if Layne had wanted to, it's practically impossible for an individual player to arrange the outcome of a football game.

"No one player, not even a quarterback, can fix a game," maintained broadcaster Harry Wismer, an original investor in the Detroit Football Company and an astute observer of the game in the postwar era. "Too many situations arise over which the players or coach [has] no control." In fact, the quarterback would be the least-likely conspirator "because his teammates and coaches would immediately suspect something if he deviated from the game plans too often or if his passes were consistently off the mark. The person I would go to would be an official. . . . If my partner in crime were the umpire, he could control the score by dropping his flag whenever the wrong team scored."

Bert Bell had a network of bookmakers and detectives in every NFL city. These contacts enabled the league to monitor unusual fluctuations in the point spread and any unsavory characters players may have been associating with, usually inadvertently. Layne was investigated. There was no evidence that he ever shaved points or threw a game.

Layne would spend five years in Pittsburgh before retiring as the league's career leader in several passing categories (including yardage, interceptions, and touchdown passes) following the 1962 season. "I know I've been accused of betting on games, especially when my team loses, but I take it with a grain of salt," he said at the time. "Losing gamblers grumble no matter what happens.

"First of all, I would have to be crazy to endanger my livelihood for a few thousand dollars. People think that all you have to do is call up and bet and collect the money week after week. I know guys who bet—who doesn't? But I owe a lot to football and to jeopardize my reputation would be ridiculous. Even if I had been betting, it would have come out in the open long ago. A coaching career and other sidelines face me when I no longer can play, and the long pull appeals to me more than the quick buck."

Why was Layne traded? Although conspiracy theorists are loath to admit it, the simplest explanation often is the correct one. Layne wasn't run out of town for being part of a gambling ring or sent packing for punching out a teammate in the alley. The trade was all about getting something while there still was something to get. Rote was two years younger, a proven winner, respected in the locker room—and, as a bonus, less likely to give management heartburn. Rote was ready to assume full-time signal-calling with a promising understudy, Morrall, in the wings.

There had been talk of impending moves all off-season. The championship game romp was barely over when some in the press began speculating that Layne, Jack Christiansen, and other fan favorites were likely to be shopped around in order to keep the team competitive. Wilson had already traded two productive veterans, Dorne Dibble and Ray Krouse. Dibble decided to retire and concentrate on his insurance business instead of reporting to the Giants, while Krouse would help Baltimore beat New York in the next two title games.

"I favor trading a player while he still has some value to the club," Wilson expressed to the *Saturday Evening Post* in a feature published the week before he traded Layne. "I wanted Parker to trade Doak Walker, Cloyce Box, and Bob Hoernschemeyer a few seasons back, but he wouldn't. Finally, all three retired and we didn't get a thing for them. I know it sounds cold and a bit cruel, but that's the way this business is—cold and cruel. You can't afford to be sentimental. A lot of teams hold onto players who are over the hill. The Lions already are behind schedule in revamping the squad."

For his part, Layne admitted to being "one confused quarterback" after the trade.

"The memories of the great teams and the great times in Detroit, and the prospect of coming cold to a new town, made me feel lousy," he said. "On the other hand, I would be rejoining Buddy Parker and have the chance to be in on a rebuilding job. And, frankly, I wasn't really happy at Detroit anymore. A lot of my pals had quit playing, and being a guy who likes to play every play, I was upset with my position as an alternate quarterback."

The Steel City, accustomed to years of mediocrity on the gridiron, was beside itself with glee. To Al Abrams, sports editor of the *Post-Gazette*, Layne was "Detroit's finest gift to Pittsburgh since the automobile." Following a blowout loss to Cleveland on the second Sunday of the season, the Steelers had scheduled a players-only meeting to clear the air. But Layne's arrival changed everything.

"We can forget that meeting now," said one Steeler. "We got our man. One Bobby Layne is worth ten meetings."

Layne, wholly familiar with Parker's offensive system, took immediate command of the huddle. He led the Steelers to a convincing win in his first start and guided the club to seven victories and a tie in his 10 games in black and gold. Pittsburgh's final 7-4-1 record in 1958 gave it a third-place finish and its first winning season since 1949. "That ol' blond fella turned us into a football team," Parker said. "He's the only guy who could have made so much of a difference so fast."

Layne was ably assisted by his old Detroit teammate and drinking buddy Tom Tracy. The stumpy back, whom Parker acquired for a draft choice just before the start of the regular season, became a fixture at the right halfback position, an all-purpose workhorse in the mode of Bob Hoernschemeyer. Over the next few seasons, Tracy regularly ranked near the top in combined rushes, receptions, and returns, and was twice selected for the Pro Bowl. He was a threat on the halfback option, throwing for more yards during his career than any non-quarterback in NFL history.

But even someone with Tracy's demonstrated endurance found it hard keeping up with Layne. During a game against Philadelphia in their first season together as Steelers, Tracy concluded a long run by crawling on all fours along the sideline, retching his guts out. He and Layne had imbibed a bit the night before, but only Tracy was feeling the after-effects. As Tracy told the story, Layne came up behind him, kicked him square in the backside, and said, "Dammit, Bomber, why don't you get in shape?"

The trading of the Lions' franchise player had other players considering the sub-message: start winning or else. During the first practice following the trade, Jimmy David took Layne's place holding the ball for the kickers.

"Hey, Hatchet, what're you doing there?" someone asked.

"Looking for job security," he joked.

With and then without Layne, the '58 Lions proved to be as big a dud as Ford's new Edsel, the overhyped "car of the future" with the unfortunate toilet-seat-shaped grille. After a 0-3-1 start, they split their next eight games, with three of the losses being by a total of 10 points.

There were some interesting moments. Against Los Angeles, Gene Gedman and Terry Barr pulled off a lateral on a kickoff return that resulted in a 104-yard touchdown, the Lions' longest scoring play of the decade. Less successful was Yale Lary's controversial fake punt against New York on a fourth-and-forever play that allowed the Giants to rally and squeak out a crucial late-season victory at frozen Briggs Stadium. Wayne Walker, who would take up placekicking and retire as the team's all-time points leader, scored the only two touchdowns of his 15-year career in 1958, returning an interception against the Rams and scooping up a fumble against the Giants.

The linebacker's most vivid memory of the season, however, was when he and several veterans tried to enter a high school field to work out during the team's West Coast trip.

"There was a fence around the field," Walker told Jerry Green. "I went out early with Tobin Rote, Charley Ane, Jim Martin, Jerry Perry, and Bob Long. The gate was locked and I was the only rookie there. They said, 'You climb over and get the caretaker and have him let us in.' I said, 'Okay.' There were about 150 people waiting to watch practice because we were world champions that year. I had on blue shorts and a gray T-shirt and football shoes. I got up on top of the fence and it was a 10-foot drop. I leaped down and my shorts hooked and when I hit the ground, I had nothing on but my jock. My shorts were still on top of the fence."

Walker's embarrassing descent was the perfect metaphor for the Lions' free fall in the standings. Demoralized and beset by injuries, the defending champs finished with a 4-7-1 mark, ahead of only the Packers. Some were inclined to write off the season as an aberration, much like the lost year of 1955, and look for a rebound in 1959. But with the departure of their spiritual leader and the graying of other favorites, the Lions' glory ride through a golden decade had coasted to a stop.

14

Football

IN A Box

After World War II, television—the "magic box" or the "boob-tube" if you will—began to come into its own and to change the living habits of all Americans. And if television's impact was felt in the field of news and entertainment, its influence on sports was and is tremendous. For boxing, it meant quick riches and a slow death. For baseball it meant the end of most of the minor leagues and the beginning of public apathy toward the game. For football, TV has been a bonanza.

—Harry Wismer

On December 28, 1958, at Yankee Stadium, Baltimore fullback Alan Ameche barged through a hole in the New York Giants' line and scored the winning touchdown in the first championship game ever to go into sudden death overtime. In a country of 175 million people, an estimated 45 million, including President Eisenhower, watched CBS's coverage of the Colts' 23–17 victory. The fierce tension and unprecedented climax hooked viewers. *Sports Illustrated* labeled it "The Best Football Game Ever Played," which even its participants admitted it wasn't. But in terms of what it meant to the future of the NFL, it may have been the most consequential. America was well on its way to becoming a nation of watchers, not participants, and the Colts-Giants spectacle, staged in the media capital of the world, helped propel that change.

Football and television were perfectly nade for each other. Unlike baseball, a laconic pastime often described as "the thinking man's game," the activity in a NFL game was constant and concentrated, with the east-west flow of action conforming nicely with the screen's "landscape" dimensions. Because NFL games were played inside ballparks whose sight lines were originally designed for baseball, most patrons were far from the action. But the camera turned every easy chair into a seat on the 50-yard line. In fact, it was easier to follow the game on TV than at the park, which was not the case with baseball.

Today it's hard to picture what the world was like before television. In the years following World War II, "video" receivers bearing such nameplates as Philco, DuMont, and Westinghouse had the same revolutionary impact that another "magic box," a computer linked to the Internet, would have a couple of generations later. At the beginning of the '50s, roughly one in 10 Detroit households had a television set. By the end of the decade that ratio had flipped, with 90 percent of homes owning at least one TV.

The medium and the league had both come a long way since the first NFL telecast in 1939, when NBC broadcast the Brooklyn Dodgers-Philadelphia Eagles game from Ebbets Field. At the time, there were about 1,000 sets in New York. The Lions made their television debut on Detroit's Channel 7 on October 9, 1948, as their night game with the Boston Yanks at Briggs Stadium capped WXYZ-TV's first day of programming. After discovering that televising home games dampened attendance, the Lions, like most pro teams, quit airing them. Road games were only sporadically broadcast.

These were primitive but exciting times for the new medium. Tom Baranski of Detroit was 10 years old when his family got its first television set, an inexpensive model with a 12-inch screen. "Dad was a real sports nut," he said, "so we had to get one. I can remember going up to the Woolworth's on Chene and seeing them put these different colored plastic sheets over the screen: blue, green, yellow. That was color TV then, I guess."

Sunday afternoons had yet to be given over to "football in a box" when the Baranskis bought their TV in 1951. That November, any Detroiters hoping to tune into the Lions-Packers game from Green Bay would have been severely disappointed. They would have instead been treated to the quiz show *Twenty Questions*—one of which might have been, "Where are the Lions?"

In fact, there was no pro football of any kind available on local TV that particular Sunday, just programming like *Meet the UAW-CIO*. A coast-to-coast system of coaxial cables, through which television signals were transmitted along with thousands of telephone calls, had just been completed, but bandwidth was limited and expensive. Some road games that season, sponsored by Goebel's on a case-by-case basis, were "piped in" via regional hook-ups. The telecast of the Lions' crucial game at San Francisco that December had to conclude at exactly 7:30 p.m., even if it meant cutting away from the game in its last gripping seconds. There was only so much electrical carrying capacity and CBS needed it to transmit the *Jack Benny Show*. It wasn't until 1954 that the Lions' entire road schedule was televised back to Detroit. By then televised NFL games on DuMont were capturing 36.3 percent of the market, up from 17.1 percent in 1951.

In 1953, DuMont began airing Saturday night games to a national audience, an experiment that foreshadowed the launch of ABC's *Monday Night Football* a couple of decades later. The first-ever prime-time evening telecast of an NFL game involved the Lions. On October 3, 1953, the defending champions beat the Colts, 27–17, in Baltimore. For the next three seasons, all of the Lions' games with Baltimore, both home and away, would be televised during prime time as part of DuMont's season-long slate of Saturday match-ups. (Among the Colts' broadcasting crew was a brush-cut announcer named Ernie Harwell.) Although DuMont was floundering, its prime-time NFL telecasts were a success, drawing nearly a quarter of all viewers.

Tom DeLisle caught football fever from his sports-loving father, Charles, an accountant with an office in the Penobscot Building. "We never missed a game on radio, until we got our first television set in 1954, which made fall Sundays even more of an event," DeLisle said. "One of the great shocks of my life followed: seeing Van Patrick on TV for the first time. I had always assumed, from hearing that booming heroic voice on the radio, that he must have looked like the guy who played Superman on the weekly adventure show. Quite a shock for a sensitive youth to see what he really looked like."

Balding, jowly, and upholstered, the impeccably dressed "Ol' Announcer" (as Patrick liked to call himself) was as integral to pro football's growing popularity in the '50s as many of the stars who suited up on Sunday.

Patrick grew up in Hicksville, Arkansas, and earned his stripes broadcasting for stations in the Southwest before moving on to Cleveland in the late '40s. He was glib, outgoing, and accustomed to a certain amount of embroidering. He said he played football with Sammy Baugh at Texas Christian University in the mid-1930s, though his name doesn't appear on the school's official list of lettermen. Detroit's WJR didn't care, hiring him in 1949.

"We didn't have any money, so we didn't get a TV until 1955," remembered Bill Grain, a retired electrician who grew up in Detroit. "What we had was one of those big tube radios—the dial lit up, the knobs lit up. Radio was exciting. You could close your eyes and imagine. As a young boy it was really something. A big part of the excitement was the announcers, Van Patrick and Bob Reynolds. These guys were a big part of my life as a kid." Reynolds began his sports media career as a reporter for the *Springfield Union* in Massachusetts, then moved to Michigan to work at Flint's WFDF after World War II. In 1952, WJR hired Reynolds to become the station's first sports director and Patrick's "color man" on broadcasts.

Patrick was the only broadcaster in a major market simulcasting the play-by-play for TV and radio. "It's my theory that you have to keep listeners interested on radio but can't overdramatize it for television," he said. However, Patrick wasn't always able to strike such a happy balance. *Sports Illustrated* grumped after the Ol' Announcer worked the 1957 title game at Briggs Stadium: "Certainly millions of professional football fans came away from the TV broadcast . . . in a mood to cuff children, because an announcer named Van Patrick doggedly persisted—in hallowed radio fashion—in telling them in detail, and without surcease, what they could already see for themselves on their own screens."

Patrick's rich, distinctive voice was the omniscient soundtrack of Lions football in the 1950s—and beyond. His death from cancer at the start of the 1974 season ended his nearly quarter-century run in the Lions' booth. By then he had introduced such now-familiar phrases as "home-run ball" (a deep pass) and "cliffhanger" (a close game) to the sports broadcasting lexicon. "I always said that if he wasn't a sports announcer he would've made a great character actor," said veteran Detroit broadcaster Ray Lane. "And maybe he was."

In 1956, CBS took over national NFL telecasts from the failed DuMont network. Broadcasts remained simple, straightforward affairs. Only two cameras were used and instant replay didn't exist. Because most sets were black and white, that season the league began its policy of having the home team wear white jerseys and the visiting team dark. Teams also were required to sew "TV numbers" on uniform sleeves to help broadcasters identify players. For night games, CBS's stricter lighting requirements meant no more white footballs after 1955, a relief for players who complained that the painted balls were too slippery to handle and often got lost in a sea of white uniforms. Roy Macklem was happy he no longer had to spend hours spray-painting the Lions' traditional silver helmets blue, a league-mandated color change intended to provide better contrast with the white pigskin. The new balls for night games were brown with white stripes. Meanwhile, the medium was turning Detroit's Thanksgiving Day traditions into national institutions. In 1957, the Hudson's parade (first aired nationally by NBC in 1952) was broadcast on ABC via 108 stations and watched by 15 million people. The Lions-Packers game that followed attracted 30 million viewers on 190 stations.

Television was instrumental in stabilizing a league accustomed to decades of franchise upheavals. By the end of the '50s, pro football was an entrenched ritual for millions, whether seated at home or in the grandstand. In 1959, NFL attendance averaged 43,617 per game, a 70 percent increase since 1950. During the decade the Lions more than doubled the size of their home crowds. The high-water mark was 1957, when they averaged 55,743 admissions per game. That winter the club sold 42,154 season tickets, a fourth straight record-breaking haul. Due largely to the weak '58 season and a lingering economic recession, the Lions would experience a dip in attendance and season ticket sales in 1959. (The fall-off also reflected the growing use of "booster" antennas, which cost bootlegging fans and businesses about $20 each, installed. Bar owners advertised "See All Games Here," with such places as Lindell's and the Willis Show Bar grabbing signals from WJRT in Flint and WJIM in Lansing. It wouldn't be until 1973 that the NFL lifted the blackout for games sold out at least 72 hours before kickoff.)

John Gordy, who had left the Lions for an assistant's job at Nebraska, returned in 1959. Although he was to enjoy a solid career as one of the best pulling guards in the league, his most consequential labor was helping to grow the fledgling NFL Players Association into a potent collective bargaining unit. Joe Schmidt was the team's representative when the NFLPA was organized over the winter of 1956–57. Detroit was the ultimate union town, but that didn't mean all sports executives believed in solidarity. While Edwin Anderson endorsed the union (noting that his players were already treated well), Jack Adams's response to Ted Lindsay's organizing efforts during this period was to trade the popular Red Wings captain to Chicago.

The initial requests by NFL players were modest: a $5,000 minimum salary, an injury clause in all contracts, and union recognition. A compromise was reached on preseason pay. As of 1957, a player could borrow $50 per exhibition, the loans being deducted from his first regular-season paycheck. Rookies who were cut could keep any advances. These were baby steps, but the union slowly gathered strength. Starting in 1961, the league, not individual clubs, negotiated TV contracts, meaning each team now got an equal slice of the pie. Players demanded their share of the ever-growing treasure. "I remember talking to the guys and they'd say, 'Oh, well, television,'" said Jerry Reichow. "Nobody in the '50s was really thinking about television. But that's where the money was. It took a while for everybody to realize it, and that's when salaries started to rise." The NFLPA today is one of the most powerful unions in the country. The deal it negotiated for the Pro Bowl is a small but illustrative example. When Schmidt played in the game following the 1959 season, he received a winner's share of $700. Sixty years later, the payout was a helmet-spinning $70,000 per man.

Harley Sewell had a country boy's knack for folksy wisdom. "When you've got holes in your shoes," the veteran guard liked to say, "your feet get cold."

That was as good an analysis as any of the 1959 Lions. Detroit's last team of the decade was on a par with the cellar-dwelling clubs of the late 1940s. The team had plenty of holes, including an aging offensive line and a set of pedestrian receivers. For the third straight September, the Lions opened their schedule with a loss at Baltimore, this time by a 21–9 score. It was just one defeat, but uneasy fans were already dreading another lost season in the making.

That was evident when boosters gathered for their first Monday luncheon of the season at the Statler. Unlike previous years, not all of the tables were filled and there were no choruses of "Gridiron Heroes." "No one sang the Fight Song," marveled George Puscas. "Even in dismal 1958, when the Lions were losing and looking mighty bad doing it, they always sang the Fight Song." One fan, an insurance agent, explained why. "We've grown so accustomed to winners around here that we're trapped when we have only losers."

In Green Bay, where Vince Lombardi had taken over as coach, the vastly improved Packers whipped the Lions, 28–10, in the second game of the season. The next Sunday the Colts spoiled Detroit's home curtain-raiser with a 31–24 victory, and a week later San Francisco crushed the Lions, 34–13. One month deep into the schedule, the team was already throwing in the towel.

Scouting director Bob Nussbaumer strained to strike an optimistic note in his periodic letters to college prospects. "As you probably know," he wrote University of Detroit halfback Bruce Maher a few days later, "the Lions have had a disappointing season so far. There will be an excellent opportunity for you to become part of our rebuilding program for next year." Maher, a Detroit boy who had grown up idolizing Doak Walker, would be one of the collegians the team depended on as it reloaded for a new decade.

As in 1958, George Wilson's squad was winless in its first four games. And once again, it finally broke into the victory column at Los Angeles, this time beating the Rams, 17–7. But after watching his team get stomped the following week in San Francisco, Wilson called a rare Monday practice as punishment. He also suspended John Henry Johnson after the fullback missed the flight back to Detroit when a California court issued a warrant on his ex-wife's complaint. Wilson stressed that he was punishing Johnson for his listless play, not because he was $2,360 behind in alimony and child support payments for his five kids.

"We don't have our old desire," Wilson said, "and we don't have the horses. Some of our guys just seem to be interested in getting their paycheck."

If Johnson's attitude hadn't already made him expendable (he would wind up in Pittsburgh, grinding out a pair of 1,000-yard seasons for Buddy Parker in the 1960s), the presence of Nick Pietrosante in the backfield would have. The big Notre Dame fullback was named the league's top rookie for his all-around play as a runner, receiver, and blocking back. Given the state of the offensive line, his 447 yards and NFL-high 5.9 average per rush were impressive figures, the latter the best of any Detroit runner in the '50s. "Pietrosante runs virtually straight-legged," observed *Sports Illustrated*, "as though his feet were moving through snow. But at 6 feet 2 and 220 pounds, he hits with considerable authority." Pietrosante would set a Lions single-season record with 872 yards the following year and leave Detroit after seven seasons as its all-time rusher.

Another bright light was Dick LeBeau, an Ohio State back who had been cut by Cleveland but would go on to become Detroit's all-time leader in interceptions, totaling 62 in 14 seasons. After that he spent a remarkable 45 seasons in coaching, winning a couple of Super Bowl rings as Pittsburgh's defensive coordinator. In 2010 he was inducted into the Pro Football Hall of Fame. He and Alex Karras are the only 1950s Lions so honored who did not play on a title team during the decade.

'In 1959, however, LeBeau was still just a rookie cornerback learning the ropes. He remembered Yale Lary, now quarterbacking a remixed secondary with the retirement of Jack Christiansen, as being "incredibly welcoming to a new player like me. I was a big sports fan growing up in Ohio," LeBeau said, "and by the time I got to Detroit, they'd already won three titles in the '50s, and I was in awe walking in there. But from the first day, he'd give me pointers—we played right next to each other. And there were so many little things he taught me. In those days the grass fields would be mostly dirt or mud late in the year because there wasn't any growing season then. So on a wet field, you'd always get your cleats clogged up with mud. Once . . . during a timeout, Yale put his arm on my shoulder to steady himself and reached into the area around his belt, and he pulled out a tongue depressor and cleaned his cleats. Got all the mud out. I looked at him. It was pretty smart. He looked at me, smiled, and crossed his fingers, like: *experience*. So for the rest of my career, on a muddy day, I always put a tongue depressor in my pants."

The Lions closed out the season, and the decade, on December 13 with a 25–14 loss to the Bears at Wrigley Field. Earl Morrall had a good Sunday in relief of Tobin Rote, his 8-yard pass to Jim Doran in the third quarter accounting for the Lions' last touchdown of the 1950s. Detroit finished with a 3-8-1 record, its only victories coming against the two last-place clubs, the Rams and Cardinals.

Several veterans had played their last game as a Lion, including Lou Creekmur, who retired for a second and final time. Creekmur actually had been given a "day" at the final home game of 1958, after which he was content to return to his job as branch manager of a local trucking firm. But then Wilson, desperate for healthy offensive linemen, talked him into coming back four games into the 1959 season. In Creekmur's first action, the Rams' Lou Michaels "just beat me to a pulp because I wasn't in good condition," he recalled. The battered tackle "crawled off the field" and two days later still couldn't lift himself out of bed. For his troubles, Creekmur got a raise above his previous year's $12,000 salary. At season's end, he retired and this time meant it. He left having played in 176 straight exhibition, regular-season, and postseason games.

Rote also made his last appearance in Detroit. Rote, reportedly paid $20,000 in 1959, had the worst season of his career, completing a miserable 38 percent of his passes while throwing 19 interceptions against five TD passes. Nonetheless, he was demanding a locked-in contract for 1960—that is, a guarantee against being traded or released. Management was uninterested. "His record shows that he has four or five really hot games a year," said an assistant coach. "We have been waiting all year for him to get hot. Next year we won't be able to wait."

The next year found Rote flinging footballs in Canada, where he would spend three seasons before moving on to the San Diego Chargers of the American Football League. In 1963, six years after his spectacular performance in the 1957 championship game, the aging Rote led the Chargers to a 51–10 rout of the Boston Patriots in the AFL title game, making him the only man ever to quarterback championship teams in the NFL and AFL.

The AFL, which began play in 1960, offered new opportunities for players and coaches. Shortly after the 1959 season ended, Buster Ramsey resigned to become head coach of the Buffalo Bills. The Bills were owned by Ralph C. Wilson, the Detroit insurance executive and minority Lions stockholder who had long dreamed of having his own team. Ramsey took assistant Bob Dove with him.

In response to the AFL invading Texas, the NFL hastened its plans for expansion. A new team would be installed in Dallas in 1960, stocked in part by cast-offs from each NFL club. Wilson was required to prepare a list of 14 players on the active roster who would be subject to being drafted by the Cowboys. Among the "touchables" was Doran—the balding veteran of nine Lions seasons, the Graham Cracker of years past, a central figure in much of the Lions' lore of the '50s.

But those heroics were so . . . *yesterday*. Doran's fate was probably already sealed when, standing wide open at the goal line in the finale against the Bears, he dropped a sure touchdown pass from Morrall.

"Doran caught the pass that brought the Lions their 1953 championship over the Cleveland Browns," Watson Spoelstra reminded readers. "It was a shame he had to go out this way. He won't be back."

CHAPTER

15

End OF A PERFECT *Thing*

I never wear a watch. When you look at a watch you see that
time is going by, and what's the use of that?

—Bobby Layne

The 1950s were over. The first season of what would be a tumultuous decade, not only for professional football but for American society as a whole, began on a small, dark note for the Detroit Football
Company. About noon on Thursday, August 11, 1960, William "Moon" Baker left
his Dearborn home. It was his day off from his job as parts manager at the Bob
Ford car dealership, and he told his wife he was going out to meet some friends.
A big weekend was coming up at Briggs Stadium, and the 50-year-old mascot
didn't intend to miss any of the fun.

At 2:40 a.m. Friday, Baker was found dead on the sidewalk in front of an old
rooming house on Winder Street, between Woodward and John R. He had cuts
across his face and his broken eyeglasses were lying nearby. His pockets had
been turned inside out, though a $5 bill was discovered on his body. Baker's car
was found parked three blocks away. His wallet, containing $338, was hidden
under a floor mat. Police described the area as sketchy and suspected foul play.

A year earlier, on the same street, a curb-crawling executive with a Dearborn trucking company had been robbed, stabbed, and left to bleed to death inside his car. The county coroner examined Baker's body and determined the official cause of death was a heart attack. Unwilling to let a quarter century of tradition die as well, Dan Baker donned his father's 25-pound lion costume and assumed mascot duties on the Detroit sidelines.

On Saturday evening, August 13, the Lions played their first game of the 1960s, an exhibition against Cleveland. It was a special occasion. The city was officially celebrating the silver anniversary of the City of Champions, with a proclamation from Mayor Louis Miriani and invitations to members of the 1935 Lions, Tigers, and Red Wings to spend a reunion weekend in town. The fans at Briggs Stadium were treated to an unprecedented sight: Dutch Clark, Ace Gutowsky, Glenn Presnell, Mickey Cochrane, Charlie Gehringer, Jack Adams, Ebbie Goodfellow, and other heroes from that memorable year of championships all sharing the same field. They also witnessed something else never seen before: a Cleveland victory at Briggs Stadium. "I'm tired of being taunted about never winning in Detroit," Paul Brown said after his team rolled over the Lions, 28–14. "We came prepared to win, now it's settled."

Following a full decade of futility, during which the Browns posted a horrendous 4-17-1 record in exhibition, regular-season, and championship games against the Lions, including a winless streak of 10 games in Detroit, the hex was declared broken. And on the 13th day of the month, no less. Buddy Parker could have warned the Lions about opening a new decade on that date. The Lions might also have been warned about the curse Bobby Layne placed on the team—if, indeed, he ever really did.

A staple of Lions lore is that the team was doomed to failure for the next half century because of the hex the departed quarterback put on the organization. The voodoo story gained traction with the advent of 24/7 sports coverage and the need to fill airtime and took off with the rise of the Internet, where conspiracy theories live forever. Asked over the years about this bit of black magic, members of Layne's family admitted they knew of no "formal" curse, as if Bobby somehow had the power to mumble the right words and turn George Wilson into a toad. If anything, the alleged curse probably was an off-handed remark the understandably upset star uttered in the aftermath of the trade, something along the lines of "The Lions won't win another championship in 50 years."

Layne was right. In fact, he was more than right—as of this writing, the Lions haven't won a championship in 62 years . . . and counting.

After getting regularly flogged on the field and in the press during the last two seasons of the '50s, the Lions rebounded in the early '60s. They finished second to Green Bay three straight years, 1960 through 1962. In some ways these Lions of a new decade resembled the championship squads of a few years back. A rock-ribbed defensive unit was the core of the club, the offense was solid if unspectacular, and the special teams were above average. In addition to holdovers like Joe Schmidt, Yale Lary, Harley Sewell, John Gordy, Terry Barr, Gil Mains, and Jim Martin, the roster included Dick "Night Train" Lane, Wayne Walker, Nick Pietrosante, ends Jim Gibbons and Gail Cogdill (the 1960 NFL Rookie of the Year), and the "Fearsome Foursome" of Alex Karras, Roger Brown, Sam Williams, and Darris McCord. What the team lacked was a dynamic quarterback, a two-minute guy who knew how to win.

At no time was this deficiency more apparent than in 1962, when the Lions fielded one of the finest teams never to play for a championship. That year the Lions compiled an 11–3 record. Their three losses were by a total of eight points: 9–7 to Green Bay, 17–14 to the New York Giants, and 3–0 to Chicago in the finale. All were agonizingly close defeats to championship-caliber teams. The Packers and Bears were destined to win the NFL title in 1962 and 1963, respectively, beating the powerful Giants each time.

The toughest defeat came in the fourth week of the season at Green Bay. Both teams were undefeated. In a bitterly contested game played on a sloppy field, the Lions had the defending world champions on the ropes, nursing a 7–6 lead with less than two minutes to play. On third down, Milt Plum—the veteran quarterback acquired before the season from Cleveland—threw an ill-advised pass. Terry Barr slipped and Herb Adderly intercepted, returning it deep into Detroit territory. That set up Paul Hornung's game-winning field goal with just seconds left. The 9–7 loss "still pisses me off," Schmidt said. "Plum never should've thrown the fucking ball. Pietrosante should've run the ball, and if he didn't make it, we had the best punter in the league, Yale Lary. Green Bay would have gotten the ball deep in their own end and with only one time-out left."

By the time the two teams met again on Thanksgiving, the Lions had fallen to the Giants, which accounted for their 8–2 record. The Packers came into the game undefeated at 10–0. In fact, reaching back into the previous season, Vince Lombardi's squad had lost only once in their previous 18 outings, and that was by a single point. Their 37–0 rout of New York in the 1961 title game was their first of an eventual five championships in seven seasons. Their aura of invincibility was underscored by the wire services' All-Pro teams, which were dominated by Packers, and magazine cover stories that proclaimed them the greatest aggregation of football talent ever to grace a gridiron.

They may have been, at that. But not on this overcast Thursday afternoon. On the Packers' first play from scrimmage, quarterback Bart Starr was swarmed under by several blitzing Lions for a 15-yard loss. It set the tone for the day. Before 57,598 wildly screaming fans and 32 million television viewers, the revenge-minded Lions practically chased the Packers back to Wisconsin. By the time it was over, Starr had been sacked 11 times and lost 110 yards attempting to pass. Jimmy Taylor, the league's leading ground-gainer, was held to a mere 47 yards. Roger Brown was credited with six sacks. The massive tackle also had a safety and delivered a jarring hit that knocked the ball out of Starr's hands; Sam Williams picked up the fumble and ran it in for a touchdown. Detroit built up a 26–0 lead early in the third quarter before coasting home, 26–14. The relatively close final score doesn't adequately convey the sense of mayhem and dominance visited upon the Packers, who the following year would end their role as Detroit's traditional holiday opponent.

Green Bay recovered from its national embarrassment to finish the season 13–1, then went on to beat New York for the title. There was no playoff system then. As the Western Conference runner-up, the Lions had to settle for a third straight appearance in the Playoff Bowl, a contrived consolation game between second-place teams in Miami. The Lions won all three times. Nobody remembers the Playoff Bowl. But the 1962 Thanksgiving Day mauling is arguably the most memorable game in Lions history, even more so than the victories that delivered titles.

On November 22, 1963, exactly one year after the Lions' rout of the mighty Packers, William Clay Ford bought the Lions for $4.5 million. At the time, major shareholders were locked in a power struggle as the team tried to recover from a gambling scandal that cost Alex Karras the entire 1963 season and his part ownership in the recently relocated Lindell A.C. Directors had approached Henry Ford II about buying the team to end the squabbling. "But he said, 'I'm too busy,'" recalled attorney Jim LoPrete. "His brother, Bill Ford, was on the slate of directors, and he said, 'I'd like to buy the club.' Which he did. That was the beginning of the demise of the team."

Ford bought the team on the day President Kennedy was shot, but otherwise his timing was exquisite. The deal was finalized on January 10, 1964, when Harry Wismer, the lone holdout among 144 shareholders, agreed to sell. Two weeks later, the NFL signed an "astounding" contract with CBS that guaranteed each team $1 million per year and instantly doubled the value of the Detroit franchise. Today the Lions are worth roughly 400 times what Ford paid.

The 1964 season was George Wilson's last as head coach. After his entire staff was fired following a 7-5-2 finish, he had no choice but to resign. "George is a fine fellow and I don't like to see him go," Ford said. "But maybe we'll both be better off for it." The club had previously allowed Don Shula, the brilliant defensive coordinator of the early '60s, to be lured away by Baltimore. Joe Schmidt and others have speculated that Detroit, which finished either first or second nine times between 1951 and 1962, would have remained a title contender for years had Shula been promoted to head coach and Wilson appointed general manager. Instead, Wilson was replaced by Harry Gilmer, one of many dubious personnel decisions that put the team on a glide path to mediocrity.

Russ Thomas assumed greater front-office responsibilities after Ford bought the team, becoming personnel director and general manager. During his 22 seasons as GM, 1967 through 1988, the team had just six winning seasons. The bulk of the winning came during Schmidt's five-season run as head coach, 1967 to 1971. The 16 years after Schmidt left were especially brutal, with just two barely winning seasons: 9–7 finishes in 1980 and 1983. The Lions lost all three playoff games during Thomas's tenure. His unusually close relationship with the owner—rumored to be the result of his helping Ford conquer alcoholism and an addiction to painkillers—made the craggy-faced executive immune to public criticism as the team floundered year after year.

Thomas retired in 1989, Ford died in 2014, and nothing really changed. Detroit remains one of only two pre–Super Bowl franchises never to have appeared in the sport's ultimate game. Ironically, Cleveland is the other. The rival powerhouses of the '50s also are the only teams to finish a season with an 0–16 record. Detroit did it in 2008, followed by Cleveland nine years later.

During this long period of competitive inertia, time has removed most of the players and coaches of the '50s. Some left earlier than others. Carl Karilivacz was only 38 when he dropped dead of a heart attack. Gene Gedman, who successfully sued the Lions for workman's compensation after a knee injury ended his career in 1958, was 44 when his own heart failed him. Les Bingaman, who fought a yo-yo battle with his weight, also was 44 when he died in his sleep. Nick Pietrosante succumbed to prostate cancer when he was 50. Bill Swiacki was 53 when he shot himself in his basement with a hunting rifle. Cancer claimed Jack Christiansen when he was 57.

Others seemed to go on forever. Yale Lary, one of five Lions selected for the NFL's official 33-man All-Decade Team of the 1950s (Layne, Schmidt, Christiansen, and Dick Stanfel were the others), was 86 when he died. Vince Banonis outlived his three sons before passing away a few months shy of turning 90, a milestone reached by Harry Gilmer, Jim Hardy, and Wally Triplett.

In his breakout season of 1950, Cloyce Box was described as "an extremely slippery customer." As a businessman who made and lost millions, the tag still applied. The large-living oilman flew his own Lear jet and owned the sprawling ranch seen in the popular prime-time soap opera, *Dallas*. He went to bed one night when he was 70 and never woke up, leaving behind a Texas-size tangle of debts and lawsuits.

Leon Hart passed away in 2002 at 73, but not before first selling his Heisman Trophy to help provide for his grandchildren's education. "I can't split the Heisman," he explained, "but I can split whatever value it has." Like many players of his era, Hart disdained the modern NFL. "They don't play football anymore. They play push-shove-pass-catch. They play the same game we play at picnics. Only difference is, they have uniforms."

Buddy Parker retired from coaching after the 1964 season and went into real estate in Texas. The originator of the two-minute offense, who as a player and a coach won four NFL titles with the Lions and Cardinals, has never truly received his due. His failure to win a third straight championship always gnawed at him, especially after the 1965–67 Packers became the first—and so far the only—team to accomplish the feat in the modern era. Parker died in 1982, age 68, after being operated on for a ruptured ulcer.

Edwin Anderson often celebrated victory as Lions president, but the aristocratic executive experienced his share of setbacks. In 1960, he failed in his bid to succeed Bert Bell as commissioner, with the ongoing turmoil among Lions directors causing owners to pull their support. The campaign to locate the nascent Pro Football Hall of Fame in Detroit also ended in disappointment. Anderson remained in the Lions' front office until 1967, quietly managing daily operations while Russ Thomas handled larger matters in the "hot seat." Anderson died in 1987, age 84. His longtime antagonist, Lyle Fife, outlived him by nearly seven years.

Long-time Lions fan Mike Cutler remembered a game sometime in the '60s when Bobby Layne and several other old-timers were introduced at halftime at Tiger Stadium, as Briggs Stadium was rebranded in 1961. Afterward, the retired quarterback invited himself into the broadcast booth, where Van Patrick practically had to wrestle the mike back from him.

"You could tell he'd had a lot to drink because his voice was all slurry," Cutler said. "So, later on, we're in the third or fourth quarter, the Lions have the ball—and all of a sudden here comes Layne running out onto the field, wearing his overcoat and fedora, wanting to take over the huddle! The refs got him out of there, but he must've had a real good buzz on to do something like that."

Layne made some concessions to age. After bouts of lip and throat cancer, he was instructed to give up smoking. His compromise was to switch from Marlboros to low-tar Merit cigarettes. While Layne stayed in Lubbock, where he oversaw various investments and businesses, Doak Walker fell in love with Colorado. He rarely visited Texas, where his four children grew up after he and Norma divorced. He subsequently married Olympic skier Gladys "Skeeter" Warner, whose brothers had worn Layne's uniform number in high school. By the time a writer for *Esquire* caught up with "the most celebrated Texas hero of the century" in 1975, Doak had grown a bit chunky, was sipping vodka on the rocks, and was reminiscing about an undistinguished assistant coaching career that ranged from the Denver Broncos to the semipro Akron Vulcans. Having been turned down for other coaching positions, including the Lions, he concentrated on his sales job with a national electrical contractor.

Layne and Walker spoke regularly by phone, calling each other by their proper names. "Ewell, is that you?" "Hello, Robert." They played in golf tournaments, visited Las Vegas, even jointly coached a high school football team for a while. "I can still see him in one of the bars with a big crowd around him," one Vegas hotel executive said of Layne. "He'd be in there telling stories and say, 'Ain't that right, Doak?' Doak would laugh and nod his head. He was pretty quiet."

Layne entered the Pro Football Hall of Fame as soon as he was eligible. Doak's election took longer, as his short career was held against him. When Walker finally was inducted in 1986, his old friend naturally presented him with his bust. Later that year, Layne made plans for his 60th birthday party. Everybody was invited. As he always told guests, "Bring a clean shirt and a $10 bill, and you won't have to change either." But he was a sick man. When he came to Detroit that November for the Lions' annual alumni gathering, he collapsed and was hospitalized for internal bleeding.

"When he was leaving for Texas, I hugged him," Dorne Dibble recalled. "I said goodbye to him. And I told my wife, 'We're never going to see him at his birthday party.' And he didn't make it. He was all skin and bones."

Layne was an alpha male accustomed to getting his own way. He hurled through life at a mile a minute, always eager for the next sensation, be it a night of drinking, a high-stakes game of cards, a swinging jazz ensemble, or a fourth-quarter comeback. But he occasionally slowed down long enough to express a bit of wistfulness. "What I miss," he once said, "is the guys. That's what I miss more than anything. I miss going to training camp. I miss the road trips and the card games. I miss the fellowship. The locker room, the places where it was a pleasure to be. The practice sessions. I miss the bar where we'd go for a beer after practice. I miss having that beer with the guys. I miss the ballgames. I mean, when you've got a whole team looking forward to everything, when you've got guys showing up for practice early and staying late—well, you've got something there. We had that perfect thing for a while."

On December 1, 1986, Layne died of cardiac arrest inside a Lubbock hospital, a victim of his fast-paced lifestyle. The night before he was buried, old teammates and friends threw a big party—a celebration, not a wake, filled with laughs, liquor, and lots of stories. "He would have loved it," Walker said. "It went on all night. Some of us stayed up, changed clothes, and went to the funeral."

The Doaker outlived Sweet Bobby by a dozen years. In 1989, Southern Methodist University created the Doak Walker Award to annually honor the college running back who best combined athletic ability, academic excellence, and citizenship. A life-size statue of Walker was erected on SMU's campus. One January day in 1998, Walker was skiing in Steamboat Springs when he catapulted over rough terrain. The accident left him paralyzed from the neck down. He died September 27, 1998, exactly 50 years to the day that he appeared on the cover of *Life* magazine. He was 71. His ashes were spread over his beloved Colorado mountains.

Texas running back Ricky Williams, a two-time winner of the Doak Walker Award, had grown friendly with the trophy's namesake. In his honor,

Williams—who would go on to win the Heisman that year—wore No. 37 in the Longhorns' upcoming game against Oklahoma. The Doaker was who he wanted to be, he said. Williams, whose controversial pro career included several failed drug tests and fathering seven children with three different women, turned out to be no Doak Walker. But then, the original had set the bar mighty high.

The staggering personal cost of playing pro football in the 1950s was evident when 16 former players gathered at a suburban Detroit hotel in June 2007 for the golden anniversary of the Lions' last championship. Jimmy David, Jim Martin, Dave Middleton, Lou Creekmur, and John Henry Johnson were no-shows; all had been institutionalized for dementia. A disoriented Terry Barr was gently steered around by a family member while a much tamer Gil Mains was coaxed through an interview by his wife. His teammates' plight, coupled with fears that he might one day wind up in the same condition, caused John Gordy to break down in tears.

Over the years, several other Lions of the '50s, including Don Doll, Bob Smith, Dorne Dibble, Fred Enke, Andy Miketa, Alex Karras, Wayne Walker, Earl Morrall, and Lew Carpenter, have died with degenerative brain disease. Although the NFL vigorously defended itself, medical researchers proved a direct correlation between the head trauma players regularly received and chronic traumatic encephalopathy (CTE), the Alzheimer's-like disease afflicting an inordinately high percentage of them.

CTE, brought on by repeated blows to the head, used to be known as *dementia pugilistica*, a condition long associated with prizefighters. Several members of the Lions' first championship team in 1935 suffered from being "punch drunk" in their latter years. "He doesn't even know his own name," a teammate sadly said of wingback Ernie Caddel, institutionalized in California. Tackle Jim Steen wandered through his Grosse Point home, a blank look on his face, unable to recall that he was a GM engineer and president of the Lion Alumni Association. Whether their dementia was the result of CTE was never determined because the condition can only be diagnosed in a postmortem examination of brain tissue. At the time, families were not requesting the procedure because nobody knew of the disease, much less its shocking scale.

Leon Hart recalled an early medical conference, with many retired players in attendance. "They asked for a show of hands: 'How many of you have had a concussion?' Many players didn't even know what a concussion was. Then they asked, 'How many of you have had your bell rung?' Then everybody's hand went up. I ran into the brick wall in left field at Wrigley Field once, reaching for the ball. I just heard a big 'gong,' like I heard a bell ring. That's the sound of your brain actually bouncing off the cranium."

By 2009, the NFL, facing a public relations nightmare and fending off lawsuits from families and the Players Association, began to tacitly accept responsibility for the repercussions of decades of medical ignorance. The league enacted a new rule that no player exhibiting symptoms of a concussion would be allowed to return to a game or practice until he had first been examined and cleared by a neurologist. The "concussion protocol" tent became a fixture of every NFL sideline.

The league also agreed to a $1 billion settlement in 2016 covering 20,000 retired players, of whom 6,000 either have been or can be expected to be diagnosed with CTE. As part of the settlement, the NFL officially admitted no fault, though in congressional testimony a league official acknowledged a direct link between football and CTE. For retirees who have yet to display outward signs of dementia, the prospect hangs like a death sentence over them and their families. A 2017 study by Boston's University's Chronic Traumatic Encephalopathy Clinic found that 110 of the 111 donated brains of former NFL players had CTE in them.

"I think it would be best for all of us guys to add our brains to the pool so they can find out if there's some conclusion they can reach or some way they can predict it," Roger Zatkoff said at the time. "I certainly had my share of concussions . . . from a scientific standpoint I think there might be something to learn. I don't know whether I'm a candidate and wind up with CTE. You guys will probably know it before I do."

The very few remaining figures from the Lions' championship era, strong lads of September now deep in December, continue to fall away, one by one, their names faintly redolent of a time and a place that can be treasured but never recaptured. Joe Schmidt, once the husky hero swept up on the shoulders of a crowd mad with joy, is a more fragile package now. He's had heart bypass surgery, a hip replacement, and shoulder and knee operations. Approaching 90, his joints creak like the hinges on an old Packard. One day he, too, will be gone, joining his teammates and those who rocked now-vanished Briggs Stadium with their boisterous cheers and off-key choruses of the fight song. "It was always a very friendly environment," he reminisced. "There was nothing like being there on a beautiful autumn day with the sun out, the smell of the freshly cut grass, and the people sitting so close it felt like you could reach out and touch them."

Among those touched was Jim Boyle Jr., whom we first met in chapter 5. Long after the ersatz Leon Hart of Highland Park last unbuckled the chinstrap of his department-store helmet, memories of the era remain warm and fortifying. A few years back, when his father was approaching a milestone birthday in poor health, Boyle settled on a meaningful way to honor him. The Lions of the Eisenhower decade had been a significant part of the connective tissue between father and son, and now he looked to revisit that link.

Over the course of several months, Boyle made repeated trips to the library, pulling down old newspaper stories about the Lions from the microfilm reader. He copied chapters from assorted sports books and wrote to the Pro Football Hall of Fame for assistance. With scissors and glue and a fair amount of patience, he assembled all of the materials into a scrapbook. It was a lot of work, but finally one day the project was done. Figuring the scrapbook needed a title, Boyle remembered the plea his father had repeatedly directed at the kitchen radio during the waning minutes of the 1953 title game. Thus the cover read: "Throw It to Doran!"

Boyle presented the scrapbook to his father on his 80th birthday. "I loved doing this," he wrote in the accompanying letter. "It brought back a lot of old memories. I loved those old Lions, just like I loved and still love my Dad."

It turned out to be the senior Boyle's last birthday. He passed away the following year, just as the leaves were starting to turn and a new season was underway. To the junior Boyle, today a retired teacher living in St. Clair Shores, Michigan, no squad wearing Honolulu blue and silver will ever tug at him like the one that so ably represented Detroit decades ago. As he expressed in the letter to his father: "Those Lions teams of the '50s are still my favorite . . . I'll love those teams 'til the day I die . . . they were the teams and heroes of my youth."

DETROIT LIONS SEASON RESULTS
1950-59

1950
Won 6, Lost 6. Fourth place, National Conference

Date	Opponent	Location (Attendance)	Result
September 17 (Sun.)	Green Bay	Green Bay (22,096)	Won, 45–7
September 24 (Sun.)	Pittsburgh	Detroit (18,707)	Won, 10–7
September 29 (Fri.)	New York Yanks	New York (12,482)	Lost, 21–44
October 8 (Sun.)	San Francisco	Detroit (17,941)	Won, 24–7
October 15 (Sun.)	Los Angeles	Detroit (32,589)	Lost, 28–30
October 22 (Sun.)	San Francisco	San Francisco (27,350)	Lost, 27–28
October 29 (Sun.)	Los Angeles	Los Angeles (27,475)	Lost, 24–65
November 5 (Sun.)	Chicago Bears	Detroit (30,410)	Lost, 21–35
November 19 (Sun.)	Green Bay	Detroit (17,752)	Won, 24–21
November 23 (Thu.)	New York Yanks	Detroit (30,206)	Won, 49–14
December 3 (Sun.)	Baltimore	Baltimore (12,059)	Won, 45–21
December 10 (Sun.)	Chicago Bears	Chicago (34,793)	Lost, 3–6

1951
Won 7, Lost 4, Tied 1. Tied for second place, National Conference

Date	Opponent	Location (Attendance)	Result
September 30 (Sun.)	Washington	Detroit (28,900)	Won, 35–17
October 8 (Mon.)	New York Yanks	*Detroit (25,554)	Won, 37–10
October 14 (Sun.)	Los Angeles	Detroit (52,907)	Lost, 21–27
October 21 (Sun.)	New York Yanks	Detroit (24,002)	Tied, 24–24
October 28 (Sun.)	Chicago Bears	Detroit (36,950)	Lost, 23–28
November 4 (Sun.)	Green Bay	Green Bay (18,165)	Won, 24–17
November 11 (Sun.)	Chicago Bears	Chicago (46,210)	Won, 41–28
November 18 (Sun.)	Philadelphia	Philadelphia (25,350)	Won, 28–10
November 22 (Thu.)	Green Bay	Detroit (33,452)	Won, 52–35
December 2 (Sun.)	San Francisco	Detroit (52,024)	Lost, 10–20
December 9 (Sun.)	Los Angeles	Los Angeles (67,892)	Won, 24–22
December 16 (Sun.)	San Francisco	San Francisco (37,776)	Lost, 17–21

*Game originally scheduled for New York; moved to Detroit due to World Series

1952
Won 9, Lost 3. Tied for first place, National Conference

Date	Opponent	Location (Attendance)	Result
September 28 (Sun.)	San Francisco	San Francisco (54,761)	Lost, 3–17
October 3 (Fri.)	Los Angeles	Los Angeles (42,743)	Won, 17–14
October 12 (Sun.)	San Francisco	Detroit (56,822)	Lost, 0–28
October 19 (Sun.)	Los Angeles	Detroit (40,152)	Won, 24–16
October 26 (Sun.)	Green Bay	Green Bay (24,656)	Won, 52–17
November 2 (Sun.)	Cleveland	Detroit (56,029)	Won, 17–6
November 9 (Sun.)	Pittsburgh	Pittsburgh (26,170)	Won, 31–6
November 16 (Sun.)	Dallas	Detroit (33,304)	Won, 43–13
November 23 (Sun.)	Chicago Bears	Chicago (37,508)	Lost, 23–24
November 27 (Thu.)	Green Bay	Detroit (39,101)	Won, 48–24
December 7 (Sun.)	Chicago Bears	Detroit (50,410)	Won, 45–21
December 13 (Sat.)	Dallas	*Detroit (12,452)	Won, 41–6

*Game originally scheduled for Dallas; moved to Detroit when league took over Dallas franchise

1952 National Conference Playoff

December 21 (Sun.)	Los Angeles	Detroit (47,645)	Won, 31–21

1952 NFL Championship

December 28 (Sun.)	Cleveland	Cleveland (50,934)	Won, 17–7

1953
Won 10, Lost 2. First place, Western Conference

Date	Opponent	Location (Attendance)	Result
September 27 (Sun.)	Pittsburgh	Detroit (44,587)	Won, 38–21
October 3 (Sat.)	Baltimore	Baltimore (25,159)	Won, 27–17
October 11 (Sun.)	San Francisco	Detroit (58,079)	Won, 24–21
October 18 (Sun.)	Los Angeles	Detroit (55,772)	Lost, 19–31
October 25 (Sun.)	San Francisco	San Francisco (54,862)	Won, 14–10
November 1 (Sun.)	Los Angeles	Los Angeles (93,751)	Lost, 24–37
November 7 (Sat.)	Baltimore	Detroit (46,508)	Won, 17–7
November 15 (Sun.)	Green Bay	Green Bay (20,834)	Won, 14–7
November 22 (Sun.)	Chicago Bears	Chicago (36,165)	Won, 20–16
November 26 (Thu.)	Green Bay	Detroit (52,607)	Won, 34–15
December 6 (Sun.)	Chicago Bears	Detroit (58,056)	Won, 13–7
December 13 (Sun.)	New York Giants	New York (28,390)	Won, 27–16

1953 NFL Championship

December 27 (Sun.)	Cleveland	Detroit (54,577)	Won, 17–16

1954
Won 9, Lost 2, Tied 1. First place, Western Conference

Date	Opponent	Location (Attendance)	Result
September 26 (Sun.)	Chicago Bears	Detroit (52,343)	Won, 48–23
October 10 (Sun.)	Los Angeles	Detroit (56,523)	Won, 21–3
October 16 (Sat.)	Baltimore	Detroit (48,272)	Won, 35–0
October 24 (Sun.)	San Francisco	San Francisco (59,600)	Lost, 31–37
October 31 (Sun.)	Los Angeles	Los Angeles (74,342)	Won, 27–24
November 6 (Sat.)	Baltimore	Baltimore (25,287)	Won, 27–3
November 14 (Sun.)	San Francisco	Detroit (58,431)	Won, 48–7
November 21 (Sun.)	Green Bay	Green Bay (20,767)	Won, 21–17
November 25 (Thu.)	Green Bay	Detroit (55,532)	Won, 28–24
December 5 (Sun.)	Philadelphia	Detroit (54,939)	Tied, 13–13
December 12 (Sun.)	Chicago Bears	Chicago (37,240)	Lost, 24–28
December 19 (Sun.)	Cleveland	Cleveland (34,168)	Won, 14–10

1954 NFL Championship

Date	Opponent	Location (Attendance)	Result
December 26 (Sun.)	Cleveland	Cleveland (43,827)	Lost, 10–56

1955
Won 3, Lost 9. Sixth place, Western Conference

Date	Opponent	Location (Attendance)	Result
September 25 (Sun.)	Green Bay	Green Bay (22,217)	Lost, 17–20
October 1 (Sat.)	Baltimore	Baltimore (40,030)	Lost, 13–28
October 9 (Sun.)	Los Angeles	Detroit (54,836)	Lost, 10–17
October 16 (Sun.)	San Francisco	Detroit (51,438)	Lost, 24–27
October 23 (Sun.)	Los Angeles	Los Angeles (68,690)	Lost, 13–24
October 30 (Sun.)	San Francisco	San Francisco (47,431)	Lost, 21–38
November 5 (Sat.)	Baltimore	Detroit (53,874)	Won, 24–14
November 13 (Sun.)	Pittsburgh	Pittsburgh (34,441)	Won, 31–28
November 20 (Sun.)	Chicago Bears	Detroit (53,610)	Lost, 14–24
November 24 (Thu.)	Green Bay	Detroit (51,685)	Won, 24–10
December 4 (Sun.)	Chicago Bears	Chicago (39,388)	Lost, 20–21
December 11 (Sun.)	New York Giants	Detroit (45,929)	Lost, 19–24

1956
Won 9, Lost 3. Second place, Western Conference

Date	Opponent	Location (Attendance)	Result
September 30 (Sun.)	Green Bay	Green Bay (24,668)	Won, 20–16
October 6 (Sat.)	Baltimore	Baltimore (42,622)	Won, 31–14
October 14 (Sun.)	Los Angeles	Detroit (56,281)	Won, 24–21
October 21 (Sun.)	San Francisco	Detroit (55,662)	Won, 20–17
October 28 (Sun.)	Los Angeles	Los Angeles (76,758)	Won, 16–7
November 4 (Sun.)	San Francisco	San Francisco (46,708)	Won, 17–13
November 11 (Sun.)	Washington	Washington (28,003)	Lost, 17–18
November 18 (Sun.)	Baltimore	Detroit (55,788)	Won, 27–3
November 22 (Thu.)	Green Bay	Detroit (54,087)	Lost, 20–24
December 2 (Sun.)	Chicago Bears	Detroit (57,024)	Won, 42–10
December 9 (Sun.)	Pittsburgh	Detroit (52,124)	Won, 45–7
December 16 (Sun.)	Chicago Bears	Chicago (49,086)	Lost, 21–38

1957
Won 8, Lost 4. Tied for first place, Western Conference

Date	Opponent	Location (Attendance)	Result
September 29 (Sun.)	Baltimore	Baltimore (40,112)	Lost, 14–34
October 6 (Sun.)	Green Bay	Green Bay (32,120)	Won, 24–14
October 13 (Sun.)	Los Angeles	Detroit (55,914)	Won, 10–7
October 20 (Sun.)	Baltimore	Detroit (55,764)	Won, 31–27
October 27 (Sun.)	Los Angeles	Los Angeles (77,314)	Lost, 17–35
November 3 (Sun.)	San Francisco	San Francisco (59,702)	Lost, 31–35
November 10 (Sun.)	Philadelphia	Philadelphia (29,302)	Won, 27–16
November 17 (Sun.)	San Francisco	Detroit (56,915)	Won, 31–10
November 24 (Sun.)	Chicago Bears	Detroit (55,749)	Lost, 7–27
November 28 (Thu.)	Green Bay	Detroit (54,301)	Won, 18–6
December 8 (Sun.)	Cleveland	Detroit (55,814)	Won, 20–7
December 15 (Sun.)	Chicago Bears	Chicago (41,088)	Won, 21–13

1957 Western Conference Playoff

December 22 (Sun.)	San Francisco	San Francisco (60,118)	Won, 31–27

1957 NFL Championship

December 29 (Sun.)	Cleveland	Detroit (55,263)	Won, 59–14

1958
Won 4, Lost 7, Tied 1. Fifth place, Western Conference

Date	Opponent	Location (Attendance)	Result
September 28 (Sun.)	Baltimore	Baltimore (48,377)	Lost, 15–28
October 5 (Sun.)	Green Bay	Green Bay (32,053)	Tied, 13–13
October 12 (Sun.)	Los Angeles	Detroit (55,648)	Lost, 28–42
October 19 (Sun.)	Baltimore	Detroit (55,190)	Lost, 14–40
October 26 (Sun.)	Los Angeles	Los Angeles (81,730)	Won, 41–24
November 2 (Sun.)	San Francisco	San Francisco (59,213)	Lost, 21–24
November 9 (Sun.)	Cleveland	Cleveland (75,563)	Won, 30–10
November 16 (Sun.)	San Francisco	Detroit (54,253)	Won, 35–21
November 23 (Sun.)	Chicago Bears	Detroit (55,280)	Lost, 7–20
November 27 (Thu.)	Green Bay	Detroit (50,971)	Won, 24–14
December 7 (Sun.)	New York Giants	Detroit (50,115)	Lost, 17–19
December 14 (Sun.)	Chicago Bears	Chicago (38,346)	Lost, 16–21

1959
Won 3, Lost 8, Tied 1. Fifth place, Western Conference

Date	Opponent	Location (Attendance)	Result
September 27 (Sun.)	Baltimore	Baltimore (55,588)	Lost, 9–21
October 4 (Sun.)	Green Bay	Green Bay (32,150)	Lost, 10–28
October 11 (Sun.)	Baltimore	Detroit (54,197)	Lost, 24–31
October 18 (Sun.)	San Francisco	Detroit (52,585)	Lost, 13–34
October 25 (Sun.)	Los Angeles	Los Angeles (74,288)	Won, 17–7
November 1 (Sun.)	San Francisco	San Francisco (59,064)	Lost, 7–33
November 8 (Sun.)	Pittsburgh	Pittsburgh (24,619)	Tied, 10–10
November 15 (Sun.)	Los Angeles	Detroit (52,271)	Won, 23–17
November 22 (Sun.)	Chicago Bears	Detroit (54,059)	Lost, 14–24
November 26 (Thu.)	Green Bay	Detroit (49,221)	Lost, 17–24
December 6 (Sun.)	Chicago Cardinals	Detroit (45,811)	Won, 45–21
December 13 (Sun.)	Chicago Bears	Chicago (40,890)	Lost, 14–25

APPENDIX B

DETROIT LIONS COMPOSITE ROSTER 1950-59

The 135 players who wore the Lions uniform for at least one game during the 1950s are listed here alphabetically. Members of the Pro Football Hall of Fame are identified with an asterisk. Complete season-by-season statistics for all players can be found at www.pro-football-reference.com.

Charlie Ane, T-C, Southern California, 1953–59; George Atkins, G, Georgia, 1955; Byron Bailey, B, Washington State, 1953–54; Vince Banonis, C-LB, Detroit, 1951–53; Terry Barr, B, Michigan, 1957–59; Ed Berrang, E, Villanova, 1951; Les Bingaman, G, Illinois, 1950–54; Bill Bowman, B, William & Mary, 1954, 1956 (Army 1955); Cloyce Box, E, West Texas State, 1950, 1952–54 (Marine Corps 1951); Howard Brown, G, Indiana, 1950; Marv Brown, B, East Texas State, 1957 (Air Force 1954–56); Chet Bulger, T, Auburn, 1950; Jim Cain, E, Alabama, 1950, 1953–55 (Army 1951–52); Stanley Campbell, G, Iowa State, 1952, 1955–58 (Army 1953–54); Lew Carpenter, B, Arkansas, 1953–55 (Army 1956); Howard "Hopalong" Cassady, B, Ohio State, 1956–59; *Jack Christiansen, DB, Colorado A&M, 1951–58; Gus Cifelli, T, Notre Dame, 1950–52; Ollie Cline, B, Ohio State, 1950–53; John Clowes, T, William & Mary, 1951; Gene Cook, E, Toledo, 1959; *Lou Creekmur, G-T, William & Mary, 1950–59; Gene Cronin, DE, College of Pacific, 1956–59; Leon Cunningham, C, South Carolina, 1955 (Army 1956–57); Peter D'Alonzo, B, Villanova, 1951–52; Jimmy David, DB, Colorado A&M, 1952–59; Dorne Dibble, E, Michigan State, 1951, 1953–57 (Air Force 1952); Don Doll, B, Southern California, 1950–52; Jim Doran, E, Iowa State, 1951–59; Bob Dove, E-G, Notre Dame, 1953–54; Tom Dublinski, QB, Utah, 1952–54; Blaine Earon, E, Duke, 1952–53; Fred Enke, QB, Arizona, 1950–51; Dick Flanagan, LB, Ohio State, 1950–52; Barry French, G, Purdue, 1951; Dom Fucci, B, Kentucky, 1955 (Army 1952–53); Sherwin "Sonny" Gandee, E, Ohio State, 1952–56; *Frank Gatski, C, Marshall, 1957; Gene Gedman, B, Indiana, 1953, 1956–58 (Army 1954–55); Jim Gibbons, E, Iowa, 1958–59; Harry Gilmer, QB, Alabama, 1955–56; Earl "Jug" Girard, B, Wisconsin, 1952–56; Bill Glass, DE, Baylor, 1958–59; John Gordy,

G, Tennessee, 1957, 1959; John Greene, E, Michigan, 1950; Rex Grossman, QB, Indiana, 1950; Bob Grottkau, G, Oregon, 1959; Bernie Hafen, E, Utah, 1950; Pat Harder, B, Wisconsin, 1951–53; Jim Hardy, QB, Southern California, 1952; Leon Hart, E, Notre Dame, 1950–57; Jim Hill, DB, Tennessee, 1951–52 (Army 1953–54); Bob "Hunchy" Hoernschemeyer, B, Indiana, 1950–55; Doug Hogland, G, Oregon State, 1958; Floyd Jaszewski, T, Minnesota, 1950–51; Walter Jenkins, E-T, Wayne, 1955; *John Henry Johnson, FB, Arizona State, 1957–59; Steve Junker, E, Xavier, 1957, 1959; Carl Karilivacz, DB, Syracuse, 1953–57; *Alex Karras, T, Iowa, 1958–59; Dick Kercher, B, Tulsa, 1954 (Army 1955–56); Karl Koepfer, G, Bowling Green, 1958; Gerry Krall, B, Ohio State, 1950; Raymond "Moose" Krouse, T, Maryland, 1956–57; *Yale Lary, DB, Texas A&M, 1952–53, 1956–59 (Army 1954–55); *Bobby Layne, QB, Texas, 1950–58; *Dick LeBeau, DB, Ohio State, 1959; Danny Lewis, B, Wisconsin, 1958–59; Jack Lininger, C, Ohio State, 1950–51; Bob Long, E-LB, UCLA, 1955–59; Gary Lowe, DB, Michigan State, 1957–59; Bob Lusk, C, William & Mary, 1956; Dante Magnani, B, St. Mary's, 1950; Gil "Wild Hoss" Mains, T, Murray State, 1953–59 (Army 1952); Jim Martin, E-G-LB, Notre Dame, 1951–59; Darris McCord, DE, Tennessee, 1955–59; Lloyd McDermott, T, Kentucky, 1950; Thurman "Fum" McGraw, T, Colorado A&M, 1950–54; Don McIlhenny, B, Southern Methodist, 1956; Dave Middleton, B-E, Auburn, 1955–59; Andy Miketa, C, North Carolina, 1954–55 (Air Force 1952–53); Bob Miller, T, Virginia, 1952–58; Bob Momsen, G, Ohio State, 1951; Earl Morrall, QB, Michigan State, 1958–59; Art Murakowski, B, Northwestern, 1951; Don Panciera, B, San Francisco, 1950; Ben Paolucci, T, Wayne State, 1959; John Panelli, B, Notre Dame, 1950; Lindy Pearson, B, Oklahoma, 1950; Gerry Perry, T, California, 1954, 1956–59 (Army 1955); Nick Pietrosante, B, Notre Dame, 1959; John Prchlik, T, Yale, 1950–53; Mike Rabold, G, Indiana, 1959; Jerry Reichow, QB-E, Iowa, 1956–59; Jim Ricca, T, Georgetown, 1955; Perry Richards, E, Detroit, 1958; Dick Rifenburg, E, Michigan, 1950; Lee Riley, B, Detroit, 1955; Dan Rogas, G, Tulane, 1951; Tobin Rote, QB, Rice, 1957–59; Ken Russell, T, Bowling Green, 1957–59; Tom Rychlec, E, American International, 1958 (Army 1957); Jim Salsbury, G, UCLA, 1955–56; Dan Sandifer, B, Louisiana State, 1950; *Joe Schmidt, LB, Pittsburgh, 1953–59; Charles "Bill" Schroll, B-LB, Louisiana State, 1950; Clyde "Smackover" Scott, B, Arkansas, 1952; Clarence Self, B, Wisconsin, 1950–51; Harley Sewell, G, Texas, 1953–59; Wayne Siegert,

T, Illinois, 1951; Jack Simmons, G-C, Detroit, 1950; J. Robert "Bob" Smith, B, Iowa, 1950–54; Robert Lee "Texas Bob" Smith, B, Texas A&M, 1953–54 (Army 1951–52); Joe Soboleski, T, Michigan, 1950; Ollie Spencer, T, Kansas, 1953, 1956, 1959 (Army 1954–55); *Dick Stanfel, G, San Francisco, 1952–55; Jim Steffen, B, UCLA, 1959; Bill Stits, B, UCLA, 1954–56; Pat Summerall, E, Arkansas, 1952; Bill Swiacki, E, Columbia, 1951–52; Ted Topor, LB, Michigan, 1955 (Army 1953–54); LaVern Torgeson, C-LB, Washington State, 1951–54; Tom "The Bomb" Tracy, B, Tennessee, 1956–57; Wally Triplett, B, Penn State, 1950 (Army 1950–51); Hal Turner, E, Tennessee State, 1954 (Marine Corps 1952–53); *Doak Walker, B, Southern Methodist, 1950–55; Wayne Walker, LB, Idaho, 1958–59; Joe Watson, C, Rice, 1950; Jim Weatherall, T, Oklahoma, 1959; Ken Webb, B, Presbyterian, 1958–59; Dave Whitsell, DB, Indiana, 1958–59; Richie Woit, B, Arkansas State, 1955; Bruce Womack, G, West Texas State, 1951; Walt Yowarsky, E, Kentucky, 1955; Roger Zatkoff, LB, Michigan, 1957–58.

NOTES

M y thanks to Bill Dow for sharing taped interviews he conducted with several former players and family members. The Dow interviews are identified as DI in the notes (for example, "DI Leon Hart"). Other frequently cited sources are abbreviated as follows: AI (author's interview), AP (Associated Press), *CT* (*Chicago Tribune*), *DFP* (*Detroit Free Press*), *DMN* (*Dallas Morning News*), *DN* (*Detroit News*), *DT* (*Detroit Times*), *LAT* (*Los Angeles Times*), *NYT* (*New York Times*), *SI* (*Sports Illustrated*), *TSN* (*The Sporting News*), and *WP* (*Washington Post*).

Introduction: Riding High

2 "Detroit has always liked": Tex Maule, "All Hail the Lusty Lions," *SI*, January 6, 1958.

2 "The fans picked me up": AI Joe Schmidt.

3 "God, we hated": Don Paul, *I Went Both Ways* (Tacoma, WA: Pro-Pacific, 1988), 134.

4 "We got sort of": Gary Cartwright, "A Sort of Superior Feeling," *DMN*, August 28, 1963.

4 "It was like walking": Bill Dow, "The Imperfect Passer," *DFP*, September 28, 2008.

4 "In our team meetings": Richard Bak, Charley Vincent, and the *Free Press* staff, *The Corner: A Century of Memories at Michigan and Trumbull* (Chicago: Triumph/ DFP, 1999), 133.

4 "We'd get the ball": George Cantor, "Three Lion Heroes from Football's Pre-Superbowl Era," *DFP Magazine*, January 13, 1974.

4 "In the early '50s": Tom DeLisle, "Cars, Bars, Booze, and the Legend of Bobby Layne," August 4, 2010, http://blog. detroitathletic.com/2010/08/04cars-bars-booze-and-the-legend-of-bobby-layne/.

4 "He was the greatest": Joe Falls, "Well, Hello Again, Buddy Parker!" *DFP*, October 31, 1972.

5 "He wasn't the fastest": "Lions Great Doak Walker Dies at 71," *DFP*, September 28, 1998.

5 "People had more than respect": Ibid.

5 "They were a living example": Jim Murray, "The Playful Little Lions," *LAT*, December 4, 1966.

5 "Maybe they all lived it up": Falls, "Well, Hello Again, Buddy Parker!"

6 "I'll never forget this": George Puscas, "It Was a Joyride Big Ol' Monte Will Never Forget," *DFP*, December 11, 1978.

6 "Those were just": Leigh Montville, "Pigskin on Turkey Day," *SI* (*Special NFL Classic Edition*), Fall 1995. In the article, Larco is mistakingly referred to as "Falco."

7 "After the first season": Bobby Layne (with Bob Drum), *Always on Sunday* (Englewood Heights, NJ.: Prentice-Hall, 1962), 60.

9 "Today the players": AI Vince Banonis.

9 "You never admitted": AI Ann Carpenter.

9 "There was a different mentality": Schmidt interview.

9 "The doctors were treating it": Layne, *Always on Sunday*, 45.

10 "Rogel was one": Ibid., 108.

10 "Well, he's an old Browns player": George E. Van, "Sports Today: Our Lions Did Browns Up Brown," *DT*, December 30, 1957.

11 "Watching that mob": AI Tom DeLisle.

Chapter 1: Two from Texas

12 "Bobby Layne and Doak Walker": AP, "Doak, Bobby Reunited," *DMN*, April 8, 1950.

13 "We want to be": Bob St. John, *Heart of a Lion: The Wild and Woolly Life of Bobby Layne* (Dallas: Taylor, 1991), 120.

13 "Playing with Bobby": Whit Canning, *Doak Walker: More than a Hero*, ed. Dan Jenkins (Indianapolis: Masters Press, 1997), 111.

13 "He didn't do": George Puscas, "Doak Walker: The Ultimate Lion," *DFP*, August 2, 1986.

13 "I'm not sure": St. John, *Heart of a Lion*, 111.

14 "I'll try": Frank X. Tolbert, "The Coach's Son," *This Week*, September 19, 1948.

14 "open the church": Stuart Leuthner, *Iron Men: Bucko, Crazylegs and the Boys Recall the Golden Days of Professional Football* (New York: Doubleday, 1988), 197.

15 "Wherever we were": Canning, *Doak Walker*, 61.

15 "He was a year": Leuthner, *Iron Men*, 193.

15 "With Bobby, it was all": Canning, *Doak Walker*, 61.

15 "It's true that": Ibid., 31.

16 "Doak isn't fast": Lyall Smith, "Walker Not Much—Just Best There Is," *DFP*, September 9, 1951.

17 "It was an unselfish": Bill Fay, "The 60th All-America," *Collier's*, December 10, 1949.

17 "a refreshing combination": Tolbert, "The Coach's Son."

17 "The way my father": Leuthner, *Iron Men*, 197.

18 "Nobody can pass": Oscar Fraley, "The Terrible-Tempered Mr. Layne," *Inside Sports*, February 1954.

18 "The board of directors": George Puscas, "Lions' Finest Hour Is in Past," *DFP*, September 4, 1983.

18 "It was a great day": Sam Blair,

"Movin' on in Motown," *DMN*, November 10, 1975.

18 "Naturally, I was happy": Ibid.

19 "It not only makes": Sam Boal, "Detroit at 250: Lusty and Young," *NYT*, July 29, 1951.

21 "A lot of college stars": Jim Warner, "Leon Is Lions' Prize Package," *DN Pictorial Magazine*, September 17, 1950.

22 "Detroit is sure to have": Charles Burton, "The Inside Story," *DMN*, March 23, 1950.

23 "as good as his name": Ken Bikoff, "A Strong 'Hunch,'" *Indiana Magazine*, November 2013.

23 "I think we had": Jack Murray, "Hunchy Building Cars," *Cincinnati Enquirer*, May 23, 1976.

23 "A slim, blond gridder": Bob Latshaw, "Bobby Layne Stamps Self as Lion Luminary in 1950," *DFP*, August 3, 1950.

23 "Playing with the Lions": Leuthner, *Iron Men*, 198.

24 "Bobby would put": AI Wally Triplett.

24 "He did like": St. John, *Heart of a Lion*, 16.

24 "I never met": Ibid., 15–16.

24 "appeared baffled": United Press, "Lions Lose Exhibition to Pittsburgh," *DFP*, August 20, 1950.

26 "We may not win": Watson Spoelstra, "McMillan: Lions Could Win 6 or 8," *DN*, September 18, 1950.

26 "We won that game": DI Leon Hart.

26 "the T-formation quarterback": Watson Spoelstra, "Lions Riding High in Seat with Bears," *DN*, September 25, 1950.

26 "the fabulous Doak": Bob Latshaw, "Fumble Helps Lions Defeat Steelers, 10–7," *DFP*, September 25, 1950.

26 "Bo is a benevolent-appearing": Arthur Daley, "Sports of *The Times*: A Mild Intrusion," *NYT*, September 28, 1950.

27 "There never has been": Bill Fay, "Bingo Bingaman—Pro Football's Immovable Object," *Collier's*, October 29, 1954.

27 "A great player": Canning, *Doak*

Walker, 109.

28 "In one preseason scrimmage": Bobby Layne (as told to Murray Olderman), "This Is No Game for Kids," *Saturday Evening Post*, November 14, 1959.

28 "I was shoeing": Lyall Smith, "As of Today: Unlucky Draw Perils Lions' Bid for 3rd Title," *DFP*, September 10, 1954.

29 "I just throw": Jeanne Hoffman, "Home Again: Former Troy Star 'Dolls' Up Ram Roster," *LAT*, September 17, 1954.

29 "I was looking": Bill Dow, "Team Put Base in Place in 1950," *DFP*, September 20, 2000.

30 "Bulger was banged up": Layne, *Always on Sunday*, 74–75.

30 "I have to feel": Tommy Devine, "Ringmaster of the Lions," *Sport*, November 1953.

30 "I remember asking": Dow, "Team Put Base in Place in 1950."

30 "Bo was a wonderful guy": Hart interview.

31 "a typical Doak Walker day": Bob Latshaw, "Lion Score: Doak 24, Packers 21," *DFP*, November 20, 1950.

31 "Doak Walker is my ideal": Charles Burton, "The Inside Story: Deacon Dan Towler Praises Doak Walker," *DMN*, February 11, 1952.

31 "I probably was": Tommy Devine, "Story-Book Touch behind Box's Rise to Fame," *DFP*, August 30, 1953.

32 "I was just about": Michael Barr, *Cloyce Box: 6'4" and Bulletproof* (College Station: Texas A&M University Press, 2017), 64.

32 "Get off the field": Layne, *Always on Sunday*, 137–38.

Chapter 2: We Can Win with Parker

34 "We know that Buddy": Bob Latshaw, "Happy News for Lions! Layne's Arm Looks OK," *DFP*, December 15, 1951.

35 "You can't do this": George Plimpton, *Paper Lion* (Guilford, CT: Lyons, 2009),

285.

35 "It is difficult": Lyall Smith, "McMillan Gives Up Job Under Fire from Directors," *DFP*, December 20, 1950. During the 1950s, the directors of the Detroit Football Company were Edwin J. Anderson (1950–59), C. E. Bleicher (1950–52), Walter O. "Spike" Briggs Jr. (1951–59), E. R. Bryant (1950–59), George A. Cavanaugh (1950–59), John J. Cronin (1951), William D. Downey (1950–59), D. Lyle Fife (1950–59), Charles T. Fisher Jr. (1950–57), William Clay Ford (1956–59), Philip A. Hart (1950–56), Arthur R. Hoffman (1950–59), Ernest Kanzler (1950–59), H. G. Little (1952–59), Joseph N. Monaghan (1955–59), Oscar L. Olson (1953–59), John K. Stevenson (1956–59), Carl F. Unruh (1950–52), and Ray M. Whyte (1950–59).

35 After all...we don't go": AP, "Ex-Lion Boss Opposed to 'Love,'" *DFP*, January 5, 1951.

35 "I'm tickled to death": "Parker Sees Lions '51 Title Contenders," *DFP*, December 21, 1950.

36 "Buddy was a great": Hart interview.

36 "Buddy never gave": Schmidt interview.

36 "I naturally thought": Stanley Frank, "He Dies for Detroit Every Week," *Saturday Evening Post*, November 13, 1954.

37 "This job is": Lyall Smith, "City of Champions Again?" *DFP*, January 17, 1951.

37 "McMillan knew football": Mickey Herskowitz, *The Golden Age of Pro Football: A Remembrance of Pro Football in the 1950s* (New York: Macmillan, 1974), 101.

37 "When we're on": Tommy Devine, "Parker Keeps It Simple," *SI*, November 15, 1954.

37 "The trouble with": Ibid., 104.

37 "Buddy liked seasoned pros": Hart interview.

38 "That was my biggest": Banonis interview.

38 "I had the brawn": Lyall Smith, "As of Today: Lions Great Champs—Banonis

Tells Why," *DFP*, December 30, 1952.

38 "No, thanks": Bill Fay, "Detroit's Castoff Champions—The Men Nobody Wanted," *Collier's*, October 2, 1953.

38 "When Harder hits": Lyall Smith, "As of Today: Harder Makes Prophet of Curly Lambeau," *DFP*, December 23, 1952.

39 "I'm going to teach": Paul, *I Went Both Ways*, 16.

39 "helped to inflame": Sam Greene, "Hiring of Harder Parker's Ace Move," *DN*, December 18, 1951.

40 "He was a low-key guy": Charlie Sanders (with Larry Paladino), *Charlie Sanders' Tales from the Detroit Lions* (Champaign, IL: Sports Publishing, 2005), 99.

40 "You can always get": Jack Newcombe, "You've Got to Be Good and Mean," *Sport*, December 1955.

40 "He wouldn't be afraid": Ibid.

40 "[Doran] has everything": Bob Latshaw, "Here's Boost for Young Lions," *DFP*, October 3, 1951.

41 "Parker, Doak Walker": Bob Latshaw, "Dibble to Keep Lions' Foes Guessing," *DFP*, August 17, 1955.

41 "the fumblingest quarterback": Al Wolf, "Sportraits," *LAT*, January 9, 1953.

41 "We worked with Layne": Raymond K. (Buddy) Parker, *We Play to Win! The Inside Story of the Fabulous Detroit Lions* (Englewood Cliffs, NJ: Prentice-Hall, 1955), 48.

42 "I told our squad": Watson Spoelstra, "Swing Triumph in 3rd Period," *DN*, September 5, 1951.

42 "We saw that": Gary Cartwright, "A Sort of Superior Feeling," *DMN*, August 28, 1963.

43 "At that time": Leuthner, *Iron Men*, 8.

44 "That is the team": Bob Latshaw, "Greene New Kind of Lion," *DFP*, October 10, 1951.

44 "Kick to the tall": Herskowitz, *The Golden Age of Pro Football*, 165.

44 "The Rams were sure": Doak Walker, "Doak's Dope," *DFP*, October 17, 1951.

44 Carol Layne and Hirsch: St. John, *Heart of a Lion*, 19–20.

45 "The treasurer's report": Tex Maule, "Lambs into Lions," *SI*, December 2, 1957.

45 "Layne has done": Bob Latshaw, "Parker Upholds Layne's Generalmanship," *DFP*, October 23, 1951.

46 "I still feel": Bob Latshaw, "'Don't Count Us Out,' Says Parker," *DFP*, October 30, 1951.

47 "He likes nothing better": Bob Latshaw, "Lucky to Have a 'Hart,'" *DFP*, November 14, 1951.

47 "My muscles would tighten": Hart interview.

47 "One time there": Jerry Green, *Detroit Lions* (New York: Macmillan, 1973), 55.

47 "The game would be": Dan Daly and Bob O'Donnell, *The Pro Football Chronicle* (New York: Collier, 1990), 130.

48 "I didn't gain": Bob Latshaw, "Joyful Lions Pat Each Other on Back," *DFP*, November 12, 1951.

48 "Even in the pro league": Bob Latshaw, "Death Brings 'McMillan Legend' to an End," *DFP*, April 1, 1952.

50 "Lotsa time": Green, *Detroit Lions*, 15–16.

50 "delirious, hilarious": Lyall Smith, "As of Today: Little Doak Becomes Giant with Chips Down," *DFP*, December 11, 1951.

51 "Any time a team": Bob Latshaw, "Lions Get LA Off Hands, Can't Get 49ers Off Mind," *DFP*, December 11, 1951.

51 "We got to win": Latshaw, "Happy News for Lions!" Through a series of coin flips involving representatives from all four contenders, Bert Bell was prepared for any contingencies. In the event of a tie between the Lions and either the Bears or Rams, Detroit would go on the road to play a special tiebreaker on December 23 to determine the conference champion. The winner of that game would play Cleveland for the title. However, the scheduling became more favorable to Detroit if there were a three-way tie among the Lions, Bears, and Rams. In round-robin fashion, Los Angeles would play at Detroit on December 23, with the winner hosting Chicago the following Sunday. The winner of that game would then host the title game on January 6, 1952. Under such a scenario, it would have been possible for the Lions to play three straight postseason games at Briggs Stadium, an unprecedented stretch of "home cooking" in an era before extended playoff tournaments became the norm.

51 "Get that bum": George Puscas, "So What's New?" *DFP*, September 21, 1990.

52 "No one really understood": Gary Cartwright, "Layne Was Toughest," *DMN*, undated [1967] clipping in author's file.

53 "The scribes themselves": Cal Wharton, "Rams Celebrate Two Victories after Game," *LAT*, December 17, 1951.

53 "We ought to have": "49ers Thwart Lions' Title Hopes, 21–17," *LAT*, December 17, 1951.

53 "As I walked off": Y. A. Tittle (as told to Don Smith), *I Pass!* (Englewood Cliffs, NJ: Prentice-Hall, 1964), 170.

54 "The most fitting thing": Sam Greene, "Dejected, They Can't Eat Parker's Cake," *DN*, December 17, 1951.

54 "We'll be back": Ibid.

54 "What sort of guys": Mark Beltaire, "The Town Crier: Lion Star Scorns Football 'Robbers,'" *DFP*, February 15, 1952.

Chapter 3: World Beaters

55 "Every son of a bitch": Myron Cope, *The Game That Was: An Illustrated Account of the Tumultuous Early Days of Pro Football* (New York: Thomas Y. Crowell, 1974), 229.

55 "Our Lions didn't": Bob Murphy, "Anderson Put Games on TV," *DT*, December 17, 1951.

55 profits and losses: AP, "Lions Announce Profit of $114,000 for '52 But Are Still in Red," *WP*, February 4, 1953.

56 "He liked people": Leuthner, *Iron Men*, 269.

57 "After I heard that": Pat Summerall (with Michael Levin), *Giants: What I Learned about Life from Vince Lombardi and Tom Landry* (Hoboken, NJ: Wiley, 2010), 31.

58 "It was a miracle": Bob Latshaw, "Infection No. 1 Worry after Doak's Injury," *DFP*, June 14, 1952.

58 "We went all out": Lyall Smith, "As of Today: All These Compliments Aren't Fooling Lions," *DFP*, August 18, 1953.

59 "The kid was": Pete Waldmeir, "The Lions' Man Friday," *Pro!* December 17, 1977.

59 "It isn't so much": Fay, "Detroit's Castoff Champions—The Men Nobody Wanted."

59 Parker's code: *Detroit Lions 1954 Facts and Team History* (Detroit: Detroit Lions Football Company, 1954), 11.

60 "the Lions gave": Bob Latshaw, "Lions at Worst for Best Crowd in Detroit History," *DFP*, October 13, 1952.

60 "Bobby just hated": Blair, "Movin' on in Motown."

60 "Kind of silly": Fraley, "The Terrible-Tempered Mr. Layne."

60 "I'm going to be": Green, *Detroit Lions*, 21.

61 "I can't sit": Ibid.

61 "This was as brutal": Bob Latshaw, "Lions Spot Rams 13–0 Lead, Roar to 24–16 Victory," *DFP*, October 20, 1952.

61 "A torn hamstring": Hart interview.

62 "What made him": Anjali J. Sekhar, "Earl 'Jug' Girard, Former Lions Player," *DFP*, January 19, 1997.

63 "Bobby's passes weren't": Banonis interview.

63 "You just give them": Steve Gelman, "Bobby Layne Lives in the Limelight," *Sport*, January 1961.

63 "Doak Walker never drank": Green, *Detroit Lions*, 124.

64 "In 'Sevens,' you just": Layne, *Always on Sunday*, 31.

65 "They're great stories": Banonis interview.

65 "I've had fellows": DI Dorne Dibble.

65 "But we never": Green, *Detroit Lions*, 126.

65 "Now, fellas": Layne, "This Is No Game for Kids."

65 "I sleep fast": Layne, *Always on Sunday*, 30.

66 "I like to be around": Ibid., 30–31.

66 "I'm a very dull": Jack Saylor, "Lions Tap 'Glory Years,' Hire Don Doll," *DFP*, February 15, 1978.

66 "Some of the back-biting": Marney Rich, "The Long Happy Hour of Bobby Layne," *Monthly Detroit*, November 1984.

66 "I've thought a lot": Fraley, "Ringmaster of the Lions."

67 "It seemed you could get": Herskowitz, *The Golden Age of Pro Football*, 101.

67 "It may seem insignificant": Fraley, "Ringmaster of the Lions."

68 "He'd tire you out": Barr, *Cloyce Box*, 62.

68 "He was a good leader": Hart interview.

68 "Stanfel does more": "Meet Your Lions," *Lion Gridiron News*, December 11, 1955.

68 "When he pulled": Bob Carroll, "Dick Stanfel," *Coffin Corner* 16, no. 2 (1994).

69 "the best holding tackle": Dick Birkett, "Former O-Lineman Is Candidate for Hall," *DFP*, January 30, 2012.

69 "Doak Walker had come": Green, *Detroit Lions*, 120.

69 "The night before": Layne, *Always on Sunday*, 140.

70 "It was a battle": Hal Middlesworth, "Hart Isn't Only Lion Hero," *DFP*, November 3, 1952.

70 "I don't feel bad": Ibid.

70 "The Layne critics": Watson Spoelstra, "Tosser Layne Now Lion-on-Loose as a Runner," *TSN*, December 10, 1952.

71 "The chances we took": Parker, *We Play to Win!* 104.

71 "If his sinewy legs": Spoelstra, "Tosser Layne Now Lion-on-Loose as a Runner."

72 "If we get": Green, *Detroit Lions*, 23.

72 "When Coach Buddy Parker": Bob Latshaw, "Put Any Lion in Any Spot; Chances Are You'll Get Good Job," *DFP*, December 11, 1952.

72 Lions-Rams playoff: Sam Greene, "Lions Master Rams—It's 3 Times and In," *DN*, December 22, 1952; Frank Finch, "Lions Down Rams in Play-off, 31–21," *LAT*, December 22, 1952.

74 "It was 'ceiling zero'": Louis Effrat, "Lions Vanquish Rams and Gain Right to Meet Browns for Pro Football Title," *NYT*, December 22, 1952.

75 "We never worked": AP, "Walker and Harder Lauded for Their Roles in Bringing Conference Honors to Detroit," *NYT*, December 22, 1952.

75 "I knew they weren't": "Couldn't Feel Any Worse—Waterfield," *LAT*, December 22, 1952.

75 "a hungry herd": Finch, "Lions Down Rams in Play-off, 31–21."

75 "Sure we'll go light": Watson Spoelstra, "Walker Again Is a-Runnin'," *DN*, December 22, 1952.

75 "They've got more guns": AP, "Brown Won't Fight Parker," *WP*, December 25, 1952.

76 "Paul Brown's Browns": Shirley Povich, "This Morning," *WP*, December 23, 1952.

76 "Anytime a club": Edward Prell, "Browns Expect 35,000 to See Duel with Lions," *CT*, December 24, 1952.

76 "reflected their city": AP, "Brown Won't Fight Parker."

76 "Do you think": Edgar C. "Doc" Greene, *Dies a Crapshooter . . . and Other Digressions* (Detroit: Marilyn Publishing, 1960), 221–25.

77 "knew all the Lions": "Death Takes Ardent Fan of Football," *DFP*, December 26, 1952.

77 Lions-Browns championship game: Edgar Hayes, "Players Heap Praise on Great Lion Defense," *DT*, December 29, 1952; Bob Latshaw, "Lions Beat Browns, 17-7, Win NFL Title," *DFP*, December 29,

1952; Sam Greene, "After 17 Years Detroit Rules Foot Ball Pros," *DN*, December 29, 1952.
77 "Doak, you rested up": Green, *Detroit Lions*, 26.
78 "If they purposely": Harold Sauerbrei, "Lions Beat Browns, 17–7, for Title," *Cleveland Plain Dealer*, December 28, 1952.
78 "Give me the ball": Layne, "This Is No Game for Kids."
78 "Box was the guy": AP, "Brown Defense Boxed by Lions," *CT*, December 29, 1952.
78 "It was a cross-buck": Blair, "Movin' on in Motown."
79 "That's pretty much": Canning, *More than a Hero*, 109.
80 "He clicked the trigger": Lyall Smith, "Lions Share Biggest Pro Payout," *DFP*, December 29, 1952.
80 player shares: Ibid.
80 "The Lions were more": H. G. Salsinger, "The Umpire: '35 Lions Better than '52 Champs," *TSN*, January 14, 1953.
81 "Winners and new champions": Bob Yonkers, "Long-Term Reign Foreseen for Lions," *TSN*, January 7, 1953.
81 "That game stands out": St. John, *Heart of a Lion*, 35.

Chapter 4: Pro Football at Its Best

82 "What I remember best": George Puscas, "New Hall of Famer Lary Recalls Lions' Glory Days," *DFP*, January 30, 1978.
82 "Did you know": "Even without Buddy Young," *DMN*, December 29, 1952.
82 "I was glad": Tommy Devine, "Sewell All-Star Standout," *DFP*, August 12, 1953.
83 "Early in the game": Bud Shrake, "No Bandage Bill for Sewell," *DMN*, August 25, 1963.
83 "After about five minutes": George Puscas, "No. 66 Plays 'Dirty'—Just Look at Him!" *DFP*, November 16, 1961.
83 "You got to be a dawg": George

Puscas, "At Last, Lions' Offensive Line Shows It Can Block," *DFP*, October 11, 1978.
84 "When Spencer moves somebody": Bob Latshaw, "Two Lions Rookies Classy but Unheralded," *DFP*, November 28, 1953.
84 "Toronto offered me": Schmidt interview.
86 "The pre-game introduction": Lyall Smith, "Champs Proved They're Ready," *DFP*, August 15, 1953.
86 "The boys just don't like": Smith, "As of Today: All These Compliments Aren't Fooling Lions."
86 "I started my pro career": Bob Latshaw, "Doll Won't Dance to Lions' Tune," *DFP*, September 15, 1953.
86 "I had the distinction": Jack Saylor, "Lions Sign No. 1 Draft Choice Lynn Boden," *DFP*, April 9, 1975.
87 "I went to camp": Schmidt interview.
87 "making tackles all over": Bob Latshaw, "Lions Bowl Over Steelers in Opener, 38–21," *DFP*, September 28, 1953.
87 "You saw it, Crowley": Harry Stapler, "Rookies Ignite Lions, but It Is Doak's Day," *DN*, September 28, 1953.
88 "Bob was trapped": Bob Latshaw, "Path to 2nd Title Thorny, Lions Find," *DFP*, October 5, 1953.
89 "Jack Christiansen grabbed": Tittle, *I Pass!*, 190.
89 "We had it coming": Lyall Smith, "As of Today: Had It Coming, Lion Veteran Admits," *DFP*, October 20, 1953.
90 "Fears had hit": George Puscas, "Lions' Stars Hart, David Left Indelible Impressions," *DFP*, May 14, 1997.
90 "Fears caught a low pass": Frank Finch, "Lion Back David Denies 'Intent' in Fears, Tittle Grid Incidents," *LAT*, October 27, 1953.
91 "I want to say": AP, "'Dirty Lions' Brings Roar from Parker," *DFP*, October 29, 1953.
91 "If I was a dirty player": Finch, "Lion

Back David Denies 'Intent' in Fears, Tittle Grid Incidents."

91 "It was the greatest": Jack Saylor, "U-M Turnout Recalls Lions' No. 1 Crowd," *DFP*, August 21, 1971.

91 "It was a knockdown": Puscas, "Lions' Stars Hart, David Left Indelible Impressions."

92 "We gathered in a little circle": Saylor, "U-M Turnout Recalls Lions' No. 1 Crowd."

92 "He should have been": Carpenter interview.

92 "He was first string": Green, *Detroit Lions*, 140.

93 "Of course, there were": Layne, *Always on Sunday*, 53.

93 "Buck never cared": Martin S. Jacobs, *San Francisco 49ers Legends: The Golden Age of Pro Football* (San Francisco: CreateSpace, 2016), 99.

93 "Buddy was the first": AI Yale Lary.

94 "Most of our success": Stan Grosshandler, "The Chris Crew," *Coffin Corner* 8, no. 3 (1986).

94 "Pass defense was": Herskowitz, *The Golden Age of Pro Football*, 164.

95 "One guy in our section": AI Fred Rice.

95 "It was just getting": Herskowitz, *The Golden Age of Pro Football*, 164.

95 "Too often the fan": Tommy Devine, "Prchlik Playing Last Year with Lions," *DFP*, August 28, 1953.

96 "Our team doesn't care": Bob Latshaw, "Nobody Straining to Be No. 1," *DFP*, December 15, 1953.

96 "How many yards": Bob Latshaw, "This Is How Runners Crumble When 340-Pound 'Bing' Moves," *DFP Roto Magazine*, August 22, 1954.

96 "strong enough to move": Bob Talbert, "A Third Michigan Winter? Ban-the-Blahs! Think Sunshine," *DFP*, November 24, 1970.

96 "He also loves to play": Bob Latshaw, "Two Lions Rookies Classy but Unheralded," *DFP*, November 28, 1953.

97 "It was more than": Louis Cook,

"Santa on Parade Carries the Day; Pilgrim Fathers Bring up Rear," *DFP*, November 27, 1953.

98 "Detroit was an elite team": AI Mike Cutler.

99 "I saw that Layne-Box": Jim Taylor, "Injured Plum Will Be Out 7–10 Days," *DFP*, October 17, 1966.

99 "We don't even eat": Clint Wilkinson, "The Wives Scream for Gold and Glory," *DFP*, December 28, 1953.

99 "My girlfriend and I": Mary Morris, "Guess What! How Mates Snared Lions," *DN*, October 30, 1953.

100 "I roomed with Harley": Schmidt interview.

100 "They'd play cards": Carpenter interview.

101 "Well, when Bobby": St. John, *Heart of a Lion*, 42.

101 "It really was": Carpenter interview.

101 "Everybody liked everybody": Canning, *Doak Walker*, 111.

101 "I loved playing": Ibid., 110.

101 "I came from": Ibid.

102 "It was a lot": Pat Smee, "8 Lions' Wives Compare Notes at 'Coffee Club,'" *DN*, October 20, 1954.

102 "I'd like to sit": Wilkinson, "The Wives Scream for Gold and Glory."

102 "Detroit was so much": St. John, *Heart of a Lion*, 41.

102 Torgeson tragedies: "Brother Lavern Torgeson, WSC Captain, Misses Finale: Tragedy Claims Cougar Hooper, Jolts Gridmen," *Oregon Statesman*, November 26, 1950; "Wife Dies; Torgeson Goes West for Funeral," *DFP*, December 5, 1953.

103 "That was the saddest": Carpenter interview.

103 "This is a close-knit team": Sanders, *Charlie Sanders's Tales from the Detroit Lions*, 169.

103 "go back to worrying": "Now Lions Will Become His Baby," *DFP*, December 9, 1953.

104 "We've beaten Cleveland": United Press, "Now for Those Browns," *DFP*,

December 14, 1953.

104 "Otto was kind of": Jack Clary, *Cleveland Browns* (New York: Macmillan, 1973), 122.

104 "I never heard Paul Brown": Alan Natali, *Brown's Town: 20 Famous Browns Talk among Themselves* (Wilmington, OH: Orange Frazer, 2001), 88.

105 "It didn't make": Ibid., 64.

105 "Bobby Layne was tough": Ibid., 242.

106 "Better than Paul Brown": Murray, "Hunchy Building Cars."

106 "great delight": Lou Groza (with Mark Hodermarsky), *The Toe: The Lou Groza Story* (Cleveland: Gray, 2003), 69.

107 "Here possibly are": Green, *Detroit Lions*, 51.

107 "There will be": Shirley Povich, "This Morning," *WP*, December 24, 1953.

107 "This should be": Arthur Daley, "Sports of *The Times*," *NYT*, December 26, 1953.

108 "a whale of a game": Lou Effrat, "Cleveland Slight Choice to Beat Detroit Today for N.F.L. Title," *NYT*, December 27, 1953.

110 "Can you still beat": Shelby Strother, "Life in the Fast Layne," January 1, 2005, www.profootballhof.com/news/1953-championship-game/.

110 "I raced toward": AP, "Bench's Aid Cited in Key Pass Play," *NYT*, December 28, 1953.

110 "Warren never got": Bak, *The Corner*, 133.

111 Lions-Browns title game: Bob Latshaw, "Our Lions Are Still Kings," *DFP*, December 28, 1953; Andy Piascik, *The Best Show in Football: The 1946–1955 Cleveland Browns, Pro Football's Greatest Dynasty* (Lanham, MD: Taylor, 2006), 276–82; Harold Sauerbrei, "Browns Lose Title Game, 17–16," *Cleveland Plain Dealer*, December 28, 1953.

111 "I made a bad pass": Lyall Smith, "As of Today: Thanksgiving Day Came Early for Lions' Banon's," *DFP*, November 26, 1953.

111 Walker's kicking shoe: "NFL May Apply Boot to Doak's Kicking Shoe," *DFP*, October 24, 1951; Bob Latshaw, "'Three Shoes' Makes One Payoff," *DFP*, November 25, 1953.

112 "C'mon, Lou": George Puscas, "Lions' Great Wonders When Fame Will Come," *DFP*, January 17, 1991.

112 "I didn't feel anything": "No Feeling at All, Says Doak," *DFP*, December 28, 1953.

112 "So we just had to": Cantor, "Three Lion Heroes from Football's Pre-Superbowl Era."

113 "It was the toughest": AP, "Bench's Aid Cited in Key Pass Play."

113 "Jest give me the time": Green, *Detroit Lions*, 52.

113 "As the fans swarmed": Lyall Smith, "As of Today: Lions Roar Because of Nerveless Layne," *DFP*, December 29, 1953.

113 "the new glamor guy": Fraley, "The Terrible-Tempered Mr. Layne."

114 "Bobby just had": Strother, "Life in the Fast Layne." Lions players voted full shares of $2,274.77 to the 33 men who suited up for the title game, as well as to equipment manager Roy Macklem, trainer Grant Foster, and the coaches. Half shares of $1,137.39 were given to Pat Harder, Bob Dove, and Blaine Earon.

Chapter 5: Gridiron Heroes

115 "Ours is a city": Michael Betzold, John Davids, Bill Dow, John Pastier, and Frank Rashid, eds., *Tiger Stadium: Essays and Memories of Detroit's Historic Ballpark, 1912–2009* (Jefferson, NC: McFarland, 2018), 240.

116 "It didn't matter what": Al Jim Boyle.

117 "I knew everything": DeLisle interview.

117 "I remember getting off": Bak, *The Corner*, 125.

117 "Sunday afternoon wrestlers": Harry Wismer, *The Public Calls It Sport* (Englewood Cliffs, NJ: Prentice-Hall,

1965), 43.

117 "He really didn't like": AI Basil "Mickey" Briggs.

118 "As an offensive end": Hart interview.

118 "The Lions sold": AI Elliott Trumbull.

119 "They were lower-deck seats": AI John Varisto.

119 "He said he had the ball": AI Marybelle Hoernschemeyer.

119 "We'd stop": Varisto interview.

120 "On blustery days": Trumbull interview.

120 "Golly, it was wonderful": Rice interview.

120 "You could actually": Trumbull interview.

120 "All that showboating": Triplett interview.

121 "Boy, he could play": Amber Arellano, "Director Changed Lions' Halftimes," *DFP*, January 18, 1994.

121 "You have no idea": Mark Beltaire, "The Town Crier: Red Prefers Having Real Cool Time," *DFP*, May 5, 1954.

121 "One day our band": AI Dick Burman.

121 "the halftime display": Mark Beltaire, "The Town Crier: Here's a Red Feather Challenge," *DFP*, October 13, 1953.

122 "Certainly I love music": Mark Beltaire, "The Town Crier: Haulaway Driver Samaritan of the Road," *DFP*, February 19, 1953.

123 "I not only missed": "Kind to Drunk," *DFP*, November 26, 1955. The All-America Football Conference (1946–49) and the American Football League (1960–69) also scheduled games on Thanksgiving. In 1966, the Dallas Cowboys started their own Thanksgiving Day tradition, adding a second game to the NFL schedule.

123 "Mullins controls": Joe Falls, "Links Strong in Lion Chain Gang," *DFP*, December 15, 1964.

124 "You never grow": William Hart, "40-Year Mascot Hangs up Fur," *DFP*,

December 18, 1977.

124 Did you ever see": "Lions Adopt Orphan, 12, as Waterboy," *DFP*, October 11, 1952.

124 "Peter was a little fellow": Bob Latshaw, "Lions' Warmest Fan Dies in Plane Crash," *DFP*, July 2, 1956.

124 "running the football team": Bud Goodman, "Crash Steals Bright Future," *DFP*, July 2, 1956.

125 "There'll be a big void": Latshaw, "Lions' Warmest Fan Dies in Plane Crash."

126 "Each year we took": AI Fred "Fritz" Wenson.

126 "You could sure hear": George Puscas, "Even in Lean Year Lions Can Lick Browns, 30–10," *DFP*, November 10, 1958.

126 "The Bears fans": Wenson interview.

126 "We had factory workers": Ibid.

127 "That's my memory": Richard Willing, "Roar No More," *DN*, November 28, 1996.

127 "The guys from Texas": AI Jerry Reichow.

128 "The wives had to sing": Jim Thomas, "HOF16: Dick Stanfel Boosted Powerhouse Detroit Teams of the 1950s," August 4, 2016, www.cantonrep.com/sports/20160804/hof16-dick-stanfel-boosted-powerhouse-detroit-teams-of-1950s.

128 "Bobby came here": Jack Saylor, "Lions Can Roar . . . And They Even Sing!" *DFP*, July 26, 1972.

128 "We heard some great": Plimpton, *Paper Lion*, 25–26.

128 "Oh, Alex": "Pro Hazing for a Rookie," *Life*, September 8, 1958.

128 "No, goddamn it": George Plimpton, *Mad Ducks and Bears* (New York: Random House, 1973), 52–54.

129 "When I was a rookie": St. John, *Heart of a Lion*, 39.

129 "Rookies in those days": Gary Cartwright, "To Play 20, Have Some Fun," *DMN*, August 29, 1963.

129 "Hi, Jolly John": Ibid.

129 "He would suck up": George Puscas, "Guinness Book of Records Calling All You Prune Eaters, Beer Drinkers," *DFP*, March 14, 1976.

130 "You had to go": DI Steve Junker.

130 "nobody was a stranger": Strother, "Life in the Fast Layne."

130 "We went to bars": Jack Saylor, "It Was a 'Love Game' for Lions' 1953 Champions," *DFP*, November 12, 1978.

130 "It was Bobby": Cantor, "Three Lion Heroes from Football's Pre-Superbowl Era."

131 "attracted many high": "Crystal Bar to Bring in Earl Belcher," *Detroit Tribune*, August 11, 1951.

131 "We got very friendly": Terry Gibbs (with Gary Ginell), *Good Vibes: A Life in Jazz* (Lanham, MD: Scarecrow Press, 2003).

131 "Bobby reminded me": St. John, *Heart of a Lion*, 57–58.

131 "He got on the field": Ibid., 57.

132 "One staggered up to": Bud Lanker, "Vice and Filth Still Flourishes on Skid Row," *DFP*, February 5, 1950.

132 "They are lured here": Dale Nouse, "Move Skid Row to Farm, City Told," *DFP*, August 13, 1953.

133 "Layne used to set up": St. John, *Heart of a Lion*, 23.

133 "You could walk in": Matt Helms and Brian Murphy, "Big-hearted Bar Owner Served Sports Legends," *DFP*, November 21, 1996.

133 "Behind the blind": George Puscas, "The Lindell: A Hangout for Athletes," *DFP*, January 8, 1963.

134 "best to watch": Plimpton, *Mad Ducks and Bears*, 136.

134 "front-runners and well-wishers": Robert W. Peterson, *Pigskin: The Early Years of Pro Football* (New York: Oxford University Press, 1997), 209.

134 "Everybody's got their groupies": Leuthner, *Iron Men*, 212.

134 "Layne was out": Tommy Devine,

"The Uneasy Coach of the Champs," *Saturday Evening Post*, September 27, 1958.

135 "On the field": Leuthner, *Iron Men*, 71.

135 "I'm a hot package": "Plot to Extort $10,000 from Grid Star Bared," *DFP*, October 22, 1950.

136 "My Triple-D Dynamo": Hoffman, "Home Again: Former Troy Star 'Dolls' Up Ram Roster."

136 "No way he cheated": Dibble interview.

136 "The sons-a-bitches had": Herskowitz, *The Golden Age of Pro Football*, 109.

137 "You didn't step": Richard Bak, *Cobb Would Have Caught It: The Golden Age of Baseball in Detroit* (Detroit: Wayne State University Press, 1991), 62.

137 "Hell, the writers": Paul Hornung (as told to William F. Reed), *Golden Boy* (New York: Simon & Schuster, 2004), 234.

137 "I don't care": Layne, *Always on Sunday*, 90.

137 "There is an opinion": Doc Greene, "Press Box," *DN*, September 18, 1957.

138 "Bobby Layne didn't give": Leuthner, *Iron Men*, 72.

138 "There was no place": Layne, *Always on Sunday*, 43.

138 "the crowds would stand up": Plimpton, *Mad Ducks and Bears*, 50.

138 "The place could hold": AI Norman Thrasher.

139 "They wanted to shut down": Bak, *The Corner*, 132.

139 "I would truly like": Jim Hawkins, "A Thumb in It," *DFP*, January 23, 1982.

Chapter 6: One of Those Things

140 "When the team loses": Frank, "He Dies for Detroit Every Week."

140 "Cheer up, Coach": Al Wolf, "West Coach Parker Gloomy over Defeat," *LAT*, January 18, 1954.

141 "We'd be playing Detroit": Natali, *Brown's Town*, 241.

141 "Nowhere in Paul Brown's": Piascik, *The Best Show in Football*, 318.

142 "New blood every year": Devine, "Parker Keeps It Simple."

142 "Lawson paints": *The Football Graphic*, September 4, 1954.

143 "Bing checked in": Waldmeir, "The Lions' Man Friday."

143 "accidentally belted": "Lions Ace Pleads Guilty in Dawn Cafe Brawl," *DT*, July 23, 1954.

144 "Five straight might be": Joe King, "What Puts the Roar in Detroit Lions?" *TSN*, December 15, 1954.

144 rule change: AP, "Football's Two-Platoon System Killed by NCAA," *DFP*, January 15, 1953.

145 "There wasn't even": Lyall Smith, "As of Today: Lopez Not Wasting Sympathy on Casey," *DFP*, August 15, 1954.

146 "I can guarantee": Arthur Daley, "Sports of *The Times*: Dress Rehearsal," *NYT*, December 19, 1954.

147 "I had a veteran team": Parker, *We Play to Win!* 148–49.

148 "It was great": O'Hara, "Dorne Dibble made his mark as a two-way player in the 1950s."

148 "Y. A. Tittle used to": Joseph Hession, "Hugh McElhenny: The King," *Coffin Corner* 8, no. 4 (1986).

149 "Any club that played": Bob Latshaw, "Lions Get Pat on Back," *DFP*, October 26, 1954.

150 "You're through": "'Tulsa Bob' Fired by Lions," *DT*, November 2, 1954.

150 "I think it is": Lyall Smith, "As of Today: Lions' Bob Smith Deserves Better Fate," *DFP*, November 4, 1954.

150 "It isn't unusual": Bob Latshaw, "Forte Tabs Mains Coming NFL Great," *DFP*, November 11, 1954.

151 "Jackson was playing": Arthur J. Donovan Jr. and Bob Drury, *Fatso: Football When Men Were Really Men* (New York: Morrow, 1987), 188.

151 "as flagrant a roughing play": Bob Latshaw, "Lions' Defense Stills Colts,"

151 "So help me Christ": Donovan, *Fatso*, 215.

DFP, November 8, 1954.

151 "We'll murder 'em": AP, "'Lions'll Murder 'em Next Time'—Parker," *LAT*, October 25, 1954.

152 "Parker was as jubilant": Hal Middlesworth, "Lions 'Greatest' in Buddy's Book," *DFP*, November 15, 1954.

152 "The game, rough all the way": AP, "Lions Extended as They Defeat Packers in Rough Game, 21 to 17," *NYT*, November 22, 1954.

152 "It was finally": Kristine Setting Clark, *St. Clair: I'll Take It Raw!* (Novato, CA: Kristine Setting Clark, 2005), 114–15.

153 "the novocaine syringe": Schmidt interview.

153 "We never had": Banonis interview.

153 "We never dispensed": Leuthner, *Iron Men*, 275.

153 "I'll throw a couple dexies": Greene, *Dies a Crapshooter*, 242.

154 "Know what I think?": Strother, "Life in the Fast Layne."

154 "Whenever Bo would": Layne, *Always on Sunday*, 136.

155 "The first people": Montville, "Pigskin on Turkey Day"

155 "It was a black-and-white": AI Armand Peterson.

156 "He had such a drawl": DI Norma Walker.

157 "Of all the pro teams": "A Pride of Lions," *Time*, November 29, 1954.

158 "It's habit-forming": Ibid.

159 "We got our first car": Carpenter interview.

160 "whacked away": Daley, "Sports of *The Times*: Dress Rehearsal."

160 "We had to snap out": AP, "Lions to Win, Says Parker; Slump Shaken," *CT*, December 22, 1954.

160 "Nowadays they change": Watson Spoelstra, "We'll Win Again, Lions Promise," *DN*, December 20, 1954.

161 "That last pass": Chuck Heaton, "Browns Halted in Last Minute, 14–10,"

Cleveland Plain Dealer, December 20, 1954.

161 "We'll see you": "Three-Hour Drama Has Grand Climax," *DN*, December 20, 1954.

161 "Wyatt Earp": Lyall Smith, "As of Today: Layne Gives Gridiron Dash of Wild West," *DFP*, December 22, 1954.

161 "Well, at least": AP, "Wily Paul Brown Refuses to Concede Title to Lions," *LAT*, December 22, 1954.

161 "We beat 'em": Jack Saylor, "Sports People: '54 Lions Alumni Rehash the Hat Trick That Wasn't," *DFP*, November 11, 1979.

161 "There are some": Arthur Daley, "Sports of *The Times*: Practice Makes Perfect," *NYT*, December 21, 1954.

162 "We're in trouble": William W. Lutz, *The News of Detroit* (Boston: Little, Brown, 1973), 170.

162 "You could just kind of see": Green, *Detroit Lions*, 126.

162 championship game: Watson Spoelstra, "Bewildered Lions Still Proud; 'We Didn't Quit,' They Insist," *DN*, December 27, 1954; Chuck Heaton, "Browns Regain Title, 56 to 10," *Cleveland Plain Dealer*, December 26, 1954; Clary, *Cleveland Browns*, 76–87.

163 "the most beautiful play": Parker, *We Play to Win!* 131.

163 "We had a standard": Don Smith, "Jack Christiansen: Crew Chief," *Coffin Corner* 6, no. 5 (1984).

163 "since we weren't": Parker, *We Play to Win!* 135–36

164 "From the roughing call": Saylor, "Sports People: '54 Lions Alumni Rehash the Hat Trick That Wasn't."

164 "Time after time": Jack Walsh, "2 Key Plays Turned Tide against Detroit," *WP*, December 28, 1954.

164 "One of the natural": Bob McClellan, "Sports Today: Lions Keyed up Bit Too Early," *DT*, December 28, 1954.

165 "A more gratifying triumph": George Strickler, "Browns Whip Lions, 56–10, for Pro Title," *CT*, December 27, 1954.

165 "Detroit has a helluva team": AP, "Graham, Brown Tell Thrill of Beating Lions," *CT*, December 27, 1954. Gate receipts for the championship game were $289,126.43. TV and radio rights brought in an additional $101,250. The winning shares were $2,478.57 per man; the losing shares were $1,585.63 each. The Lions voted to divide their loot into 41½ shares, with all 33 active players getting a full share, as well as Dick Kercher (sidelined by a broken elbow), the coaches, equipment manager Roy Macklem, and trainer Grant Foster. Bob Smith, kicked off the team in midseason, received a half-share of $792.82. Clubhouse attendant John Hand received $500 and $125 was earmarked for gifts for office personnel. Bob Latshaw, "Bingaman, Too Old at 28, Calls It Quits," *DFP*, December 23, 1954.

165 "Hell, we all went": St. John, *Heart of a Lion*, 47.

165 "I guess when": Ibid.

165 "With that lopsided margin": Parker, *We Play to Win!* 136.

166 "Nobody hit me": AP, "'Luck Ran Out on Us,' Says Lion Coach."

Chapter 7: Sorry, Buddy
183 "Doak was the real": Dibble interview.

183 "I wanted to quit": Natali, *Brown's Town*, 65.

184 "We've never haggled": "Walker Can't Make Up Mind on Pro Game," *DMN*, April 6, 1955. According to the U.S. Census Bureau, the median salary for American workers in 1955 was $4,418.

184 "Wouldn't it be terrible": Ibid.

185 Lions salaries: Lyall Smith, "Doak Signs . . . for $27,500," *DFP*, July 30, 1955; Vartan Kupelian and Mike O'Hara, "Behind the Scenes: Players Didn't Get Rich in Old Days," *DN*, May 3, 1998.

185 "Doak's popularity": Jack Newcombe, "The Little Guy Who Fooled the Pros," *Sport*, January 1956.

185 "He would stand": "Lions Great Doak Walker Dies at 71."

185 "one of the finest": Canning, *Doak Walker*, 109.

186 "Just his name": Newcombe, "The Little Guy Who Fooled the Pros."

187 "I wasn't certain": Lyall Smith, "As of Today: Canadian Bid Tempting, but Box Stays a Lion," *DFP*, June 12, 1952.

188 "offered me more money": Jacobs, *San Francisco 49ers Legends*, 59–60.

189 "Mains liked to hang out": AI Jim LoPrete.

189 "I had played": Marshall Dann, "Forced to Move—Dublinski," *DFP*, March 26, 1955.

190 "I'm glad to be back": Lyall Smith, "Canadian Football Not for Gil Mains," *DFP*, September 19, 1955.

191 "special disciplinary practice": AP, "Walker, Layne Disciplined by Lions' Coach," *CT*, August 12, 1955.

192 "It's curfew": Arthur Daley, "Sports of *The Times*: Pedestal for the Doaker," *NYT*, December 1, 1959.

192 "Bobby Layne, who always was": Ibid.

193 "He was so popular": Cecil Hurt, "Harry Gilmer was a Tide Superstar," *Tuscaloosa News*, August 20, 2016.

193 "Maybe some of us": Michelle Kaufman, "Out Like a Lion: Hired to be Fired," *DFP*, September 6, 1990.

193 "He was always looking": Alex Karras, "Few Vets Give All during Training," *DFP*, August 1, 1972.

194 "I'll be darn": Jimmy Smothers, "Atkins' Greatest Coaching Success Not with Auburn," *Gadsden Times*, August 28, 2007.

194 "Detroit would part": David Condon, "In the Wake of the News," *CT*, August 24, 1955.

194 "I went to meet": Dave Klein, *The Game of Their Lives* (New York: Random House, 1976), 69.

194 "But he'll never fit": Lyall Smith, "As of Today: Young Bobby Layne Throws Dad for Loss," *DFP*, August 5, 1955.

194 "our little Les": Lyall Smith, "As of Today: Don't Write Off Lions, Parker Cautions," *DFP*, August 4, 1955.

195 "used every able-bodied player": Bob Latshaw, "Pro Champs Go Down to 19–3 Loss," *DFP*, September 11, 1955.

195 "This definitely is": Lyall Smith, "As of Today: Skip the Crying Towel, Parker Won't Use One," *DFP*, September 11, 1955.

195 "I'm glad they're all": Jack Walsh, "Everybody Expecting Detroit to Take a Dip Except Coach and Lions Themselves," *WP*, August 28, 1955.

195 season tickets: "Lions Set Ticket Mark," *DFP*, September 27, 1955.

195 "If Lee and Crockett": Mark Beltaire, "The Town Crier: 25-Cent Switch KO'd Such Crust III," *DFP*, August 12, 1955.

196 "I can remember Y. A.": AI Roy Schairer.

196 It was crazy": Cliff Christi, "An Oral History—Gary Knafelc," November 12, 2014, www.packers.com/news-and-events/article-1/An-Oral-History——Gary-Knafelc/ff9ce7a5-bf28–4d0a-a18a-f86643ef5ddc.

197 "They just beat hell": Bob Latshaw, "Parker: Colts Best in NFL since '35," *DFP*, October 3, 1955.

197 "We call him": Watson Spoelstra, "Big Hart Learns Plays at Fullback," *DN*, September 28, 1955.

197 "I always tried": Irv Goodman, "Sportalk," *Sport*, December 1955.

197 "I guess the fellows": Tommy Devine, "Lions Sniff NFL King Role Again, Jockeyed by Whip-Cracking Layne," *TSN*, October 31, 1956.

197 "If we could win one": Watson Spoelstra, "No Champion Has Fallen as Fast as Forlorn Lions," *DN*, October 14, 1955.

198 "Officially, 51,438 watched": Edward Prell, *CT*, October 17, 1955.

198 "Parker was an extreme introvert":

Leuthner, *Iron Men*, 269.

198 "a seething hulk": Devine, "Parker Keeps It Simple."

198 "After every game": Leuthner, *Iron Men*, 29.

199 "I moved to defense": Green, *Detroit Lions*, 118–19.

199 "First time I carried": Mark Beltaire, "The Town Crier: Nose No Camping Ground," *DFP*, November 17, 1954.

200 "More and more players": United Press, "Walker of Lions Backs Graham Charges of 'Dirty Football' in National League," *NYT*, November 16, 1955.

201 "Ah, Victory!": Bob Latshaw, "Layne, Walker and Defense Rays of Sunshine for Lions," *DFP*, November 7, 1955.

201 "Look, you can have": Newcombe, "The Little Guy Who Fooled the Pros."

201 "Most of the time": Leuthner, *Iron Men*, 198.

202 "If you were ahead": St. John, *Heart of a Lion*, 56.

202 "Nice tackle": Leuthner, *Iron Men*, 202.

202 "I could see it": Herskowitz, *The Golden Age of Pro Football*, 90.

202 "On one play": Bobby Layne (as told to Booton Herndon), "All Quarterbacks Are Crazy," *True*, October 1957.

203 "made a dangerous move": Watson Spoelstra, "How Good? 1955 Bears 'Not Great,'" *DN*, November 21, 1955.

203 "The shabby luck": Bob McClellan, "Injured Layne May Miss Last Game," *Detroit Reporter*, December 6, 1955.

204 "It hurts sometimes": St. John, *Heart of a Lion*, 55.

204 "Detroit will say goodbye": Marshall Dann, "The Doaker's Day," *Polish Daily News*, December 10, 1955.

205 "It was a very exciting day": Walker interview.

205 "But most of all": Bill Dow, "Premature Retirement: Doak Walker Quit the Lions at Age 28," *DFP*, December 14, 2005.

206 "In all, I had eight concussions":

Murray, "Hunchy Building Cars."

206 "I have a lot": George Maskin and Don Lee, "It's Short and It's Newsy," *Detroit Reporter*, January 6, 1956.

207 "positively final": International News Service, "Pro Bowl to Draw 85,000 in L.A.," *Polish Daily News*, January 15, 1956.

207 "I loved football": Canning, *Doak Walker*, 112.

207 "He was very restless": Walker interview.

207 "I want to get": Goodman, "Doak."

208 "disappeared as fast": Dow, "Premature Retirement."

208 "They were worrying": Dibble interview.

208 "Sorry, Buddy": Goodman, "Doak."

Chapter 8: Tackling Jim Crow

209 "I didn't take nothing": Leuthner, *Iron Men*, 225.

210 "I did stumble": Coleman Young and Lonnie Wheeler, *Hard Stuff: The Autobiography of Mayor Coleman Young* (New York: Viking, 1994), 158.

211 "I just hadn't been": Bill Matney, "Detroit Lions Get Johnson," *Chicago Defender*, May 25, 1957.

211 "Johnson is the kind": Ibid.

212 "We'll start signing": Thomas G. Smith, "Outside the Pale: The Exclusion of Blacks from the National Football League, 1934–1946," *Journal of Sport History* 15, no. 3 (1990). For a concise list of African American milestones in pro football, including the first black fielded by each NFL and AAFC team, see Joe Horrigan, "Early Black Professionals," *Coffin Corner* 7 (1985).

212 "Younger people don't know": Triplett interview.

213 "Of course, the opposing players": Myron Cope, *The Game That Was: An Illustrated Account of the Tumultuous Early Days of Pro Football* (New York: Thomas Y. Crowell, 1974), 213.

213 "had more colored gridmen": "Report Hoosiers Had 8 Gridders," *Afro American*,

December 6, 1947.

214 "the Negro bundle": "Lions Lose Again but Don't Blame Doak," *DFP*, September 4, 1950.

214 "I just thought": DI Bill Dudley.

214 "Bo told us": Michael Ranville and Gregory Eaton, "Bob Mann Arrives in Detroit after Stellar Career at U of M," *Michigan Chronicle*, November 1, 2005.

215 "This was not": Triplett interview.

215 "It was an unusual city": Andy Piascik, *Gridiron Gauntlet: The Story of the Men Who Integrated Pro Football in Their Own Words* (Lanham, MD: Taylor, 2009), 42.

215 "Segregation was bad": Ibid.

216 Mann and Goebel: Charles K. Ross, *Outside the Lines: African Americans and the Integration of the National Football League* (New York: New York University Press, 1999), 123–24.

216 "just a whole lot": Piascik, *Gridiron Gauntlet*, 43.

216 "I must have been blackballed": Russ J. Cowan, "Russ' Corner," *Chicago Defender*, November 11, 1950.

216 "While Bob is just": Ibid.

216 "Green Bay was": Triplett interview.

217 "I was hailing": Bill Dow, "Mann Pioneer Player in NFL," *DFP*, January 11, 2002.

217 "was kind of reticent": Triplett interview.

217 "We would just get": Piascik, *Gridiron Gauntlet*, 140.

218 "I hit their quarterback": Triplett interview.

218 "how things go": Pete Waldmeir, "Schott's Crime Was Bigoted, but the Punishment Was Strictly Bush League," *DN*, February 5, 1993.

218 "No jiggs with Briggs": Bak, *Cobb Would Have Caught It*, 104.

219 "when season ticket": Waldmeir, "Schott's Crime Was Bigoted, But the Punishment Was Strictly Bush League."

219 "I don't think the coaches": Schmidt interview.

219 "So strictly from": Parker, *We Play to Win!* 186.

219 "To demonstrate the importance": Ibid., 181.

220 "We take these tips": Ibid., 185.

220 "Ray Dillon, the huge": Bob Latshaw, "Squad Cuts Tax Coaches' Wisdom," *DFP*, August 6, 1952.

220 "He said, 'Radar'": James LaCombe, "Galveston Island Icon: 'Tank' Dillon, 1st Black Galvestonian Drafted into NFL, Shares Memories," *Galveston News*, September 28, 2014.

221 "I intended to play": Lyall Smith, "As of Today: New 'Rhubarb' Threatens NFL-Canada Relations," *DFP*, June 20, 1954.

221 "husky Negro tackle": Bob Latshaw, "Lions Obtain Offensive Aces in NFL Draft," *DFP*, January 28, 1955.

221 "I'll tell you why": Scott Fisher, "Calgary Stampeders Edwin Harrison's Grandfather Calvin Jones Was a Solid Player," *Calgary Sun*, November 1, 2012. Although blacks found opportunities playing in Canada, they still encountered discriminatory practices in the sport and in society at large. For an overview, see Neil Longley, Tedd Crosett, and Steve Jefferson, "The Migration of African Americans to the Canadian Football League during the 1950s: An Escape from Discrimination?" *International Journal of the History of Sport 25*, no. 10 (2008).

222 "We don't have": Ron Bellamy, "Wings of Fire," *Register-Guard* (Eugene, OR), February 6, 2005.

222 "He goes to this room": Ibid. In addition to teaching for many years in California, Davis worked as a scout for NFL teams, including the Lions. He died in 2008.

223 "I was playing offense": Piascik, *Gridiron Gauntlet*, 221–22.

224 "Bootsy would wake": Johnny Sample (with Fred J. Hamilton and Sonny Schwartz), *Confessions of a Dirty Ballplayer* (New York: Dial, 1970), 104.

224 "I know you had": Ibid., 102.

224 "I ain't gonna tell you": Dan Daly, *The National Forgotten League* (Lincoln: University of Nebraska Press, 2012), 255.

225 "Some of the guys": Leuthner, *Iron Men*, 224–25.

225 "making monkeys": Jack Walsh, "All-Stars' 35–19 Upset of Lions Complete, Totally Unexpected," *WP*, August 17, 1958.

225 "Actually both teams": Howard Gould, "25th All-Star Game Exciting," *Chicago Defender*, August 18, 1958.

227 "I don't think these": Leuthner, *Iron Men*, 224.

227 "Man, I'm glad": Piascik, *Gridiron Gauntlet*, 45.

Chapter 9: Muggings and Mayhem

228 "There's a fine line": Hart interview.

228 club profits: Bob Latshaw, "Last-Place Lions Find Profits Dip," *DFP*, February 8, 1956.

228 attendance records: Marshall Dann, "Chicago's 'Dirty Football' Beat Us—Parker," *DFP*, December 17, 1956.

229 "We found that": LoPrete interview.

229 "We're not going to sell": AP, "Detroit Lions Offer to Buy Tigers, Stadium," *WP*, April 12, 1956.

229 "It's time pro football": Robert S. Lyons, *On Any Given Sunday: A Life of Bert Bell* (Philadelphia: Temple University Press, 2009), 241.

230 salary survey: Bill Levy, "What Are Your Chances of Making a Living in Sports?" *Sport*, January 1956

230 team salaries: Craig R. Coenen, *From Sandlots to the Super Bowl: The National Football League, 1920–1967* (Knoxville: University of Tennessee Press, 2005), 184.

230 "In those days": Reichow interview.

230 "wore $39,500 smiles": Charles Burton, "Eagles, Lions, Sponsors Happy over Pro Tilt," *DMN*, August 21, 1955.

231 "We get more": Bob Latshaw, "Pro Football More Fun than College Brand," *DFP*, December 9, 1956.

231 "It was tough": Reichow interview.

232 "You dealt with old Nick": Junker interview.

232 "The quarterbacks drive": Newcombe, "You've Got to Be Good and Mean."

232 "Nick, you and I": David Condon, "In the Wake of the News," *CT*, December 11, 1970.

233 "a tremendous person": Cope, *The Game That Was*, 232.

233 "A nice crisp hundred": Kupelian and O'Hara, "Behind the Scenes: Players Didn't Get Rich in Old Days."

233 "Nick got guys": Cope, *The Game That Was*, 232.

233 "That '53 title game": Bak, *The Corner*, 129.

233 "I did substitute teaching": Triplett interview.

234 "I always worked": Bill L. Roose, "Hopalong: Buckeyes to the Bronx," *DFP*, March 9, 2000.

234 "It was always hard": Carpenter interview.

234 "At first I didn't work": Peterson, *Pigskin: The Early Years of Pro Football*, 209.

234 "It seems a shame": Watson Spoelstra, "Sidelines Cited as Factor in Lions' Limp," *TSN*, November 9, 1955.

235 "I only hope": Bob Latshaw, "Lions Finally Corral Hoppy," *DFP*, July 20, 1956.

236 "I didn't know what": Bob Christ, "Reichow Has Had Quite a Run," *Albuquerque Journal*, January 3, 2015.

236 "Hoppy disappeared": Dibble interview.

236 "See, in college": Roose, "Hopalong: Buckeyes to the Bronx."

237 "Couldn't help feeling": Lyall Smith, "Radio-Control Defense Gets Only Cool 'Okay' from Lion Coaches," *DFP*, October 15, 1956.

238 "There is some": Lyall Smith, "As of Today: Tigers Get Brain's Message Too Late," *DFP*, September 18, 1956.

238 "I'm for it solidly": Buck Rogers, "Schmidt Gets His 'Space Ship,'" *DN*, October 12, 1956.
239 "The Rams said": Lyons, *On Any Given Sunday,* 241.
239 "in case Parker": Rogers, "Schmidt Gets His 'Space Ship.'"
239 "All electronic devices": "Bell Tells Pros: No More Radio, Play It Straight," *DFP*, October 19, 1956.
239 "Charley was provoked": Green, *Detroit Lions,* 121.
240 "has played with": Tommy Devine, "Lions Sniff NFL King Role Again, Jockeyed by Whip-Cracking Layne," *TSN*, October 31, 1956.
240 "You can win": Ibid.
241 "Bobby had an affinity": Green, *Detroit Lions,* 118.
241 "Well, he called a timeout": Cantor, "Three Lion Heroes from Football's Pre-Superbowl Era."
241 "I never yelled": Gary Cartwright, "A Sort of Superior Feeling," *DMN*, August 28, 1963.
242 "I saw all the great": AI Gene Cronin.
242 "Schmidt's was not": Plimpton, *Paper Lion,* 62–63.
242 "He was so quick": Paul Hornung (as told to Al Silverman), *Football and the Single Man* (New York: Doubleday, 1965), 230.
243 "I could hear him": Ibid.
243 "He's the kind": Bob Latshaw, "New Linesmen Add to Lions' Strength," *DFP*, August 13, 1956.
243 "loved to give": Fran LaBelle, "Tackle to Tack: Miller Adjusts," *Sun-Sentinel,* January 20, 1989.
244 "We had it coming": Bob Latshaw, "Bowman, McIlhenny Due Back," *DFP*, November 13, 1956.
244 "I went back to pass": Ed Fitzgerald, *Johnny Unitas* (New York: Bartholomew House, 1960), 87.
245 "This was like": Marshall Dann, "My Boys Just the 'Greatest'—Parker," *DFP*,

December 3, 1956.
245 "They roughed us": Arthur Daley, "Sports of *The Times*: Operation Rebound," *NYT*, December 16, 1956.
246 "Tell 'em to keep": Lyall Smith, "As of Today: Lions Will Have to Be 'Ready for Anything,'" *DFP*, December 11, 1956.
246 "We all ate together": Herskowitz, *The Golden Age of Pro Football,* 109.
246 "I was with Bobby": Cantor, "Three Lion Heroes from Football's Pre-Superbowl Era."
247 "I really don't know": Dann, "Chicago's 'Dirty Football' Beat Us—Parker."
247 "I broke his nose": Green, *Detroit Lions,* 121.
248 "Knees, elbows and fists": Bob Latshaw, "Bears Maul Lions, 38 to 21," *DFP*, December 17, 1956.
248 "I was mad": Edgar C. Greene, "Lions Bitter in Defeat, Rip Bear 'Blackjack' Tactics," *DN*, December 17, 1956.
248 "You can't tell me": Cantor, "Three Lion Heroes from Football's Pre-Superbowl Era."
248 "I thought Bobby": Dann, "Chicago's 'Dirty Football' Beat Us—Parker."
248 "This is still America": Edgar C. Greene, "No Slugging, Movies Show," *DN*, December 18, 1956.
249 "The Lions have two": "Lions Called 'Dirtiest' by Fears," *DFP*, December 21, 1956.
250 "The team that I really": Larry Mayer, "Smith Thrilled to Meet Bears' First African American Player," February 14, 2012, www.chicagobears.com/news/article-1/Smith-thrilled-to-meet-Bears-first-African-American-player/1BFACE62-E9D9-43D6-8432-24391D403A97.
250 "When I was with": AI Dom Moselle.
250 "We play rough": "A Pride of Lions."
250 "Our boys get enthusiastic": Latshaw, "Pro Football More Fun than College Brand."
250 "all the older guys": Berry Stainback,

"Is It Dirty Football?" *Sport*, July 1963.

250 "I can remember": Herskowitz, *The Golden Age of Pro Football*, 165.

250 "It was always": Clary, *Cleveland Browns*, 115.

250 "his groin ripped open": "A Pride of Lions."

250 "Pro football is getting": Ibid.

251 "We used to ride": Leuthner, *Iron Men*, 68.

251 "I'll never forget": Natali, *Brown's Town*, 177.

251 "A lot of us": Leuthner, *Iron Men*, 44.

252 "I felt a little funny": Frank Eck, AP, "Justice, Walker Top AP's All-America," *St. Petersburg Times*, December 2, 1948.

252 "When was the last time": Leuthner, *Iron Men*, 145–46.

252 "Forearms, clotheslines": Ibid., 50

253 "We're not trying to hurt": "Savagery on Sunday," *Life*, October 24, 1955.

253 "You'd be down": Piascik, *Gridiron Gauntlet*, 62.

253 "Everybody waited around": Daly and O'Donnell, *The Pro Football Chronicle*, 143.

253 "During the 1950s": Donovan, *Fatso*, 180.

254 "If you go back": Leuthner, *Iron Men*, 73.

254 "a cleaner game": Hart interview.

254 "With those gadgets on": "Confessions of a Dirty Football Player," *Sport*, December 1955.

254 "If you're scared": Norman Nicholson, "Pro Football: Doak Walker Is a Small Man among the Giant Pros," *SI*, October 3, 1955.

254 "has reached the stage": Alfred Wright, "The Pros Hit the Clover," *SI*, September 5, 1955.

255 "Those two games": Green, *Detroit Lions*, 126.

255 "Bobby never lost": There are several variations of Walker's quote. See Daley, "Sports of *The Times*: Pedestal for the Doaker," for an early (1959) example.

Chapter 10: Pro Bowls and Army Legs

256 "I think the Pro Bowl": Herskowitz, *The Golden Age of Pro Football*, 165.

256 "What the hell": Jeff Davis, *Papa Bear: The Life and Legacy of George Halas* (New York: McGraw-Hill, 2004), 243.

257 "I remember the first": Donovan, *Fatso*, 128.

257 "In those more innocent": Paul, *I Went Both Ways*, 54.

258 "the most fabulous array": Frank Finch, "Pro Bowl to Lure 60,000 to Coliseum," *LAT*, January 14, 1951.

258 "studded by a long list": "Hollywood Celebrities to Appear at Pro Bowl," *LAT*, January 14, 1951.

258 "The Lion ballhawk": "Doll Shades Van Brocklin for Most Valuable Trophy," *TSN*, January 21, 1953.

259 "He was dressed": Nolan Bianchi, "Family of Late Lions Defensive Back Doll Races Against Time for Hall of Fame Honor," *DN*, December 20, 2019.

259 "other commitments": AP, "Change Pro Bowl Date," *DFP*, November 18, 1951.

260 "A lot of ballplayers": Lyons, *On Any Given Sunday*, 294.

260 "The owners always said": Summerall, *Giants*, 131.

260 "That wasn't a football game": Shirley Povich, "This Morning," *WP*, January 12, 1953.

260 "If Coach Buddy Parker's": Lyall Smith, "As of Today: Back-Slapping OK— But Not for Pro Grid," *DFP*, January 20, 1954.

261 "Hey, I thought": Herskowitz, *The Golden Age of Pro Football*, 165.

262 "I was miserable": Triplett interview.

262 "They called Lewis": Carpenter interview.

263 "That training camp": Al Marv Brown.

264 "Everybody up in Detroit": Schmidt interview.

264 "I made some": O'Hara, "Dorne

Dibble Made His Mark as a Two-Way Player in the 1950s."

264 "You had guys": Schmidt interview.

Chapter 11: The Last Great Season

265 "I just hope next season": Richard Bak, *A Place for Summer: A Narrative History of Tiger Stadium* (Detroit: Wayne State University Press, 1998), 273.

265 "Bobby Layne was always": AI Harry Mageski.

265 "Some may be outraged": George E. Van, "Sports Today: Great Athletes Mortal Like All," *DT*, September 19, 1957.

266 "I remember one time": Dave Lewis, "Once Over Lightly: Bingaman Returns to Lions as Line Coach," Long Beach *Independent*, January 23, 1960.

266 "Once, we're at": Wenson interview.

266 "All I asked": Green, *Detroit Lions*, 133–34.

267 "I just hope": Joe Stiglach, "No. 14: John Henry Johnson," *Contra Costa Times*, March 13, 2006.

267 "happy-go-lucky": Triplett interview.

267 "He was a competitor": Moselle interview.

268 "Each of them": Lyall Smith, "As of Today: Buddy Parker's Rich . . . And Happy Too!" *DFP*, July 28, 1957.

268 "Who ever complained": Devine, "Parker Keeps It Simple."

268 "This club is fabulous": Watson Spoelstra, "Lions to Face Old Teammate," *DN*, December 4, 1957.

268 "In blond, strong Joe": Tex Maule, "Sudden Death in San Francisco," *SI*, December 23, 1957.

269 "Fife had a suite": Herskowitz, *The Golden Age of Pro Football*, 110.

269 "We went to the Statler": Jerry Green, "Rote, Not Layne, Was the Lions' Last Championship Quarterback," *DN*, September 15, 1996.

269 "I have a situation": Tommy Devine, "Buddy Parker Says: 'I Quit,'" *DFP*, August 13, 1957.

270 "We didn't know": Brown interview.

270 "He said, 'I've been'": Green, *Detroit Lions*, 127.

271 "I think we have": Bob Latshaw, "Lions, Wilson Get First Test," *DFP*, August 14, 1957.

271 "You didn't talk": AI Ken Russell.

271 "Breaking into professional football": AI John Gordy.

272 "I play football": "Layne Offers to Quit Lions after Arrest," *DT*, September 17, 1957.

272 "After a little": "Lion Star Is Halted at 2 A.M.," *DN*, September 17, 1957.

273 "I know what": "Layne Offers to Quit Lions after Arrest."

273 "You're a big man": Ibid.

273 "We parked and walked": St. John, *Heart of a Lion*, 12.

273 "I think Layne": Jack Berson, "Lions Back Layne in 'Hour of Need,'" *DT*, September 18, 1957.

274 "I've got the itch": Arthur Daley, "Sports of *The Times*: The Reluctant Dragons," *NYT*, October 20, 1957.

274 "I know Halas": Herskowitz, *The Golden Age of Pro Football*, 110.

275 "We should see": Jim Hock (with Michael Downs), *Hollywood's Team: Grit, Glamor, and the 1950s Los Angeles Rams* (Los Angeles: Rare Bird, 2016), 292. In the book, Gedman is mistakenly identified as Bob Hoernschemeyer, who by then had been retired two years.

275 "He wasn't a very big guy": Roose, "Hopalong: Buckeyes to the Bronx."

276 "When he waves": George Puscas, "'Hoppy' Wants to Roam—Lions Ready to Oblige," *DFP*, October 15, 1958.

276 "I knew something": George Puscas, "It Was Fantastic, Incredible—It Was Insane!" *DFP*, October 21, 1957.

276 "It was the greatest comeback": Junker interview.

276 "I wonder what": Doc Greene, "Press Box: Still a Bit of Unbelief," *DN*, October 21, 1957.

276 "I play 'em": Ibid.

277 "Finally, I could wait": Tittle, *I Pass!* 206–7.

277 "Fans collapsed everywhere": Jacobs, *San Francisco 49ers Legends*, 241.

277 "We're not out of it": Green, *Detroit Lions*, 64.

278 "Let's go, Bobby": Layne, *Always on Sunday*, 104–5.

278 "A quarterback has to be": St. John, *Heart of a Lion*, 71.

278 "It was the maddest": Green, *Detroit Lions*, 65.

278 "You're no coach": Bob Latshaw, "'I'll Help Others Beat the Lions!'" *DFP*, December 3, 1957.

279 "It could be hard": Triplett interview.

279 "Layne had this": Junker interview.

280 "how could they know": Gerry Johnson and Tom Houston, "Texas Drawl Wins Acquittal for Layne," *DFP*, December 7, 1957.

280 "I'm familiar with": "You All Are Not Guilty, Jury Tells Drawling (Not Brawling) Bobby Layne," *DT*, December 7, 1957.

280 "How many more": Johnson and Houston, "Texas Drawl Wins Acquittal for Layne."

280 "This was during": LoPrete interview.

280 "The question is whether": Johnson and Houston, "Texas Drawl Wins Acquittal for Layne."

280 "I voted for acquittal": Ibid.

280 "The least he could have": "You All Are Not Guilty, Jury Tells Drawling (Not Brawling) Bobby Layne."

281 "You son of a bitch": Paul, *I Went Both Ways*, 133–34.

281 "win one for Bobby": Ibid.

281 "They wanted to operate": Cronin interview.

282 playoff scenarios: Watson Spoelstra, "Colts Get Break in Playoffs," *DN*, December 3, 1957.

283 "I couldn't get it": Junker interview.

283 "We'll whip 'em": United Press, "'We'll Beat Lions,' SF Coach Brags," *DFP*, December 16, 1957.

284 "He was a nervous wreck": Reichow interview.

284 "You could hear": Dave Birkett, "When the Walls Talked: Inside Detroit Lions' Improbable 1957 Title Run," *DFP*, September 8, 2017.

284 "We were like": Green, "Rote, Not Layne, Was the Lions' Last Championship Quarterback."

284 "When we were down": United Press, "49ers Didn't Realize What They Were Losing, Says Lion Tackle," *LAT*, December 23, 1957.

285 Lions-49ers playoff: Joe Falls, "Lions Unload Potent 'Bomb' on Frisco," *DT*, December 23, 1957; Green, *Detroit Lions*, 62–69.

285 "I remember Buster": Schmidt interview.

285 "They pushed us": Tittle, *I Pass!* 208.

285 "It's not over": Green, *Detroit Lions*, 68.

285 "I had been warned": Bill Dow, "Golden Roar," *DFP*, September 28, 2007.

286 "I don't believe it": Doc Greene, "Press Box," *DN*, December 22, 1957.

286 "I think they broke": Lyall Smith, "'49ers Did Right Thing in Going for Field Goal,'" *DFP*, December 23, 1957.

286 "No comment": AP, "Buddy Speechless after Lions Win—or at Least Silent," *DN*, December 23, 1957.

288 "I have to protect": Louis Effrat, "Browns Favored to Beat Lions in Title Game Today," *NYT*, December 29, 1957.

288 "No, no, a thousand times": Tommy Devine, "Bell's Battle Cry: 'No, No and No,'" *DFP*, December 29, 1957.

288 "We were able": AI Mike Dalessandro.

288 "first Super Bowl party": AI Tony Dalessandro.

289 "The crippled Lions": Maule, "All Hail the Lusty Lions."

289 "Cleveland isn't a hard team": Ibid.

289 "I was sitting there": Schmidt interview.

290 Lions-Browns title game: Bob

Latshaw, "Lions Win, 59–14!" *DFP*, December 30, 1957; Sam Greene, "Lions Give Brown Worst Defeat," *DN*, December 30, 1957.

290 "We'd been working": Russell interview.

290 "God, don't drop it": Junker interview.

290 "I thought those guys": Russell interview.

291 "Remember last Sunday": Maule, "All Hail the Lusty Lions."

291 "Sure, we talked": Joe Falls, "'Bell's Blackout' Hit Wrong City," *DT*, December 30, 1957.

291 "Detroit partisans": Chuck Heaton, "Lions Crush Browns, 59–14," *Cleveland Plain Dealer*, December 30, 1957.

291 "We couldn't hear": AP, "Brown Philosophical about 59–14 Licking," December 30, 1957, in Richard M. Cohen, Jordan A. Deutsch, Roland T. Johnson, and David S. Neft, *The Scrapbook History of Pro Football* (Indianapolis: Bobbs-Merrill, 1976), 152.

292 "It was euphoria": Schairer interview.

292 "Here's a time-capsule": DeLisle interview.

292 "He must have had": Birkett, "When the Walls Talked: Inside Detroit Lions' Improbable 1957 Title Run."

292 "a drunk crawled out": DeLisle interview.

Chapter 12: Cardboard Lions

293 "The 1954 Bowman NFL cards": Tom DeLisle, "Lions, and Tigers, and Wings . . . Oh My," October 16, 2010, www.detroitathletic.com/blog/2010/10/16/lions-and-tigers-and-wings- . . .-oh-my/.

297 "to get them off": Terry Dickson, "Would-Be Star Called an Audible," *Florida Times-Union*, July 27, 2008.

298 "some dumb-ass kid": Tom DeLisle, "A Detroit Tigers-Red Wings-Lions Fan's Rite of Passage in the Fall of 1954," August 27, 2011, www.detroitathletic.

com/blog/2011/08/27/a-detroit-tigers-red-wings-lions-fans-rite-of-passage-in-the-fall-of-1954/.

299 "Topps took what appeared": Dean Hanley, *The Bubble Gum Card War: The Great Bowman & Topps Sets from 1948 to 1955* (Lexington, KY: Mighty Casey Books, 2015), 142–43.

299 "I don't need money": Lyons, *On Any Given Sunday*, 238.

299 "We'll have a thing": Ibid.

300 "Contrary to what": Dave Jamieson, *Mint Condition: How Baseball Cards Became an American Obsession* (New York: Grove Press, 2010), 129.

300 "The best part": DeLisle, "Lions, and Tigers, and Wings . . . Oh My."

Chapter 13: Goodbye, Two-Minute Guy

301 "In football you can't stay": Cope, *The Game That Was*, 233.

301 "I think we can": "Newcomers Important to Sewell," *DMN*, July 21, 1958.

301 "Our best football team": Reichow interview.

302 "I have a report": Alex Karras (with Herb Gluck), *Even Big Guys Cry* (New York: Holt, Rinehart & Winston, 1977), 7.

303 "You respected these guys": Green, *Detroit Lions*, 146.

303 "Rookie, from now on": Plimpton, *Mad Ducks and Bears*, 48–49.

304 "The coaches never liked": Ibid., 48.

304 "I could have cared": Green, *Detroit Lions*, 146.

304 "He wasn't a gentleman": DeLisle interview.

304 "After 1953": Cope, *The Game That Was*, 229.

305 "Do the Lions": George Puscas, "Lions, Now's the Time," *DFP*, September 28, 1958.

305 "It wasn't Bobby's fault": "Bad One to Lose—But How Bad?" *DFP*, October 6, 1958.

306 "Bobby Layne is a bundle": Watson

Spoelstra, "Jittery Layne Fails Lions in Clutch," *DN*, October 6, 1958.

306 "I've got four girls": George Puscas, "What Veteran Lions Think of Layne Trade," *DFP*, October 7, 1958.

307 "Layne probably had": AP, "Wilson Denies Feud Led to Layne Trade," *WP*, October 11, 1958.

307 "I'll bet they": Edgar Hayes and George E. Van, "Layne Gone, Rote Hurt; Hot Spot for Morrall," *DT*, October 7, 1958.

307 "Bobby is still": "Warning! Better Start Winning," *DT*, October 7, 1958.

308 "Great quarterbacks will come": Greene, *Dies a Crapshooter . . . and Other Digressions*, 244.

308 "I couldn't figure": Schmidt interview.

308 "Openly they got": George Puscas, "Layne Traded to Steelers," *DFP*, October 7, 1958.

308 "They were two": Russell interview.

308 "No one player": Wismer, *The Public Calls It Sport*, 54–55.

308 "I know I've been accused": Layne, *Always on Sunday*, 132.

310 "I favor trading": Devine, "The Uneasy Coach of the Champs."

310 "The memories of the": Layne, *Always on Sunday*, 123.

310 "Detroit's finest gift": Al Abrams, "Can Layne Swing Tide?" *Pittsburgh Post-Gazette*, October 14, 1958.

310 "We can forget": Al Abrams, "Layne Shows Old Ability," *Pittsburgh Post-Gazette*, October 9, 1958.

310 "That ol' blond fella": St. John, *Heart of a Lion*, 83.

311 "Dammit, Bomber": Ibid, 81–82.

311 "Hey, Hatchet": George Puscas, "Lion Morale Hits Bottom After Trade," *DFP*, October 8, 1958.

311 "There was a fence": Green, *Detroit Lions*, 146.

Chapter 14: Football in a Box
313 "After World War II": Wismer, *The*

Public Calls It Sport, 55.

313 "The Best Football Game": Tex Maule, "The Best Football Game Ever Played," *SI*, January 5, 1959.

314 "Dad was a real": AI Tom Baranski.

315 "We never missed": DeLisle interview.

316 "We didn't have any": AI Bill Grain.

316 "It's my theory": Hal Middlesworth, "Van Patrick: Sports' Voice," *DFP*, August 29, 1954.

316 "Certainly millions": "Events & Discoveries," *SI*, January 13, 1958.

316 "I always said": AI Ray Lane.

318 "I remember talking": Reichow interview.

318 "When you've got holes": George Puscas, "Lions' Feet Getting Colder and Slower," *DFP*, December 7, 1987.

318 "No one sang": George Puscas, "Lions Haven't Started," *DFP*, September 29, 1959.

319 "As you probably know": Bob Nussbaumer to Bruce Maher, October 22, 1959. Author's collection.

319 "We don't have": George Puscas, "Angered Wilson Suspends Johnson," *DFP*, November 3, 1959.

319 "Pietrosante runs virtually": "A Man and a Hope," *SI*, November 19, 1962.

320 "incredibly welcoming": Peter King, "RIP Yale Lary," May 15, 2017, www.si.com/mmqb/2017/05/15/buffalo-bills-sean-mcdermott-brandon-beane-nfl-peter-king.

320 "just beat me": Green, *Detroit Lions*, 120.

320 "His record shows": George Puscas, "Rote May Return—But on Lion Terms," *DFP*, December 15, 1959.

321 "Doran caught the pass": Watson Spoelstra, "Rote's Exit Almost Certain after 'Last Chance' Flop," *DN*, December 14, 1959.

Chapter 15: End of a Perfect Thing
322 "I never wear": Plimpton, *Mad Ducks*

and Bears, 63.

322 Moon Baker: "Lion Mascot Found Dead on Sidewalk," *Dearborn Independent*, August 18, 1960; "Mascot of Lions Found Dead," *DFP*, August 13, 1960.

323 "I'm tired of being": George Puscas, "Lions Discouraged?—I Should Say Not!" *DFP*, August 15, 1960.

324 "still pisses me off": Schmidt interview.

325 "But he said": LoPrete interview.

326 "George is a fine fellow": Joe Falls, "'Surprised Me'—Ford," *DFP*, December 24, 1964.

327 "an extremely slippery customer": Barr, *Cloyce Box*, 55.

327 "I can't split": Hart interview.

328 "You could tell": Cutler interview.

328 "the most celebrated": Goodman, "Doak."

328 "I can still see him": St. John, *Heart of a Lion*, 198.

329 "Bring a clean shirt": Ibid., 7.

329 "When he was leaving": Dibble interview.

329 "What I miss": Cope, *The Game That Was*, 234.

329 "He would have loved": St. John, *Heart of a Lion*, 2.

330 "They asked for": Hart interview.

331 "I think it would be": Dave Birkett, "Fears of the Worst," *DFP*, September 10, 2017.

331 "It was always": Bak, *The Corner*, 129.

332 "I loved doing this": Boyle scrapbook.

INDEX

Abrams, Al, 310
Adams, Jack, 158, 317, 323
Adderly, Herb, 324
Adrian College, 268
Afflis, Dick, 217
Afro American, 213
"The Aggie War Hymn," 127
Akers, Stanley, 288
Akron Vulcans, 328
Albert, Frankie, 49, 93, 187-88, 218, 283
Al Horvay Trio, 275
All-America Football Conference (AAFC), 17, 18, 21-22, 40, 85, 144, 152, 187, 206, 213-14, 268
All-Decade Team (1950s), 327
"Alley-Oop" pass, 277, 283, 286
Ameche, Alan, 197, 242-43, 313
American Broadcasting Company (ABC), 31, 187, 203, 315, 317
American Charcoal Company, 234
American Football League (AFL), 226, 321
amphetamines, 153-54
Anderson, Clifford, 123
Anderson, Edwin J. (Andy), 20, 34-35, 52, 55, 72, 100, 134, 143, 162, 189, 216, 228-29, 248-49, 271, 289, 307, 308, 327-28
Ane, Charlie, 84, 99, 127, 136, 145, 166, 200, 234, 241, 247, 268, 311
Ane, Charlie (Kale), 99
Ane, Marilyn (Dolan), 99, 101, 136
Arenas, Joe, 53-54, 89, 90
Arizona State University, 222
"army legs," 263
Arrow shirts, 157
Atkins, Doug, 107, 111, 112, 203-4
Atkins, George, 193-94
Auburn University, 36, 193, 194, 270
automobile industry, 158, 159, 304
aviation accidents, 125, 222

Bailey, Maureen, 97-98

Baker, Al (Bubba), 227
Baker, Dan, 127, 323
Baker, LaVern, 138
Baker, Sam, 243
Baker, William (Moon), 123-24, 127, 322-23
Baltimore Colts, 22, 32, 39, 40, 87-88, 96, 99, 127, 141, 150-51, 196-97, 201, 219, 222, 237, 242-43, 244, 274-76, 277, 278, 281, 282, 283, 298, 304-5, 313-14, 315, 318-19
Banonis, Pete, 37, 95
Banonis, Vic, 86
Banonis, Vince, 9, 37-39, 63, 64-65, 68, 69-70, 78, 80, 87, 93, 95, 97, 111, 112, 124, 134, 143, 153, 200, 234, 296
Baranski, Tom, 314-15
Barney, Lem, 226
Barr, Terry, 290, 311, 324, 330
Bassett, Mo, 163
Batchelor, Eddie, 205
Baugh, Sammy, 193, 316
Bednarik, Chuck, 302
Beech-Nut Gum, 5, 156
Bell, Bert, 17, 45-46, 72, 107, 111, 135, 144, 145, 147, 152, 190, 229, 239, 248-49, 253, 257, 259-60, 282, 287-88, 298, 299, 309, 327
Bell, Marty, 16, 18
Beltaire, Mark, 120, 195
Berger, Sy, 295, 299
Berle, Milton, 133
Berry, Chuck, 127
Berry, Raymond, 305
Bert Bell Benefit Fund, 299
Bible, Dana X., 16
Billingsley, Arthur, 276
Bingaman, Les, 6, 27-28, 46, 47, 54, 71, 72, 88, 132, 136, 144, 157, 194, 198, 200, 221, 232, 243, 297, 327
    bar owner, 266, 272, 279
    drinking, 63, 65, 129-30, 266
    popularity, 6, 96
    size, 6, 27-28, 143
Bingaman, Lois, 136
Birmingham, Alabama, 25, 224

Birmingham High School (Michigan), 266
Blackbourn, Lisle, 267
Blanda, George, 32, 71, 97, 103, 247, 282
Bloomfield Rams, 244
"Bobby Layne curse," 11, 323-24
Bolling Air Base, 143, 263
Betty Boop, 288
Boston Patriots, 321
Boston Redskins, 212. *See also* Washington Redskins
Boston Yanks, 17, 314. *See also* New York Yanks
"bottle gangs," 132
Bowling Green University, 268
Bowman, Bill, 142-43, 147-48, 152, 162, 164, 194, 199, 211, 235, 247, 262, 296, 298-99
Bowman Gum Company, 293-99
Bowman, J. Warren, 294, 295
Box, Cloyce, 22, 25, 31-32, 35, 59, 61, 62, 72-73, 78,86, 88, 92, 99, 109, 110, 129, 136, 144, 156, 159, 187, 200, 217, 220, 258, 262, 310, 327
Box, Fern, 99, 136
Boyd, Bob, 89, 91
Boykin, Richard, 214
Boyle Sr., Jim, 116, 331-32
Boyle Jr., Jim, 115-16, 331-32
Boyle, Tom, 115-16
Brachman, Bob, 277
Brady, Tom, 114
Brass Rail, 275
Bratkowski, Zeke, 145
Brazil, Bo-Bo, 298
Brewster, Darrell, 80, 164
Brewster the Goebel Rooster, 49, 64
Briggs Manufacturing, 19
Briggs Stadium, 6, 8, 26, 44, 49, 42, 72, 74-75, 77, 84, 89, 96, 103, 113, 117, 132, 147, 148, 154, 155, 185, 197, 198, 201, 209, 228-30, 238-39, 243, 244, 245, 267, 268, 275, 276, 277, 311, 314, 322-23
    assessed value, 229
    attendance, 5-6, 29, 41-42,

45, 60, 69, 108, 118, 151–52, 198, 205, 228
bleachers, 120, 205, 291–92
"chain gang," 123
"cheater" seats, 118–19
configuration of gridiron, 117
fans, 61, 89, 96, 98–99, 151–52, 159, 204–5, 291–92
footballs kicked into stands, 119, 292
game programs, 253
goalposts, 8, 118
halftime shows, 120–21
neighborhood, 8, 132–34
preparing field for football, 117–18
rental fee, 229
seating, 102, 117, 218–19
ticket prices, 45, 106, 108, 288
Briggs Sr., Walter O., 23, 117, 218–19
Briggs Jr., Walter O. (Spike), 229
Briggs, Basil (Mickey), 117
Brodie, John, 281
Brooklyn Dodgers (baseball), 229
Brooklyn Dodgers (football), 23, 229, 314
Brown Derby, 258
Brown, Earl, 36, 40, 234
Brown, Ed, 203, 244, 282
Brown, Hardy, 199, 250, 253
Brown, Howard, 252
Brown, Jimmy, 94, 281, 290, 291
Brown, Marv, 262, 269
Brown, Paul, 3, 24, 38, 183–84, 195, 200, 213, 287, 291, 323
  AAFC seasons, 17, 144, 268
  record vs. Detroit, 141–42
  rivalry with Buddy Parker, 38, 41–42, 69–70, 75–76, 104–6, 140–42, 146–47, 161, 165, 237, 258
Brown, Roger, 226, 324, 325
Brown vs. the Board of Education of Topeka, 210
The Bubble Gum Card War (Hanley), 299
bubble gum trading cards, 176–81, 293–300
Buffalo Bills, 286, 321
Buhl Building, 189
Bulger, Chet, 29–30
Bull 'n Bush, 134, 258

"Bull Elephant Backfield," 44
Burman, Dick, 121
Butsicaris, Jimmy, 133–34
Butsicaris, Johnny, 133–34
Butsicaris, Meleti, 133

Caddell, Ernie, 330
Cadillac Asphalt Paving Company, 157
Caesar, Sid, 61
Cain, Bob, 262
Caldwell, Jim, 227
Calgary Stampeders, 187–88, 222
Camel cigarettes, 154
Camp Pendleton, 263
Campbell, Milt, 290
Campbell, Stan, 9, 241, 262, 306
Canadian Football League (CFL), 84, 186–91, 194, 222, 226, 296, 321
"Cardinal Puff," 63–64
Carl's Chop House, 66
Caroline, J. C., 245
Carpenter, Ann, 9, 92, 100, 101, 159, 234, 262
Carpenter, Lew, 9, 84, 87, 100, 145, 148, 155, 159, 162, 194, 203, 262, 291, 297, 330
Carpenter, Ken, 79, 112
Casares, Rick, 145, 244, 256–57
Cason, Jim, 54
Cassady, Howard (Hopalong), 6, 201, 208, 235–36, 237, 259, 270, 275–76, 282, 304
Cassidy, William (Hopalong), 235
Centre College, 20
"chain gang," 123
Chapman, Dick, 142, 296
"cheater" seats, 118–19
Chesterfield cigarettes, 154
Chesterfield Lounge, 217
Chevrolet, 159
Chevrolet Gear & Axle, 19
Chicago Bears, 4, 17, 29, 32, 37, 46, 47–48, 50, 51, 71, 72, 97, 103, 105–6, 122, 124, 126, 142, 144, 147–48, 150, 160, 195, 203–4, 214, 240, 244–45, 246–49, 255, 256, 274, 278, 282, 320, 324
Chicago Cardinals, 25, 37–38, 56, 90, 146, 246, 249, 262, 267
Chicago Defender, 225

Chicago Hornets, 21
Chicago Rockets, 26
Chicago Tribune, 85, 165, 198, 225
Childers, Elijah, 221
Childress, Joe, 270
"Chris's Crew," 7, 93–95, 107, 117, 269
Christensen, Jack, 40, 58, 89, 91, 93–95, 107, 157, 187, 200, 232, 233, 244, 250, 256, 259, 261, 269, 277, 282, 297, 309, 320, 327
  as punt returner, 44, 48, 71, 149, 155, 163
  as running back, 72–73, 93, 145
Christman, Paul, 146
Christmas Carol, 97–98
chronic traumatic encephalopathy (CTE), 9–10, 330–31
Chronic Traumatic Encephalopathy Clinic, 331
Chrysler Freeway, 210
Chrysler Stamping, 19
Cifelli, Gus, 22, 39, 68, 84, 214, 252
"City of Champions" reunion (1960), 323
City Stadium, 152, 153, 196
Civic Stadium, 274
Civil Rights Act, 226
Clark, Dutch, 206, 323
Clark, Ernie, 226
Clark, William (Tex), 221
Cleveland Browns, 24, 38, 39, 49, 126, 146–47, 160–61, 183–84, 195, 200, 201, 219, 263, 269, 281, 319, 326
  AAFC seasons, 17, 21–22, 40, 51, 75, 144, 213, 268
  championship games, (1950) 218, (1951) 53, 218, (1952) 75–81, (1953) 9, 106–14, 321, (1954) 160–66, (1955) 206, (1957) 2, 10–11, 287–92
  rivalry with Detroit, 2–3, 10–11, 41–42, 69–70, 104–7, 161, 305, 323
Cleveland Indians, 146–47
Cleveland Plain Dealer, 78, 291
Cleveland Rams, 43
Cline, Ollie, 40, 51, 90

Cobo, Albert, 132
Cobo Hall, 7
Cochran, Red, 237
Cochrane, Mickey, 323
Coca, Imogene, 61
Coconut Grove, 258
Cogdill, Gail, 324
Cole, Emerson, 38
College All-Star Game, 37–38, 68, 235, 257; (1936) 85–86, (1951) 42, (1953) 85–86, (1954) 144–46, (1955) 183, 185, (1958) 225, 301–2
college draft, 17, 142–43, 235, 296
College of William & Mary, 28, 56, 127, 142
Collier, Blanton, 105
Collier's, 6, 17, 27, 157
Collins, Charles (Rip), 304
Collins, Ray, 54
Colo, Don, 281, 292
Colorado A&M University, 28, 40, 58, 99
Columbia Broadcasting System (CBS), 313–14, 316–17
Comiskey Park, 38
concussions, 9–10, 23, 52, 149, 206, 330–31. See also chronic traumatic encephalopathy (CTE)
Cone, Fred, 196
Conerly, Charlie, 257
Congress Tool & Die, 19
Connor, George, 204
Cook, Louis, 97–98
Cooper, Gary, 66
Costello, Charley, 138
Cotton Bowl (game), 267
Cotton Bowl (stadium), 16, 25, 146, 184, 191
Cowans, Russ, 211, 216
Cracker Jack, 294–95
Cranbrook Academy, 268, 270, 271, 272
Crazylegs (film), 43
Creekmur, Lou, 9, 27, 47, 68–69, 85, 107, 135–36, 145, 164, 187, 200, 233, 234, 235, 241, 257, 258, 268, 281, 284, 289, 291, 297, 307–8, 320, 330
    fights, 152, 247
    as middle linebacker, 199
    tactics, 69, 239–40

Crest Lanes, 127, 131
Crisis Club, 126
Crockett, David, 195
Cronin, Gene, 242, 281, 293
Crosby, Bing, 43
Crowley, Joe, 87
Crystal Show Bar, 131
Cutler, Mike, 98–99, 328

Dalessandro, Mike, 288
Dalessandro, Tony, 288
Daley, Arthur, 26–27, 107, 160, 162
Dallas, Texas, 11, 99, 191, 222
Dallas (TV series), 327
Dallas Cowboys, 156, 321
Dallas Morning News, 12
Dallas Texans, 68, 71, 72–73, 82, 87, 122
Daly, Dan, 224
Dann, Marshall, 204–5
David, Jimmy, 7, 57–58, 89–92, 93–95, 99, 114, 130, 233, 237, 244, 250, 257, 269, 277, 311, 330
David, Shirley, 99
Davis, Dick, 15
Davis, Glenn, 43
Davis, Milt, 221, 222
Dearborn, Michigan, 211
DeLisle, Charles, 11, 292, 315
DeLisle, Tom, 4, 11, 115–17, 292, 293–94, 298–300, 315
Delvecchio, Alex, 158
Denver Broncos, 328
Detroit, Michigan, 19, 42, 158, 210
    industry, 7–8, 19, 159, 212, 304
    national image, 7, 19, 158, 159
    newspaper strike, 133, 204–5
    race relations, 210–12, 215, 218–19
    skid row, 132–34
    suburbs, 159, 210–11
Detroit Athletic Club, 34, 133
"Detroit Destroyers," 96
Detroit Diesel, 19
Detroit Football Company. See Detroit Lions
Detroit Free Press, 23, 44, 48, 50, 60, 72, 97–98, 103, 132, 133, 150, 201, 204, 240, 260–61, 288
Fresh Air Fund Game, 41–42

Detroit Heralds, 131
Detroit Lions (Green), 92
Detroit Lions, 49, 145, 221, 325–26
    attendance, 5–6, 29, 45, 55, 118–119, 156, 205, 317
    broadcast revenue, 10, 287
    camaraderie on team, 4, 42, 59, 63–66, 77, 82, 100–103, 127–35, 157, 235–36, 275, 304
    championship games, (1952) 75–81, (1953) 9, 106–14, 321, (1954) 160–66, (1957) 2–3, 10–11, 287–92, 316
    College All-Star Games, (1953) 85–86, (1954) 144–46, (1958) 225, 301–2
    college draft, 21, 38, 40–41, 57–58, 68, 82–84, 142–43, 213–14, 219–21, 226, 235, 270, 278–79
    competition with Canadian leagues, 186–91
    conditioning, 152–54, 191–92, 197
    defensive formations and strategy, 56, 92–96, 163, 165, 199, 242, 284–85
    directors, 18, 19–20, 34–35, 51, 124, 135, 136–37, 208, 228–29, 231, 269, 270, 307, 325
    "dirty football" accusations, 89–92, 151, 249–51
    divisional playoffs, (1952) 72–75, 106, (1957) 283–86
    equipment, 199–201, 317, 320
    exhibition games, 24–25, 41–42, 58–59, 65, 86–87, 105, 128, 191, 195, 214, 224, 304–5
    fans, 29, 52, 61, 76–77, 95–96, 108, 126–27, 195, 204–5, 266, 291–92, 306, 331–32
    mascots, 123–24, 127, 322–23
    national following, 6–7, 154–58
    night games, 24, 59, 87, 96, 201, 237, 314
    1948 season, 20–21, 314
    1949 season, 21, 214–16
    1950 season, 23–33, 34–35, 209
    1951 season, 35–54, 55

1952 season, 56–81, 82
1953 season, 82–114
1954 season, 140–66, 220
1955 season, 183–206, 209, 221, 228
1956 season, 222, 228–55
1957 season, 265–92
1958 season, 301–12
1959 season, 318–21
1962 season, 324–25
1964 season, 326
1966 season, 192
offensive formations and strategy, 36, 66–68, 70–71, 78, 108, 148, 201–2, 235, 268, 278, 303–4
players lost to military, 143, 194, 235, 261–64
President's Trophy (MVP), 9, 162
profits and losses, 45, 55, 228
radio broadcasts, 62, 83, 116, 152, 155, 287, 315–16
radio-equipped helmets, 237–39
reunions, 49, 323, 330
rivalry with Cleveland, 2–3, 10–11, 38, 41–42, 69–70, 75–76, 104–7, 140–42, 161, 165, 258, 287–92, 305, 323
rookie hazing, 127–30, 235–36, 243, 271–72, 302, 303
salaries, 184–87, 216, 230–34, 283
scouting, 41, 226, 319
season ticket sales, 6, 45, 195, 228, 317
shareholders, 55, 308, 326
television, 10, 31, 49, 61, 72, 83, 99, 107–8, 122–23, 148, 155, 160, 241, 247, 287–88, 301–2, 314, 315, 317, 326
Thanksgiving Day games, 28–29, 31, 48, 71–72, 97–99, 122–23, 155, 203, 244, 250, 267, 278, 317, 324–25
tickets, 45, 51, 106, 108, 287
training camp (Cranbrook), 207–8, 268, 269, 271, 272
training camp (Ypsilanti), 23–25, 84–87, 142–46, 191–92, 194, 216, 220, 235–36, 262

valuation, 10, 203, 326
Detroit News, 39, 76, 80, 137, 210, 239, 306
Detroit Osteopathic Hospital, 89, 99, 281
Detroit Pistons, 307
Detroit Red Wings, 158, 187, 317, 323
Detroit Reporter, 133
Detroit Tigers, 29, 117, 118, 158, 210, 218–19, 229–30, 243, 323
Detroit Times, 55, 133, 137, 143, 165, 218, 265
Detroit Times Building, 133
Devine, Tommy, 198, 240
Dibble, Betty, 108, 130–31
Dibble, Dorne, 4, 40–41, 48, 65, 69, 89, 90, 103, 112, 130–31, 136, 143, 145, 147, 148, 160–61, 162, 183, 208, 235, 236, 241, 246, 248, 262, 264, 303–4, 310, 330
"Dick the Bruiser" (Dick Afflis), 217
Dillon, Ray Dohn, 220
DiMaggio, Joe, 308
Dinan Field, 26, 37, 117
"Dirty Shirts," 96
Doak Walker Award, 328–29
Doak Walker Day, 204–5
"Doak's Dope," 44
Dr. Pepper, 5, 156
Dodge Main, 19
Dohring, Bud, 123
Doll, Diana, 136, 259
Doll, Don, 28–29, 66, 79, 86, 129, 136, 252, 258–59, 330
Donovan, Art, 68, 127, 151, 253
Dooley, Jim, 282
Doran, Jim, 9, 40, 70, 71, 79, 93, 152, 162, 187, 233, 235, 243, 268, 276–77, 291, 305, 306, 320, 321, 332
Dove, Bob, 90, 144, 151, 250, 321
Driscoll, Paddy, 244
Dublinski, Tom, 58, 60, 85, 145, 146, 149, 152, 159, 160, 164
  bubble gum card mix-up, 298
  salary, 188, 191
  with Toronto, 188–91, 234
Dudley, Bill, 32, 214
DuMont Network, 77, 107–8, 155, 259, 314, 315, 316

Saturday night telecasts, 315
Durham, Bob, 132
Dwyer, Jack, 91

Earon, Betty, 101
Earon, Blaine, 74, 92, 101
East Texas State University, 263
East-West Game, 219
Eastern Michigan University, 268. See also Michigan Normal College
Eaton's, 158
Edgecomb, Charley, 126
Edgewater Beach Hotel, 246
Edsel automobile, 311
Effrat, Louis, 74
Eisenhower, Dwight D., 224, 261, 313
Elder High School, 22
Ellington, Duke, 215
Eliot, Sonny, 133
Elliott, Carlton (Stretch), 152
Enke, Fred, 18, 31, 45, 51, 58, 252, 330
Evangelista, Pete, 288
Ewbank, Weeb, 141, 274
Ex-Cell-O plant, 116

face masks, 69, 108, 199–201, 254
Falb, Kent, 155
fans, 49, 76–77, 91–92, 95–96, 115–20, 125–27, 152, 185, 205, 225, 291–92, 296, 306
Farr, Mel, 226
Fatso (Donovan), 151
Fay, Bill, 17, 27
Fears, Tom, 74, 89–90, 91, 216, 249
"Fearsome Foursome," 324
Federal Aviation Authority, 125
Fife, D. Lyle, 20, 126, 269, 270, 328
Finch, Frank, 91, 258
Finks, Jim, 87
Fisher Body, 19
Flame Show Bar, 138–39, 217, 272, 273
Flanagan, Dick, 46, 72, 79, 86, 87, 129
Fleer Chewing Gum Company, 294
The Football Graphic, 142

Forbes Field, 24
Ford, Edsel, 19
Ford Field, 3, 227
Ford, Henry (football player), 223
Ford, Henry (industrialist), 7, 37
Ford II, Henry, 325
Ford, Len, 39, 107, 108, 110
Ford Motor Company, 95, 150,
    233, 311
Ford Rotunda, 160
Ford Rouge plant, 19
Ford, William Clay, 11, 325-26
Fort Benning, 263
Fort Eustis Wheels, 263
Fort Knox, 264
Fort Leonard Wood, 264
Forte, Aldo, 30, 36, 51, 68, 72, 78,
    84, 151, 237, 243
Foster, Grant, 96
Franklin, Aretha, 139
Franklin, Rev. C. L., 139
Frolic Show Bar, 217

Gandee, Marilyn, 101
Gandee, Sherwin (Sonny), 152,
    191-92, 203, 266, 298
Gatski, Frank, 10-11, 107, 146,
    268, 278, 297
Gedman, Gene, 84-85, 87, 97,
    104, 131, 134, 138, 143,187,
    194, 235, 245, 247, 261, 275,
    285, 286, 290, 306, 311, 326-27
Gehringer, Charlie, 323
General Motors, 159, 304
Genoff, Lucille, 135-36
Gentile, Joe, 120, 126
George A. Fuller Company, 184
George Halas Trophy, 258-59
Georgetown University, 86
Gibbons, Jim, 297-98, 324
Gibbs, Ron, 61, 249
Gibbs, Terry, 131
Gifford, Frank, 205, 298
Gillette razors, 156
Gillom, Horace, 163, 258
Gilmer, Harry, 154, 189, 191,
    192-93, 198, 205, 245, 246,
    247, 297, 326
Girard, Earl (Jug), 62, 71, 72,
    102, 127, 150, 152, 160-61,
    196, 206, 266
Girard, Joan, 102
Glass, Bill, 187

Goebel Brewing Company, 20, 49,
    64, 216, 307, 315
Golden Gloves tournament, 85
Goodfellow, Ebbie, 323
Gordy, John, 268, 271-72, 283,
    317, 324, 330
Gordy, "Poppa John," 271
Gorgal, Ken, 109
Gotham Hotel, 215
Gould, Howard, 225
Grace Hospital, 52, 61
Graham, Otto, 70, 76, 77-80,
    104-9, 112, 113, 140, 160-65,
    183-84, 195, 200, 206, 237,
    240, 258, 287, 302
Grain, Bill, 316
Grange, Red, 31
Grayson's, 158
Graystone Ballroom, 212
Great Lakes Steel, 19
Greco, Buddy, 257
Green, Jerry, 92, 311
Green Bay Packers, 25, 30-31,
    46, 69, 84, 96, 103, 144,
    216-17, 236-37, 241, 267, 269,
    275, 277, 283, 296, 305-6, 311,
    315, 327
    Thanksgiving Day games, 48,
        71-72, 97-99, 155, 203, 244,
        250, 278, 317, 324-25
The Green Hornet (radio show), 7
Greenberg, Hank, 304
Greene, Edgar C. (Doc), 76, 133,
    137, 252, 276, 308
Greene, John, 24, 25, 34, 41, 214
Greene, Sam, 39
Gridiron Gauntlet (Piascik), 223
"Gridiron Heroes," 111, 120, 318
Groomes, Mel, 213
Grosse Pointe, 20, 211, 266
Groza, Lou, 32, 76, 107, 108, 109,
    110, 112, 140, 250
Gutowsky, Ace, 206, 323

Haelen Laboratories, 295-96, 299
Haggar slacks, 156
Halas, George, 17-18, 22, 47, 244,
    245, 248, 250, 271, 274
Hamilton Air Force Base, 51
Hampton, Lavinia, 13-14
Hampton, Wade, 13-14
Handler, Phil, 38
Hanley, Dean, 299

Harder, Pat, 33, 38-39, 48, 52,
    54, 61, 71, 74, 75, 80, 84, 92,
    143, 200, 259, 264
Hardy, Jim, 58-59, 60, 85, 327
Harlem Globetrotters, 215
Hart, Leon, 6, 25, 29, 30, 35,
    46-47, 48, 50, 52, 68, 70, 86,
    89, 96, 104, 116, 118, 145, 159,
    233, 246, 254, 259, 270, 297,
    304, 330-31, 332
    commercial endorsements, 156
    as defensive end, 42, 47,
        149-50, 197
    as fullback, 196, 235
    and Heisman Trophy, 6, 21,
        327
    injuries, 47, 60-61, 109, 331
    with Notre Dame, 6, 21, 39, 47
    salary, 30, 232
Hart, Philip, 19-20
Harwell, Ernie, 315
Hasel, Joe, 31
Hawaii All-Stars, 259
Hayes, Edgar, 137, 218
Hayes, Woody, 221, 235
Heaton, Chuck, 291
Hecker, Norb, 90
Heisman Trophy, 6, 16, 21, 187,
    197, 221, 302, 327
helmets, 116, 199-201, 237-39,
    254, 317
Herzog, Henry, 225
Highland Park High School,
    12-13, 15
Hill, Harlon, 203, 245
Hill, Jim, 194, 262
Hillsdale College, 268
Hirsch, Elroy (Crazylegs), 41,
    43-44, 50, 51, 73, 90, 275
Hoerner, Dick, 44, 50-51, 298
Hoernschemeyer, Bob (Hunchy),
    7, 23, 31, 46, 48, 50, 53, 61,
    62, 71, 72, 74, 78, 88, 89, 96,
    105, 106, 110, 119, 131, 144,
    147, 149, 194, 196, 197, 200,
    241, 297, 310
    AAFC career, 22-23
    concussions, 23, 52, 206
    fights, 5, 134, 143
    owns bar, 206, 266
    retirement, 206, 235
    statistics, 31, 206
Hoernschemeyer, Marybelle, 119

Hoffa, Jimmy, 7
Hog's Heaven, 57
Holiday, Billie, 215
Hollywood, 43
"Hollywood Rams," 43–44
Hooper, Sen. Warren G., 135–36
Hope, Bob, 43
Horne, Lena, 215
Hornung, Paul, 137, 242–43
Houser,.Bob, 275
Houston, Cisco, 132
Houston Oilers, 286
Howe, Gordie, 7, 158
Howland, Ed, 123
Howley, Bob, 138
Howton, Billy, 72, 244, 261
Hubbard, Orville, 211
Hudson, J. L., 97–98, 122, 158
    Thanksgiving Day parade,
        97–98, 122–23
Hudson Motors, 19
Huffman, Dick, 187
Hula Bowl, 207, 259–60
"Hunks of Granite," 96
Hutson, Don, 31, 206

"Ida Red," 127, 303
Indiana University, 20, 22, 213
Iowa State University, 40, 114
Iron Men (Leuthner), 135
Ironton Bengals, 214

Jack Benny Show (TV show), 315
Jackson, Ken, 151
Jagade, Harry (Chick), 77, 79,
    108, 109
Jamieson, Dave, 300
Jarmoluk, Mike, 251, 252
Jaszewski, Floyd, 46, 157
Jayne Field, 32
J. C. Higgins footballs, 156
Jenkins, Walter, 211
John's Rendezvous, 134
Johnson, Calvin, 227
Johnson, John Henry, 149, 275,
    276, 278, 281, 282, 285, 305,
    319, 330
    and racism, 209, 219, 222,
        223–24, 227
    traded to Detroit, 211, 267
    with Pittsburgh, 223–24
Jones, Calvin, 187, 220–21
Jones, Charles Robert, 135–36

Jones, Dub, 76, 112
Junker, Steve, 265, 268, 275, 276,
    279, 283, 284, 286, 290, 291,
    298

Kaline, Al, 7, 158
Kanzler, Ernest, 19–20
Karilivacz, Carl, 84, 90, 94, 100,
    112, 148, 159, 160, 163, 164,
    277, 297, 326
Karras, Alex, 134, 286, 302, 319,
    324, 325, 330
    and Bobby Layne, 128–29, 286,
        303–4
Kelley, Millard, 56, 153–54, 198
Kelly, Jimmy, 131
Kelly's Bar, 129, 131
Kelsey-Hayes, 19
Kelvinator plant, 19
Kennedy, John F., 11, 326
Kentucky State University, 225
Kerbawy, Nick, 18, 45, 54, 56,
    57, 59, 60, 66, 84–85, 91, 96,
    145, 150, 162, 184, 186, 187,
    188, 198, 206, 231–33, 253,
    273, 280, 307
Kercher, Dick, 220
Kern's department store, 98, 159,
    283
Keys, Brady, 223
Kezar Stadium, 52, 90, 240, 250,
    283–86
Kieban. Len, 238
Kilroy, Francis (Bucko), 199, 252
King, B. B., 139
King, Joe, 144
King, Rev. Martin Luther, 210
Kissell, John, 76
Knafelc, Gary, 196
Knorr, Fred, 229–30
Knute Rockne, All American, 281
Konz, Ken, 105, 141, 290, 291
Kopcz, Josephine, 280
Korean War, 158, 261–62, 304
Krall, Jerry, 56
Krouse, Ray (Moose), 243, 244,
    310
Kuenn, Harvey, 158
Kuhn, Jean, 135–36

Lafayette Park, 210
Lahr, Warren, 78, 109, 110, 161
Lambeau, Curly, 38

Lane, Dick (Night Train), 73, 226,
    324
Lane, Ray, 316
Lanker, Bud, 132
Larco, Mark, 6
Larco, Pete, 6
Larco's Inn, 6
Lary, Janie, 99, 136
Lary, Yale, 57–58, 79, 82, 88, 90,
    93–95, 107, 110, 121, 127, 128,
    129, 136, 139, 157, 243, 259,
    269, 276, 320, 324, 327
    and Bobby Layne, 4, 201, 282
    in military, 143, 261, 262
    as punter, 90, 94, 311
Latshaw, Bob, 23, 48, 61, 72, 88,
    124–25, 220, 248
Lavelli, Dante, 104–5, 107, 108
Lawson, Bob, 142
Layne, Beatrice, 12–13
Layne, Bobby, 3, 4–5, 19, 22, 23,
    24–25, 28, 29–30, 33, 35, 40,
    43, 44, 45, 46, 47–48, 49, 50,
    51–53, 55, 57, 60, 67–68,
    69–70, 72, 74, 77–81, 82–83,
    85, 86, 87–91, 96, 99, 100, 101,
    103, 104–5, 107, 108–110,
    112–14, 115–16, 127, 132–33,
    140, 149, 152, 155, 160, 161,
    162–65, 191–92, 193, 201,
    202–4, 222, 231, 232, 235, 236,
    237, 238, 239–41, 242, 243,
    245–49, 252, 262, 268, 270,
    275–78, 286, 301, 305–6, 322
    amphetamine use, 154
    awards, 162, 193, 255, 327
    as ball carrier, 16, 26, 70–71,
        72, 240
    "Bobby Layne curse," 323–24
    bubble gum trading cards,
        293–94, 297
    childhood, 12–15
    college career, 16–17, 193
    commercial endorsements,
        154, 156
    competitiveness, 15, 24, 60,
        113, 158, 255
    death, 329
    drinking, 4, 5, 63–66, 85,
        129–31, 165, 235–36, 246,
        256–57, 265–66, 271–73,
        279–80, 303, 306–7, 310–11,
        328

drunk driving case, 272-73, 279-80

gambling, 24, 308-9

Hula Bowl, 259-60

injuries, 51-52, 62-63, 93, 149, 192, 196, 198, 201, 203-4, 236-37, 240, 247-49, 278, 281, 286, 302

with New York Bulldogs, 17-18, 216

nightlife, 24, 129-31, 134-35, 137-39, 217, 265-66, 272-73

with Pittsburgh, 154, 260, 309-311

popularity, 6-7, 70-71, 115-16, 138, 157, 293-94

post-football career, 328

Pro Bowl, 256-57, 259

public image, 4, 137-38, 157, 159, 161, 265-66

and rookie hazing, 127-30, 235-36, 243, 271-72, 302, 303

salary, 146, 185, 230, 232-33

smoking, 64, 154, 236, 328

statistics, 70, 71, 113, 114, 164, 204, 240, 246

Texas drawl, 279-80

traded to Detroit, 18, 216, 271

traded to Pittsburgh, 306-310

two-minute offense, 4, 67-68

Layne, Carol, 13, 16, 44, 99-102, 306, 308

Layne, Sherman, 12

Leahy, Frank, 21

LeBeau, Dick, 297-98, 319-20

Ledbetter, Toy, 134

Lee Plaza, 30, 100

Lee, Robert E., 195

LeForce, Clyde, 18

Leland Hotel, 133

Leuthner, Stuart, 135

Lewis, Danny, 225, 226, 297-98

Lewis, Wallace (Bootsy), 223-24

Lewis, Woodley, 91

Life, 329

Lillywhite, Verl, 53

Lindell A. C., 133-34, 138, 317, 325

Lindell Hotel, 133

Lindsay, Ted, 158, 317

Lion Alumni Association, 330

Lion Gridiron News, 253

Lions Bleacher Club, 126-27, 266

Lions Den, 206, 265

Lipscomb, Gene (Big Daddy), 223, 244

Little, Jack, 151

Little Rock, Arkansas, 224, 225

Little Rock Central High School, 224, 225

Livonia, Michigan, 211

Lombardi, Vince, 318, 324-25

The Lone Ranger (radio show), 7, 14

Long, Bob, 237, 285, 290, 311

Look, 6, 157

LoPrete, Jim, 189, 280, 325

Los Angeles Dons, 214

Los Angeles Publishers Association, 257

Los Angeles Rams, 5, 29, 32, 43-44, 50-51, 53, 59, 60-61, 72-75, 91-92, 105-6, 134, 148, 149-50, 197, 198, 206, 218, 219, 237-39, 240, 261-62, 269, 275, 276, 283, 311, 319, 320

Los Angeles Times, 5, 44, 53, 252, 258

Louis, Joe, 7, 158, 183-84

Louisell, Joseph W., 273, 279-80

Lowe, Gary, 264

Lubbock Hubbers, 16

Luckman, Sid, 17-18, 29, 52, 240

Lucky Strike cigarettes, 154

Lujack, Johnny, 17-18

Lynch, Budd, 203

Maccabees Building, 14

Macklem, Roy (Friday), 46, 59, 64, 87, 92, 124, 128, 143, 194, 280, 317

Macon, Eddie, 250

Macy's department store, 97

Mandel, Fred, 19

Magnani, Dante, 154

Maher, Bruce, 319

Mains, Gil (Wild Hoss), 127, 221, 241-42, 271, 286, 297-98, 305, 330

fights, 151, 248

reputation as dirty player, 7, 151, 250, 252-53

with Toronto, 188-89, 191

Majeski, Harry, 265

Malvern Hotel, 92, 100

Mann, Bob, 98, 213-17, 227

Mantle, Mickey, 308

marching bands, 47, 98, 120-21

Marietta, William T., 200

Marlboro cigarettes, 154, 328

"Marlboro Man" ad campaign, 154

Marshall, George Preston, 212

Martin, Billy, 133

Martin, Gloria, 99

Martin, Jim, 39, 46, 47, 68-69, 79, 99, 103, 141, 152, 153, 233, 244, 269, 277, 305, 311, 330

as kicker, 39-40, 240, 271, 285, 289, 292

military service, 39, 252

with Toronto, 188, 191

versatility of, 39, 72, 93

Maryland Eastern Shore University, 226

mascots, 49, 123-24, 127, 322-23

Massey, Carlton, 166

Masters, Norm, 267

Matney, Bill, 211

Matson, Ollie, 230

Matuszak, Marv, 307

Maule, Tex, 2, 137, 269, 289

Maxwell Award, 18, 21, 235

Maxwell Club, 16

"Maybelline," 127

Mays, Willie, 261

Mazeroff, Dave, 135-36

McCants, Howard, 215, 220-21

McClellan, Bob, 125, 165, 203

McClung, Willie, 223, 226

McCollouch, Earl, 226

McCord, Darris, 234, 243, 286, 297-98, 324

McCormack, Mike, 164

McElhenny, Hugh, 88, 90, 149, 150, 230, 239, 253, 277, 281, 284, 285, 297

McGraw, Beryl, 108

McGraw, Thurman (Fum), 27, 28, 40, 42, 71, 79, 96, 127, 151, 157, 194, 198, 258

McIlhenny, Don, 235, 236, 239, 245, 250, 267, 297

McLouth Steel, 19

McMillan, Alvin (Bo), 20, 23, 24, 26-27, 30-33, 34-35, 37, 45, 48, 65, 88, 154, 213-15, 232,

251, 271, 299
McNally, Vince, 230
Meadows, Ed, 202–3, 247–49
Meet the UAW-CIO (TV show), 315
Melvindale High School, 215
Memorial Coliseum (Los Angeles), 7, 50, 53, 91, 140, 240, 257, 260
Michaels, Lou, 320
Michaels, Walt, 251
Michigan Avenue (Detroit), 4, 84–85
Michigan Central Station, 77, 80
Michigan Normal College, 23, 85, 268. *See also* Eastern Michigan University
Michigan State University, 40, 142
Middlesworth, Hal, 152
Middleton, Dave, 194, 198, 203, 219, 235, 243, 245, 281, 282, 291, 330
Midnighters, 138
Miketa, Andy, 143–44, 193, 330
military draft, 261-64
Millen, Matt, 3
Miller, Bob (Detroit Lions), 72, 233, 234, 243, 253
Miller, Bob (Detroit Tigers), 243
Miller Brewing Company, 107-8
Miller High School, 244
"Million Dollar Backfield," 149
Millner, Wayne, 48
Mint Condition (Jamieson), 300
Miriani, Louis, 323
Mitchell, Bobby, 302
Modzelewski, Dick, 250
Monaghan, Hart and Crawmer, 188, 189, 229
Monday Night Football (TV show), 315
Montana, Joe, 114
Montgomery bus boycott, 210
Moore, Herman, 227
Moore, Lenny, 244, 276
Moore, Terry, 43
Morabito, Tony, 277
Morrall, Earl, 297, 307, 309, 320, 321, 330
Moselle, Dom, 250, 267
Motley, Marion, 40, 77, 79, 94, 107, 146, 213
Mullins, Moon, 123

Municipal Stadium (Cleveland), 146, 160–61, 164
Muntz television, 155
Murakowski, Art, 251–52
Murphy, Bob, 55
Murray, Jim, 5
Murray State College, 151
Mutual radio network, 155

Nancarrow, Jack, 272–73
National Broadcast Company (NBC), 187, 259, 287, 317
National Collegiate Athletic Association (NCAA), 22, 109, 144–45, 187, 302
National Football League (NFL), 114, 212
  African American players, 209–27
  attendance, 7, 254, 317
  championship games, (1950) 32, 218, (1951) 218, (1952) 75–81, (1953) 9, 106–14, 321, (1954) 160–66, (1955) 206, (1956) 255, (1957) 316, (1958) 313–14
  college draft, 193, 212, 213–14, 219–20, 278–79
  concussions, 9–10, 330–31
  conferences renamed, 22, 105
  divisional playoffs, (1950) 32, (1952) 72–75, (1957) 283–86
  face masks, 199–201, 254
  merger with AAFC, 21–22
  military draft, 261-64
  option clause in player contracts, 188-90, 206
  passer rating, 114
  roster size, 9, 302
  rule changes, 46, 199–201, 253–54
  salaries, 10, 230, 232
  seven-point touchdowns proposed, 46, 111
  steroids, 153–54
  sudden death overtime, 45–46, 313
  television, 122–23, 259, 313–18
  violence, 8, 39, 61, 92, 151, 199–200, 247–54, 256, 260–61
  white footballs, 8, 317
National Football League Players

Association, 260, 317–18, 331
Navin Field, 118
Neal, Jim, 142, 296–97
Neale, Earle (Greasy), 41
New Orleans, 214, 226
New York Bulldogs, 17–18, 41
New York Giants (baseball), 15, 147
New York Giants (football), 4, 32, 103–4, 111, 194, 205, 219, 243, 244–45, 255, 287, 311, 313, 324
New York Times, 19, 26–27, 74, 107, 160
New York World-Telegram, 144
New York Yanks, 17–18, 26, 28, 31, 45, 216. *See also* Boston Yanks and New York Bulldogs
New York Yankees, 144, 229, 308
Newcombe, Jack, 185
Newhouser, Hal, 7
Ninowski, Jim, 302
Nisby, John, 223
Noll, Chuck, 107
Northland shopping mall, 98, 159
Northwood Golf Club, 58
Novocain, 152–53
Nussbaumer, Bob, 220, 278, 319

Oakwood Hospital, 103
O'Brien, Pat, 281
O'Connell, Tommy, 287, 290
Ohio State University, 6, 56, 221, 235
Olszewski, Johnny, 194
Olympia Stadium, 273
O'Malley, Tom, 25
Ontario Court of Appeals, 190
Osborn, Don, 272
Ottawa Rough Riders, 84, 266
Our Lady of Good Counsel, 293–94
Outland Trophy, 221, 302
Overgard, Dr. Graham T., 120–21
Owen, Steve, 103
Owens, R. C., 277, 283

Packard plant, 19
Page, Patti, 132
Palo Alto, California, 283
Panelli, John, 24, 38, 214
Paper Lion (Plimpton), 242
Paradise Valley, 215
Parilli, Vito (Babe), 98, 238

Park Shelton, 100
Parker, Bobby, 191-92
Parker, Jane, 36, 140
Parker, Raymond (Buddy), 4-5,
    30, 38-40, 43, 45-49, 51, 52,
    54, 58, 61, 62, 85, 91, 92, 97,
    102, 103, 109, 128, 134-35,
    136-37, 140-48, 149, 150, 152,
    160-61, 188, 189, 191-97, 206,
    208, 234-35, 245, 248-50,
    260-61, 323
  accused of spying, 141, 145
  background, 35-37, 85-86
  and Bobby Layne, 4-5, 41, 52,
    60, 65, 69, 165, 192, 204,
    240, 246, 248, 255, 266, 268,
    269, 270, 306-7, 310
  with Chicago Cardinals, 34, 38,
    249
  coaching philosophy, 5, 8-9,
    36-37, 59-60, 65, 66-68, 72,
    163, 165, 201-2, 235, 266
  competitiveness, 60, 140-41,
    158
  contracts, 35, 56, 255
  death, 327
  drinking, 165-66, 198-99, 270
  innovations, 67-68, 93-94,
    237-39
  with Pittsburgh, 193, 223-24,
    274, 278-79, 286, 287,
    306-7, 310, 311, 319
  quits Lions, 5, 269-71
  racial views, 211, 215, 223-24
  rivalry with Paul Brown, 38,
    41-42, 69-70, 75-76, 104-6,
    140-42, 146-47, 161, 165,
    237, 258
  superstitions, 36, 96, 125, 144,
    147, 223-24
  two-minute offense, 4, 67-68
Parkhurst Products, 298
Parks, Rosa, 209-10
Patrick, Van, 62, 83, 96, 116, 117,
    120, 152, 259, 315-16, 328
Paul, Don, 164, 257-58
Pellington, Bill, 305
Pennsylvania State University,
    212, 214
Penobscot Building, 315
Pentecost, Paul, 83
Perry, Gerry, 151, 312
Perry, Joe, 52, 53, 88, 90, 149,

    200, 211, 253, 286
Peterson, Armand, 155
Petok, Ted, 253
Pietrosante, Nick, 297-98, 319,
    324, 327
Philadelphia Eagles, 25, 38, 41,
    48, 86, 144, 159, 214, 230, 251,
    277, 302, 311, 314
Philco, 314
Philip Morris, 154
Piascik, Andy, 141, 223
Pittsburgh Post-Gazette, 310
Pittsburgh Steelers, 24, 71, 72,
    87, 126, 193, 202-3, 223-24,
    246, 274, 287, 306-7, 310-11,
    319
Playoff Bowl, 325
Plimpton, George, 134, 242
Plum, Milt, 287, 324
Polish Daily News, 204-5
Polo Grounds, 26, 103
Pool, Hamp, 59, 72, 75
Portsmouth Spartans, 268
Povich, Shirley, 76, 107, 260
Powell, Charlie, 217, 239-40
Powers, Jimmy, 90, 91
Prairie View College, 220, 221
Pratt, Lemmie, 272, 273
Prchlik, John, 22, 40, 46, 61, 71,
    95-96, 129, 143
Prell, Edward, 198
Presbyterian College, 305
President's Trophy, 9, 162
Presley, Elvis, 261
Presnell, Glenn, 323
Prest-O-Lite batteries, 156
Prestone Anti-Freeze, 156
Pro All-Star Game, 257
Pro Bowl, 28, 54, 65, 86, 104,
    140-41, 142, 207, 256-61, 269,
    311, 318
Pro Football Hall of Fame, 7,
    94-95, 107, 267, 319, 327, 328,
    332
"Production Line" (hockey), 158
Purple Gang, 135-36
Puscas, George, 133, 305, 318

Quaker Oats cereal, 156
Quinlan, Skeets, 91, 149-50

radio broadcasts, 14, 62, 152, 155,
    287, 315-16

Raikovitz, Joe, 123
Ramsey, Garrard (Buster), 56,
    96, 143, 150, 224, 237-38, 243,
    284, 321
Ratterman, George, 113, 238
Rauch, Johnny, 17
Rawlings sporting good, 156
Reichow, Jerry, 127, 187, 230,
    231, 235-36, 240, 246, 284,
    291-92, 297-98, 301, 318
Renfro, Ray, 80, 109, 140, 164
Reserve Officers Training Corps
    (ROTC), 262
Retzlaff, Pete, 86
Reuther, Walter, 7, 158
Reynolds, Billy, 162, 164
Reynolds, Bob, 62, 120, 269, 316
Ricca, Jim, 194-95, 198-99
Rice, Fred, 95, 120
Rice University, 142, 267
Richards, G. A. (Dick), 19, 268
Richards, Ray, 194
Richter, Les, 253
Riddell Sporting Goods, 200
Ridgeland Apartments, 36
River Rouge High School, 215,
    220
Roberts, Gene (Choo-Choo), 186
Robinson, Jackie, 213
Robinson, (Sugar Ray), 158
Robinson, Will, 226
Robustelli, Andy, 43-44
Rogas, Dan, 45, 46
Rogel, Fran, 9-10
Rogers, Buck, 239
Rogers, Shaun, 227
Rooney, Art, 274
Rose Bowl, 193
Rosenbloom, Carroll, 274
Rote, Tobin, 4, 25, 71-72, 222,
    240, 259, 269, 275, 276-78,
    281, 282, 284, 302, 303, 305,
    308, 309, 311, 320, 321
  postseason performances,
    284-86, 289-92, 321
  success vs. Detroit, 196, 244,
    255, 267
  traded to Detroit, 267
Rush, Jerry, 226
Russell, Jane, 43, 258
Russell, Ken, 268, 271, 308

St. Aloysius Church, 69

St. Clair, Bob, 267
St. Francis Hotel, 54
St. Louis Cardinals (baseball), 58
Sales, Soupy, 7, 159
Salesmanship Club of Dallas, 184
Salsbury, Jim, 241, 267
Salsinger, Harry, 80
Sample, Johnny, 223-24
San Diego Chargers, 321
San Francisco Examiner, 277
San Francisco 49ers, 22, 29, 46,
    49, 52-54, 59, 60, 88-89,
    90-91, 103, 105-6, 120,
    148-49, 151-52, 196, 197, 198,
    199, 217, 218, 239, 240, 250,
    267, 276-77, 281, 283-86, 319
Sanders (confectionary), 158
Sanders, Barry, 227
Sanders, Charlie, 226
Saturday Evening Post, 6, 157, 310
Sauerbrei, Harold, 78
Sawchuk, Terry, 158
Sax Club, 266, 272, 273
Schairer, Roy, 195-96, 292
Schemansky, Norb, 153
Schenkel, Chris, 117
Schmidt, Joe, 2, 4, 5, 9, 10-11,
    84, 87, 92, 100, 107, 108, 127,
    128, 129, 131, 132-33, 135,
    138, 146, 153, 157, 162, 164,
    185, 187, 195, 199, 200, 207-8,
    219, 234, 237-39, 244, 251,
    253, 254, 268-69, 275-76,
    284-86, 297, 308, 317, 324,
    326, 327, 331-32
  coaching career, 326
  competitiveness, 96, 242
  military service, 264
  Pro Bowl, 257, 259, 318
  salary, 84, 233, 264, 283
  switches to middle linebacker,
    241-43
Schmidt, Marilyn, 136
Schmidt, William, 251
Senior Bowl, 219
Seward Hotel, 100
Sewell, Harley, 82-83, 100, 101,
    127, 128-29, 145, 154, 163,
    185-86, 193, 196, 241, 268,
    285, 301, 318
Shamrock Hotel, 42
Shaw, Buck, 93, 218
Shaw, George, 237

Sheraton-Cadillac Hotel, 69, 278
Shibe Park, 48
Shore, Dinah, 258
Show of Shows, 61
Shubot, Maurice, 195
Shurford, Harry, 15
Simmons, Jack, 252
Sims, Billy, 227
Sinatra, Frank, 195
Singer, Jack, 252
single-wing offense, 16, 43-44
"Skid Row Boogie," 132
Smith, Bob (Texas Bob), 200,
    263-64
Smith, Bob (Tulsa Bob), 9-10,
    28-29, 42, 46, 50-51, 75, 79,
    90, 97, 143, 150, 330
Smith, Lyall, 50, 113, 150, 161,
    260-61
Smith, Ray, 203
Smith, V. T. (Vitamin T), 75
Soldier Field, 38, 85, 146, 301-2
Soltau, Gordy, 52, 53, 88-89, 140,
    283, 284
Sonne, Ben, 46
Sonny Gandee's Celebrity House,
    266
South Dakota State University, 86
Southern Methodist University, 6,
    15, 27, 206-7, 235
Speedie, Mac, 76, 186-87
Spencer, Ollie, 83-84, 143, 219,
    235, 247, 261, 267, 268, 297
Spinney, Art, 244
Spoelstra, Watson, 70-71, 203,
    306, 321
Sport, 185, 230
The Sporting News, 243, 258
Sports Illustrated, 2, 6, 137, 157,
    221, 236, 254, 269, 289, 313,
    316, 319
Sprinkle, Ed, 46, 71
Stadium Bar, 4, 63-64, 127,
    130-31, 236, 304, 308
Stafford, Matthew, 12
Stanfel, Dick, 68-69, 78, 107,
    127-28, 145, 152-53, 162, 187,
    196, 232, 327
Stanford University, 283
Starr, Bart, 114, 325
Statler Hotel, 269-70, 306
Steen, Jim, 330
steroids, 153-54

Stits, Bill, 118, 142, 150, 157, 163,
    211, 296
Strickler, George, 165
Strode, Woody, 213
Stryzkalski, John, 53
Studstill, Pat, 99
Stydahar, Joe, 44, 59
Sugar Bowl, 193
Summerall, Pat, 57, 86, 106, 246,
    260
Sweetan, Karl, 99
Swiacki, Bill, 43, 59, 78, 188,
    252, 327
Syracuse University, 84

Taseff, Carl, 305
Tatum, Jim, 145
Taylor, Altie, 226
Taylor, Jimmy, 325
television, 7, 31, 49, 77, 155, 160,
    187-88, 203, 241, 247, 301-2,
    313-18, 325
  blackout rule, 72, 151-52,
    287-88, 317
  booster antennae, 288, 317
  closed-circuit, 288
  coaxial cable, 52, 315
  growth, 313-18
  night games, 8, 87, 96, 148,
    201, 314, 315
  revenue, 10, 187, 318, 326
  "television numbers," 316-17
Terkel, Studs, 251
Texas A&M University, 57, 127,
    263
Texas Christian University, 316
"Theme from Limelight," 63
Thomas, Russ, 56-57, 84, 326,
    327-28
Thompson, Bobby, 226
Thompson, Dr. Richard, 89, 281
Thrasher, Norm, 138-39
Tidwell, Billy, 152
Time, 6-7, 157, 159, 250
Timken Axle, 19
Tittle, Y. A., 52, 53, 88-89, 90-91,
    149, 196, 198, 277, 283, 284-85
Tonnemaker, Clayton, 69
Topps Chewing Gum Company,
    294-96, 298-300
Torgeson, LaVern, 45, 75, 102-4,
    145, 194, 198, 234, 297
Torgeson, Mary Lou, 102-4

Torgeson, Robert, 102
Toronto Argonauts, 84, 186, 188-91, 221, 296
Towler, Dan (Deacon), 30, 44, 74, 94, 149
Tracy, Tom (The Bomb), 5, 266, 285-86, 297, 310-11
Trebotich, Ivan (Buzz), 22
"Tribe Fight Song," 127
Triplett, Wally, 24, 120, 212-13, 215, 217, 233, 261-62, 267, 279, 327
Tripucka, Frank, 18
Trout, Bob, 189
Truman, Harry, 261
Trumbull, Elliott, 118
Tsoutsouvas, Sam, 22
Tuller Hotel, 189, 272
Tunnell, Emlen, 258
Turner, Harold (Hal), 211, 219, 220
Twenty Questions (TV show), 315
two-minute offense, 4, 67-68
two-minute warning, 67

University of California-Los Angeles (UCLA), 142, 213, 221
Unitas, Johnny, 127, 237, 244, 274-75, 304-5
United Auto Workers (UAW), 158, 210
University of Alabama, 192-93
University of Arkansas, 57, 84
University of Detroit, 26, 37, 266
University of Florida, 145
University of Georgia, 145
University of Illinois, 28
University of Iowa, 221
University of Kansas, 83-84
University of Michigan, 39, 213, 214, 235, 269, 290
University of North Carolina, 143
University of Notre Dame, 21, 29, 39, 66, 214
University of Pittsburgh, 84
University of San Francisco, 68
University of Southern California, 29, 84
University of Tennessee, 268
University of Texas, 16, 82-83, 193, 329-30
University of Utah, 58
University of Virginia, 243

University of Washington, 102
University of Wisconsin, 38, 62, 197, 226
Uremovich, Emil, 22

Van, George, 265
Van Brocklin, Norm, 43, 44, 70, 74, 89, 91, 148, 149, 230, 275
Van Buren, Steve, 94
VanDeKeere, Michael, 77
Varisto, John, 119
Verhougstraete, Blanche, 123-24
Vesper Club, 278
Vessels, Billy, 187
Vietnam, 261, 263
Vitalis Hair Tonic, 5, 156
Voting Rights Act, 226

Waldmeir, Pete, 218-19
Walker Jr., Ewell (Doak), 5, 22-23, 24, 26, 27, 28, 30-31, 33, 34, 41, 43, 44, 46, 50, 56, 59, 69, 70, 71, 73, 74, 77-80, 82, 86, 87, 88, 91, 100, 101, 103, 107, 110-12, 121, 129, 136, 145, 147-48, 151, 152, 159, 161, 163, 196, 197, 198, 200, 203, 217, 220, 235, 254, 264, 310
    attempted comeback, 207-8
    awards, 6, 16-17, 31, 207
    and Bobby Layne, 5, 12, 13, 15-16, 18, 24-25, 26, 50, 63, 77-80, 82, 96, 108-9, 112, 130, 146, 155, 192, 201, 202, 203, 241, 255, 257, 328-29
    bubble gum trading cards, 293-94, 297, 298
    childhood, 12-16
    college career, 16-17
    commercial endorsements, 5, 156, 200
    competitiveness, 15, 202
    death, 329
    as defensive back, 160, 164, 201
    Doak Walker Award, 328-29
    Doak Walker Day, 204-5
    injuries, 29, 36, 58, 61-62, 90
    kicking shoe, 111
    popularity, 15-17, 27-28, 183, 185-86, 191, 222, 298, 319
    post-football career, 207-8, 328, 329

Pro Bowl, 257, 258
    public image, 5, 16-17, 183, 185-86, 202, 329-30
    retirement, 204-8, 240
    salary, 184-86
    size, 27, 201
    statistics, 31, 79, 148, 201-2, 206
    versatility, 148, 160, 201
Walker Sr., Ewell, 17, 185, 207
Walker, Norma, 17, 99, 136, 156, 185, 205, 207-8
Walker, T-Bone, 138
Walker, Wayne, 117, 303, 311-12
Walsh, Jack, 164-65
Walston, Bobby, 148
Walton, Larry, 226
Ward, Arch, 85, 145
Warner, Gladys (Skeeter), 328
Washington, Dinah, 138
Washington, Kenny, 213
Washington Post, 76, 107, 164-65, 260
Washington Redskins, 25, 31, 40, 43, 58-59, 86, 189, 194, 212, 226, 243
Washington State University, 220
Wasserman, Morris, 138
water boys, 124-25
Waterfield, Bob, 29, 43, 44, 50, 75, 113, 206
Watkins, Bobby, 282
Watson, Joe, 26
Wattrick, Don, 49
Watts, John D., 279-80
Wayne University, 221
We Play to Win! (Parker), 197, 219
Webb, Ken, 305
Webster, Alex, 194
Wedgwood Room, 138
Weiss, Rube, 97-98
Weissmuller, Johnny, 43
Welty, Billy, 124
West Texas State College, 31
Westinghouse, 314
Weston, Fred (Fritz), 126-27, 266
WFDF (Flint station), 316
Wheaties, 156
White, John, 215
White Spot restaurant, 143
Whiting, Margaret, 42
Whorton, Cal, 53, 252
Whyte, Peter, 124-25

Whyte, Ray, 124–25
Wightkin, Bill, 46
William, G. Mennen (Soapy),
   204, 288
Williams, Fred, 278
Williams, Ricky, 329–30
Williams, Sam, 324, 325
Williams, Ted, 304
Willis, Bill, 107, 146, 213
Willis Show Bar, 317
Willow Run Airport, 283
Wilson, Billy, 52, 91
Wilson, Camp, 18
Wilson footballs, 156
Wilson, George, 30, 31–32, 36, 90,
   92, 103, 197, 255, 270
     as Lions head coach, 271, 273,

274, 276–79, 281, 282, 289,
   290, 302, 303–4, 306–7,
   309–10, 319–21, 323, 326
Wilson, Jackie, 7, 138
Wilson, Ralph C., 321
Wilson, Tommy, 83
Winnipeg Blue Bombers, 187, 222
Wismer, Harry, 117, 203, 308–9,
   313, 326
WJBK (Detroit station), 49, 77, 126
WJIM (Lansing station), 288, 317
WJR (Detroit station), 19, 49,
   62, 316
WJRT (Flint station), 317
Wojciechowicz, Alex, 22
World Series, 147
World War II, 16, 153–54, 212–13,

251–52, 257, 262
Wrigley Field, 32, 97, 124, 126,
   160, 203, 246–47, 320
WXYZ (Detroit station), 14, 314

Xavier University, 268

Yankee Stadium, 255, 313
Yonkers, Bob, 81
Young Jr., Coleman, 210
Younger, Paul (Tank), 44, 94
Yowarsky, Walt, 194–95
Ypsilanti Farm Bureau, 143

Zagers, Bert, 189
Zatkoff, Roger, 269, 274, 284, 286,
   297, 331